The Human Brain and its Disorders

The Human Brain

and its disorders

Edited by:

Doug Richards, Tom Clark,
and Carl Clarke

OXFORD
UNIVERSITY PRESS

OXFORD
UNIVERSITY PRESS

Great Clarendon Street, Oxford OX2 6DP

Oxford University Press is a department of the University of Oxford.
It furthers the University's objective of excellence in research, scholarship,
and education by publishing worldwide in

Oxford New York

Auckland Cape Town Dar es Salaam Hong Kong Karachi
Kuala Lumpur Madrid Melbourne Mexico City Nairobi
New Delhi Shanghai Taipei Toronto

With offices in

Argentina Austria Brazil Chile Czech Republic France Greece
Guatemala Hungary Italy Japan Poland Portugal Singapore
South Korea Switzerland Thailand Turkey Ukraine Vietnam

Oxford is a registered trade mark of Oxford University Press
in the UK and in certain other countries

Published in the United States
by Oxford University Press Inc., New York

British Library Cataloguing in Publication Data

Data available

Library of Congress Cataloging in Publication Data

Data available

Typeset by Graphicraft Limited, Hong Kong
Printed in Great Britain
on acid-free paper by
CPI Bath Ltd, Bath

ISBN 9780199299843

1 3 5 7 9 10 8 6 4 2

Preface

About this book

The human brain is probably the most complex creation known to humanity, and one that controls every aspect of our existence from movement, feeding, and reproduction, through to our memories of the past, our aspirations for the future, our personalities, our moods, and our emotions. Little wonder, then, that when the brain malfunctions, the consequences on our lives can be devastating.

Neuroscience, the study of the brain and the nervous system, is one of the most rapidly advancing areas of scientific endeavour. Excellent textbooks are constantly being updated to keep pace with these rapid developments at the forefront of both the basic sciences and in clinical medicine.

However, there is also a need for textbooks to cater for students and health professionals interested in understanding neuroscience as part of a wider programme of health-related study, where the level of background knowledge may not yet be ready for comprehensive neuroscience or medical textbooks.

The purpose of this book is to first provide an introduction to normal brain structure and function, and the mechanisms that underlie this, before then addressing some of the neurological and psychiatric disorders that may affect our brains. Each chapter is written by experts in their field, but in a style accessible to the non-specialist.

Using this book

To help the reader to make best use of the information in the book, we have provided a number of learning features.

- Medical and scientific terminology can often be a barrier to the non-specialist, so **key words** are emboldened, with definitions being provided in an extensive **glossary** towards the end of the book.

> Arteries can slowly fur up, like lime scale in a kettle. The substance narrowing the artery is called **atheroma** and the process is called **atherosclerosis** (look at the top of Figure 5.3). Atheroma is made up of fatty deposits, but how this stems from the vascular risk factors discussed above is not known in detail.
>
> Alternatively, arteries can suddenly become blocked. This happens when a blood clot forms on a deposit or plaque of atheroma, so-called **thrombosis**. Sudden occlusion of an artery can occur if a clot of blood from an atheromatous plaque breaks loose and floats further down the narrowing vessel, eventually becoming lodged as shown in the middle diagram of Figure 5.3. This clot is called an **embolism**.

- To help consolidate important facts and concepts, **key points** are used throughout chapters to reinforce important messages.

> With repeated relapses of the disease, the process of remyelination is imperfect and nerve impulse transmission along the axon does not fully recover. In time individual axons die and scar tissue forms at the site of the inflammatory plaque. Impulse transmission along the nerve does not return. This corresponds to the progressive stage of MS, when disability accumulates.
>
> **MS arises because of damage to the blood–brain barrier and activation of the immune system within the CNS.**

SELF-CHECK 10.5

What therapies are available to control symptoms in MS?

immobility in joints can be eased with non-steroi patients report that cannabis can relieve paroxysn toms in MS and further detail of this is given in Box illegal in the UK. It is anticipated that this will be cl to be effective in future clinical trials.

Overwhelming tiredness is a frequent symptom in M treat. Recent studies with modafinil, an agent develop of **narcolepsy**, have shown some success. Selec (SSRIs) can sometimes help in treating fatigue, in commonly seen.

- **Self-check questions** are also provided, with brief answers towards the end of the book, so that students can check their understanding of important concepts before moving on to the next section.

- For each of the clinical chapters, we consider such matters as how common the condition is, its causes, underlying pathology and mechanisms, the symptoms, diagnosis, treatment alternatives, and likely outcomes.

case study: Puerperal psychosis

BOX 14.4

A 28-year-old single woman, delivered her first child, a girl, at term by a normal vaginal delivery 4 days before her presentation to the GP.

Her partner first became concerned when he noticed that she was not sleeping at all and that she was neglecting the newly born child. Her mood appeared to be shifting from being cheerful to unprovoked inconsolable tearfulness. She had also stopped eating.

Her partner became very worried when she started to say that their daughter was the Devil's child, and had brought an evil presence to their home. The partner became con-

- **Case studies** have been included to illustrate the real-life consequences of brain disorders.

extension: Use of CT and SPECT in the diagnosis of AD

Researchers from Oxford (OPTIMA) discovered that by tilting the axis of cross-sectional CT imaging, they could produce images of the entire medial temporal lobe, the structure affected very early in AD. This can be se Figure 7.3.

- For those requiring more in-depth information, **extension boxes** have been provided throughout all chapters.

Excitatory and inhibitory amino acid neurotransmission are introduced in section 2.2.4 on page 29.

Further discussion of the role of these transmitter systems in epilepsy can be found in section 6.6 on page 117.

In the last few years, scientists have identified ove epilepsy. Many of these are genes encoding for va or inhibitory amino acid signalling systems in the br

Thus, mutations of the genes for the NMDA and AMF mitter glutamate, and the GABA$_A$ and GABA$_B$ rece GABA, have been associated with epilepsy. Howeve other genes implicated in epilepsy, is not clear, and for a few types of epilepsy, there are many other forr remains unknown.

- The chapters are extensively **cross-referenced**, both to help the student link basic mechanisms to disease processes, and to highlight how similar mechanisms or concepts may be associated with very different clinical outcomes.

SUMMARY

- A stroke is a sudden loss of brain function lasting for more than 24 hours resulting from perturbation of its blood supply.
- A transient ischaemic attack (TIA) is a cerebral ischaemic event with all symptoms and signs disappearing within 24 hours.
- The two carotid and two vertebral arteries supply

- Patients who have suffered a battery of investigations in ECG, and a CT brain scan.
- CT imaging should be do severe stroke to ensure th and to exclude haemorrhag
- Treatment of stroke includ tive measures, rehabilitatio

- Finally, each chapter concludes with a **summary** of its main points . . .

FURTHER READING

E. M. Manno. Subarachnoid haemorrhage. *Neurologic Clinics* 2004: **22**; 347–366.
A general overview of latest developments in the diagnosis and treatment of subarachnoid haemorrhage.

Neurology in practice: Issue 1—Stroke. *Journal of Neurology, Neurosurgery and Psychiatry* 2001; **70**(Suppl. 1).
More advanced discussion of current issues in stroke management.

C. Warlow, C. Sudlow, M. Dennis **362**: 1211–1224.
An excellent overview of all aspe

- . . . as well as a suggested **further reading** list which directs the interested reader seeking further information to appropriate primary literature references, textbooks, or electronic resources.

Acknowledgements

Our grateful thanks go to the various reviewers who commented on initial drafts of each of the chapters and who have helped us to improve the finished version of the book. At OUP, a very special thanks to Jonathan Crowe, our commissioning editor, who has guided us through the maze of the writing and publishing process with just the right balance of criticism, patience, and encouragement. Finally, and most importantly, our thanks to our contributors; the clinicians and scientists whose hard work and enthusiasm for their topics has resulted in excellent chapters that we hope will introduce the fascinating world of neuroscience to a wider audience.

Contents

Contributors

Dr Tom Clark	Reaside Clinic, Birmingham Great Park, Bristol Road South, Rubery, Birmingham, B45 9BE
Dr Carl E. Clarke	Department of Neurology, City Hospital, Dudley Road, Birmingham, B18 7QH
Dr Alison J. Cooper	Division of Neuroscience, School of Medicine, University of Birmingham, Edgbaston, Birmingham, B15 2TT
Dr Ed Day	Department of Psychiatry, University of Birmingham, Queen Elizabeth Psychiatric Hospital, Mindelsohn Way, Edgbaston, Birmingham, B15 2QZ
Dr John Fox	Department of Neurophysiology, Division of Neuroscience, Queen Elizabeth Hospital, Edgbaston, Birmingham, B15 2TH
Dr Barbara Hoggart	Solihull Hospital, Lode Lane, Solihull, B9 2JL
Professor John G. R. Jefferys	Department of Neurophysiology, Division of Neuroscience, School of Medicine, University of Birmingham, Edgbaston, Birmingham, B15 2TT
Dr Lisa A. Jones	Department of Psychiatry, University of Birmingham, Queen Elizabeth Psychiatric Hospital, Mindelsohn Way, Edgbaston, Birmingham, B15 2QZ
Dr Mary Keen	Department of Pharmacology, Division of Neurosciences, Medical School, University of Birmingham, B15 2TT
Professor Karen E. Morrison	Division of Neurosciences, Medical School, University of Birmingham, Edgbaston, Birmingham, B15 2TT
Dr Zsuzsanna Nagy	Department of Clinical Neurosciences, Division of Neuroscience, Medical School, University of Birmingham, B15 2TT
Professor Femi Oyebode	Department of Psychiatry, University of Birmingham, Queen Elizabeth Psychiatric Hospital, Mindelsohn Way, Edgbaston, Birmingham, B15 2QZ
Dr Alessandra Princivalle	Department of Pharmacology, Division of Neurosciences, Medical School, University of Birmingham, B15 2TT
Dr Spyros Sgouros	Birmingham Children's Hospital, Steelhouse Lane, Birmingham, B4 6NH
Dr Martin Vreugdenhil	Department of Neurophysiology, Division of Neuroscience, School of Medicine, University of Birmingham, Edgbaston, Birmingham, B15 2TT

Abbreviations

AADC	amino acid decarboxylase
ACTH	adrenocorticotrophic hormone
AD	Alzheimer's disease
AMPA	alpha-amino-3-hydroxy-5-methylisoxazole-4-propionic acid
ApoE	apolipoprotein E
APP	amyloid precursor protein
ATP	adenosine triphosphate
AVM	arteriovenous malformation
CBT	cognitive behaviour therapy
CRH	corticotrophic releasing hormone
CSF	cerebrospinal fluid
CT	computed tomography.
DISC1	disrupted-in-schizophrenia gene
DNA	deoxyribonucleic acid
ECG	electrocardiograph
ECT	electroconvulsive therapy
EE	expressed emotion
EEG	electroencephalogram
EPSP	excitatory postsynaptic potential
ESR	erythrocyte sedimentation rate
fMRI	functional magnetic resonance imaging
GABA	gamma-amino butyric acid
GAD	generalized anxiety disorder
GCS	Glasgow coma score
HD	Huntington's disease
5-HIAA	5-hydroxyindole acetic acid
5-HT	5-hydroxytryptamine (also known as serotonin)
HPA	hypothalamic-pituitary-adrenocortical
ICP	intracranial pressure
IIH	idiopathic intracranial hypertension
IPSP	inhibitory postsynaptic potential
IPT	interpersonal psychotherapy
LACS	lacunar syndrome
LP	lumbar puncture
LTP	long-term potentiation
MAOI	monoamine oxidase inhibitor
MHPG	3-methoxy-4-hydroxyphenylglycol
MMT	methadone maintenance therapy
MND	motor neuron disease
MPTP	1-methyl-4-phenyl-1,2,3,6-tetrahydropyridine
MRI	magnetic resonance imaging
mRNA	Messenger ribonucleic acid
MS	multiple sclerosis
MT	microtubules
NARI	noradrenaline reuptake inhibitor
NMDA	N-methyl-D-aspartate
NSAID	non-steroidal anti-inflammatory drug
OCD	obsessive compulsive disorder
PACS	partial anterior circulation syndromes
PD	Parkinson's disease
PET	positron emission tomography
PFC	prefrontal cortex
PHF	paired helical filaments
PHN	postherpetic neuralgia
POCS	posterior circulation syndrome
PTA	post-traumatic amnesia
PTSD	post-traumatic stress disorder
RNA	ribonucleic acid
SAD	seasonal affective disorder
SAH	subarachnoid haemorrhage
SPECT	single photon emission computed tomography
SSRI	selective serotonin reuptake inhibitor
TACS	total anterior circulation syndrome
TBI	traumatic brain injury
TCA	tricyclic antidepressant
TENS	transcutaneous electrical nerve stimulation
TIA	transient ischaemic attack
tPA	tissue plasminogen activator
TSE	transmissible spongiform encephalopathy
TSH	thyroid stimulating hormone
TTH	tension-type headache
WHO	World Health Organization

CHAPTER ONE

Brain basics

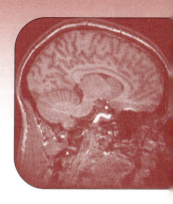

John Jefferys and Alison Cooper

INTRODUCTION

The aim of this chapter is to introduce some basic concepts about how the brain works and to define and explain words and phrases you will need to learn about the nervous system. This will act as a basis for you to go on to understand the brain disorders or diseases presented in the subsequent chapters.

We start by outlining how the human nervous system is organized in the body before focusing in on the brain. We go on to consider some of the defining features of the cells that make up the brain and how these cells function to enable us to carry out complex tasks.

1.1 What is the human nervous system?

The human nervous system is divided up into the **central nervous system** (CNS) and the **peripheral nervous system** (PNS). The CNS comprises the brain and the spinal cord which we can think of as being the overriding controllers of the body. The PNS acts as the link between the CNS and the various tissues and organs of the body.

The PNS is divided into somatic and autonomic divisions. The somatic division controls the activity of muscles which are attached to the skeleton; the **somatic nervous system** is sometimes called the voluntary nervous system because we can consciously alter its activity, for example, to move muscles in the legs when we want to walk. In contrast, the **autonomic nervous system** is sometimes called the involuntary nervous system since it controls functions in the body over which we have no conscious control such as heart rate, gut motility, and sweating.

> The CNS is made up of the brain and spinal cord.

1.2 What is the brain made of?

Like all the other organs in the body, the brain is made up of the basic unit of biological activity—the cell. Cells of the brain can be classified into two major types called **neurons** and **glia**.

1.2.1 Neurons

Neurons are the cells that enable the nervous system to carry out all the complex computational functions we know that it does. Each is only a few tens of micrometers (millionths of a metre) across at its thickest point, so it was only with the invention of the microscope that we realized that the human brain (which can be as big as 1.5 litres, weighing about 1.3 kg) was actually made up of these tiny cells, each of which weighs less than a microgram (one millionth of a gram). Estimates of how many neurons the human brain contains are in the range of 20–100 billion! Although we can't see individual neurons with the naked eye, if we slice a brain in half, we can see that the tissue is not uniform but has some darker areas (known as **grey matter**) and some paler areas (known as **white matter**, which will be discussed later in this section). The grey matter represents

---

extension: Brain vs computer

BOX 1.1

If the brain is made up of such a large number of calculating units (neurons), does it work just like a very large computer? There are some parallels between the brain and a computer. The brain receives information, stores some of this information in memory, performs calculations, and produces an output. There are important differences too. Most obviously, digital computers are made of silicon chips which have a fixed structure once they are made, whereas brains are made of living tissue—fats, proteins, nucleic acids—and continuously modify their detailed structure in response to previous activity.

In terms of performance, brains are much less precise than digital computers: they cannot compete on tasks such as finding large prime numbers or calculating square roots. That said, some estimates of the computational activity of the brain puts it at 100 million MIPS (million instructions per second), which is better than a high-end PC. Where brains really score over digital computers is in tasks such as pattern recognition, coping with unpredictable events, and developing original ideas.

Perhaps the most important differences are in the massively parallel structure of the brain and the modifiability of its component parts. Powerful computers today probably have around 1000 processors. The equivalent of the computer processor in the brain is less clear, but could be something like a cortical module of up to 1000 neurons, which would suggest we have hundreds of millions of them. The basic unit in the brain is the neuron, which receives between 1000 and 10 000 inputs from other neurons, which is much more complex than the transistor or its equivalent element in a computer chip which has just a few.

There are useful analogies between digital computers and brains, which are helping developments in understanding both systems, but we must not lose sight of the fact that they are very different.

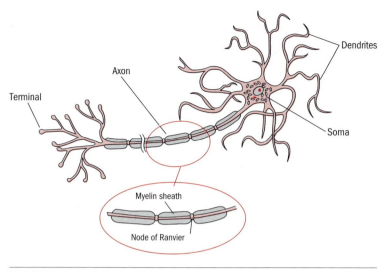

Figure 1.1 Stylized drawing of a motor neuron.

collections of neurons which have related functions and connectivity (each collection is known as a **nucleus**).

If we look at neurons through a microscope it is clear that they can appear to be different shapes. However, all neurons have the same basic plan, with different regions of the cell having specialist functions. This arrangement is shown in Figure 1.1.

The **dendrites** receive the incoming signals from other neurons. These many inputs then converge and are integrated together in the **soma**. The **axon** is a very fine, and some-times long, process that originates in the soma and conveys the information, in the form of electrical signals, along its length to the **terminals**, where chemical substances known as **neurotransmitters** can be released to allow communication with adjacent neurons.

The length of the axon varies between different neurons. Hence, even though they are very small in diameter, neurons can extend over long distances. For example, the giraffe has neurons that stretch for about 2 metres from its neck to its foot. This presents the neurons with a problem; they need to allow one end of the cell to communicate with the other end which may be some distance away. Neurons have developed a means of trans-mitting electrical signals to solve this problem. The processes involved in transmitting these electrical signals throughout the neuron will be discussed in more detail in the next chapter.

SELF-CHECK 1.1

Why do the different regions of a neuron have different functions?

One of the unique properties of the nervous system is that in order for it to perform its function of producing coordinated activity, the individual neurons must form networks which require them to be able to communicate with other neurons involved in the same function. The mechanisms by which neurons are able to do this will also be discussed in Chapter 2.

The axons which allow one neuron to communicate with others some distance away, tend to be bundled together in the brain in what are known as **tracts**. Looking at Figure 1.2,

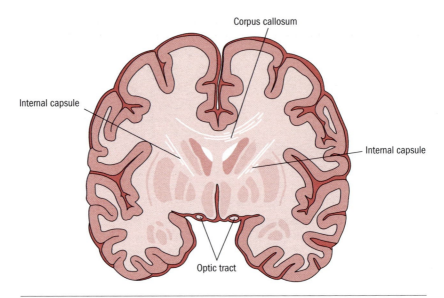

Corpus callosum

Internal capsule

Internal capsule

Optic tract

Figure 1.2 Coronal slice through the human brain showing some of the major tracts. Reproduced with permission from A. Siegel and H. N. Sapru. *Essential Neuroscience.* Baltimore, MD: Lippincott, Williams & Wilkins, 2005.

we can see that if we slice the brain in half, there are pale areas (known as white matter) visible with the naked eye; these are the bundles of many thousands of axons which we can see even though each individual axon is microscopic. This is an indication of how important the connectivity between neurons is.

> Neurons are connected to each other in large networks so they can process information and produce an appropriate response.

1.2.2 Glia

Glial cells are often described as the supporting cells of the nervous system. However, this description hides the extremely important role they play in allowing the nervous system to work properly. Indeed, it is estimated that the average human nervous system contains up to 10 times more glial cells than neurons. There are different types of glia which have different functions; here, we will consider two types that are found in the brain which are known as **astrocytes** and **oligodendrocytes**.

> Glia have diverse functions, all of which allow the neurons to perform optimally.

Astrocytes

These glial cells work to maintain an optimal environment for the neurons to function. For example, the astrocytes take up neurotransmitters and ions released by the neurons themselves. Recent evidence suggests that astrocytes may also play some role in modifying the activity of neurons by releasing some of the transmitters they take up. Furthermore, these cells act to regulate which substances can enter the brain from the blood system, allowing uptake of nutrients whilst providing some protection against, for example, invading microorganisms.

Oligodendrocytes

Oligodendrocytes play an extremely important role in facilitating the electrical signalling that is vital for allowing neurons to communicate with each other over long distances, as we will learn in the next chapter. They do this by wrapping their cell membranes around the axon to form what is known as a **myelin sheath**; we can see this in Figure 1.1. This myelin sheath is largely composed of lipids, which gives the pale colour to the bundles of axons and the white matter described above. The important property of the myelin sheath is that it acts as electrical insulation, which helps to increase the speed at which the electrical signals travel. It is clear that if the **myelination** of axons is defective, then neurons of the brain will not be able to communicate effectively.

 Multiple sclerosis is a disease characterized by defective myelination, and the mechanisms of this are discussed in section 10.3 on page 205.

1.2.3 Meninges and ventricles

The brain is a delicate structure and, as we shall see throughout this book, performs many critical functions. Therefore it is not surprising that it is well protected from damage. The **meninges** are the membranes that wrap and protect the brain. Between the bony skull and the neural tissue lie three layers of connective tissue, which are known as the dura mater, arachnoid mater, and pia mater.

The **dura mater** is a highly fibrous layer that lies next to the skull; in some disease states the space between the dura mater and the skull may become filled with fluid. Projections extend from the inner surface of the dura mater into the neural tissue and prevent gross movement of the brain within the skull when the head moves. The largest of these projections lies between the two **cerebral hemispheres**. The **pia mater** is attached to the brain itself and closely follows the contours of the folded surface of the brain. The **arachnoid mater** lies between the dura mater and pia mater. Between the arachnoid mater and the pia mater is the **subarachnoid space**, and strands of tissue that traverse the space.

The subarachnoid space is filled with **cerebrospinal fluid** (CSF), which, together with the strands of tissue traversing the space, cushions the brain against shear forces within the skull. In the healthy brain, the composition of CSF is constant, being broadly similar to blood serum, although lacking protein. However, certain pathological situations, for example CNS infection and multiple sclerosis, result in detectable changes in the composition of CSF which may form the basis of diagnosis.

 The procedure for obtaining a sample of CSF, and a description of its potential diagnostic value, is given in Box 5.8 on page 101.

The CSF is made by the **choroid plexus**, a specialized vascular lining of the fluid spaces that extend throughout the brain. These four fluid spaces are known as the **ventricles**. CSF slowly flows unidirectionally through the ventricles, from the lateral ventricles in each hemisphere, into the third ventricle in the centre of the brain, and then into the fourth ventricle in the brain stem. From here, it exits into the subarachnoid space from which it is reabsorbed at specialized sites in the brain and spinal cord.

SELF-CHECK 1.2

What are the differences between the functions of neurons and glia in the brain?

The brain is further protected by the **blood–brain barrier**, a physical barrier formed from the junctions between brain capillary endothelial cells, which are tighter than those between capillary endothelial cells in other parts of the body. Facilitation of the transport of certain key molecules into the brain, such as sugars and amino acids, or blockade of undesirable molecules from crossing this barrier, provides control of the chemical environment in the brain, and also excludes many unwanted compounds as well as infectious agents.

1.3 What are the key components of the nervous system?

The nervous systems of all animals exist to detect things that might affect the survival of themselves as individuals and their species—locating food, spotting predators, finding a mate, and so on—and to organize the appropriate responses. Nervous systems have a **sensory division**, responsible for detecting events and conditions, a **motor system**, responsible for allowing the animal to move and eat, and a **processing system** between the two.

Sensory nerves have specialized endings that convert some physical energy into signals that can then be carried along nerves. These sensory endings can be as complex as the eye and ear—that is, organs of special senses—or the nerve endings found in the skin that convert mechanical stimuli into senses of touch or pressure, or into potentially damaging stimuli that will be perceived as pain.

Motor nerves connect with muscles, making them contract (some invertebrates have motor nerves that can make muscles relax, but vertebrates such as humans do not).

The circuitry that links the sensory and motor systems may be rather simple, such as in a jellyfish, or it can be extremely complex, most dramatically in our topic—the human brain.

1.4 How is the brain organized?

Now that we understand the types of cells that make up the nervous system, we need to know how they are organized. The human brain comprises three regions: the cerebral hemispheres, the **cerebellum**, and the **brain stem**. If we look at an intact human brain, as illustrated in Figure 1.3, the most striking feature is the wrinkled surface of the cerebral hemispheres (known as the cerebral **cortex**) and the smaller grooved structure at the back of the brain known as the cerebellum.

The many millions of neurons in the brain need to be highly organized so that neurons with similar functions are close together.

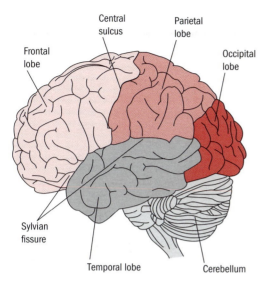

Frontal
lobe

Central
sulcus

Parietal
lobe

Occipital
lobe

Sylvian
fissure

Temporal lobe

Cerebellum

Figure 1.3 External view of brain showing the lobes of the cerebral hemispheres and the cerebellum. Reproduced with permission from M. F. Bear *et al.*, *Neuroscience: Exploring the Brain*, 3rd edn. pp. 11–13. Baltimore, MD: Lippincott, Williams & Wilkins, 2006.

---

extension: Do we only use 10% of our brains?

BOX 1.2

There is an urban legend that we only use 10% of our brains. In reality we each use all of our brain, as shown by electrical recordings and by functional brain imaging. It is true that large areas of the cortex are relatively adaptable, so that the roles of damaged areas can be taken over by surviving tissue, as happens following a stroke. This flexibility of function is important both as insurance against injury and illness, and as a means of coping with novel environments and situations—we did not evolve brain functions to deal with keyboards and computer monitors, or for driving cars, but the adaptability of our brains allows us to learn these and many other new tasks.

Where the notion that we only use 10% of our brains came from is not exactly clear. It was restated in *Uri Geller's Mind-Power Book*: 'In fact, most of us only use about 10% of our brains, if that', but it may originate from one or more of the following:

- Early studies of brain function found clear roles for relatively limited areas of cortex (notably the primary motor and sensory areas, and the speech areas), but researchers working then lacked the tools to find out what other parts of the cortex were doing.

- Karl Lashley's work in the 1930s showing that rats could still learn specific behavioural tasks even when large parts of their cortex had been removed, but this reflects the adaptability of the surviving cortex rather than the lack of function of the lost cortex.

- A misquote from Albert Einstein.

1.4.1 **The brain has two hemispheres**

If we look at the brain from above, as shown in Figure 1.4, it is clear that it is divided into two parts from front to back. Although the two halves of the brain, known as hemispheres, look identical, they can have different functions. For example, the nineteenth-century French

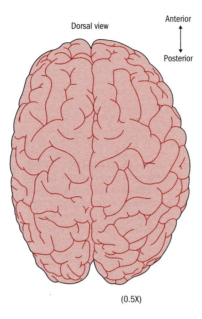

Dorsal view

Anterior

Posterior

(0.5X)

Figure 1.4 External view of the brain from the top showing the two hemispheres. Reproduced with permission from M. F. Bear *et al.*, *Neuroscience: Exploring the Brain*, 3rd edn. pp. 11–13. Baltimore, MD: Lippincott, Williams & Wilkins, 2006.

neurologist Paul Broca discovered that patients who had suffered a stroke that involved specific parts of the left hemisphere subsequently suffered from a problem with language, which was not seen in patients who had suffered a stroke in the right hemisphere.

About one third of left-handed people have their speech centres in the right hemisphere instead of the left. Overall the left hemisphere seems to be linked with behaviours involving mathematics and logic as well as language, whereas the right hemisphere seems to have more to do with spatial skills, music, and imagery. These differences only become clear in the few people who have the two hemispheres disconnected—the so-called 'split brain' operation, occasionally used to treat epilepsy. In the rest of us the two hemispheres work closely together.

> Many functions of the brain are mirrored in the two halves but some are specific to one side: perhaps the best example is language.

1.4.2 Cerebral cortex

Although the cerebral cortex appears to be uniform all over, in terms of function it is clear that different parts play distinct roles. Indeed, visual inspection of the cerebral cortex allows us to divide the cortex up into anatomical regions known as **lobes**, and these are illustrated in Figure 1.3.

During the early twentieth century, extensive microscopic investigations allowed the German neurologist Korbinian Brodmann to develop a more detailed classification of cortical areas into many different kinds (these are known as **Brodmann's areas**). These histological differences map onto functional specializations, so that Brodmann's number system is still used by researchers.

The grey matter containing the neuron cell bodies, dendrites, and final parts of axons, that is most of the computational structure, is only a very thin layer—about 2 mm thick —on the surface of the cerebral hemisphere. The white matter—essentially the cabling that joins the different parts of the cortex and other parts of the brain together—makes up a much larger volume. The reason the cortex is so extensively folded in humans is to increase its surface area without increasing its volume to a size at which the infant skull would be incapable of passing down the birth canal.

Much of our understanding of the localization of function to different cortical lobes has come from studying people who have suffered brain damage, perhaps as a result of traumatic injury or through clinical incident such as stroke. Clinical observations of such patients identified the parts of the cortex most directly concerned with sensory or motor function. The remaining parts of the cortex, the **association areas**, were more difficult, with the notable exception of the work by Broca and others on language.

More recently, with the development of imaging tools we can actually visualize the areas of the brain that become active when a person is undertaking a particular activity.

Frontal lobes

This is the largest lobe of the human cerebral cortex. Indeed, its size may be fundamental to aspects of brain function that we regard as uniquely human. It includes areas that play crucial roles in high level processes such as reasoning, planning, emotions, speech and problem solving. At its posterior end, next to the parietal lobe, is the primary motor area which is shown in Figure 1.5.

The primary motor area contains some of the largest neurons in the brain, the so-called **Betz cells** or **upper motor neurons**, which have axons that descend to neuronal networks responsible for the direct control of the muscles, down in the spinal cord and in the motor nuclei of the cranial nerves. As with most other pathways in and out of the brain, these descending motor axons cross over to the other side of the body by the time they reach the spinal cord, so the left frontal cortex controls the muscles of the right side of the body.

The primary motor area lies just in front of the central sulcus—the fold that separates the frontal and parietal lobes, as shown in Figure 1.3. It runs from the junction with the

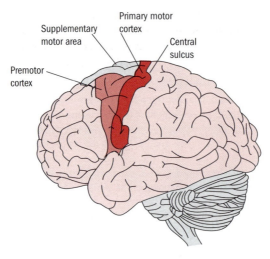

Figure 1.5 Location of the regions of the cerebral cortex which are concerned with motor control. Reproduced with permission from A. Siegel and H. N. Sapru. *Essential Neuroscience.* Baltimore, MD: Lippincott, Williams & Wilkins, 2005.

opposite hemisphere, near the top of the brain, in a narrow strip down the side of the brain until it reaches the Sylvian fissure, which separates the frontal lobe from the temporal. The primary motor area is organized in a somatotopic map (**somatotopy** simply refers to the fact that different regions of the body are represented by discrete regions of the cerebral cortex), so that the feet are represented at the end nearest the midline and the mouth nearest the temporal lobe. As we can see in Figure 1.6, this map is often represented as a **homunculus**—a distorted drawing of the body in which the area of the body region is proportional to the amount of brain tissue that represents it.

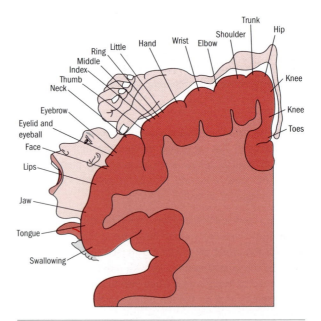

Figure 1.6 The motor homunculus. Reproduced with permission from A. Siegel and H. N. Sapru. *Essential Neuroscience.* Baltimore, MD: Lippincott, Williams & Wilkins, 2005.

The primary motor cortex does not directly control the muscles in most cases; instead, it controls the operation of groups of muscles. At least two areas further forward in the frontal lobe have important roles in initiating and sequencing complex movements of the muscles. These areas are called the **association areas** of the motor cortex—the premotor area and the supplementary motor area—and they can be seen close to the primary motor cortex in Figure 1.5.

An example of a simple movement is repeatedly touching the thumb to the forefinger, which can be done without appreciable changes in activity in the association motor areas. An example of a more complex movement is touching the thumb to each of the other fingers in turn: still not exactly a difficult task, but hard enough to need activation of the supplementary motor area as well as the hand region of the primary motor cortex. Rehearsing the movement in the mind, without actually executing it, results in activity in the supplementary motor area but not in the primary motor area. A similar disconnection of 'planning' movements from their execution happens during dreaming.

Other parts of the frontal lobe have more complex functions, including aspects of memory and strategic planning of behaviour—which often means inhibiting behaviours that would seem immediately rewarding. For instance, you are reading this book to help deliver a longer-term goal of learning more about the brain, and are probably inhibiting behaviours that would result in more immediate gratification.

The classic case that illustrates the kinds of roles played by the prefrontal lobes (the part of the frontal lobes closest to the front of the brain) is that of Phineas Gage. He was a mining engineer who had an unfortunate accident with a rod used to compress explosives in narrow holes and lost much of his prefrontal cortex, as shown in Figure 1.7. He survived, but radically changed in behaviour, losing most of his social graces, and his ability to plan his life more than a few minutes ahead.

SELF-CHECK 1.3

What are the main functions of the frontal lobes?

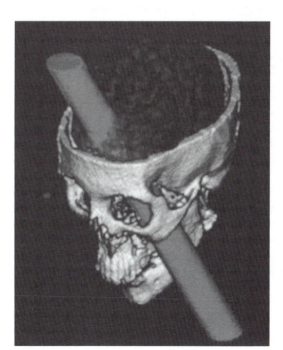

Figure 1.7 Illustration of Gage's head and tamping iron. Reprinted with permission from H. Damasio *et al.*, *Science* **264**: 1102–1105. Copyright 1994 AAAS.

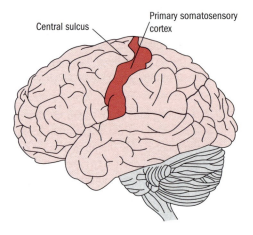

Central sulcus

Primary somatosensory cortex

Figure 1.8 Location of the primary somatosensory cortex. Reproduced with permission from M. F. Bear *et al.*, *Neuroscience: Exploring the Brain*, 3rd edn. pp. 11–13. Baltimore, MD: Lippincott, Williams & Wilkins, 2006.

Parietal lobes

The parietal lobes are largely concerned with sensory perception. The primary **somatosensory system** (that is the sensory areas that respond to receptors in the skin, muscles, and joints) lies just behind the central sulcus and is shown in Figure 1.8. There are several somatotopic maps, or homunculi, that roughly parallel the motor equivalents on the other side of the central sulcus, as we saw in Figure 1.6. The pathway from the skin, muscles, and joints travels up the spinal cord, crossing to the other side of the body, so that the central representation of the body is on the opposite side.

The sensations detected by the somatosensory system are touch, pressure, temperature, pain, and a less obvious faculty called **proprioception**—information on the positions of joints, lengths of muscles, and similar matters. Each of these kinds of sensation has its own specific receptors tuned to translate a specific kind of physical energy into neural signals. The different sensations are decoded into conscious perceptions in slightly different parts of the somatosensory cortex, but the details of this are beyond the scope of this book.

The rest of the parietal lobe is another association area, which combines information from several sensory systems, particularly the visual and somatosensory, providing an integrated perception of the outside world. Damage to these areas produces a strange syndrome called **sensory neglect** in which patients deny the existence of the part of the body or the sensory region affected.

Occipital lobes

The occipital lobes are at the back of the brain and are concerned with vision. They include the primary visual areas that were so elegantly delineated by Inouye, as described in Box 1.3, and by others more recently. The primary visual areas receive inputs from visual pathways that start in the retina of the eye, and pass through a structure called the **thalamus** (see section 1.4.3 below) where some processing occurs, before arriving at the primary visual cortex.

The primary visual cortex has what is called a **retinotopic map**, so that the visual field is laid out across the surface of the cortex in a systematic manner. It detects edges,

extension: Colour constancy

BOX
1.4

Wavelengths in the light that illuminates our world vary with the time of day and with artificial illumination. V4 corrects for this variation. The end result is that people do not look as though they have jaundice when illuminated by the relatively yellow light of tungsten bulbs, nor do they look frozen in the middle of the day when the illumination is biased to the blue end of the spectrum. Essentially V4 estimates the balance of wavelengths in the visual scene as a whole, and uses that information to estimate the colour of objects by the wavelengths reflected from them. The brain does this so easily, we usually do not notice the process. That there is a problem can be seen from pictures taken with outdoor film indoors (which will look yellower than expected) or indoor film outdoors (which will look bluer than expected).

movements, and different wavelengths of light which are then sent on to higher or association visual cortices. The higher visual cortices have less precise retinotopic maps than the primary areas, and they are responsible for rather complex calculations.

So, there is an area called V5 (or sometimes MT) that specializes in detecting the movement of objects. Another area, called V4, carries out the difficult calculations needed for colour constancy, as described in Box 1.4.

A large part of the cortex, perhaps one third of its area, representing at least 30 extensively interconnected areas, is concerned with vision. The ability of our brains to integrate the massive computations performed by these areas and to produce such a deceptively effortless perception of the outside world is truly remarkable.

Temporal lobes

The temporal lobes have the main sensory area devoted to hearing—the auditory cortex. Perhaps related to this is the presence of areas involved in language. Different parts of the temporal lobe contain higher visual areas associated with tasks such as recognizing and categorizing faces, objects, animals and so on; these are discussed in a little more detail below.

The temporal lobes contain regions that are essential for learning and memory, as we will see below when discussing the **hippocampus**. These memory skills differ on the two sides of the brain: damage to the left temporal lobe impairs memory for verbal content, whereas damage to the right impairs memory for non-verbal material such as music and images. Finally, the temporal lobe contains regions important in emotions, personality, and sexual behaviour.

Epileptic seizures in the temporal lobe can affect many of these functions, resulting in abnormal emotions, aggression, paranoia, and strange speech.

 Temporal lobe epilepsy is discussed in more detail in section 6.4.2 on page 111.

> The cerebral cortex contains many regions which have highly specific functions such as processing sensory information and controlling motor behaviour.

1.4.3 **Inside the cortex**

If we were to cut the brain in half between the two hemispheres, we would discover that beneath the cortex there are further specialized regions of grey matter.

Basal ganglia

The basal ganglia are a group of nuclei, as shown in Figure 1.9, which are extensively interconnected, both with each other, but also with other regions of the brain associated with controlling voluntary movement. Hence the output of the basal ganglia is directed towards the thalamus, which then sends the message on to the regions of the frontal lobes discussed above. The exact function of the basal ganglia in the normal brain is not fully understood. However, from studying humans who have damage to their basal ganglia, it is clear that they play a critical role in movement control. The best-known disorders associated with basal ganglia damage are Parkinson's disease and Huntington's disease.

Parkinson's disease is covered in detail in section 8.1 on page 151, and Huntington's disease in section 8.3 on page 171.

Hippocampus

The hippocampus is part of the temporal lobe. It is on the inward-facing, or medial, part of the lobe. It has long been a popular area for brain researchers. Although it is continuous with the rest of the temporal cortex, it has a slightly simpler cellular organization. It plays a crucial role in learning and memory, as most dramatically revealed by the famous case of HM, outlined in Box 1.5.

Work on experimental animals has shown that the hippocampus plays a crucial role in spatial navigation. The hippocampal neurons seem to signal when the animal is in

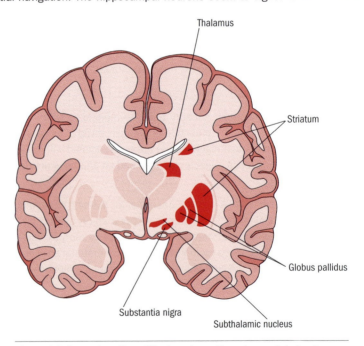

Figure 1.9 Coronal section of the basal ganglia and associated regions. Reproduced with permission from M. F. Bear *et al.*, *Neuroscience: Exploring the Brain*, 3rd edn. pp. 11–13. Baltimore, MD: Lippincott, Williams & Wilkins, 2006.

case study: Humans with damage to their hippocampus— the case of HM

BOX 1.5

In 1953, HM had surgery to cure him of epilepsy. (Case reports of patients conventionally use initials to identify them for the literature while retaining anonymity for the individual.)

As we will see in Chapter 6, surgery can be an effective treatment for some kinds of epilepsy. HM had severe epilepsy that failed to respond to the drugs available at that time. He had the hippocampi and adjacent mesial temporal lobe structures removed on both sides of the brain. At the time no one had any idea what the hippocampus did. The surgery cured the epilepsy but left HM with a permanent inability to remember anything that happened to him after the operation—a condition called **anterograde amnesia**. His case shows that memory comes in many forms. He had no losses in short-term memory, long-term memory from before the surgery, or procedural memories (things like learning to ride a bike), and he did not have marked changes in personality or IQ.

The surgery performed on HM removed a large amount of brain tissue around the hippocampus, and there have been considerable debates about which of the removed structures really were necessary for the memory loss. More recent patients have narrowed this down. One example was RB who had a stroke and then developed anterograde amnesia. When he died his brain was very carefully examined and the only substantial damage was within the hippocampi, arguing that in his case at least, this part of the brain is necessary for laying down long-term memory.

particular places in its environment. Recently, recordings from hippocampal neurons in humans revealed similar spatial properties (these recordings were made to prepare for surgery—to make sure the correct hippocampus was removed to cure temporal lobe epilepsy). The role in spatial navigation is probably a particular example of the general role of the hippocampus in what is called **declarative memory**; that is memory that you can speak about—memory for events or facts.

The hippocampus is also involved in emotion. It is part of the **limbic system** (see below). At first sight it can be difficult to reconcile these two roles: memory and emotion. There is some evidence that these roles are to some extent segregated along the length of the hippocampus, although it is true that memories can trigger emotions and emotions can affect memory.

Thalamus

The thalamus (shown in Figure 1.9) is a key relay station between the major sensory inputs—vision, touch/proprioception, hearing—and the cerebral cortex. The inputs from the sensory organs—eyes, skin/muscle, ears—all make synapses in their dedicated regions of the thalamus. These inputs allow some processing to take place before the signal passes on to the cortex. The thalamus also has other inputs. The cortex 'feeds back' to the thalamus, allowing some control over the stream of information, for instance allowing the focusing of attention on specific sensory inputs. Several brain stem structures also send inputs to the thalamus, changing the way it transmits information on to the cortex, and helping regulate states of arousal.

Hypothalamus

The hypothalamus, which lies below the thalamus, is evolutionarily an old part of the brain that is responsible for some of the basic functions that keep us alive; for example, by maintaining the body temperature via actions on the autonomic nervous system, and in regulating intake of food and drink. The hypothalamus also has an important role in regulating hormonal functions throughout the body as it interacts with the pituitary gland.

The limbic system

More details of the circuitry of the limbic system and its role in anxiety are given in section 13.3.4 and Figure 13.2 on page 276.

The limbic system is a collection of highly interconnected but dispersed structures, including the hippocampus, hypothalamus, amygdala, and cingulate cortex. This system appears to be involved in functions associated with emotional control. For example, people who suffer damage to these regions may show an altered ability to experience fear, and epileptic seizures can trigger fear and other emotional responses. For this reason the limbic system is sometimes described as providing emotional colouring to consciousness, a process that depends on its connections to the autonomic nervous system via the hypothalamus, and to the **neocortex** via the cingulate cortex.

1.4.4 Other regions of the brain

Cerebellum

The cerebellum is the smaller grooved structure illustrated in Figure 1.3, which is behind and below the cerebral cortex and attached to the brain stem. Its functions are mostly related to the coordination of movement, especially the timing of movements and the learning of new patterns of movement. Given its role in controlling movement, it has important links with both primary and association motor cortices, via the pons in the brain stem and the thalamus, and with the spinal cord. Recent work, using non-invasive imaging, shows that the cerebellum is also involved in cognitive as well as purely motor functions.

Brain stem

SELF-CHECK 1.4

Can you name three regions of the brain that contribute to motor control?

The brain stem can be considered as connecting the spinal cord with the rest of the brain. It consists of three regions: the **medulla**, the **pons**, and the **midbrain**. These regions are evolutionarily ancient, being found in organisms more primitive than mammals. This reflects the fact that they control some of the most basic functions required to keep an organism, including humans, alive. Examples of these functions include regulation of the cardiovascular system, regulation of the respiratory system, and the level of arousal which is concerned with the process of sleeping.

1.5 How does the brain process information?

In order for the brain to perform its functions, it needs to receive information about both the external environment and the internal environment of the body. This information then needs to be processed to attach meaning to it, which will allow the brain to then coordinate a suitable response. Broadly speaking, the information that the brain receives is classed as sensory information and the response that is made is classed as motor information.

1.5.1 The visual system as an example of sensory input leading to motor output

Vision is our dominant sense. Consider an apparently simple task such as catching a ball.

First, the ball needs to be identified: the visual input is processed to separate the ball from its background by features such as its shape, colour, texture, and movement—each of which is processed by a dedicated part of the visual cortex. These different features need to be immediately combined to provide the perception of the ball. They will allow some estimation of its properties based on memory and how it moves through the air —catching a fast-moving cricket ball or baseball is a very different task from catching a soft foam ball.

This visual information, along with information from the somatosensory cortex on the position of the body and limbs, reaches the association cortex that plans how to catch the ball—a process that needs prediction of its trajectory, and calculations of how to move the hand to the correct location to catch and hold it. The output then drives the motor system to move the arm and hand into the correct position, and then to grip the ball when it makes contact. Even a simple task such as this requires coordinated activity across large parts of the brain.

1.6 The plastic brain

From what we have discovered so far, you may be tempted to think that the brain is 'hard wired' or fixed in the way that it processes information. In fact the brain is able to adapt to new situations. Flexibility, or **plasticity**, of the connections in the brain is essential for our ability to learn and adapt to changing conditions.

It also is important when the brain is injured. Stroke is probably the most common way that the brain suffers localized injury, and we will cover this in more detail in Chapter 5. The key point here is that patients benefit from therapy and training for many years after the stroke occurred. This late recovery is largely due to the plasticity of the surviving brain tissue that allows it to take over some functions of the damaged tissue.

Similar kinds of plasticity can allow people who become blind to link their somatosensory system (the touch sense in their fingers) to their visual centres in the occipital lobes— a remarkable reassignment of function.

> **SELF-CHECK 1.5**
>
> Can the adult brain change its properties?

1.7 Neurons—from birth to death

1.7.1 Brain development

It is clear that in order to perform its extraordinary functions, the human brain needs to contain a vast number of neurons that are correctly interconnected. During brain development in the human fetus there are a number of key phases which must occur in the correct sequence. The complex details of these phases are beyond the scope of this book, but a summary of the key stages is given below.

The first phase is cell division or proliferation, which involves the massive increase in numbers of neurons. It has been estimated that at the peak, about 250 000 neurons are generated per minute.

During the **migration** phase these newly created neurons need to move away from the site of generation to take up their appropriate positions in relation to each other. In the case of the neocortex, the dividing **progenitor** cells are in a layer next to the ventricles. The cells destined to be neurons then migrate, along scaffold-like extensions of specialized glia, towards the cortical surface. The cells that will form the deepest part of the cortex arrive first so that those forming more superficial layers have to migrate past them. This process is orchestrated by coordinated chemical signals that tell the future neurons where to travel and when to stop.

Once the neurons are at their final positions they undergo **differentiation**, which results in them taking up their characteristic neuronal appearance, producing dendrites and extending axons, for example. These axons cannot be allowed to extend in random ways but must make connections with appropriate neurons. To facilitate this, there are a number of factors in the environment surrounding the axons which act to guide the axons to the appropriate target.

The final phase requires the formation of synapses (**synaptogenesis**) to allow the neurons to communicate with each other. The strengthening of useful synapses and the pruning of those that are less useful are crucial kinds of synaptic plasticity that allow the brain to wire up correctly during development.

> Brain development is very complex and needs to be precise. Errors cannot be corrected and can lead to a permanent disruption of function.

1.7.2 'Good' neuronal death

The death of neurons sounds like bad news, and indeed it is in many of the diseases we will introduce later in this book. However, neuronal death is also a key aspect of brain development. As we have just seen, neurons are 'born' and migrate to their correct locations. Wiring them up is a hugely complex process. One solution to this problem is to produce too many neurons and then to discard those that do not end up connected correctly.

Neurons secrete special chemicals called **neurotrophins**, or growth factors, which tell one another whether or not they have made the correct connections. If a neuron fails to detect the appropriate growth factors it will die, leaving only those neurons that do receive the necessary factors.

This kind of neuronal death is called programmed cell death. It is not just the cell dying and falling apart, but instead is an active, highly controlled sequence of changes known as **apoptosis**. Apoptosis depends on a complex series of intracellular chemicals, or signalling molecules, which ultimately allow the cell to break up into smaller fragments while keeping its outer membrane intact. (This is extremely important, because if the outer membrane breaks, it releases the cell contents, including enzymes and other potentially damaging material.) The small cell fragments can then be mopped up by scavenger cells and safely disposed of.

1.7.3 'Bad' neuronal death

Apoptosis is essential for normal development, but it can be triggered inappropriately, resulting in one of several neurodegenerative diseases, such as Parkinson's disease, or it may also follow some other pathological event such as stroke.

Apoptosis uses metabolic energy. If the cell's energy mechanisms are disrupted, and in particular the operation of its 'powerhouses', the **mitochondria**, then events that would otherwise trigger apoptosis result in the much more damaging process of **necrosis**, which is often associated with an excess production of free radicals (see Box 1.6). The release of cell contents during necrosis can kill neighbouring cells and also can trigger inflammatory responses, both of which make the damage worse.

One final class of cell death is especially important in the brain—**excitotoxicity**. Glutamate is the most common excitatory neurotransmitter in the brain, and we shall learn much more about this in Chapter 2. Unfortunately, it can also be toxic. If too much glutamate accumulates, as can happen during prolonged epileptic seizures or after the loss of blood supply as a result of a stroke, then it activates receptors that allow calcium ions to enter the neuron. This can trigger several enzymes that directly destroy the cell contents, or lead to the release of free radicals (see Box 1.6) that will also kill the neuron.

> **SELF-CHECK** 1.6
>
> What are the two main ways that neurons can die? How do they differ from each other?

---

extension: Free radicals

BOX 1.6

Free radicals are highly reactive chemicals that cells make as part of their production of energy from glucose. The mitochondria safely keep them contained and away from vulnerable parts of the cell. Cells contain enzymes to protect themselves from any free radicals that may spill out into the cytoplasm. One of these is called superoxide dismutase, which features in one form of motor neuron disease (see Chapter 8). If the enzymatic protective mechanisms break down, or the mitochondria are damaged, or too many free radicals are produced, then the excess free radicals will react with the cell contents and kill the cell.

Several components of our diet, such as vitamins C and E, are effective free-radical scavengers and can help protect us from damage associated with ageing and some diseases—which is a good reason for eating a varied diet.

SUMMARY

- The human nervous system can be subdivided into the central nervous system and the peripheral nervous system, the latter of which can be further divided into the somatic and autonomic divisions.

- Neurons and glia are the two major types of brain cell.

- Nervous systems have a sensory division for detecting events and conditions, a motor division that allows the species to respond, and a processing system between the two.

- The human brain is comprised of three regions: the cerebral hemispheres, the cerebellum, and the brain stem.

- The brain has two halves, or hemispheres, and some functions are specific to one side.

- The cerebral cortex can be divided into a number of anatomical regions known as lobes, and different lobes have specific functions.

- Beneath the cortex are further specialized regions such as the basal ganglia, hippocampus, thalamus, hypothalamus, and the limbic system, and again these are associated with specialized functions.

- The cerebellum is largely concerned with the co-ordination of movement.

- The brain stem consists of the medulla, the pons, and the midbrain and controls basic functions such as the cardiovascular system and respiration.

- Far from being 'hard wired', the brain can constantly adapt to new situations or diseases by making new internal connections; a feature known as plasticity.

- During development, new neurons are produced in vast numbers and complex chemical signalling ensures they move to the right position and make appropriate connections.

- Sometimes the brain may remove unwanted neurons through a programmed and regulated series of events known as apoptosis. However, in some disease states, neuronal death may also occur through necrosis and excitotoxicity.

FURTHER READING

The contents of this and the next chapter cover a vast area of our current understanding of neuroscience, and are intended only to provide the reader with sufficient background knowledge to allow them to understand the terminology and concepts presented in the clinical chapters that follow.

For those seeking a more detailed knowledge of the neurobiology of the brain, the following textbooks are recommended:

M. F. Bear, B. W. Connors and M. Paradiso. *Neuroscience: exploring the brain*, 3rd edn. Baltimore, MD: Lippincott, Williams & Wilkins, 2006.

A. Siegel and H. N. Sapru. *Essential neuroscience*. Baltimore, MD: Lippincott, Williams & Wilkins, 2005.

CHAPTER TWO

Brain function: from membrane to memory

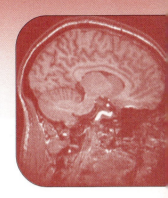

Martin Vreugdenhil

INTRODUCTION

We have seen in the previous chapter that our brain is not like a big computer; millions of processes can be run in parallel and the brain shows both flexibility and adaptability. In this chapter we look a little deeper into brain function.

We may see a single neuron as a sophisticated calculator; adding, subtracting, multiplying, and dividing inputs from other cells and responding with its own unique output. However, whereas a calculator always gives the same answer to an input, a neuron is more moody; sometimes sensitive to inputs, sometimes unresponsive, and it takes recent events into account in its calculations, as if it has memory. In a sense, each of our single neurons is a bit like our brain. In this chapter we look in more detail at how a single neuron works, and what determines these features.

We have also seen that our brain is not just a collection of individual neurons, but that they are interconnected, forming an intricate network that sends messages along many miles of axons. In this chapter we look at the way neurons communicate with one another, and how this communication can adapt to new demands. Finally, we consider how a neuronal network may store information as a basis for perception, learning, and memory.

2.1 What makes a neuron different from other cells?

Since it was shown at the end of the eighteenth century that the movement of dead frog legs was induced by 'animal electricity', various hypotheses have been proposed as to how the wire-like nerves might propagate electric signals and how this could cause muscular contraction.

In many ways a neuron is very similar to other cell types. What distinguishes a neuron from, let's say, a liver cell are two key features:

- The cell membrane is **excitable**; that is, it has special properties enabling it to generate electrical signals as a basis for communication.
- Neurons can vary in shape and can be very long. Although neurons come in a staggering array of different shapes, they all have the same basic elements of dendrites, soma, axon, and synaptic terminals as shown in Figure 1.1 on page 3, and have the ability to transmit an electrical signal from one end to the other.

> Two main features distinguish neurons from other types of cells in our body. These are the excitability of the cell membrane and the varied shape.

2.1.1 Excitable membranes

Historically, electrical activity in a nerve cell was thought to be analogous to electrical potential passing through connected wires. In reality, neurons turned out to be very different. If we apply an electrical potential at one end of an insulated wire, we can measure instantaneously almost the same potential at the other end, less a small potential drop due to electrical resistance.

A neuron, though, has a relatively high resistance because of the low conductivity of the cytoplasm, and, even worse, the membrane is not a good insulator. If we apply an electrical potential to one end of a neuron, most of the current escapes, and we measure next to nothing at the other end. So what makes the neuron so leaky?

The cell membrane is made of lipids that form an isolator which, like an electrical capacitor, can store electrical charge. At rest, the inside of the membrane is negatively charged: the membrane is polarized; it has a negative **membrane potential**. If we add positive charge to the inside of the membrane, the membrane potential will become less negative (we call this **depolarization**). However, the membrane potential will not stay depolarized, because the neuronal membrane is full of proteins that form pores, or **leak channels** that let the excess of charged ions escape from the cell. The ability to store added charge, and then lose it slowly through leak channels, is crucial for neuronal function and is further explained in Box 2.1.

2.1.2 Potassium channels

In addition to these non-selective leak channels, the membrane also has channels that let only potassium ions (K^+) through, and then only under specific conditions. **Ion pumps** keep the K^+ concentration inside the neuron 30–40 times higher than that outside.

If we look at the left panel of Figure 2.2, we can see that K^+ will diffuse out of the neuron through these **K^+ channels** from a region of higher concentration to one of lower concentration. This K^+ outflow makes the inside of the cell more negative than the outside, but this is not unlimited. Because the positively charged K^+ are attracted to the negatively charged inside of the neuron (remember, opposite charges attract), there will be a membrane potential where K^+ ions are no longer flowing out, even when the K^+

extension: Bucket analogy of a neuronal membrane

BOX 2.1

The neuronal membrane consists of a capacitor (lipids) and a conductance (leak channels). We will use an analogy for charging and discharging the membrane capacitor to appreciate how this determines neuronal membrane properties.

If we look at Figure 2.1, we can see the membrane as a leaky bucket; the size of the bucket equates to the capacitance of the membrane, and the holes in the bucket are the leak channels. The water flowing from the tap is like current that adds charge to the inside of the membrane and the water level in the bucket equates to the membrane potential

The empty bucket (panel a) represents the resting membrane potential. When we open the tap (panel b), the water levels

initially increase at a speed dependent on the current amplitude (how far the tap is turned on) and the size of the bucket, but as the water level rises, the water pressure through the holes increases until the leak current is equal to the injected current and the water level remains stable (panel c). If we turn off the tap, initially water rushes out and empties the bucket quickly (panel d), but as the water pressure falls, the last water just trickles out (panel e).

Note also from Figure 2.1, that the voltage change (bottom line) follows the current changes (top line) with a delay essential for neuronal function, as we will see in section 2.2.5.

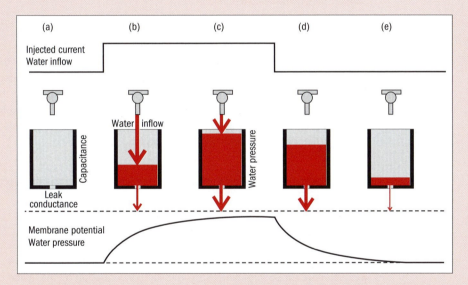

Figure 2.1 Bucket analogy of passive membrane properties. A useful analogy of the electrical properties of a neuronal membrane is a bucket with a hole, where the diameter of the bucket represents the capacitance and the size of the hole represents the inverse of the resistor. Injected current fills the capacitor/bucket (b) until an equal amount of current leaks out (c). It takes time to release the charge after the current is switched off (d,e).

channels remain open (Figure 2.2 middle), and normally this is about −80 millivolts (mV). So the membrane potential of a hypothetical neuron with only K$^+$ channels will be near −80 mV at rest.

The K$^+$ channels in neurons are special: they can open and close all the time, like garden gates in the wind, but the chance that they are open increases with the membrane potential. Therefore, we call these channels **voltage-gated**. In the complex structure of the channel protein there are voltage-sensitive parts that actually move when the

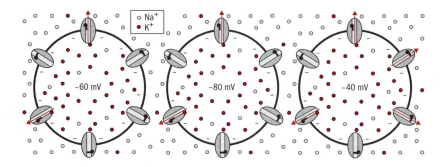

Figure 2.2 Potassium movement at different membrane potentials. Potassium ions (K⁺) ions will move down their concentration gradient through K⁺ channels out of the cell, unless (at −80 mV) the negative charge on the inside of the membrane attracts the positively charged K⁺ with a force equal to the diffusion force. When the membrane is depolarized (−40 mV) the net driving force for K⁺ increases and more voltage-gated K⁺ channels open; resulting in a large K⁺ current (coloured arrows).

membrane potential changes, thus opening and closing the K⁺-selective pore. This complicates the picture, because when we add positive charge to the inside of the neuron, the membrane potential depolarizes, and as a result of this, more voltage-gated K⁺ channels open. As we see in the right panel of Figure 2.2, K⁺ is less attracted to the membrane inside and now rushes out. This will cause the membrane potential to become more negative (**hyperpolarized**) towards −80 mV. So, voltage-gated K⁺ channels function as a negative feedback, counteracting depolarization.

> Opening of voltage-gated K⁺ channels hyperpolarizes the neuronal membrane potential.

2.1.3 Sodium channels

In addition to voltage-gated K⁺ channels, neuronal membranes also have channels that are selective for sodium ions (Na⁺). The Na⁺ concentration on the inside of the neuron is 10 times lower than that on the outside , which lets Na⁺ flow in unless we reach the potential where the inside of the membrane becomes so positive that no positively charged Na⁺ ion can enter (this is about +50 mV). Without influence from outside, most Na⁺ channels in a neuronal cell membrane will be closed, so some K⁺ will flow out, but very little Na⁺ flows in. The resulting membrane potential at rest is about −65 mV, and this is known as the **resting membrane potential**.

Like K⁺ channels, these **Na⁺ channels** are voltage-gated and the chance of opening the gate increases with membrane depolarization. So if the membrane potential increases, some Na⁺ channels open, Na⁺ flows in, further depolarizing the membrane, which then opens even more Na⁺ channels. So, Na⁺ channels function as a positive feedback, like a snowball effect, depolarizing the membrane close to +50 mV, where Na⁺ can no longer enter.

When we have both Na⁺ and K⁺ channels in a neuron, pulling the membrane potential in different directions, who will win? The answer to this is first the Na⁺ channels, and then the K⁺ channels. The different properties of Na⁺ and K⁺ channels (see Box 2.2

extension: Na$^+$ versus K$^+$ channels and the action potential

BOX 2.2

Na$^+$ channels differ from K$^+$ channels in two ways: First, Na$^+$ channels respond much quicker to membrane depolarization than K$^+$ channels. If we look at Figure 2.3, this illustrates the states of the Na$^+$ and K$^+$ channels and their currents in different phases of an action potential. Each phase takes about 1 ms.

In the resting condition (at 0 ms), most K$^+$ channels and almost all Na$^+$ channels are closed. A small depolarization can open some Na$^+$ channels, and before the K$^+$ channels are activated, the positive feedback process of the Na$^+$ current has depolarized the membrane potential within one millisecond to almost +50 mV (1 ms). Although Na$^+$ channels are still open, little Na$^+$ flows in because there is no longer the driving force.

If we now look at the 2 ms situation in Figure 2.1, we see that the membrane depolarization has eventually opened the slower K$^+$ channels, which now have a strong driving force for K$^+$ out of the cell (see also Figure 2.2), and soon the net flux of positively charged ions (cations) is outwards, which makes the inside of the membrane more negative. This will regain the driving force for the Na$^+$ channels, and you would expect that these Na$^+$ channels would regain strength.

However, the second key difference between Na$^+$ and K$^+$ channels is that Na$^+$ channels cannot stay open longer than about 1 ms, because they have two gates that need to be open at the same time for ion flow. The 'front door' opens quickly with depolarization, but the 'back door' closes slowly with depolarization, allowing for only a brief period of actual ion flow.

We see now that after 3 ms, when K$^+$ channels are still open and Na$^+$ channels all closed, the membrane potential will come close to -80 mV. In the whole process the membrane potential has changed from resting membrane level to almost +50 mV and back to -65 mV in about 2 ms.

Once the Na$^+$ channel 'back door' is closed, it takes some time at or below resting membrane potential (about 4 ms) before it opens, and allows another action potential to be started.

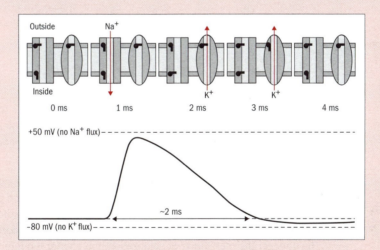

Figure 2.3 Action potential generation: the battle between Na$^+$ channels and K$^+$ channels. The state of the Na$^+$ channels (square, with two gates) and K$^+$ channels (oval, with a single gate) during sequential phases of action potential generation: The outside gates of both channels open with depolarization, the inside gate ('back door') of Na$^+$ channels closes with depolarization, allowing the characteristic membrane potential change in time called **action potential**.

for more details) cause a fixed sequence of events that is illustrated in Figure 2.3. We start with a net inflow of positive charged ions, followed by a net outflow of charge. This sequence causes rapid membrane depolarization followed by hyperpolarization. This whole process takes less than 1/500 of a second (2 ms), and is called **action potential generation**.

> Opening of voltage-gated Na^+ channels depolarizes the neuronal membrane potential.

SELF-CHECK 2.1

What are the most distinctive properties of excitable membranes?

> The presence of voltage-gated Na^+ and K^+ channels enables the neuronal membrane to generate action potentials.

2.2 How do neurons communicate?

In section 2.1 we have seen how neurons can generate action potentials. These action potentials allow neuronal messages to be sent around the brain, and in this section we look at the processes involved in the transmission of a message from one neuron to its target neuron.

2.2.1 How is the message coded?

Every time the neuronal membrane potential depolarizes (for reasons we discuss in section 2.2.5 below), and reaches the potential at which the Na^+ inflow is stronger than the K^+ outflow, this initiates the whole process of action potential generation. We call this membrane potential the **firing threshold**.

Once initiated, the action potential generation is an all-or-nothing process; that is, the amplitude and the timings of the changes underlying an action potential are fixed, so a message cannot be coded by varying the amplitude. Therefore, if the membrane remains depolarized above the firing threshold, several action potentials are generated. The stronger the membrane depolarization, the shorter the interval between consecutive action potentials (as can be seen if we look at panel (a) of Figure 2.4). In other words, depolarization of the membrane potential above firing threshold is translated into a signal of a variable number of action potentials coming at a variable rate. Small depolarizations result in low-frequency action potential firing; strong depolarizations result in high-frequency firing (panel (b) of Figure 2.4 shows us this relationship). This is called **frequency coding**.

Next we need to understand how this frequency-coded message is sent to other neurons and how they can receive and decode the action potential pattern.

SELF-CHECK 2.2

How is the neuronal message coded?

> The level of depolarization determines the firing frequency of the neuron.

2.2.2 How is the message conveyed?

The generation of action potentials is something that happens locally in a small patch of neuronal membrane that has been depolarized above threshold. However, the current that depolarizes this piece of membrane does not remain local but spreads, thus causing adjacent patches of membrane to depolarize above threshold as well. These patches will then go through the whole action potential generation process, which in turn pushes their neighbouring patches over the threshold, and so on.

In panel (a) of Figure 2.5, we can see the whole process of action potential generation similar to that shown in Figure 2.3, but now the different stages are happening at different places at any one time. This process is called **action potential propagation**.

The Na$^+$ channels in the wake of the activity cannot be activated again for a few milliseconds because these channels are now in the inactivated state (as shown in Figure 2.3).

(a)
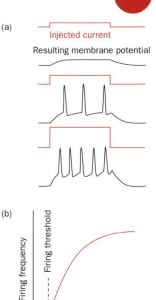

(b)

Figure 2.4 Neuronal message is frequency coded: (a) The response of a neuron (membrane potential: black lines) to increasing depolarizing current injection (coloured lines). The stronger the depolarization, the higher the frequency. (b) The theoretical relationship between depolarizing current and firing frequency.

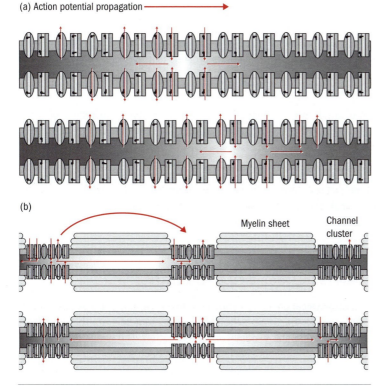

Figure 2.5 Action potential propagation: (a) The different stages of channel opening and currents (arrows) that underlie action potential generation (Figure 2.3) happen at the same time at different places along a neuronal membrane. The bottom graph gives the situation a fraction of a millisecond later and illustrates the wave of depolarization (light colours) followed by a wave of hyperpolarization (dark colours). (b) To speed up action potential propagation axons are partly covered by a myelin sheath with clusters of voltage-gated channels uncovered. Current influx in one cluster can now depolarize and activate channels in the next and, compared with the situation in panel (a), a much larger distance is crossed in the same time.

We could compare the process of action potential propagation with lighting the fuse of a firework. Once lit, the heat spreads and ignites the next bit and the spark moves steadily along the length of the fuse. Although the heat can also spread backwards, the burnt patch will not ignite again. However, if we consider the real speed at which an action potential moves along an axonal membrane, the fuse analogy pales. In some axons the action potential propagates at 100 m/s—as fast as a sports car. However, this speed can only be achieved by a special adaptation of the axon; fast-conducting axons are wrapped in many layers of membranes of glial cells (oligodendrocytes).

→ The role of oligodendrocytes and other glial cells is described in section 1.2.2 on page 4.

The **myelin** sheath and voltage-gated channels are clustered on uncovered bits of the axon, known as the **nodes of Ranvier**. The myelin sheath serves as an insulator; making the membrane of the axon less leaky. As we can see in the lower panel of Figure 2.5, the current that flows in through the Na^+ channels does not just depolarize the adjacent membrane, but activates the next cluster of Na^+ channels. The action potential thus jumps from one cluster to the next, a process known as **saltatory conduction**.

→ The consequences of impaired action potential propagation in multiple sclerosis are discussed in section 10.3.1 on page 205.

In multiple sclerosis, the insulating myelin sheet is destroyed. Without its insulator, the current cannot jump to the next cluster of Na^+ channels, and the action potential fails to propagate.

The fuse analogy fails also because the process is irreversible in a fuse, whereas in an axon, action potentials follow each other tirelessly, wave after wave, at rates of up to 400 a second.

The axon of a neuron is designed for fast and reliable propagation of action potentials towards the **synaptic terminal**. How then does the message pass to the receiving neuron?

> If one part of a neuronal membrane is depolarized above firing threshold, the action potential spreads quickly like a wave along the axon to convey the frequency-coded message to other neurons.

2.2.3 How is the message transmitted?

As there is no physical connection between two neurons, the message has somehow to cross the gap to the neuron the message is targeted at. This junction between nerve cells is known as the **synapse** or **synaptic cleft**. The end of an axon is called the **synaptic terminal**, and this is specialized to turn each action potential into a chemical message that can then cross the gap between the two neurons, in order to transmit the message onwards.

The chemicals specialized for this task are called **neurotransmitters**. Neurotransmitters are stored in the synaptic terminal in small spheres made of the same material as the cell membrane. These are called **synaptic vesicles** and are located close to the cell membrane lining the synaptic cleft.

In Figure 2.6, we can follow the processes that happen when an action potential (a) arrives at the synaptic terminal. The membrane depolarization in the synaptic terminal opens voltage-gated channels (b) that are selective for calcium ions (Ca^{2+}). Normally,

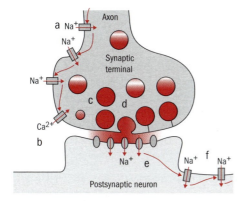

Figure 2.6 Neurotransmitter release: the chemical message. The presynaptic action potential (a) opens voltage-gated Ca^{2+} channels (b). Synaptic vesicles filled with neurotransmitter fuse with the membrane (d) by a process (c) triggered by Ca^{2+}. The neurotransmitter diffuses and binds to postsynaptic receptors, which open and (for glutamate receptors) depolarize the postsynaptic membrane (e), which can activate a postsynaptic action potential (f).

the Ca^{2+} concentration is kept very low in the neuron, but the influx of Ca^{2+} activates Ca^{2+}-dependent enzymes that trigger a complicated chemical cascade (c), causing some of the synaptic vesicles to fuse with the membrane (d).

These vesicles turn themselves inside out and release their content into the synaptic cleft, where the concentration of neurotransmitter may increase by almost a million times. The neurotransmitter diffuses across to the other side of the cleft, reaching the receiving neuron within a staggering 1 ms after arrival of the action potential.

> **SELF-CHECK** 2.3
>
> How is the neuronal message transmitted to the receiving neuron?

2.2.4 How is the message received?

At the receiving side of the synaptic cleft are specialized membrane proteins called **receptors**. Neurotransmitter molecules have a specific structure which fits into these receptor proteins, rather like a key in a lock. What happens next depends on which type of neurotransmitter is released, and to what type of receptor it binds to.

However, before considering the various classes of neurotransmitter and their receptors, it is important to point out that leaving such huge concentrations of the neurotransmitter in the synaptic cleft would cause problems. Receptors would quickly lose sensitivity and this would prevent a new message getting through. Mechanisms for dealing with this potential problem are considered in Box 2.3.

There are many different chemicals that can act as a neurotransmitter in the brain, but there are three major categories:

- amino acids, such as glutamate, gamma-aminobutyric acid (GABA), and glycine
- neuropeptides, such as vasopressin, somatostatin, and neurotensin
- monoamines (noradrenaline, dopamine, and serotonin) plus acetylcholine.

In the brain the peptides, monoamines, and acetylcholine have specialized modulating functions. We will learn more about these in Box 2.4 below and in section 2.3.4.

For now, we will consider the two major 'workhorses' of the brain; glutamate and GABA. A neuron or synapse utilizing glutamate as its neurotransmitter is termed **glutamatergic**. A neuron or synapse utilizing GABA is termed **GABAergic**. These two play opposing roles.

extension: How is neurotransmitter action terminated in the synaptic cleft?

BOX 2.3

As mentioned above, postsynaptic receptors would quickly lose sensitivity if left exposed to the huge concentrations of neurotransmitter resulting from synaptic release. There are three major ways in which the resting conditions may be restored and these are illustrated in Figure 2.7.

- Neurotransmitter may diffuse away as shown by (a) in the figure. This is relatively slow and takes place only at the fringes of the synaptic cleft.

- Neurotransmitter may be degraded by an enzyme, as shown by (e) in Figure 2.7. This is especially important in the neuromuscular junction where the neurotransmitter acetylcholine is removed rapidly by hydrolysis with the enzyme acetylcholinesterase, making sure the synapse is ready for its next action.

- An important way of removing neurotransmitter from the synaptic cleft is the active reuptake by **neurotransmitter transporters**, and again this can be seen if we look at Figure 2.7. The neurotransmitter may be taken up by the neuron itself (b)

or into adjacent glial cells (c). For GABA, for example, uptake into glial cells may be followed by conversion to an inactive metabolite (d), which is handed back to the synaptic terminal (f), which then converts it back to the neurotransmitter (h). Similarly, the enzymatic breakdown products of acetylcholine (see above) may be taken up into the synaptic terminal (g) and converted back into the neurotransmitter (h)

Drugs that block these reuptake mechanisms are important in the treatment of a number of diseases as they increase the concentration of, and prolong the presence of, the neurotransmitter in the cleft. For example, GABA reuptake blockers are used in the treatment of epilepsy. Another example is the monoamine transporter that recovers noradrenaline and serotonin from the synaptic cleft. Blocking this transporter increases monoamine levels in the brain, an objective in the treatment of depression. In contrast, the blockade of the reuptake of dopamine by recreational drugs, such as cocaine, can give a pleasurable sensation but can lead to drug dependence.

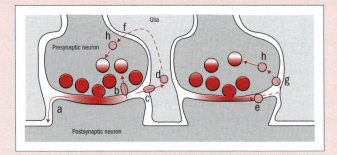

Figure 2.7 The fate of neurotransmitters. After release into the cleft, the neurotransmitter (solid arrows) can diffuse away (a) or be taken up by transporters into the terminal (b) or into glia (c). Neurotransmitter can be converted by an enzyme into an inactive metabolite (dashed arrows) in glia (d) or in the cleft (e). This metabolite then either diffuses (f) or is actively taken up (g) into the synaptic terminal, where it is converted back into the neurotransmitter (h).

Glutamatergic excitation

If we look again at Figure 2.6, we can see what happens when glutamate binds to a receptor on the postsynaptic neuron. Proteins in the membrane change shape to form a channel permeable for cations only. At rest mainly Na^+ flows into the postsynaptic neuron, which transiently depolarizes the postsynaptic membrane (shown as (e) in Figure 2.6) and this temporarily increases the chance that the receiving neuron responds with an action potential (shown as (f) in Figure 2.6). This is therefore called the **excitatory postsynaptic potential** (EPSP).

The glutamate receptor type that is mostly used in fast communication between neurons is the **AMPA receptor** (named after the compound that was first identified to activate this type of receptor). AMPA receptors are like the voltage-gated Na$^+$ channels described before; they open quickly but stay open only briefly. Even if there is still glutamate around, the channel closes, in a similar fashion to the inactivation gate of the Na$^+$ channel that closes when the membrane is still depolarized.

The other important glutamate receptor type is the **NMDA receptor** (again named after a compound that selectively activates it). NMDA receptors are more like the K$^+$ channels described before; they open slowly and remain open as long as glutamate is around. Along with Na$^+$, some Ca^{2+} ions also enter the cell through the NMDA channel, and this can increase the intracellular Ca^{2+} concentration triggering a wide variety of processes that involve Ca^{2+}-dependent proteins, some of which we will consider later in section 2.3.3.

GABAergic inhibition

When GABA binds to the postsynaptic **GABA$_A$ receptor**, it opens a channel through which chloride ions (Cl$^-$) flow into the neuron, because the intracellular concentration of Cl$^-$ is kept low. The result of a net influx of negatively charged ions into the post-synaptic neuron is a transient hyperpolarization of the membrane. This temporarily decreases the chance that the postsynaptic neuron fires, and is therefore called the **inhibitory postsynaptic potential** (IPSP).

> The frequency-coded message of the presynaptic neurons causes the release of neurotransmitter that activates receptors on the postsynaptic neuron, before it is removed from the synaptic cleft.

 More details of the structure and function of the NMDA receptor are described in Box 6.10 on page 126.

 More details of the structure and function of the GABA$_A$ receptor are given in Box 6.9 on page 125.

 The drug treatment of epilepsy is described in more detail in section 6.7.2 on page 123.

 The use of uptake inhibitors in the treatment of depression is described in section 14.7.1 on page 300.

 The role of dopamine in drug dependence is covered in section 16.3.1 on page 328.

2.2.5 How is the message translated?

The ultimate goal of neuronal activity is of course to pass the message on; that is to get the postsynaptic neuron to respond with one or more action potentials. This requires a postsynaptic depolarization that reaches the firing threshold.

As we can see in panel (a) of Figure 2.8, presynaptic activity causes a very brief gluta-matergic depolarizing current, which causes a slightly longer EPSP. If we return to our analogy of the leaky bucket (as described in Box 2.1), the depolarizing current resulting from the activity of one glutamatergic synapse is like adding a small cup of water; when emptied into the bucket it only causes a tiny increase in water levels. A single EPSP is not nearly sufficient to reach the firing threshold.

There are two basic ways by which we can generate an EPSP that is large enough to cross the firing threshold and trigger an action potential and these are known as **temporal summation** and **spatial summation**.

Temporal summation

Temporal summation makes the most of the slow time course of an EPSP as we can see in panel (a) of Figure 2.8. When a synapse is repeatedly activated at high frequency, the second depolarizing current arrives before the first EPSP has gone and its EPSP will add up. In the analogy of the leaky bucket, this equates to adding a second cupful

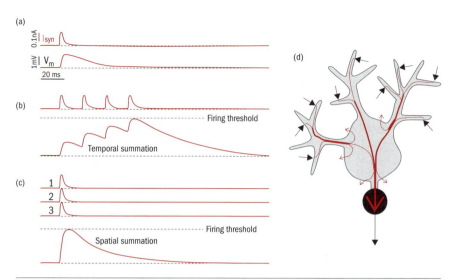

Figure 2.8 EPSP summation: (a) In line with the bucket analogy (see Box 2.1) the duration of an EPSP (black lines) is longer than the depolarizing current (coloured lines). (b) EPSP amplitude can be increased by temporal summation when the interval between synaptic currents is shorter than the EPSP duration, or (c) by spatial summation when the depolarizing currents of different presynaptic neurons coincide. (d) The flow of current from the synaptic sites to the soma illustrated as the flow of water into a lake, but because lots of current leaks out, the cell can only reach firing threshold (fill the lake) by collaboration of many synapses.

of water before the water of the first cup has leaked out. As we can see in panel (b) of Figure 2.8, a sequence of presynaptic activity generates a large staircase-like EPSP, so, the higher the firing frequency of the presynaptic neuron, the stronger the postsynaptic depolarization and the higher the chance of triggering an action potential (see frequency coding in section 2.2.1).

Spatial summation

The other way to reach the firing threshold is collaboration between glutamatergic synapses; a process we call spatial summation. If a few glutamatergic synapses are active at the same time, the charge of these small depolarizing currents adds up to cause a much larger EPSP, as we can see in panel (c) of Figure 2.8. In our leaky bucket analogy, this equates to emptying several different cups of water into the bucket at the same time.

Because glutamatergic synapses are spread all over the dendrites, we can consider the small dendrites as small brooks with the water (that is, the charge) converging into larger streams, which converge into rivers that eventually empty into a lake (this is illustrated in panel (d) of Figure 2.8). However, synaptic currents usually last only a few milliseconds. In our new analogy, the river bed and lake bed are porous (they leak) and the water dissipates steadily. Therefore, in order to generate a depolarization of the soma sufficient to cross the firing threshold, all of the collaborating depolarizing currents need to coincide for the charge to add up.

SELF-CHECK 2.4

What is the effect of synaptic release of glutamate and of GABA on the postsynaptic cell?

> EPSPs in the soma are small, but can evoke an action potential by temporal summation or by spatial summation.

Neuronal arithmetic

We have now seen that a neuron can make additions by spatial or temporal summation of EPSPs. In the same light we can see the activity of an inhibitory GABAergic synapse as a subtraction. When GABAergic and glutamatergic synapses are localized on a single dendrite, the net result of the activity of glutamatergic and GABAergic inputs determines the amount of charge that flows to the soma (or the lake in our analogy), as shown in panel (d) of Figure 2.8.

Many GABAergic synapses are located on the soma. If they are active, the 'lake bed' in panel (d) of Figure 2.8 becomes even more leaky, causing more of the depolarizing charge flowing from the dendrites into the soma to dissipate. The activation of these somatic GABAergic synapses can therefore be seen as division; it halves or decimates the amount of charge that otherwise would reach the axon.

If we consider that a single neuron receives information from about 10 000 glutamatergic synapses, on top of several thousand GABAergic synapses, we must realize that the frequency-coded messages of thousands of presynaptic neurons are converted into the graded postsynaptic membrane potential change, which is then in turn transformed into a new frequency code (as described in section 2.3.1)

> The frequency-coded message of many presynaptic neurons is integrated and translated into a graded synaptic depolarization by the postsynaptic neuron, which in turn converts this back into a frequency-coded message.

> **SELF-CHECK** 2.5
> Which factors determine whether or not a cell responds with an action potential to synaptic inputs?

2.3 How can neurons adapt to new situations?

Now we have discussed the way neurons communicate, we will next consider the reasons they need to do so.

What distinguishes animals and humans from plants is that they have survival aims, such as obtaining food, reproduction, and safety, and that they have mobility in order to reach these aims. The ability to adapt is essential. Our brains receive information about the environment, filter out the irrelevant information, and compare it with existing information in our memory. Aims and goals are identified, and achieving these may require different actions each time. Fortunately, our brain is perfectly designed to find solutions for every situation, by its ability to learn new tricks and to store useful experience or knowledge.

In contrast to computers, our brains make numerous misjudgements, but compensate for it by being creative and adaptable as they learn from mistakes.

In this section, we will use the example of a simple network to consider the ability of neurons to adapt to new situations. This property is called **synaptic plasticity**.

2.3.1 Association and changing neuronal connectivity

We will first consider the famous observation made by Ivan Pavlov around 1900, who trained dogs to salivate in response to a sound by pairing the otherwise neutral sound of a bell with offering of the dog's favourite food. After some time the bell became associated with the food, and the sound of the bell alone was now sufficient to make the dogs drool.

This was an adaptation of the way the brain circuits work; somehow the neurons responsible for salivation now received strong signals in response to the activity of the neurons activated by the sound of a bell, whereas before the training, this input to the salivation neurons was either non-existent or ineffective.

How can this **associative learning** be achieved by a group of neurons in a network? The psychologist Donald Hebb postulated in 1949, long before there was any scientific evidence for it, that if a cell A often fires at the same time as cell B, the connection between A and B becomes stronger. In short, 'neurons that fire together, wire together'.

We can consider this concept for the example with Pavlov's dog. Looking at the left-hand panel of Figure 2.9, we can imagine that before conditioning, the neuron responsible for salivation received an effective synaptic input from the neuron responding to the smell of food, but an ineffective input from the neuron responding to the bell ringing. After conditioning (right-hand panel), the connection between the 'bell-ringing neuron' and the 'salivation neuron' was made stronger, because it was (by pairing the inputs) made to fire together with a the 'food smell neuron', which already had a functional connection with the 'salivation neuron'. So the associated firing of the 'bell-ringing neuron' and the 'food smell neuron' eventually caused the 'bell-ringing neuron' to activate the 'salivation neuron' on its own; the dog had learned to associate the bell ringing with food.

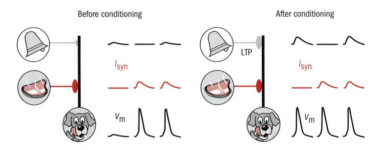

Figure 2.9 Plasticity in the brain of Pavlov's dog. Schematic representation of the simplest neuronal network that can account for learning to associate the bell with food. Before conditioning the synaptic current (grey lines) of the 'bell-ringing neuron' was too small to depolarize the membrane potential of the 'salivation neuron' (black lines) beyond firing threshold. After conditioning (pairing with the effective synapse of the 'food smell neuron' (coloured lines)) the strength of this synapse is increased and is now sufficient to activate the 'salivation neuron'. Before conditioning the EPSC of the 'food smell neuron' was able to evoke an action potential in the 'salivation neuron' but the 'bell ringing neuron' could not. After conditioning (pairing with the effective synapse of the 'food smell neuron'), the strength of this synapse is increased by LTP and is sufficient to activate the 'salivation neuron'.

There are two possible ways that this **Hebbian plasticity** might be achieved: by making new connections between simultaneously active neurons, and/or by changing the strength of the existing connections.

> Associative learning requires functional reorganization of neuronal connections.

First, we should consider how the connections were made in the first place. It is most unlikely that all of the billions of neurons in our brain receive instructions from our genome for making contacts with approximately 10 000 other cells. Some gross connectivity is definitely genetically determined, but most connections at the level of individual neurons seem to be widespread and rather random at an early stage of development.

A summary of the early stages of brain development is given in section 1.7.1 on page 17.

During a critical early period of development, new connections are formed dependent on activity, and unused connections are pruned. During later development and in the adult brain, physical growth of new connections is mainly associated with pathological conditions, such as trauma, stroke, or epilepsy, all of which we will consider in later chapters. However, in the adult brain, the strength and effectiveness of the connections can be modified, dependent on use and experience. Thus, detailed connectivity adapts and allows self-organization of the brain.

SELF-CHECK 2.6

Explain how synaptic modification may underlie associative learning.

2.3.2 **The Hebbian synapse**

The **Hebbian synapse**, which has the ability to modify its strength when presynaptic activity and postsynaptic activity coincide, has been centre stage for decades of brain research.

An early observation of synaptic modulation was made in a defining experiment where the synaptic response to the electrical activation of presynaptic axons was increased for several days after evoking a high-frequency train of activity in the same axons. This phenomenon was called **long-term potentiation (LTP)**.

Hebb had postulated that changes in synaptic strength require coinciding pre- and postsynaptic activity. LTP can be induced in many ways, but critical to all is that the stimulus needs to cause firing in the postsynaptic neuron. Simultaneous recordings from two connected neurons showed that evoking action potentials in one neuron or the other was not sufficient to modulate the strength of the synapses between them. LTP only occurred when the presynaptic and postsynaptic neurons are made to fire at the same time. So we see that synapses where glutamate is released around the time that the postsynaptic neuron fires are strengthened.

Hebb had postulated that changes in synaptic strength are synapse-specific. Experiments with intracellular recordings of two presynaptic neurons connected to a third (postsynaptic) neuron showed that only the synapse that released glutamate at the time the postsynaptic neuron fired showed LTP, leaving the other unchanged. So we see that only those synapses involved in the activation of the postsynaptic neuron are strengthened. Once again; neurons that fire together, wire together through LTP.

We know that a single EPSP is not sufficient to cause a postsynaptic action potential, but in section 2.2.5 we saw that, through spatial summation, coinciding activity in different synapses can trigger the required firing in the postsynaptic neuron. So presynaptic neurons need to cooperate in order to become strengthened. This is important because it allows association of different inputs.

If we return now to Pavlov's learned association between the sound of a bell and food (see section 2.3.1), let's think it through on a cellular level. Whenever the 'bell-ringing neuron' in Figure 2.9 is active together with the 'food smell neuron', the glutamate release at the 'bell-ringing neuron'–'salivation neuron' synapse coincides with an action potential in the 'salivation neuron'. Because the criteria for LTP are met, this synapse is strengthened until it is strong enough to make the 'salivation neuron' fire even without the input from the 'food smell neuron'.

SELF-CHECK 2.7

Under what circumstances does a Hebbian synapse change its strength?

> Associative learning takes place if a weak synapse is strengthened by pairing it with synapses strong enough to make the postsynaptic neuron fire.

2.3.3 What mechanisms underlie a Hebbian synapse?

Now that we have seen that LTP fulfils the requirements for associative learning proposed by Hebb, we will discuss the cellular and molecular mechanisms underlying LTP.

A naive synapse between cells that have not yet established meaningful connections has mainly NMDA-type glutamate receptors and only a few AMPA-type receptors. We can see in panel (a) of Figure 2.11 that when the postsynaptic neuron fires an action potential that coincides with the release of glutamate by this synapse, NMDA receptors are activated and allow Ca^{2+} to enter the cell (see Box 2.4 for more detail on how this occurs).

The resulting increase in intracellular Ca^{2+} concentration activates Ca^{2+}-dependent protein kinases, which are enzymes that trigger a complicated cascade of cellular events

---

extension: Coincidence detector

BOX 2.4

Much LTP research has concentrated on the CA1 region of the hippocampus, a structure critically involved in learning and memory. The synapse of axons of CA3 cells releases glutamate and the strength of the synapse can be potentiated. The activation of the NMDA receptor (Figure 2.10) requires simultaneous action of both the presynaptic neuron (agonist release/binding) and postsynaptic depolarization (action potential generation).

The reason for the second requirement is that the cation channel opened by binding of the agonist (glutamate/NMDA) is normally plugged by Mg^{2+} ions that are attracted by the negative inside of the membrane. To get rid of the Mg^{2+} plug, two things need to happen simultaneously: glutamate release/binding and postsynaptic depolarization.

The increased positive charge on the inside of the membrane repels the positive charged Mg^{2+} plug. Because the NMDA gated channel is also permeable to Ca^{2+}, a versatile intracellular messenger, the NMDA receptor becomes a **coincidence**

detector that increases the intracellular Ca^{2+} concentration, only when and where pre- and postsynaptic activity coincide.

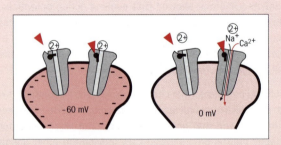

Figure 2.10 The NMDA receptor as coincidence detector. The NMDA receptor requires coincidence of presynaptic neuron firing (binding of glutamate) and postsynaptic depolarization, which expels the positively charged Mg^{2+} from the pore. The resulting influx of Ca^{2+} can 'switch on' Ca^{2+}-dependent processes required for synaptic plasticity (see Figure 2.11).

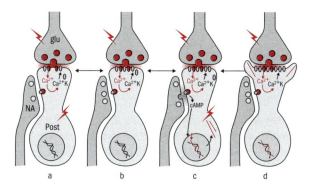

Figure 2.11 Long-term potentiation. The elements required for long-term potentiation are a presynaptic neuron, releasing glutamate (glu), a synaptic terminal releasing noradrenaline (NA) and a postsynaptic neuron (post) with receptors for glutamate and noradrenaline. A weak synapse (b) contains NMDA receptors (coloured) and a few AMPA receptors (grey). When glutamate is released coinciding with an strong depolarization of the postsynaptic cell, Ca^{2+} enters through NMDA receptor activation and triggers Ca^{2+}-dependent kinases (Ca^{2+} K) that facilitate insertion of AMPA receptors in the membrane (b). This potentiation of the synaptic strength is reversible unless the adrenergic receptor is co-activated and cyclic AMP is produced that activates transcription factors that cause the production of new proteins (c), which are used to consolidate the increased strength of the active synapse (d).

that eventually leads to an increase in the number of AMPA-type receptors inserted into the membrane (as shown in panel b of Figure 2.11). As a result, the next time glutamate is released by this synapse the EPSP will be bigger, and we have LTP.

But what do we mean by long term? If nothing else happens, the number of AMPA receptors and the resulting EPSP amplitude are restored to baseline levels within hours, whereas experiments have shown that LTP lasts for many days.

> Neurons that fire together wire together through use-dependent modulation of the synaptic strength, thus adjusting existing networks.

SELF-CHECK 2.8

How can an NMDA receptor function as a coincidence detector?

2.3.4 What determines the duration of LTP?

For longer-term potentiation we need structural changes, for example, in the amount of receptor proteins and the size of the synapse. To achieve this, it was discovered that the postsynaptic neuron needed an increase in the production of **cyclic AMP**, another important intracellular messenger molecule.

In panel (c) of Figure 2.11, we see that cyclic AMP activates nuclear proteins that cause a change in the transcription of genes and the production of new proteins, which are responsible for long term (hours to days) changes in the properties of synapses, but only those synapses that just have been potentiated (see panel d). An increase in cyclic AMP can be caused by activating the receptors for modulatory neurotransmitters like noradrenaline or dopamine.

The processes illustrated in Figure 2.11 demonstrate that we need three elements in order to potentiate synapses for longer than 2 hours:

- presynaptic activity
- simultaneous postsynaptic activity
- the release of modulatory neurotransmitters.

Noradrenaline is released from axons of neurons in deeper parts of the brain that are responsible for arousal. If something is behaviourally and/or functionally important for you because, for example, it is frightening or exciting, noradrenaline is released and those synapses that undergo Hebbian potentiation at that time will be potentiated for a long time, assuming that these inputs were relevant to what was causing the fright or excitement.

A different functional importance comes from experiences that are perceived as pleasurable. Nicotine, alcohol, recreational drugs, and sex all lead to the release of dopamine, which can also cause the increase in cyclic AMP required for LTP. Therefore, synapses that undergo Hebbian potentiation coinciding with the perception of pleasure will remain stronger, assuming that they are involved in processing information relevant for providing you pleasure.

SELF-CHECK 2.9

What determines whether synaptic modification will last?

> For consolidation of Hebbian modulation of the synaptic strength, the adjusted connections must be functionally and/or behaviourally relevant.

2.4 Memory: the search for the engram

LTP can change the strength of the connections between neurons, but what is this good for? Most scientists agree that synaptic plasticity provides at least a theoretical basis for learning and memory. It offers, for example, an explanation for associative learning (such as with Pavlov's dog). We can apply this principle of association of different inputs in many different situations, for example associating a red traffic light with danger.

Further subdivisions of long-term memory stores are described in section 4.4.2 on page 76.

Learning is the ability of the brain to both store information in memory, and to retrieve information from memory. There is a principal difference between **short-term memory** that we use for instance for remembering a telephone number we dial once, and **long-term memory** that we use for instance to remember our own telephone number.

Whereas short-term memory most likely represents the limited period of activity in a group of connected or related neurons, long-term memory requires the long-term modulation of the connections between neurons that respond to features in our environment in such a way that these connections represent relations and associations between these features. In this section we consider how this can be achieved.

There is widespread agreement that the process of retaining information over time requires some sort of structural change within the nervous system. This 'memory trace' or **engram** was originally defined as 'a permanent change wrought by a stimulus on any living substance'. Experience, in other words, must somehow make its mark upon the brain. However, opinions as to the nature of this engram continue to differ.

2.4.1 Barlow's grandmother cell theory of engrams

When we consider possible ways of how memory could be stored in cortical networks, a likely guess might be that we have a neuron specific for every individual feature of the world outside. A neuron representing an angle fires when it receives a message from neurons that fire in response to two different line orientations. A few neurons representing different angles may activate a neuron that is specific for a diamond shape, and the message from neurons representing a rectangle and two diamonds activates a neuron specific for a three-dimensional cube. The activity of the cube neuron combined with the activity of cells representing certain arrangements of dots makes a 'dice neuron' fire. Following this line of thinking, one can imagine building cells with more and more complex response properties. Eventually we end up with cells that respond only to one feature, for example, your grandmother. That is why this idea was dubbed the '**grandmother cell**' theory.

Recently, incredible specificity was shown in cells in the association cortex of the temporal lobe that responded only to pictures or drawings, or even the written name, of a famous actress. However, the 'grandmother cell' theory is challenged because it implies that we have a neuron for each possible (or even impossible) feature of the outside world, including for example, a purple banana.

Furthermore, you would forget your grandmother instantly if the cell that responded only to her accidentally died. On the contrary, lesion studies have shown that losing cells leads to little memory loss, and that other areas can take up the function of the damaged area.

2.4.2 Hebb's neuron assembly theory of engrams

As we have seen, Hebb proposed that neurons that fire together, wire together. He assumed that neurons that are simultaneously active have something in common. They may all have been activated by the activity of neurons that respond, say to the smell and the sight of a particular kind of food (remember Pavlov's dog). All the neurons that are now active will strengthen the connections they have between them, because the LTP criterion of coinciding pre- and postsynaptic activity has been met there. As a result this **assembly** of neurons with strong interconnectivity will form a functional unit that is active every time this food is perceived; this is the engram.

So learning is 'engraining' the memory engram in the brain through the generation of these assemblies. Every time the assembly of neurons forming the engram for this food is active, we perceive or remember this food. The number of neurons engaged in an engram of a mental object is not known: estimates range from tens to tens of thousands.

One interesting feature of this (hypothetical) engram concept is that even when the input is only partial—for example, when we smell food that we can't see—a significant number of the neurons in the engram for this food are activated directly by inputs conveying the olfactory (smell) message. Other neurons that would normally be activated by inputs conveying the visual message may now be activated through the potentiated connections with already active neurons in the assembly. It means that a partial input can give the full **perception**; you can almost 'see' the food when you only smell it.

extension: Grandmother cell versus neuron assembly

BOX 2.5

As we see in Figure 2.12, there are two ways of assigning sensory information to neurons. The left-hand diagram shows how five single grandmother cells (vertically orientated) would be activated by unique sensory information from each family member (horizontally orientated). In the right-hand diagram the same information activates a number of different cells.

Suppose we have only 5 cells to remember our family. If they act as 'grandmother' cells they can each respond to a family member; say your Gran, Dad, Mum, brother, and sister. With the same

5 cells, you can make 26 different assemblies of 2 or more active cells in the neuron assembly model (just 5 examples are shown in Figure 2.12), and this would allow you to store your whole extended family. So distributed memory is more 'economical'.

Memory distributed over different cells is also less vulnerable. If one neuron dies, say neuron 3 in the graph, we still have a unique set of cells active for each family member, whereas we would have lost the memory of Gran if memory was stored by 'grandmother' cells.

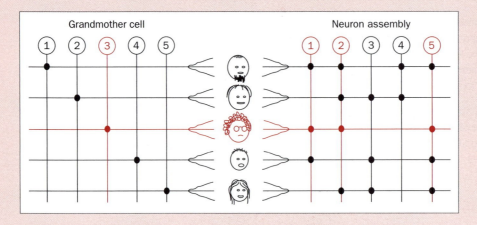

Figure 2.12 Alternative assignments of sensory information to neurons.

➡ The clinical features of Alzheimer's disease are discussed in section 7.2 on page 132.

Cells can also be part of more than one engram (as illustrated in Box 2.5), which allows an almost infinite number of memory engrams being formed in the vast number of interconnected cortical neurons in our brain. Another aspect is that, in contrast to 'grandmother cells', you won't lose a memory if a few cells of an engram are lost, although disorders such as Alzheimer's disease demonstrate that there is a limit to the number of cells that you can lose.

> The memory trace or engram of a feature is formed by strengthening connections between the assembly of neurons activated by the feature.

The cells forming an engram can be widely distributed throughout the cortex. Recent studies have revealed that even the perception of a 'simple' object causes widespread activity throughout the cortex. For an example, have a look at the left-hand panel of Figure 2.13 (but cover the right-hand panel). You may recognize a Dalmatian sniffing around in leaves. The black blobs initially did not activate an engram, but once you have given significance to this arrangement of black blobs, activated neurons distributed over your visual cortex potentiate their mutual connections and form a new engram. Next time you will recognize the Dalmatian in Figure 2.13 almost instantly.

SELF-CHECK 2.10

How does Barlow's grandmother cell theory differ from Hebb's assembly theory of the memory engram?

2.4.3 'Bottom-up' processing

The primary visual cortex receives frequency-coded information from the thalamus about basic features of a picture like intensity and contrast. The widely distributed neurons that respond to this information send a message to neurons in the visual cortex that respond selectively to, for example, lines at certain angles or blobs of a certain size. This information is then carried on to 'higher' visual areas in the cortex, which has groups of neurons that respond to more complex shapes.

This '**bottom-up**' processing of visual inputs can activate engrams for objects or letters, which in turn activate engrams for complex objects or words and, at a higher stage, scenes, faces, or poems. Another line of visual information processing activates engrams for different aspects of time; like movement, velocity, and acceleration. Where is the object in time and space? Where is it within a sequence of events? (Do you remember the cricket ball in section 1.5.1?). When did it happen? What does it lead to?

2.4.4 'Top-down' processing

Of course we can only perceive a Dalmatian in Figure 2.13 if we have seen a Dalmatian before, and already have an engram representing Dalmatians that provides an expectation of what to perceive. Neurons that make up the engram for a Dalmatian in 'higher' cortical areas have connections with neurons in 'lower' visual cortical areas. Because all these neurons have been active simultaneously when you studied the picture, LTP has strengthened the so-called '**top-down**' connections between higher and lower cortical engrams.

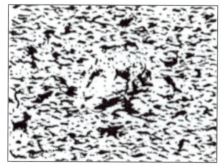
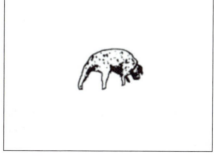

Figure 2.13 Distributed engrams. (a) Monochrome picture of an animal. Individual black areas activate neurons widely distributed over the visual cortex that together can give the perception of a Dalmatian wandering in the park. (b) The Dalmatian lifted out of (a) to help you perceive it. Adapted with permission from C. Tallon-Baudry *et al.*, *Journal of Neuroscience*, 1997; **17**: 722–734. Copyright Society for Neuroscience, 1997.

As a result the neurons of the lower visual cortex engram for a Dalmatian receive not only 'bottom-up' sensory inputs, but also 'top-down' inputs that represent the expectation or prediction of a Dalmatian. This increases the chance that the neurons in this lower level of the engram will actually respond to a rather low-quality image. So the brain tries to match 'bottom-up' sensory information to a 'top-down' template of what is expected or predicted from memory. This activates the whole of the engram for this Dalmatian, consisting of neurons distributed over different cortical areas. It is therefore difficult to locate a particular memory trace.

In the human brain, large areas of the cortex have no clear sensory or motor function, but are mutually connected with almost all other parts of the cortex, which allows all possible or impossible associations to be made. The volume of white matter (the axons) far exceeds the volume of grey matter (the cell bodies, dendrites, and synapses), which enables us to associate any input with anything already stored in engrams, and so continuously create new engrams through LTP. If the new engram is meaningful, behaviourally relevant, leads to improved survival and pleasure, or is for the good of others, it will be consolidated and becomes an established memory trace. As a result you may have even now connected some neurons into an engram for this concept.

SELF-CHECK 2.11

What is the role of long-term potentiation in the formation of memory?

SELF-CHECK 2.12

What is the role of top-down information processing?

> The coincident firing of neurons activated by a 'bottom-up' specific input will form an engram that embodies the memory for that input. Addition of 'top-down' inputs will help to activate the right engram which leads to the perception of the memory.

SUMMARY

In the first part of this chapter, we have seen what makes a neuron so special:

- Its excitable membrane, which enables it to fire action potentials that travel down the axon towards target cells.
- Its synaptic contacts on the dendrites of the target cell, which enable it to translate the frequency-coded message into membrane potential changes in the target neuron.
- Its integrative properties, which enable the cell to weight all synaptic inputs and to generate a new frequency-coded message.

In the second part of the chapter we have seen that synaptic plasticity provides:

- strengthening of synapses from neurons that are together able to cause their target neuron to fire
- neuron groups that fire and wire together to embody the perception of a memory
- formation and self-organization of 'bottom-up' and 'top-down' connections based on experience, relevant to help us to reach our goals.

FURTHER READING

The content of this and the previous chapter cover a vast area of our current understanding of neuroscience, and are intended only to provide the reader with sufficient background knowledge to allow them to understand the terminology and concepts presented in the clinical chapters that follow.

For those seeking a more detailed knowledge of the neuro-biology of the brain, the following textbooks are recommended:

M. F. Bear, B. W. Connors and M. Paradiso. *Neuroscience: exploring the brain*, 3rd edn. Baltimore, MD: Lippincott, Williams & Wilkins, 2006.

A. Siegel and H. N. Sapru. *Essential neuroscience*. Baltimore, MD: Lippincott, Williams & Wilkins, 2005.

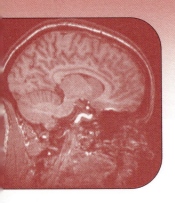

CHAPTER THREE

The genomics of brain disorders

Mary Keen and Alessandra Princivalle

INTRODUCTION

The science of genetics, the study of how characteristics are passed from one generation to another, is an old one, which has gained enormous momentum with the techniques of molecular biology and the sequencing of the human genome. We now have a draft of the entire genetic blueprint that encodes a human being, and we can understand that code, at least to a limited extent.

3.1 Introduction

A genetic sequence is the sequence of bases (adenine, thymine, guanine, and cytosine) found in **deoxyribonucleic acid** (DNA). This sequence of bases determines the amino acids which will be inserted into each and every protein; a region of DNA which encodes a single protein is called a **gene**.

> Genetic information consists of a sequence of bases in DNA. This sequence determines the structure of proteins.

DNA has a double helix structure, which consists of two strands of DNA linked together by **base pairing**, in which adenine is always paired with thymine, and guanine always paired with cytosine. Figure 3.1 shows the structure of these base pairs, and the overall helical structure of the DNA molecule. Base pairing is essential to the function of DNA; it allows faithful copies of the sequence of bases to be made in new DNA molecules, and it allows the synthesis of the template that is required for protein synthesis, a molecule of **messenger ribonucleic acid** (mRNA).

> Messenger RNA is a 'copy' of the DNA sequence which is required for the synthesis of protein.

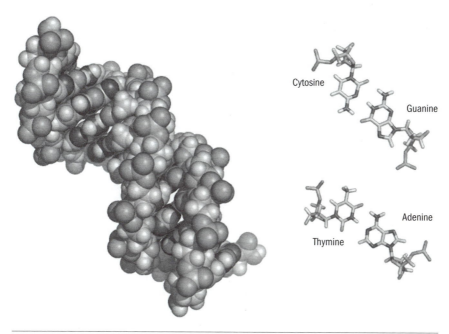

Figure 3.1 A space-filling model (where each atom is shown as a sphere) of the DNA double helix structure. Also shown is the structure of the cytosine–guanine and adenine–thymine base pairs, orientated as they are in the complete molecule and drawn to the same scale. These diagrams were derived from the real three-dimensional structure of DNA using the open-access molecular graphics programme PyMOL (DeLano Scientific LLC).

We understand the code that determines which amino acid is inserted into a protein, and we are starting to understand the information contained in the **non-coding regions** of the genes. These non-coding regions do not determine protein structure, but control when, and how much of, a particular protein is made, or expressed. We are, however, a very long way from understanding how all this genetic information is put together, or how changes (**mutations**) in individual genes affect the functioning of the organism as a whole. To put this into genetic jargon, we do not yet fully understand the way in which an organism's **genotype** (its genes) determines its **phenotype** (the way the organism looks and behaves).

3.2 Is there a genetic basis for brain disorders?

It has been clear for a great many years that some brain disorders are inherited; Huntington's disease (discussed in more detail in section 3.4.1 below, and in Chapter 8) is clearly passed from parent to child, with the offspring of an affected parent having a 50:50 chance of inheriting this devastating disorder. However, since the advent of molecular biology, there has been a greater and greater emphasis on the possible genetic basis of disease, be it diabetes, heart disease, or our tendency to develop depression, schizophrenia, or even alcoholism and aggression.

The genetic basis of disease is extremely complicated and is as yet rather poorly understood. For the purposes of this chapter we have divided the causes very broadly into three categories: chromosomal abnormalities, single-gene disorders, and multiple-gene disorders.

> Many brain disorders have a genetic component, but how important this component is, varies enormously.

3.3 What are chromosomal abnormalities?

The normal human cell has 46 **chromosomes**, in 23 pairs, one chromosome of each pair being inherited from each parent. Under most circumstances, the chromosomes are packaged in the nucleus, and cannot be teased apart. However, during cell division, the separate nature of the chromosomes becomes apparent under microscopic examination, and a skilled operator can distinguish the various chromosomes on the basis of their size and sort them into their various pairs.

This provides a basis for determining sex (the human female having two X chromosomes and the male one X and one Y chromosome) and also a mechanism for detecting any gross problems with the chromosomes, such as too few, too many, or any major malformations of the chromosome structure.

This **karyotype analysis** is usually done on fetal cells obtained from the amniotic fluid during pregnancy, or on the white blood cells. Figure 3.2 shows the full set of chromosomes obtained from an individual with Down's syndrome, as there is an extra copy of chromosome 21 (we discuss this in more detail in section 3.3.1 below). Can you work out what sex this individual is?

Figure 3.3 shows the unusual structure of a **fragile X** chromosome; a mutation in a single gene produces the constriction near the tip of the long arm of the chromosome. We consider this condition further in section 3.4.2.

How do chromosomal abnormalities occur? The proper answer to this is that we don't yet know, but most seem to occur as a result of errors during the separation of the parental chromosomes into egg or sperm cells, during the process known as **meiosis**.

> We possess 23 pairs of chromosomes which together contain all our genes. One chromosome from each pair is inherited from each parent.

Unsurprisingly, most abnormalities of chromosome number are fatal, resulting in death of the fetus before birth; more than 70% of spontaneous abortions occurring in the first 3 months of pregnancy are thought to occur as a result of chromosomal abnormalities. However, a few chromosomal abnormalities can be sustained, and 1 in 200 babies are born with such an abnormality.

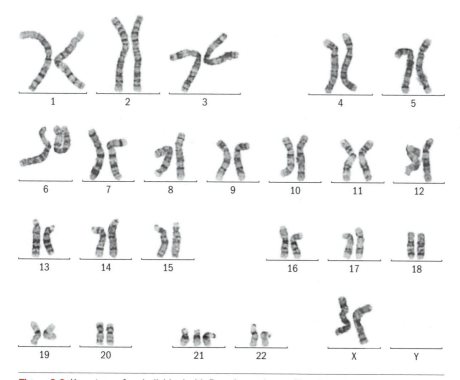

Figure 3.2 Karyotype of an individual with Down's syndrome. The chromosomes have been separated and arranged in their individual pairs. Picture courtesy of the Regional Genetics Laboratory, Birmingham Women's NHS Trust, UK.

Down's syndrome or **trisomy 21**, which results from having three copies of chromosome 21 (see Figure 3.2), is perhaps the best known of the chromosomal abnormalities, but there are others. Trisomy of chromosomes 13 and 18 can occur; they result in very severe mental retardation and many physical abnormalities, with more than 90% of affected children dying before the age of 1 year. Abnormalities of the sex chromosomes seem to be the best tolerated.

> Too many (or too few) chromosomes results in too many (or too few) copies of all the genes on that chromosome. Unsurprisingly, this can result in severe abnormalities.

3.3.1 **Down's syndrome**

Most people are familiar with Down's syndrome, which affects up to 1 in 700 children, the incidence increasing dramatically with maternal age. People with Down's syndrome have characteristic facial features, with slanting eyes, small ears and nose, and a large tongue, which tends to protrude. Mental retardation is mild to moderate and a variety of other problems may or may not be present, including heart defects, epilepsy, hypothyroidism, and coeliac disease. The severity of Down's syndrome can vary enormously; about two thirds of Down's syndrome fetuses abort spontaneously whereas many affected individuals

Figure 3.3 A 'fragile X' chromosome. The arrow shows the 'fragile' site. Picture courtesy of the Regional Genetics Laboratory, Birmingham Women's NHS Trust, UK.

can lead full and happy lives, living until 40 or 50 years old. Unfortunately there is a very high risk of older people with Down's syndrome developing Alzheimer's disease.

Most cases of Down's syndrome are due to trisomy of chromosome 21, and it seems that in 90% of cases the abnormality occurs during formation of the egg. How the non-disjunction of the chromosome occurs, and why it should occur much more frequently in older women, is not understood.

In 3–4% of cases there is a **translocation** of part of chromosome 21 to another chromo-some, often 14. In these cases, the total number of chromosomes is normal, but there are still three copies of the genetic material from part of chromosome 21, giving rise to a partial trisomy.

In an even smaller minority of cases, mis-sorting of the chromosomes occurs during development of the embryo, giving rise to 'mosaic' Down's syndrome, in which some cells have the normal 46 chromosomes, while others have 47, with trisomy of chromosome 21. Some forms of **mosaicism** arise from a normal embryo whereas others arise from an embryo with trisomy. On average, the symptoms of mosaic Down's are less severe than the non-mosaic forms, presumably because not all the cells in the body are affected.

> Down's syndrome is caused by the presence of an extra copy of chromosome 21.

---

extension: Genes involved in Down's syndrome

BOX 3.1

It has been recognized since 1959 that an extra copy of chromosome 21 is the cause of Down's syndrome, but which particular genes are responsible as yet remains unknown. It seems likely that no single gene is either necessary or sufficient to cause all the symptoms of Down's, but rather that various genes seem likely to be involved. Some of the genes which have come under particular scrutiny include:

- *SOD1*, a gene for superoxide dismutase, whose overexpression may give rise to the premature ageing associate with Down's syndrome
- *COL6A1*, one of the collagen genes, which may be implicated in the development of heart defects
- *CRYA1*, the gene for crystallin alpha-1, which is one of the key proteins in the lens in the eye; its overexpression may have a role in the premature development of cataracts, which commonly occurs in Down's
- *IFNAR*, a gene for the interferon receptor, whose overexpression might well be expected to interfere with the functioning of the immune system and other organ systems.

It is unclear why there should be such variation in the symptoms of Down's syndrome. Some mild cases may be due to duplication of an extremely small region of chromosome 21, such that fewer genes are affected. However, the severity of the full trisomy form also varies enormously. It may well be that some variant forms of the affected genes are more (or less) damaging than others. It is also likely that the affected genes will interact with other genes, and variation in these genes will affect the **penetrance** of the overexpressed genes. Even for a syndrome as comparatively well characterized as Down's, there is a great deal that we do not know.

3.3.2 Abnormalities of the sex chromosomes

Abnormalities of chromosomes 13, 18, and 21 appear to be comparatively well tolerated because these chromosomes carry rather a small number of genes. Abnormalities of the sex chromosomes seem to be even better tolerated. In the case of the Y chromosome, this is presumably because it carries very few genes.

The X chromosome, on the other hand is large, and replete with genetic information. However, cells have developed a mechanism to cope with the overabundance of X chromosome genes that would otherwise occur in all XX females: the phenomenon of **X inactivation** whereby one X chromosome in every cell is inactivated by **DNA methylation**.

> The X and Y chromosomes, which determine sex, are unusual in that these 'paired' chromosomes do not carry the same genes.

X chromosome abnormalities

Turner's syndrome occurs in about 1 in 2000 girls. It occurs when a girl inherits only one X chromosome, having the so-called XO genotype. Girls with Turner's syndrome are short and may have some physical abnormalities, including heart defects and a webbed neck. Unless treated with hormones, these girls will not undergo puberty.

Trisomy of the X chromosome can also occur, again in about 1 in 2000 girls. Girls with three X chromosomes tend to be taller than average, but they undergo normal puberty and are fertile. Learning difficulties are relatively common.

Y chromosome abnormalities

Maleness depends on the possession of a Y chromosome; thus individuals with Klinefelter's syndrome (two X chromosomes and one Y chromosome) are male. Like XXX females, they are taller than average, but these men are infertile. One in a thousand males has one X chromosome and two Y chromosomes. These XYY males tend to be tall and extremely physically active. They may experience learning problems, with delayed mental maturation and possibly delayed speech.

Do these syndromes affect the brain? They seem to, which is not surprising given the complexity of brain function and development. Thus although individuals with sex chromosome abnormalities are generally of normal intelligence, specific learning difficulties are very common.

For example, girls with Turner's syndrome typically have problems with mathematics and spatial concepts, whereas boys with Klinefelter's syndrome often exhibit poor judgement and impulse control. There have been studies suggesting that XYY men are slightly over-represented in the prison population, but the link between this condition and criminal behaviour is extremely questionable.

> Abnormalities of the sex chromosomes are well tolerated, but they are not without effect.

3.3.2 Other chromosomal disorders

Improved testing methods are allowing the detection of smaller and smaller chromosomal abnormalities, including translocations (where part of one chromosome becomes attached to another chromosome), inversions (where part of one chromosome is incorporated 'upside down'), and deletions (in which part of the chromosome is lost). Microdeletions can now be detected that reflect the loss of very small portions of the chromosome, which may in some cases reflect the loss of single genes.

Two distinct conditions can arise from small deletions in the long arm of chromosome 15; Prader–Willi syndrome and Angelman syndrome.

Prader–Willi syndrome

This syndrome is characterized by muscle weakness and **hypotonia**, borderline to moderate learning difficulties, small stature, incomplete sexual maturation, characteristic behaviours (including temper outbursts, stubbornness, and repetitive thoughts and mannerisms) and most notably, a constant and irresistible urge to eat, which, if unchecked, results in extreme obesity and early death due to conditions such as high blood pressure, diabetes, or respiratory problems.

Angelman syndrome

Angelman syndrome (which has also gone by the graphic, if politically incorrect, name of 'happy puppet syndrome') is characterized by severe developmental delay, near absence of speech, jerky and tremulous movements, hyperactivity, and frequent laughter and smiling. Affected individuals give every appearance of being genuinely happy. Epileptic seizures are also common and many people with this syndrome have a fascination with, and attraction to, water.

While they are interesting in their own right, what is particularly fascinating about these two quite different conditions is that they can both arise from identical deletions of the q11–q13 region of chromosome 15. How can the loss of the same region of genetic material give rise to such different phenotypes? It turns out that it depends on whether the deletion affects the chromosome inherited from the mother or from the father; a phenomenon known as **imprinting**.

> Prader–Willi and Angelman syndromes both arise from deletion of the same region of chromosome 15.

What is imprinting?

Surprisingly, all DNA is not equivalent. Some regions of your DNA carry an 'imprint' (a kind of memory) that depends on whether that chromosome was inherited from your mother or your father. Neither the reason for imprinting, nor the molecular mechanisms underlying it are completely understood, but it can clearly have important effects.

Imprinting results in inactivation of various genes; thus in the region of chromosome 15 affected in Prader–Willi and Angelman syndromes, different genes will be active in the maternal and paternal chromosomes. For example, *UBE3A*, the gene for ubiquitin ligase, an enzyme important for regulation of the levels of various proteins in cells, is inactivated in the paternal chromosome. Therefore, if this gene is deleted in the maternal chromosome, Angelman syndrome will occur; loss of the gene from the paternal chromosome would have no effect.

> Imprinting inactivates particular genes in a small region of a chromosome, depending on whether that chromosome was inherited from the father or the mother.

SELF-CHECK 3.1

What is meant by a chromosomal abnormality?

3.4 What are single-gene disorders?

Single-gene disorders occur when a mutation in a single gene has such a dramatic effect on the phenotype that affected individuals are noticeably 'abnormal'. Amongst these disorders are some that are inherited by classical **Mendelian genetics**. Huntington's disease, an **autosomal dominant** disorder, is one of the best known examples of these. However, the inheritance of other single-gene disorders can be decidedly more complex.

3.4.1 Huntington's disease

This inherited condition which results in selective death of nerve cells in the caudate nucleus, giving rise to choreoform (dance-like) movements, rigidity, and dementia, which typically appear between the ages of 40 and 50. The disease occurs as the result of mutation in a single gene on chromosome 4; the *huntingtin* gene.

In common with a number of other genes, the *huntingtin* gene contains a region of 'triplet repeat' in which three nucleotides (CAG in *huntingtin*) may be replicated many times. The size of the repeat region varies enormously within individuals, and up to 26 repeats can be found in the normal population. More than 40 repeats are associated with the development of Huntington's disease.

In *huntingtin*, the CAG repeat occurs in the protein-encoding region of the gene, and increasing numbers of CAG repeats leads to a corresponding increase in the length of a chain of glutamine residues in the huntingtin protein. There is a tendency for the length of triplet repeat regions to increase with subsequent generations, and in Huntington's disease, this is associated with the earlier and earlier onset of symptoms.

Quite why the mutant huntingtin protein leads to neurodegeneration is at present unclear. However, the mutant protein is more resistant to proteolytic breakdown than the normal protein, and its accumulation within neurons appears to underlie its neurotoxicity.

More information on the incidence and clinical manifestations of Huntington's disease is given in section 8.3 on page 171.

> Huntington's disease is due to expansion of a triplet repeat in the *huntingtin* gene.

3.4.2 Fragile X syndrome

Fragile X syndrome is the commonest form of inherited mental retardation, affecting about 1 in 2000 males. It is apparent from very early childhood and is characterized by moderate to severe mental retardation, large ears and testicles, a prominent jaw, and high-pitched, playful speech. Sufferers also tend to be hyperactive, and may exhibit connective tissue abnormalities such as heart valve problems.

Like Huntington's disease, fragile X occurs as the result of expansion of a triplet repeat in a single gene; in this case a CGG triplet in the *FMR-1* gene, found at position q27.3 on the X chromosome. However, in fragile X syndrome, the mutation does not affect the protein-encoding region of the gene; it is in the non-coding region. Thus the fragile X mutation does not affect the structure of the FMR-1 protein, rather it affects the way in which expression of this protein is regulated.

The normal population have in the region of 15–75 CGG repeats in the *FMR-1* gene. Fragile X syndrome occurs when the number of repeats is greater than 200. The disease seems to occur as a result of the 'silencing' of the *FMR-1* gene, probably via DNA methylation. Thus in fragile X syndrome, no FMR-1 mRNA or protein is expressed. The normal cellular function of the FMR-1 protein is not fully understood, but it is a cytoplasmic protein, found predominantly in neurons, and is likely to have a role in regulating mRNA expression.

> Fragile X syndrome occurs when expansion of a triplet repeat in the *FMR-1* gene results in the silencing of that gene, so that no FMR-1 protein is produced.

3.4.3 Fragile X tremor/ataxia syndrome

Interestingly, there is another disease syndrome associated with these same CGG repeats in the *FMR-1* gene. Parents and grandparents of boys affected by fragile X frequently have a 'pre-mutation' of *FMR-1*, with more than 80 CGG repeats. This pre-mutation results in a 2–4-fold elevation in the level of FMR-1 mRNA, although the levels of FMR-1 protein are normal, or somewhat reduced.

Carriers of the pre-mutation appear perfectly normal until they reach late middle age. However, from the age of about 50, they develop so called fragile X tremor/ataxia syndrome. Sufferers have severe intention tremor, parkinsonian symptoms, staggering, and generalized brain atrophy. Men with the condition also exhibit dementia, but for some reason women seem to be relatively protected from this particular manifestation of the syndrome. However, the pre-mutation is associated with premature ovarian failure in women; this does not occur in women who are carriers of the full mutation.

Thus it seems that a moderate number of CGG repeats in the *FMR-1* gene result in overproduction of FMR-1 mRNA and that this overproduction is associated with neurodegenerative changes. Why this should occur is unknown, but it seems likely that the excessive amounts of FMR-1 mRNA disrupt normal cell function in some way.

SELF-CHECK 3.2

What is the genetic basis of Huntington's disease?

This raises the intriguing possibility that the silencing of the *FMR-1* gene with the full mutation actually occurs as an attempt to limit the damage produced. Although this may be fine in women, who have another copy of the *FMR-1* gene, it is clearly a problem for men!

3.5 What are multiple-gene and multifactorial disorders?

An enormous number of different disorders seem to be associated with the effects of multiple genes, often in combination with lifestyle and/or environmental factors. Thus, although an individual gene may be a risk factor in developing a particular condition, the condition may not be manifest unless a person also has a number of other, quite different, susceptibility genes, plus the right (or rather, wrong) precipitating factors in their environment, such as stress, or a viral infection, as illustrated in Figure 3.4.

This means that it is not possible to predict with any certainty an individual's chance of developing a particular disorder, simply because they are known to possess one of the susceptibility genes. In addition, for many disorders, such as epilepsy, it seems that a whole variety of genes can be risk factors, so that mutation of any one of many different genes can give rise to essentially the same condition.

Although these complex disorders often cluster in families, they do not have a clear-cut pattern of inheritance. This makes it difficult to determine a person's risk of inheriting or passing on these disorders. Complex disorders are also difficult to study and treat because the specific factors that cause most of these disorders have not yet been identified. Such complex disorders include heart disease, diabetes, alcoholism, Alzheimer's disease, epilepsy, and schizophrenia.

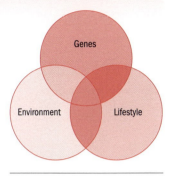

Figure 3.4 Multifactorial disorders occur when the presence of one, or a number, of susceptibility genes is combined with appropriate environmental and/or lifestyle triggers.

> Multifactorial disorders depend on genes, environmental factors, and lifestyle.

3.5.1 Epilepsy

Epilepsy (which is considered in detail in Chapter 6) is a chronic disorder of brain function characterized by periodic convulsive seizures, or 'fits'. Epilepsy seems to occur as a result of an imbalance between excitatory and inhibitory mechanisms in the brain, which give rise to the excessive and uncontrolled neuronal firing that constitutes a seizure. Electrical activity in the brain can be measured by surface electrodes to yield an EEG (electroencephalogram). Figure 6.2 on page 108 shows the EEG waveforms characteristic of someone undergoing an epileptic seizure.

In over half the cases of epilepsy, the cause is unknown. However, predisposing factors in other cases include damage to the brain due to a tumour or head injury, alcohol withdrawal (a lifestyle factor), infections such as meningitis (an environmental factor), and family history, which strongly suggests a genetic component. In this section, we will focus on these genetic factors.

 More information on other aspects of epilepsy can be found in Chapter 6.

The most common forms of inheritance in epilepsy are **multifactorial**, meaning that it is caused by several genetic and environmental factors acting together. Evidence for the role of genetic factors comes from the observation that people who have a parent or sibling with epilepsy are more likely to have epilepsy than someone in the general population. In the general population, about 1 in 100 (1%) of people have epilepsy, but for someone who has a close relative with the disease, the chances are increased to about 2–8%, depending on the specific type of epilepsy. On the other hand, there is a 92–98% chance for the close relative of someone with epilepsy of *not* having the same condition.

> Epilepsy, a chronic disorder of the brain that results in recurrent seizures and arises from an imbalance between excitatory and inhibitory neurotransmission in the brain, is an example of a multifactorial disorder.

Excitatory and inhibitory amino acid neurotransmission are introduced in section 2.2.4 on page 29.

In the last few years, scientists have identified over two dozen genes associated with epilepsy. Many of these are genes encoding for various components of the excitatory or inhibitory amino acid signalling systems in the brain.

Thus, mutations of the genes for the NMDA and AMPA receptors for the excitatory transmitter glutamate, and the GABA$_A$ and GABA$_B$ receptors for the inhibitory transmitter GABA, have been associated with epilepsy. However, the exact function of these, and other genes implicated in epilepsy, is not clear, and although these genes may account for a few types of epilepsy, there are many other forms of the condition where the cause remains unknown.

Further discussion of the role of these transmitter systems in epilepsy can be found in section 6.6 on page 117.

More recently, microarray technology (see section 3.6.2 below) has identified many genes which encode for a normal protein, but whose expression is either increased (up-regulated) or decreased (down-regulated) in epilepsy. Once again, many of these proteins are associated with either excitatory or inhibitory neurotransmission.

Thus, genes for NMDA, AMPA, GABA$_A$, and GABA$_B$ receptors have all been shown to be up-regulated in epilepsy. Also up-regulated in this disorder are *GAD-65* and *GAD-67*, the genes for glutamate decarboxylase, the enzyme that converts glutamate to GABA.

---

extension:　**Other genes involved in epilepsy**　　BOX 3.2

A whole variety of different genes have been implicated in epilepsy, including the genes for various neurotransmitter receptors, as outlined above. In addition, it seems that although the proteins encoded by various other genes may be normal, the amount of these proteins appears to be either too high (up-regulation) or too low (down-regulation). Some other examples of these genes include:

- **calmodulin**—an omnipresent calcium-binding protein that mediates a variety of cellular responses to calcium, and that is reported to be down-regulated in epilepsy

- **calponin**—an abundant actin-binding protein in smooth muscle reported to be up-regulated in epilepsy

- **fibroblast growth factor 1**—involved in the induction of cell growth or proliferation; has been reported to be both up- and down-regulated in epilepsy

- **haem oxygenase**—an enzyme responsible for the breakdown of haem (an important component of haemoglobin, the red pigment in blood cells carrying oxygen to tissues) and which is widely overexpressed in CNS tissue in a variety of brain diseases, including epilepsy.

With regard to some of the proteins responsible for the uptake of these neurotransmitters from the synapse, EAAT3 (an uptake protein for glutamate) is up-regulated, whereas GAT-1 (an uptake protein for GABA,) is down-regulated. All of the genes encoding for these proteins may be involved in some way in the generation or progression of epilepsy.

> Many genes are directly or indirectly associated with epilepsy.

3.5.2 Schizophrenia

Schizophrenia (which is considered in detail in Chapter 15) is really a group of severe mental disorders, characterized by distortions of reality, which result in unusual thought patterns and behaviours. In this section we will focus on the genetic factors associated with this condition.

 For more information on the role of genetic factors in schizophrenia, see section 15.3.1 on page 311.

The cause of schizophrenia is unknown. Genetic factors appear to be involved in producing susceptibility to the condition, as studies among identical twins show a 30–50% concordance rate; that is, if one twin has schizophrenia, the other twin is also affected in 30–50% of cases. Medical imaging studies have revealed various physical and physiological anomalies in some patients. Other research implicates mistiming of neural responses to stimuli in the brain. It seems likely that schizophrenia is due to a combination of influences, including the possession of susceptibility genes, and such environmental factors as viral illness or malnutrition in the patient's mother during pregnancy.

Recently, several specific genes have been convincingly associated with schizophrenia risk in a number of populations around the world. Some of the genes that have been studied most extensively include:

- catechol *O*-methyltransferase (*COMT*) (chromosome 22q), an enzyme that inactivates catecholamine neurotransmitters such as dopamine, adrenaline and noradrenaline
- *dysbindin-1* (chromosome 6p) and *neuregulin 1* (chromosome 8p), both associated with glutamate neurotransmission
- metabotropic glutamate receptor 3 (*GRM-3*) (chromosome 7q), a type of glutamate receptor
- *glutamate decarboxylase 1* (chromosome 2q), the enzyme that converts glutamate to GABA
- disrupted-in-schizophrenia 1 (*DISC1*) (chromosome 1q), essential for maintaining a complex of microtubule-associated protein at the centrosome.

> Schizophrenia, a brain illness characterized by disordered perception, thought disturbances, and disorganized speech, is another example of a multifactorial disorder.

3.5.3 Alzheimer's disease

Alzheimer's disease (which is considered in detail in Chapter 7) is a progressive disease of the brain that is characterized by impairment of memory, and a disturbance in at least one other thinking function (for example, language or perception of reality). It is not a normal part of ageing and is not something that inevitably happens in later life. Rather, it is one of the dementing disorders, which are a group of brain diseases that result in the loss of mental and physical functions.

The possible mechanisms underlying Alzheimer's disease are discussed in section 7.5 on page 144.

Alzheimer's disease is characterized histopathologically by the presence of two hallmark brain lesions: extracellular deposits of beta-amyloid in neuritic plaques, and intracellular neurofibrillary tangles. One explanation for the cause of Alzheimer's disease is that it results from an increase in the production or accumulation of the beta-amyloid protein which leads to nerve cell death.

Most cases of Alzheimer's disease do not appear to have a genetic cause. However, mutations in the amyloid precursor protein (APP) gene on chromosome 21, which is the gene responsible for the formation of beta-amyloid, and in the two presenilin genes on chromosomes 14 and 1 (*presenilin-1* and *presenilin-2*), are clearly associated with familial, early onset forms of the disease.

Mutations of the two presenilin genes account for about 5% of all cases of Alzheimer's disease. The presenilin-1 (PS1) and presenilin-2 (PS2) proteins are 467 and 448 amino acids long, respectively. Both are membrane proteins with multiple transmembrane regions and show a high degree of similarity in amino acid sequence between species, and thus also in protein structure. Their precise function is currently unknown.

SELF-CHECK 3.3

What is meant by a multifactorial disorder?

> Alzheimer's disease is a further example of a multifactorial brain disorder.

3.6 Gene hunting

Many years of research have demonstrated that vulnerability to brain illnesses, such as schizophrenia, bipolar disorder, early-onset depression, anxiety disorders, autism, epilepsy, and Alzheimer's disease, has a genetic component. Researchers are 'hunting' these disease genes because they are likely to be a vital key to deciphering what goes wrong in the brain in neurological or psychiatric illness, and may provide ideas for new therapies.

> Gene hunting is the seeking of the sequences responsible for, or involved in, a particular disorder.

3.6.1 Linkage studies

The traditional method of gene hunting involves linkage studies, in which the inheritance patterns of known sections of DNA (called **markers**) can be compared to an affected family's transmission of a particular disorder. If a known marker can be correlated with the presence or absence of the disorder, this finding narrows down the chromosomal location of the suspect gene.

Clearly, linkage studies are easier if large families are available who are heavily affected by the disease of interest. Studies in populations who are geographically or culturally isolated have been particularly useful. In these isolated populations, it is likely that the susceptibility genes for a particular disorder arose in one or two founding members. Furthermore, as a result of the isolation, fewer individuals make up the community's family trees and therefore there should be fewer variations of the disease genes within the population, which makes the search for these susceptibility genes a bit easier. Similarly, the genetic markers that are near the susceptibility genes are also likely to have limited variation, which further simplifies the search.

In many cases it appears that members of the family who do not have the disorder share genes with their ill relatives, which predispose them to similar but much milder characteristics. For example, relatives of people with autism or schizophrenia, although undoubtedly 'normal', may still display subtle cognitive problems.

Once a candidate gene has been identified, association studies are used to determine whether those people who exhibit the disorder really possess a version of the gene that is different from those without the disorder.

However, these studies often yield rather disappointing results; the complexity of many human brain disorders means that genes which may cause a disease within one family are very often absent from unrelated individuals with the same disease.

> Linkage studies assist in defining the region of DNA associated with a disorder. To do linkage studies, two genes must be considered; one a known marker and the other the gene for a disease, the location for which is unknown.

SELF-CHECK 3.4

What are linkage studies, and under what conditions are they best done?

3.6.2 Microarrays

One of the most up-to-date methods of hunting genes is a microchip array or **microarray**. Microarrays allow the detection of thousands of genes at once in a relatively straight-forward and cost-effective manner.

In simple terms, a microarray consists of a matrix, which may be a glass slide or a microchip, on to which thousands of minute 'dots' of known sequences are precisely placed, usually by robotic machinery. Research workers may then take RNAs from a tissue homogenate or single cell (such as a neuron), transform the RNAs back into DNA, and label them with, for example, a fluorescent chemical, and then apply this to the microarray matrix. If the cells under study are expressing a particular gene, it will bind with the complementary DNA 'dot' on the matrix, thus making it more or less fluorescent according to the level of expression of that particular gene. The dots on the array can then be read by specialized scanner equipment which can quantify the level of expression of each of the individual 'dots' (genes) on the matrix.

We can see the sort of output obtained from a microarray in Figure 3.5. This technique represents a major advance, because it is by no means easy to isolate potential disease-causing genes from the enormous number of genes that are expressed in the human brain, particularly when any disease may require the expression of multiple genes, each of which makes only a small contribution to the overall effect.

SELF-CHECK 3.5

With respect to gene hunting, what are the advantages of microarrays compared to other techniques?

> A microarray is a tool used to examine the expression levels of many genes simultaneously, and the intertwined interactions amongst them.

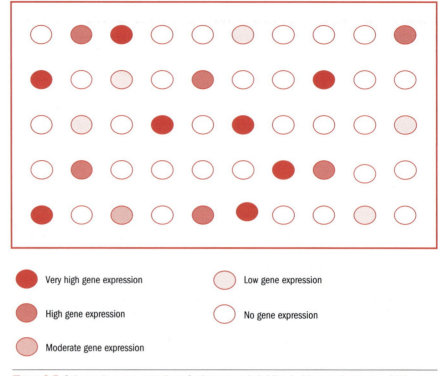

Very high gene expression

High gene expression

Moderate gene expression

Low gene expression

No gene expression

Figure 3.5 Schematic representation of microarrays hybridized with complementary DNA probes from a single neuron. Each dot on the matrix contains a known gene sequence, and we can see if the cells we are investigating are expressing the corresponding gene and to what extent.

Genome sequencing

The successful completion of the Human Genome Project has provided the precise sequence of the 3 billion DNA bases—adenine (A), thymine (T), cytosine (C), and guanine (G)—that make up the 24 human chromosomes. This has revealed the estimated 20 000–25 000 genes possessed by all humans, as well as the complex **non-coding** regions that control them. The availability of this information is already having an enormous impact on the study of human disease.

The sheer scale of the task of sequencing the human genome acted as an incentive to develop automated techniques for sequencing DNA, and these techniques are now well established. The various steps in sequencing are outlined in Box 3.3.

In genetics, sequencing is the determination of the primary structure of a bio-polymer. This results in a symbolic linear depiction summarizing the structure of the sequenced molecule. In the case of DNA, this consists of a sequence of A, C, G, and T bases.

extension: The various stages of DNA sequencing to determine a complete genome sequence.

BOX 3.3

1. The large sequences of DNA which make up each chromosome (50–250 million base pairs) are broken into much shorter pieces. This is referred to as the **subcloning step**.

2. Each of these short pieces is then used as a template to generate a set of fragments that differ in length from each other by a single base. These are the **template preparation** and **sequencing reaction steps**.

3. The fragments in each set are separated using a technique called **gel electrophoresis** (the **separation step**).

4. In this **base-calling step**, the final base at the end of each fragment is identified. Thus the original sequence of A, T, C, and G bases can be determined for each of the short pieces generated in stage 1. Automated sequencer machines are used to analyse the results; their output is a chromatogram in four colours showing 'peaks' that represent each of the four DNA bases.

5. Stage 4 yields blocks of sequence of about 500 bases long; the so called 'read length'. Powerful computers are then used to assemble these blocks into long continuous stretches representing complete chromosomes. These sequences are then analysed to detect any errors, protein-encoding regions, and other characteristics.

6. Finally, the completed sequence is submitted to one or more of the major public sequence databases, such as GenBank. In this way, sequence data from the Human Genome Project is made freely available to anyone around the world.

Therapeutic potential

The genomic revolution is producing a wealth of information regarding the influence of genes on our susceptibility to disease, but the promise of improved therapies for these diseases has not so far been forthcoming. The question remains: what good is all this new information?

One area in which the identification of a candidate disease-causing gene can have an immediate impact is in diagnosis. If your grandfather develops Huntington's disease, it is no longer necessary to spend your life in agonized limbo, watching for the first signs of the disease in your parent, and then yourself. You can have a test, and know, once and for all, with 100% certainty, whether or not you will develop the condition. Hhmm, maybe that's not such a simple decision after all? And what about conditions in which the genetic cause and effect is not so clear cut? There is already much debate of the ethics of deciding to abort a child known to be affected with Down's syndrome. What if we could test our unborn children for the gene for aggression, or laziness?

> Genetic testing for susceptibility to a disease is relatively easy to do, once a gene has been identified.

The great hope for understanding the genetic basis of disease is that it will improve therapy, either by gene therapy (replacing or repairing the defective gene) or by allowing the development of better-targeted conventional drug treatments. If we know the protein that is malfunctioning in a particular disease, it might be possible to develop drugs that specifically target the faulty protein, for example.

Much research effort, and even more money, is being expended in these areas, but so far without any marked therapeutic benefits. It seems to be a fact of life that genetic information can be obtained much more quickly and easily than information about what the proteins that are the products of those genes actually do.

> It is hoped that genetic information may provide new treatments for disease, but these are not yet making much of an impact.

It is not only in our susceptibility to disease that our genes make a difference, but also in the way in which we respond to drugs. **Pharmacogenomics** (the study of the impact of genes on our sensitivity to drugs) may well soon be making an impact in the way in which drugs are prescribed to treat, for example, depression or schizophrenia.

Many drugs used in the treatment of mental illness are metabolized by a particular enzyme, P450 mono-oxygenase CYPD26. There is considerable variation between individuals in the sequence of the gene for this enzyme, a situation known as **genetic polymorphism**, and in about 7% of the population CYPD26 is virtually inactive. This means that these individuals are unable to eliminate a variety of drugs effectively, and if given a 'normal' dose of these drugs they are likely to experience excessive and disabling side effects. There are plans to introduce routine testing for CYPD26 polymorphisms for psychiatric inpatients in the very near future.

SELF-CHECK 3.6

In what ways might understanding the genetic basis of brain disorders help in the treatment of these conditions?

> Genetics play a large role in determining how we respond to drugs.

SUMMARY

- Many brain disorders have a genetic component.

- Chromosomal abnormalities occur when there are too many, or too few, copies of a particular chromosome. Individuals with Down's syndrome have an extra copy of chromosome 21. An alternative name for the condition is trisomy 21.

- A variety of disorders of the sex chromosomes can occur, including Turner's syndrome (XO) and Klinefelter's syndrome (XXY).

- Small areas of chromosomes may also be duplicated, deleted, or inverted, which can also give rise to chromosomal abnormalities.

- Two very different conditions, Prader–Willi and Angelman syndromes, arise from deletion of the same region of chromosome 15. The different syndromes result because different genes are inactivated in this region, depending on whether the chromosome came from the mother or the father. This process is known as imprinting.

- Huntington's disease and fragile X disease both arise as a result of mutations in single genes. These are *huntingtin* and *FMR-1*, respectively.

- Most brain disorders appear to be multifactorial. These disorders will only be manifest if the patient possesses several susceptibility genes, and if they have been exposed to particular environmental or lifestyle factors.

- New disease genes (or genes that make one susceptible to a particular disease) are being identified all the time.

- The main therapeutic impact of these discoveries has been in the development of genetic tests.

- It is hoped that knowledge about disease genes will help provide improved treatments for these diseases in the future.

- Information regarding the genetic basis of variation in responsiveness to drugs is likely to be used in the near future to inform the use of conventional drugs in many conditions.

FURTHER READING

B. Alberts, A. Johnson, J. Lewis *et al. Molecular biology of the cell*, 4th ed. New York: Garland Science, 2002.
A comprehensive textbook of cell biology. The first chapter is particularly recommended as an introduction to the structure and function of DNA.

D. Stekel. *Microarray bioinformatics.* Cambridge: Cambridge University Press, 2003.
Everything you might ever have wanted to know about microarrays, plus useful instructions for using the wealth of genetic information available on the World Wide Web.

National Centre for Biotechnology Information <*www.ncbi.nlm.nih.gov/*>
This website provides access to the wealth of information available on DNA sequences and the effect of mutations in particular genes. OMIM (Online Mendelian Inheritance in Man) is exceptionally useful for finding out what is known about the genetics of any number of conditions. Genbank is one of the main sources for genome sequence information on humans (and other species).

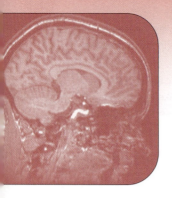

CHAPTER FOUR

Basic psychiatric concepts

Femi Oyebode and Tom Clark

INTRODUCTION

Psychiatry is the branch of medicine that deals with morbid psychological experiences. It is concerned with disorders of the mind, or **mental disorders**. There are some issues which distinguish psychiatry from other branches of medicine, and we look at these controversies first of all. Then we look at biological and psychological approaches to understanding mental disorders. Finally we look at some of the most important psychiatric symptoms and clinical concepts, before briefly considering the classification of mental disorders. There is further explanation of many of these topics within the later chapters which deal with particular types of mental disorder.

4.1 The nature of psychiatry

The roots of modern psychiatry lie in neurology, and many early psychiatrists began their careers within neurology. But for a variety of reasons, psychiatry is more complex than other medical specialities in terms of its influences, scope, and boundaries. We'll consider some of these issues in this section.

4.1.1 What is the mind?

This is a complicated question, which has no equivalent in other medical specialties. It is easy for a hepatologist to define the liver, or for a neurologist to define the central nervous system. But the mind is a nebulous and abstract concept, the nature of which is a matter for philosophy as much as for doctors.

The ideas of the philosopher Descartes have been particularly influential. As we can see in Box 4.1, Descartes formulated the idea that there is a fundamental distinction between the body (including the brain) and the mind, implying that there is no link between the two. This **dualism** finds resonance in many religious or spiritual philosophies and has been influential in medicine and psychiatry, leading to a split between physical medicine

extension: René Descartes and Cartesian dualism   BOX 4.1

The idea that the mind (or soul) is entirely separate from the body and of a different nature to the body was influentially endorsed by the philosopher René Descartes (1596–1650). Descartes has been described as the founder of modern philosophy. He invented the philosophical method of **systematic doubt**, according to which he determined that he would believe nothing that could in any way be doubted. In this manner he gradually rejected everything until he was convinced that the only existence of which he could be absolutely certain was his own. But he was even able to doubt that he had a body. Perhaps his body was some illusion created by an evil demon—a very unlikely scenario, admittedly, but nonetheless possible. On the other hand, he must still exist, because if he did not, it would not be possible for such a demon to deceive him. So the only aspect of himself of which he was absolutely certain, was his act of doubting. This led to the often-quoted maxim 'I think, therefore I am'.

So Descartes considered that the mind was fundamentally different in nature to the body, capable of existing separately from the body. In this sense he was very much a man of his time, when the idea of a separate soul, distinct from the body, was commonplace. This tended to lead to the assumption that disorders of the mind were also fundamentally different from those of the body, and that mental disorders would not be susceptible to physical medicine.

(which ignored psychological aspects of disease) and psychiatry (which ignored the importance of the biology of the brain in producing mental illness).

But Descartes' ideas have become much less influential in recent decades. Now the mind may be considered to be the activity of the brain, so everything that we see, feel, hear, think, believe, and otherwise experience is the mind. This conceptualization links the brain and the mind inextricably. So disorders of the mind must have origins within the brain, and disorders of the brain (or indeed the body) must also have a mental or psychological aspect.

 We will look at this split between biological and psychological medicine again in section 4.1.5 on page 66.

SELF-CHECK 4.1

What is the relationship between the brain and the mind?

4.1.2 How do we know when the mind is disordered?

The mind cannot be observed in the same way as the brain or other organs of the body. It is not susceptible to blood tests or other physical investigations. Brain scanning is of increasing importance in psychiatry, but cannot be said to be visualizing the mind itself. Clinical psychiatric examination is dependent upon carefully asking a patient about their subjective experiences—asking them to use their mind to examine their mind! So the assessment is intrinsically subjective and any **pathology** is itself liable to colour the way in which that pathology is presented to the examining doctor.

Furthermore, normal human experience is vast and wide-ranging, varying between individuals and between cultures. Determining what is within the realm of normal human experience and what is outside it, is not straightforward. Box 4.2 gives examples of how this can be a problem for a practising psychiatrist.

case study: Two examples of cases in which it might be difficult to tell whether apparent symptoms are pathological

BOX 4.2

A 42-year-old man was brought up in northern Pakistan. He married a UK citizen and came to live in England with his wife about 10 years ago. Since then he has continued to live predominantly within Pakistani communities and speaks very little English. Both of his parents have died recently in close succession. In addition he recently lost his job because the factory closed down. He appears to have developed a mental illness, perhaps in consequence to these stresses. He has come to believe that these bad things have happened to him because he has been cursed by djinns (spirits or demons). He now believes that his wife is in danger too. His wife agrees with him that djinns exist and may affect people in this way. But she thinks he is overly preoccupied with these thoughts and certainly doesn't consider that she is in any danger.

A 75-year-old woman has recently been widowed after 45 years of marriage. She is low in mood and has frequent thoughts that she may as well be dead too. She feels guilty about her husband's death and thinks she should have done more to care for him while he was ill. She finds it difficult to sleep and her appetite is poor. She often hears the voice of her husband talking, and on several occasions has thought that she has seen him walking around the house.

Pragmatically, psychiatric diagnosis relies on:

- demonstrating the presence of a defined **syndrome**—that is to say, a number of individual symptoms that are recognized as tending to occur together. It is unlikely that any single symptom would be sufficient to justify a diagnosis. Syndromal diagnoses occur in all branches of medicine but all psychiatric diagnoses are syndromal.

- considering the degree to which these symptoms are interfering with a patient's personal or social functioning, or the degree of distress they are causing the patient.

> All psychiatric diagnoses are syndromal in nature.

4.1.3 Why are some people opposed to mainstream psychiatry?

The reliance on syndromal diagnoses, together with the other conceptual complexities referred to above, leaves psychiatry in a vulnerable position. The absence of independent and objective criteria for establishing diagnosis lays psychiatry open to the criticism that clinical judgements are subjective and rely solely on the authority of the clinician. A psychiatrist would argue that the presence of a syndrome implies some form of illness or disease, but for others, the absence of a demonstrable underlying physical pathology implies that no such pathology is present.

The anti-psychiatry movement had its heyday in the 1960 and 1970s, but remains active today. Proponents argue that the whole concept of mental illness is flawed, that

> **extension:** The anti-psychiatry movement and abuses of psychiatry
>
> **BOX 4.3**
>
> --
>
> The anti-psychiatry movement is really a collection of individuals or bodies who share a variety of concerns about the practice of psychiatry, rather than being a single coherent movement. But they have in common a fundamental challenge to the basis of psychiatry, particularly biological psychiatry. The movement developed in the context of 1960s counter-culture, with leading proponents such as R. D. Laing in the UK and Thomas Szasz in the United States.
>
> Anti-psychiatrists argue that mainstream psychiatry relies too much on a biological paradigm for understanding mental illness, stigmatizes people by using categorical diagnoses, and does not qualify as a science according to usual criteria. They also argue that emotional and psychological problems or individual differences should not be considered as illness. For example, R. D. Laing stated, 'the experience and behaviour that gets labelled schizophrenic is a special strategy that a person invents in order to live in an unliveable situation', illustrating his view that severe mental illness should be seen as a strategy to communicate distress, rather than being labelled as illness.
>
> Other issues that are important to the anti-psychiatry movement include a perceived vulnerability of psychiatry to being influenced by large pharmaceutical companies, and the use of physical treatments, particularly electroconvulsive therapy.
>
> But perhaps the most controversial issue is the use of mental health legislation to detain people against their will. Although most psychiatrists would argue that this is occasionally necessary, for some it is wholly unjustified. There are certainly examples of situations in which psychiatry has been misused, often for political ends. The detention of political dissidents in psychiatric hospital in the former USSR and in China are often given as examples. In recent years the UK government has proposed detaining people with **personality disorder** who are considered to pose a risk to other people, even when no effective treatment is available. Some mainstream psychiatrists consider this to be ethically unacceptable.

psychiatrists inappropriately medicalize social problems, and that psychiatry is a tool of social control rather than a legitimate branch of medicine. You can read more about the anti-psychiatry movement in Box 4.3.

SELF-CHECK 4.2

Why is psychiatry more vulnerable to challenge than other branches of medicine?

4.1.4 What is the scope of psychiatry?

The scope of psychiatry may be said to include:

- minor emotional disturbances that are understandable reactions to environmental or psychosocial stress
- profound psychological change that is unheralded by significant or meaningful stress
- disturbances of personality that have a pervasive influence on behaviour such that the person or others suffer
- psychological changes that are directly the consequences of demonstrable organic brain change
- psychological and behavioural consequences of the use of substances such as alcohol, cannabis, cocaine, or heroin.

But this is not without controversy and disagreement, even among psychiatrists. For example, a woman may be struggling with bereavement after the death of her husband; perhaps she is finding it difficult to cope with looking after her young children and is weighed down by the various practical issues that need to be resolved. Her emotional state may be considered entirely understandable and even usual, but should this preclude her from receiving support from mental health services?

Another individual might experience repeated episodes of severe **psychosis** because he has schizophrenia. Clearly, such a patient should receive all the help and treatment that mental health services can offer. But if his psychotic episodes are in part precipitated by his persistent drug misuse, does he still warrant such treatment? It is very important that psychiatry avoids the value-laden judgements that such debates tend to produce.

Some people believe that the scope of psychiatry should include giving a complete account of human behaviour, not simply of clinical disorders but also of human motivation and behaviour in social and political life, and in art and religion. Such an expansion in scope would embrace all branches of human knowledge such as history, anthropology, literature, and art, and is likely to render the task of psychiatrists unduly large. A particular area of importance is in the understanding of criminal behaviour. Psychiatrists frequently provide evidence to the criminal courts about such issues and some take on a role in treating criminal behaviour, the most common example being sexual offending. But this is controversial, and not within the realm of mainstream psychiatry.

4.1.5 Psychology or biology?

Modern psychiatry was born out of neurological practice in the second half of the 1800s, fuelled by the demonstration of biological pathology for diseases which caused severe psychiatric symptoms, such as epilepsy and late-stage syphilis infection. In 1873, the famous English psychiatrist Henry Maudsley stated, 'the battle has been won and the victory is complete; no one . . . pretends now that [mental illnesses] are anything more than the deranged functions of the supreme nervous centres of the body'. But this biological, brain-based, and reductionist approach to mental illness was short-lived.

As the 1900s approached, Sigmund Freud abandoned his previous neurological practice and began to develop his theories of psychoanalysis, treating patients with various psychological problems, though not those with the most severe forms of mental illness. Nonetheless his theories of the mind became enormously influential and were applied by others across the whole spectrum of psychiatric disorders. This led to a dramatic paradigm shift in psychiatry and a resurgence of a dualist approach—the brain was forgotten and all mental illnesses were understood solely in psychological terms.

Cartesian dualism is discussed in section 4.1.1 on page 63.

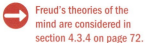
Freud's theories of the mind are considered in section 4.3.4 on page 72.

Since the 1970s mainstream psychiatry has re-embraced the importance of the brain and biology, leading to a resurgence of biological investigation and treatment of mental disorder.

The debate over whether a psychological or biological paradigm is the most appropriate approach for understanding mental disorder continues around the fringes of psychiatry today. But mainstream psychiatry has finally adopted a more mature position, recognizing that mental illnesses may be conceptualized in a variety of ways that are not mutually exclusive. So when considering the causes of mental illness in a patient, psychiatrists adopt an eclectic approach encompassing biological, psychological, and social factors. Similarly, these same groups of factors may be used in developing treatment plans for patients. For some patients and for some illnesses, one or other approach may seem to hold the most promise, but none is ever irrelevant.

> Clinical psychiatry often uses an inclusive biopsychosocial paradigm to understand mental disorder.

We next consider biological and psychological ways of investigating and understanding mental illness; these topics are covered in more detail with regard to specific disorders in later chapters.

4.2 What biological factors are important in understanding mental illness?

Although psychiatric diagnoses are all syndromal in nature, so diagnoses do not encompass theories of aetiology, there are a variety of ways of investigating biological correlates of mental illness. We will take an initial look at these here, but they are all covered in more detail with regard to specific disorders in subsequent chapters.

4.2.1 Are mental illnesses genetically determined?

Many psychiatric disorders are known to run in families. This is demonstrated by family studies. Other forms of genetic study such as twin and adoption studies confirm that for many disorders, particularly bipolar affective disorder and schizophrenia, this familiality is genetically mediated, rather than being due to a similar upbringing. Box 4.4 explains these types of study in more detail.

More recently, molecular genetic studies have begun to produce promising results in relation to these genetically mediated psychiatric disorders. Molecular genetic studies actually look at variations in the chromosomes and the genes they contain to see if particular variations can be linked to the presence of a disorder. These types of study hold much promise for our future understanding of the pathophysiology underlying psychiatric disorder.

It is important to appreciate that the demonstration of a genetic contribution to aetiology does not mean that genes are the whole story. There are no psychiatric disorders which are due to a single gene or chromosomal abnormality that is necessarily passed from parent to child (as is the case in Huntington's disease for example).

The genetic basis of Huntington's disease is considered in section 3.4.1 on page 51, and the manifestations of the disease in section 8.3 on page 171.

For psychiatric disorders, the offspring of sufferers merely have a greater risk of developing the illness than the general population. For most psychiatric disorders there may be a number of different genes involved in conferring a genetic predisposition (or **diathesis**) on an individual to develop a particular disorder. Whether the individual actually goes on to develop the disorder is due to other factors, such as environmental stressors. This

extension: A closer look at studies of genetic contribution to illness

BOX 4.4

There are three types of study that are used to investigate whether or not an illness or disorder is genetically mediated: family studies, twin studies, and adoption studies.

Family studies

Family studies compare the rate of disorder in relatives of **probands**, with the rate of illness in the general population or **controls**, or in the relatives of controls. If there is an increased risk of the disorder among the relatives of probands, then the disorder may be said to run in families.

It may well be that this is because genetic factors are important in causing the disorder. On the other hand, it might be that some environmental factor common to a family predisposes each member of that family to develop the disorder. This might be sharing a similar upbringing or other life experience. Therefore, family studies can only demonstrate that a disorder is familial, not that it is genetic.

The relative contribution of genes and environmental factors to this familiality is investigated by two types of natural experiments: twin studies and adoption studies.

Twin studies

Twin studies investigate rates of the disorder among identical (monozygotic) and fraternal (dizygotic) twins. They are based on the assumption that while monozygotic twins are genetically identical and dizygotic twins share, on average, half their genes, both types of twin share their environment to the same degree. In these studies individuals who have the disorder in question are identified (probands) and the rate of the disorder in their co-twins is ascertained. The results are reported as **concordance** rates. So if every co-twin of a proband also has the disorder, the concordance rate is 100%. If only half the co-twins have the disorder, the concordance rate is 50%.

If a twin study shows that there is a difference in concordance rate between monozygotic and dizygotic twin pairs, that difference must be due to the differing genetic similarity, because both types of twin pair share their environment to the same degree. So if the concordance rate is higher for monozygotic twins than for dizygotic twins, this is strong evidence for a genetic contribution to the disorder in question.

Adoption studies

These studies take advantage of the changes in environment brought about by adoption. Adoption creates pairs of relatives who share: (1) genes but not environment (biological relatives);

or (2) environment but not genes (adoptive relatives). There are three approaches:

- **Adoptee studies** compare the rate of disorder in adopted-away offspring of affected parents with the adopted away offspring of controls.
- **Adoptee family studies** compare the rate of disorder in biological and adoptive relatives of affected probands.
- **Cross-fostering studies** compare rates of disorder among adoptees with affected biological but unaffected adoptive parents, with rates of disorder among adoptees with affected adoptive but unaffected biological parents.

Each of these three approaches distinguishes between genetic and environmental influences in a slightly different way. Genetic influences are suggested by:

- increased risk of disorder in the adopted-away offspring of affected parents compared to controls in adoptee studies
- increased risk of disorder in the biological relatives of probands compared to the adoptive relatives in adoptee family studies
- increased risk of disorder in adoptees with affected biological parents compared to adoptees with affected adoptive parents in cross-fostering studies.

Both twin and adoption studies have methodological limitations. Both types of study are particularly vulnerable to problems associated with small sample sizes and ascertainment biases. Also, some researchers argue that the experience of being a twin and the experience of being adopted are so unusual that such samples are not representative of the general population.

In adoption studies, it is often hard to account for factors such as age at adoption, and there may well be incomplete separation from biological relatives. Additionally, adopted-away offspring have shared an environment with their biological mother for 9 months prenatally.

The validity of the 'equal environments' assumption inherent in twin studies is questioned by some who argue that the experience of being an identical twin is very different from being a non-identical twin. However, this can be tested by looking at monozygotic and dizygotic twin pairs who have been reared apart since birth (this is a combination of twin and adoption methodologies). Such twins have not shared postnatal environmental factors and thus, in these cases, the equal environments assumption should be more valid.

However, where these studies are replicated and where the evidence from twin and adoption studies goes in the same direction, they often provide powerful evidence for a genetic effect.

conceptualization is sometimes known as the **diathesis–stress model** and is a useful way of thinking about many psychiatric disorders. According to the model, an individual with a strong diathesis for a particular disorder may become ill following some fairly minor stressor, but someone with a much weaker diathesis would not become ill unless exposed to a severe stressor.

 See Chapter 3 for a more detailed introduction to the genomics of brain disorders.

> There is unequivocal evidence of a genetic contribution to the aetiology of bipolar affective disorder, schizophrenia, and some other mental disorders.

SELF-CHECK 4.3

What is the diathesis–stress model of illness?

4.2.2 Can biochemical changes be demonstrated in mental disorder?

The role of **neurotransmitters** in psychiatric disorder is of great importance because pharmacological treatments for mental illness are designed to manipulate neurotransmitter function. The success of these treatments is very good evidence of the importance of neurophysiology in causing psychiatric disorder. But studies of neurotransmitter function are difficult to do, because it is not possible to take direct samples of brain tissue from patients.

Therefore biochemical investigations in humans either depend on post-mortem brain research, which is vulnerable to certain **confounders**, or on using **proxy measures** of neurotransmitter function. Such measures include measuring the concentration of neurotransmitters in the **cerebrospinal fluid** (CSF), or looking at the levels of metabolites of neurotransmitters which are excreted in urine. Although important findings do come from these studies, it is difficult to be certain of the exact relationship between the proxy measures and the real situation in the brain.

The neurotransmitters most commonly implicated in psychiatric disorder are **serotonin** (also known as 5-hydroxytryptamine, 5-HT) and **noradrenaline** in mood disorders (leading to the monoamine theory of depression) and **dopamine** in schizophrenia (dopamine hypothesis of schizophrenia). But this is a great simplification. A wide variety of other neurotransmitters are also likely to be important, and they each interact with each other, meaning that the true picture is exceedingly complex.

> The development of pharmacological treatments for mental disorder is based on studies demonstrating neurotransmitter abnormalities.

4.2.3 Neuropathological changes in mental disorder

The early demonstration of ventricular enlargement in post-mortem brains of people who had had schizophrenia has been followed by the use of brain imaging techniques to investigate the structure and function of the brain in people with mental illness during life. Structural imaging techniques are commonly used in clinical psychiatry, MRI scanning superseding the earlier use of CT scans. More recently, functional imaging techniques such as SPECT and **functional magnetic resonance imaging** (fMRI) have been used increasingly in clinical research, though they have little place in clinical practice at present.

 These imaging techniques are described in more detail in later chapters: see Box 5.4 on page 91 for CT, Box 6.2 on page 108 for MRI, and Box 8.3 on page 159 for SPECT.

These areas of the brain have already been introduced in sections 1.4.2 and 1.4.3 on pages 8 and 16. The limbic system is also considered in further detail in section 13.3.4 on page 276.

The areas of the brain in which abnormalities are most often demonstrated for psychiatric disorder are the temporal lobes and to a lesser extent the frontal lobes. The limbic system, which is important in emotion and mood regulation, memory, aggression, and sleep, is also commonly implicated.

4.2.4 What about hormonal changes?

In many **endocrine** disorders, there is an increased incidence of psychiatric disorders. For example, depression is more common in disorders of the thyroid gland and the adrenal glands. Furthermore, a number of abnormalities of endocrine function have been demonstrated in psychiatric disorders, though it is often unclear whether these represent causes or consequences of the mental illness.

4.2.5 Are there changes in the electrical activity of the brain?

The **electroencephalogram** (EEG) measures the electrical activity of the brain via electrodes placed on the scalp or, very occasionally, placed closer to the brain in the **sinuses** of the skull. It is most important in the investigation of epilepsy, in which characteristic changes can be demonstrated. It has also been used in the investigation of other psychiatric disorders, but with limited success in terms of clinical utility.

> Most biological investigations are important in clinical research into the cause of mental disorder, rather than being of immediate importance to clinical practice.

4.3 What psychological approaches are used to understand mental illness?

In this section we introduce some basic psychological concepts, which may be used to understand, conceptualize, and treat psychiatric disorder. The interested reader may find it useful to learn more about these topics from a basic psychology textbook, as suggested in the further reading section on page 83. In this section we focus on learning and conditioning, cognitive and behavioural approaches, and psychodynamic theory.

4.3.1 What is the relevance of learning and conditioning theory?

Classical conditioning

The neuronal basis of Pavlov's experiments is discussed in section 2.3.1 on page 34.

This was first studied in detail in the famous experiments of Pavlov (1849–1936), in which he demonstrated that a dog that salivated in anticipation of being given food could learn to associate the ringing of a bell with food, and then would salivate in response to the bell.

This ability to associate two stimuli with each other has been used to understand the development of phobic anxiety disorders, in which a patient experiences irrational anxiety in response to some objectively benign stimulus.

Phobic anxiety disorders are explained further in section 13.2.3 on page 269.

Operant conditioning

Operant conditioning refers to the way in which behaviour is modified according to its consequences, leading to a change in the frequency of the particular behaviour. **Reinforcement** occurs when something leads to an increased frequency of the behaviour. A **positive reinforcer** is a pleasant consequence of the behaviour, such as giving a child a sweet as a reward for good behaviour. A **negative reinforcer** is an unpleasant condition, removal of which leads to increased frequency of the behaviour, such as taking painkillers for a headache. This is distinguished from **punishment**, which is designed to reduce the frequency of an unwanted behaviour. Learning that a behaviour avoids something unpleasant is dependent on these principles. The concept of avoidance is very important in perpetuating anxiety disorders.

Avoidance and anxiety disorders are discussed further in Chapter 13.

Social or observational learning

Social learning theory is a more general approach to the explanation of human behaviour which makes use of conditioning principles. The process of learning occurs through **modelling**, in which an individual learns a new behaviour through observing and replicating the behaviour of someone else. It differs from strict **behaviourism**, which would be based on conditioning theory, in that it allows for learning to occur without any change in behaviour.

> Behavioural models, based on learning theory, may be used to understand some forms of mental disorder.

4.3.2 What about cognitive approaches?

Cognitive approaches to understanding and treating psychiatric disorder have become prominent in clinical psychology over the last few decades, overtaking the behaviourist approach of classical and operant conditioning theory. There are a wide range of clinical interventions, theories, and therapeutic methods which are considered to be cognitive, but it is difficult to characterize them as a group and they have little to do with formal cognitive psychology research. But they all seek to explain symptoms in terms of how individuals acquire and use information, and they assume a link between how we think and how we feel emotionally.

SELF-CHECK 4.4

What is the difference between cognitive and behavioural approaches?

4.3.3 What about cognitive behavioural approaches?

Cognitive behavioural approaches assume a link between how we think, how we feel, and how we act. The cognitive behavioural therapist seeks to modify how an individual is feeling emotionally by manipulating the way they think and behave. Cognitive behavioural approaches are very commonly used clinically to treat neurotic disorders such as depression and anxiety disorders.

Cognitive behavioural approaches to treating neurotic disorders are considered further in sections 13.5.2 on page 280 and 14.7.1 on page 301.

4.3.4 What is psychodynamic theory?

Psychodynamic psychopathology explains current abnormal experience as deriving from early childhood experience, particularly the relationships with parents. It was pioneered by Sigmund Freud (1856–1939) who in the last years of the nineteenth century developed a new method of understanding psychological phenomena, which relied on interpretation and analysis of what a person says or omits to say while freely associating under instruction to report his thoughts without reservation. For Freud, **free association**, and subsequently dreams, offered a window through which the unconscious mind could be accessed.

His achievement was to demonstrate that psychological phenomena, which might be easily dismissed as accidental or meaningless, could be explained by reference to past experiences, particularly childhood experiences. In this way early experiences, long forgotten by the conscious mind, could be brought to light and current psychological symptoms could be understood.

Freud wrote extensively about these issues and introduced a number of new concepts, such as the **Oedipus complex** and **infantile sexuality**. He developed a number of models of the mind and gave the first descriptions of psychological **defence mechanisms**. We can see more about these topics in Box 4.5.

Some of the evidence in support of the existence of an unconscious mind is presented in section 4.4.1 on page 74.

---

extension: Freud's theories of the mind and some common defence mechanisms BOX 4.5

Topographical model of mind (1900)

This was Freud's first major theory of mind, in which he considered that the mind consisted of three parts:

- The **Conscious** is the part of the mind in which information from the external world or the body is brought into awareness. It is the subjective experience that can be communicated by means of language or behaviour. It consists of everything of which an individual is immediately aware.
- The **Preconscious** is composed of the mental events that can be brought into awareness by the process of attention. It is the interface between the conscious and the unconscious.
- The **Unconscious** consists of the mental contents that are kept from awareness through the force of censorship.

Structural theory of mind (1920)

Freud developed his topographical theory, particularly in terms of the unconscious aspects of the mind, until he produced this alternative model, in which the mind also consisted of three parts:

- The **Id** refers to a reservoir of inchoate and unorganized instinctual drives. It lacks the capacity to delay or modify the instinctual drives.
- The **Ego** is conceived as the executive organ of the psyche and controls contact with reality. It uses the defence mechanisms to delay or modify the expression of drives.

- The **Superego** is an agency of moral conscience that dictates what a person should not do.

Defence mechanisms

Defence mechanisms are psychological strategies which are used mostly unconsciously to reduce anxiety. They are considered very important to normal human experience, enabling us to tolerate situations or conflicts that may otherwise be overwhelming.

- **Denial** is the avoidance of painful aspect of reality by negating sensory data.
- **Projection** is reacting to unacceptable aspects of inner impulses as though they were outside the self.
- **Regression** is the return to an earlier phase of functioning in order to avoid tension and conflict evoked by the present level of development.
- **Displacement** is the shifting of an emotion from one idea or object to another that resembles the original in some aspect or quality.
- **Repression** is the withholding from consciousness an idea or feeling.
- **Sublimation** is the transformation of a socially unacceptable aim into a socially acceptable one.

A psychoanalyst may explain psychological distress in terms of maladaptive defence mechanisms, and would treat the **neurosis** by helping the patient to develop this understanding of their distress. It is important to note that psychoanalytic theories may be helpful in understanding and treating patients with neurotic disorders, particularly those that affect their relationships with other people. But they are of little benefit for patients with severe mental illnesses such as schizophrenia or other psychoses.

4.3.5 What is descriptive psychopathology?

Descriptive psychopathology is rather different from the other psychological approaches described above, in that it does not seek to explain, but simply describes and categorizes the abnormal experience. It has roots in **phenomenology**, a philosophical tradition associated with Husserl (1859–1938) that inquires into consciousness and its processes without any preconceptions about external causes and consequences. The aim is to inquire into the reality of experienced phenomena in order to exhibit their universal character.

There are two distinct parts to descriptive psychopathology: empathic assessment of subjective experience, and the observation of behaviour. Thus, descriptive psychopathology categorizes abnormal experience and, on the basis of this categorization, clinical diagnosis is made. We'll look at some of these categories of symptoms now, and the relationship between symptoms and particular diagnoses will be examined in later chapters.

4.4 What are the key psychiatric symptoms?

In this section we look at some important groups of psychiatric symptoms. Most of them are covered in further detail in the chapters relating to particular psychiatric disorders.

Psychiatrists often distinguish between two types of symptom:

- **Psychotic** symptoms are symptoms which, from an objective viewpoint, are categorically different from normal human experience. Psychotic symptoms are intrinsically pathological and usually the patient will not appreciate their pathological nature.

- **Neurotic** symptoms on the other hand, are familiar to all of us. They become pathological when they are particularly extreme, or occur in inappropriate situations. They are on a continuum with normal human experience.

We can see examples of psychotic symptoms and neurotic symptoms in Table 4.1. Some disorders, such as schizophrenia, are defined by the presence of psychotic symptoms. Others, such as anxiety disorders, do not include psychosis, and in others, such as the mood disorders, the presence of psychosis may be considered an indicator of severity.

> The presence of psychosis is an indicator of severity for some disorders.

SELF-CHECK 4.5

What sort of disorders tend to be most appropriately understood using psychodynamic principles?

SELF-CHECK 4.6

What is the difference between psychosis and neurosis?

Table 4.1 Some psychotic and neurotic symptoms

Psychotic symptoms	Neurotic symptoms
Delusions	Low mood
Hallucinations	Anxiety
Loosening of associations	Obsessions and compulsions
Lack of insight	Phobic anxiety
	Sleep disturbance
	Overvalued ideas

4.4.1 What symptoms are related to consciousness and disturbed consciousness?

The term **consciousness** as used in the clinical setting refers to the state of awareness of the self and the environment. There are three dimensions of consciousness:

Normal alertness to coma

People who are severely ill, whether from some major infection or other systemic disease or from some gross brain pathology, may show diminution of consciousness along this dimension. The patient becomes drowsy and shows impaired attention and concentration, orientation, and judgement. Then they begin to drift off to sleep without sensory stimulation, their actions become slowed and their speech slurred. Further progression leads to coma, shown by reduced muscular reflexes, unconsciousness, and reduced or absent responses to painful stimuli. This dimension ends with death.

Wakefulness to sleep

When an individual is asleep, they are unconscious. There is a continuum from full wakefulness, through feeling tired or drowsy, when the level of vigilance is impaired, to the early stages and then the late stages of sleep. As an individual progresses through these stages, they become increasingly less aware of their surroundings and less rousable.

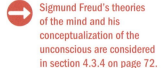
Sigmund Freud's theories of the mind and his conceptualization of the unconscious are considered in section 4.3.4 on page 72.

The conscious and the unconscious mind

We have already seen that Sigmund Freud was influential in developing the idea that for each of us there is a part of our mind of which we are not immediately aware. We can see some of the evidence for the existence of an unconscious mind in Box 4.6.

Qualitative changes in consciousness

Delirium is an acute disturbance of consciousness in which there is a particular impairment of attention and concentration, leading to impaired orientation and memory disturbance. Additional symptoms include disturbance of the usual sleep–wake cycle (tending to be awake at night and sleepy during the day), mood changes with irritability or

---

extension: Evidence for the existence of an unconscious mind

BOX 4.6

- **Dreams**—the content of dreams commonly refers to daily events or real issues
- **Artistic and scientific creativity**—we may struggle with a problem for a long time. It is only when we put it aside and do not consciously attend to it, that the solution suddenly comes to mind.
- **Post-hypnotic phenomena**—an individual will carry out some simple task as instructed while hypnotized, but will be unable to explain why he did so.
- **Parapraxes**—the so-called 'Freudian slip' is a good example. One accidentally substitutes a meaningful word into speech as a slip of the tongue. An obvious example would be accidentally calling one's partner by someone else's name.
- **Subliminal perception**—this refers to the idea that a signal or message may not be perceived by the conscious mind, but nonetheless may influence behaviour, demonstrating that it has been assimilated unconsciously.

---

suspiciousness, perceptual symptoms by way of illusions, distortions and hallucinations, and **delusions**. It signifies some general disturbance of brain function, caused either by some general systemic disorder or by some intracranial pathology. Patients with **dementia** are particularly likely to suffer from delirium.

Dissociation refers to a state in which there is a lack of the normal connection between coexisting mental processes, resulting in a failure of the normal integration of thought and experience into consciousness. This may lead to a patient presenting with physical symptoms, such as pain or paralysis, with no determinable physical cause. The symptom is considered to be psychologically mediated, but the mental process resulting in the symptom is dissociated from other conscious processes. More dramatically, in **dissociative fugues**, an individual may travel large distances in a state of altered consciousness. To casual observers their behaviour appears entirely normal, but if one were to engage them in conversation it would quickly become apparent that they were not fully aware of their surroundings. This explains the occasional appearance of an individual with apparent memory loss who cannot identify themself. This type of dissociation is usually related to some stress or life problem and is usually self-limiting. A similar situation, though usually with less complex behaviours, may occur following epileptic seizures.

Hypnosis induces a trance-like state in which the field of consciousness is narrowed and directed towards the hypnotist, reality-testing is diminished, and suggestibility is increased. The change in consciousness is similar to that in dissociative states. It is notable that some individuals are more susceptible to hypnosis than others. The subject must be willing, able to relax and have a high capacity for fantasy.

Sensory distortions, illusions, and hallucinations are described in section 4.4.3 on page 77. Delusions are described in section 4.4.4 on page 79.

Changes in the quality of consciousness occur in a wide variety of psychiatric disorders, physical disorders, and non-pathological situations.

4.4.2 What about memory disturbance?

Memory is a cognitive function concerned with the retention and reproduction of learnt information. There are a number of different ways of understanding the normal structure and organization of memory. Schemes used in clinical practice often differ from those used in neuropsychological research and theory.

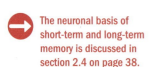

The neuronal basis of short-term and long-term memory is discussed in section 2.4 on page 38.

In one scheme, commonly used in clinical practice, and illustrated in Figure 4.1, **immediate memory** (or **sensory memory**) refers to the retention of information for less than 1 second, usually in the form in which the information is perceived, either in visual (iconic) or auditory (echoic) form. **Short-term memory** is limited to approximately 15–30 seconds unless the material is rehearsed, and only 6–7 items can be retained. **Long-term memory** has the capacity to hold information that has been selected for long-term storage for many years.

Figure 4.1 also shows the further subdivisions of the long-term memory store. **Implicit or procedural memory** refers to the memory of how to do things. This form of memory may often be used without consciously thinking about it—riding a bike is a good example. **Declarative or explicit memory** refers to our knowledge of facts, and is further divided into **semantic memory**, which stores general knowledge, and **episodic memory**, which stores events. So, for example, you now know that immediate memory lasts for less than 1 second (this is your semantic memory), and you know that you learnt that today while reading this book (this is your episodic memory). These different forms of memory are important clinically, because they may be differentially affected by lesions in different areas of the brain.

Our ability to retrieve information from memory stores may be manipulated. **Recall**, the spontaneous and active retrieval of information at will, is distinguished from **recognition**, the passive identification of stored material when subsequently presented. Recognition is much easier than recall, so using cues such as mnemonics is helpful. Also when one learns an array of new information, that which was learnt first (primacy) and last (recency) is subsequently retrieved more easily than that in the middle.

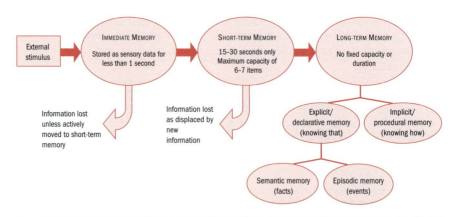

Figure 4.1 A model of memory.

Recall is also dependent upon mood and context. So one will retrieve information more easily in the same circumstances in which it was originally learnt. Clinically this is seen in depressed patients who are more likely to recall unhappy memories.

The topic of **recovered memories** is also important. This refers to a situation in which an individual, usually while undergoing psychotherapy, 'remembers' sexual abuse from their childhood, of which they had previously been unaware. This is a controversial subject. It seems likely that although some of these recovered memories may be valid, many are not, and are due to suggestibility within the relationship the patient has with their therapist.

Disturbances of memory

It is interesting that, generally speaking, memory disturbance is not thought of as being a central feature of most psychiatric disorders, though there are exceptions, such as the severe dissociative states described above. But in fact, memory disturbance is usual in many psychiatric disorders. In particular, a subjective impairment of memory, which is probably rooted in impaired attention and concentration rather than memory itself, is a common symptom of depression. It is also common for patients with mania or severe psychosis to show a significant subsequent amnesia for the period of illness.

- **Anterograde amnesia** describes a period of impaired new learning following (for example) a head injury. At the time it will be apparent that new learning is impaired on testing. After resolution of the amnesia, the patient will continue to have an amnesic gap for that period of time. The duration of this period is an important prognostic indicator following head injury.

- **Retrograde amnesia** refers to the time between the moment of sustaining a head injury, and the last clear memory before the head injury. It is usually fairly short, but may be persistent.

- Memory disturbance is a central feature of dementias, in which there is impaired new learning and a retrograde amnesia with a **temporal gradient**.

- In the **amnesic syndrome**, which is most commonly associated with vitamin B_1 deficiency secondary to alcoholism, there is a selective and specific impairment of new learning, without the more general cognitive impairment seen in global dementias.

> Memory disturbance is a very common feature of psychiatric disorders.

4.4.3 What are the common abnormalities of perception?

Our senses receive impressions from the external world. Sensation is the first stage in this process and consists of mere sensory data that are yet to become meaningfully organized. **Perception** is the process by which sensory data is made meaningful, by eliminating what is irrelevant and by associating with other sensory data or internal data. Abnormalities of perception may be sensory distortions or false perceptions (**illusions** and **hallucinations**).

Sensory distortions

Sensory distortions are particularly common in mood disorders. Depressed patients often complain that the intensity of perception is diminished, such that everything looks dull or food tastes bland. Manic patients, on the other hand, may find that their experience of colour is heightened, such that everything looks bright and more colourful, music sounds clearer, and everything around them seems more vivid and alive. Less commonly, objects seem smaller (micropsia), or bigger (macropsia), than they are, or occasionally they appear distorted on one side only (dysmegalopsia). These latter symptoms may occur in various brain disorders including schizophrenia, or with drug intoxication.

Illusions

Illusions are false perceptions that arise from real sensory data in the external world. There are three types of illusion:

- In **affect illusion**, the predominant affect influences the perception of the external world. For example, while walking on a dark night, anxiety may influence our perception of a tree such that it is perceived as a dangerous person lurking in the shadows.
- A **completion illusion** depends on inattention and involves the perception of an incomplete pattern to form a meaningful whole. The most common example is our tendency not to notice misspellings in the newspaper because we perceive the word as though it were spelt correctly.
- **Pareidolic illusions** are meaningful images created out of random patterns; for example, perceiving a human face in a random cloud formation. They differ from the other types in that they are potentiated by attention.

Hallucinations

An hallucination is a false perception in the absence of an external stimulus. From the subjective viewpoint it is indistinguishable from a normal perception in every respect. Hallucinations can occur in any sensory modality so that there are auditory, visual, olfactory (smell), gustatory (taste), and tactile hallucinations.

True visual hallucinations are relatively uncommon in psychiatric disorders. They may range from simple flashes of light or colour to complex images.

The most important types of hallucinations in psychiatry are auditory. Hearing voices is often thought of as being the hallmark of mental disorder, but auditory hallucinations may also consist of other sounds or music. When sufferers hear voices, they may hear their own thoughts spoken out loud, they may hear a voice speaking to them in the second person, or they may hear a voice talking about them in the third person. We can see examples of this in Box 4.7. Audible thoughts and third-person auditory hallucinations are considered to be characteristic of schizophrenia.

It is important to note that these symptoms are not always pathological or indicative of mental illness. Sensory distortions may occur in the context of normal variations in mood or with fatigue, and illusions are common in everyday life. Hallucinations are more likely to be of pathological significance, but may not be so. More than 50% of the normal population report having heard their own name spoken when alone. It is also common for people to experience hallucinations as they move from wakefulness to sleep (hypnagogic hallucinations) or from sleep to wakefulness (hypnopompic hallucinations). These are often auditory or tactile in nature.

> **SELF-CHECK** 4.7
>
> What is a hallucination and how does it differ from a normal perception?

Hallucinations are usually, though not always, pathological.

---

extension: Examples of auditory hallucinations

BOX 4.7

Second-person auditory hallucinations

A depressed man complained of hearing the voices of his parents talking to him when he was alone. They said unpleasant things such as 'we always knew you wouldn't make much of yourself', 'you might as well do away with yourself', and 'you're a failure'.

Third-person auditory hallucinations

A man with schizophrenia persistently heard a voice talking about him, commenting on his actions. For example, they would say 'he's going downstairs now, he's putting the kettle on, now he's making his breakfast.' This was interspersed with two voices talking about him amongst themselves, for example 'he's a foolish man isn't he?'; 'hasn't he worked it out yet?'.

4.4.4 What are the common abnormalities of thought?

Abnormalities of flow of thought

In some psychiatric disorders the flow of thought is disturbed. Of course, this cannot be observed directly, so it is examined through the proxy of speech. For example, depressed patients often think (and speak) slowly and may answer questions monosyllabically. By contrast, patients who are elated through mania may think and speak very quickly. Manic patients also tend to have difficulty maintaining the overall direction of their thinking, tending to jump from topic to topic, making it hard to follow their train of thought.

Loosening of associations

This type of disordered thinking is characteristic of schizophrenia. The usual links (or associations) between sequential thoughts are lost, so thoughts do not follow each other in a usual or predictable way. When mild, this leads to a subtle sense in the listener that he is not quite grasping the meaning of what the patient is saying. When it is severe the patient's speech may be utterly nonsensical, with a fluent stream of apparently unconnected individual words.

Delusions

A **delusion** is a belief that is held with conviction despite evidence to the contrary, and which is out of keeping with the person's educational, cultural and social background. Delusions are usually incorrigible and recalcitrant to counter-argument. The content of the delusions varies, but common themes are:

- Delusions of persecution, in which the sufferer believes that some person or persons, or some other agency, are against them.
- Delusions of grandiose identity or ability, in which a person may believe that he is related to royalty or has some special power, strength, or intelligence.
- Delusions of love or jealousy, in which a person believes that another person is in love with him, or believes that their partner is being unfaithful.

- Nihilistic delusions, in which the patient believes that something doesn't exist. This may be a delusion of poverty, or may be a belief that his marriage is over, his career is finished or even that he himself is dead.

- Delusions of guilt when a person erroneously believes they have committed some terrible crime or sin, or believes that some minor error is in fact an issue of enormous importance for which they should be punished.

- Delusions of reference are characteristic of schizophrenia and occur when a patient perceives a link between himself and some unconnected event or experience. A common example occurs when a patient watches television and believes that the presenter or the programme is taking about him or in some way relates to him.

- Delusions of passivity (or delusions of control) are also characteristic of schizophrenia. They may relate to the person's thoughts, volition, impulse, or feelings, which are experienced as being controlled by some external agency.

SELF-CHECK 4.8

Which two types of delusion are particularly characteristic of schizophrenia?

Delusions of jealousy are particularly noteworthy because they are significantly associated with violent attacks on the sexual partner or on the imagined lover. They also illustrate the point that a delusional belief is not always erroneous. It is often reported that the partner of a man with delusional jealousy may become unfaithful because of the stress and tension within the relationship. So it is not that the belief itself is wrong, but that the process by which the belief comes to be held that is abnormal.

Overvalued ideas

An overvalued idea is an idea that is not necessarily false, but with which an individual is unduly preoccupied, and which comes to dominate an individual's life. Disturbances of body image often involve this kind of abnormal thought, such as the thought that one's nose is too big.

Overvalued ideas are also common in personality disorders. An individual with paranoid personality disorder may engage in a civil law suit against the neighbour whose fence is in poor condition. An issue like this may be irritating, but most people would maintain some perspective and would not resort to the law.

Obsession and compulsions are described in more detail in section 13.2.5 on page 272.

> Overvalued ideas often occur in the absence of mental illness, and are a manifestation of an individual's personality or disposition.

Obsessions

SELF-CHECK 4.9

Which abnormalities of thought are considered to be psychotic symptoms?

An obsession is a thought, image, or impulse that repeatedly forces its way to the front of a person's mind, so that despite his best efforts he cannot help experiencing it. It usually causes anxiety and tension and is accompanied by a compulsion, which is a behaviour designed to reduce the anxiety associated with an obsession.

4.4.5 What are the common abnormalities of mood?

Psychiatrists often distinguish between two related concepts:

- **Mood** refers to a pervasive and sustained (prolonged) prevailing state or disposition.

- **Affect** is a person's present emotional responsiveness, usually inferred from their facial expression and the amount and range of emotional expression.

Abnormalities of mood and affect are probably the most common symptom of psychiatric disorder. Apart from the mood disorders, in which changes in mood are the paramount symptom, mood changes are common in almost all psychiatric disorders. Commonly described subjective mood states include anxiety, depression, elation, euphoria, anger, and perplexity. Of course these are all features of normal human life, but the severity or persistence of the state is abnormal in psychiatric disorders.

Some people complain of abnormalities in the variability of their mood. For example in mania the mood state is often labile, which means that it fluctuates rapidly and dramatically between mood states. In contrast, depressed patients complain of flattening of mood, in which they do not experience a usual variability or reactivity of mood.

4.4.6 What is insight?

The term **insight** is used by psychiatrists to describe the degree to which a patient with a mental illness is aware of the pathological nature of their problem. It is an important concept in psychiatry because some psychiatric disorders, particularly psychoses, directly impact upon a patient's capacity to appreciate the nature of their illness.

For example an individual with schizophrenia who is labouring under the delusional belief that MI5 is following him with a view to arranging his death, will not appreciate that he is ill. So it is unlikely that he will agree to accept psychiatric treatment—he will be more concerned with evading his persecutors! This is why it is occasionally necessary to treat people against their will, using mental health legislation.

But the concept of insight refers to more than just knowing whether or not one is 'ill'. A doctor will also want to know how the patient conceptualizes their various symptoms, what they think has caused their symptoms, and what sort of treatment the patient thinks might be necessary.

> The concept of insight is of great importance to the clinical management of a patient with mental disorder.

4.5 How are psychiatric disorders classified?

We have seen that all psychiatric disorders are syndromal, and investigations to confirm psychiatric diagnoses are lacking. In order to reduce unreliability in psychiatric diagnosis, psychiatrists rely on operationally defined clinical criteria for reaching diagnosis.

The World Health Organization (WHO) publishes the *International Classification of Diseases*, which is currently in its tenth edition (ICD-10) and the American Psychiatric Association publishes the *Diagnostic and Statistical Manual* which is currently in its fourth edition (DSM-IV). These standardized criteria have improved the reliability of clinical diagnosis in psychiatry, but until there are objective and independent criteria, the validity of the diagnostic categories will remain open to challenge.

ICD-10 and DSM-IV are very similar and contain the same broad categories of psychiatric disorder:

1. Acute and chronic mental illnesses. These include:

   a Schizophrenia and related disorders

   b Mood disorders

   c Anxiety disorders and related disorders

2. Dementia, delirium and related disorders

3. Disorders due to substance misuse, including intoxication, dependence, and related syndromes

4. Personality disorders

5. Disorders of childhood, including conduct disorders, hyperkinetic disorder and pervasive developmental disorders such as autism

6. Learning disability, previously known as mental retardation.

We will learn much more about the acute and chronic mental illnesses and about substance misuse in Chapters 13–16.

SUMMARY

- Psychiatry is that branch of medicine which is concerned with disorders of the mind.

- In comparison to other medical specialties, the mind is a complicated concept, and defining when it is disordered takes on great complexity.

- All psychiatric diagnoses are syndromal, leaving psychiatry vulnerable to attack from those who disagree with the fundamental basis of psychiatry within medicine.

- Psychiatrists consider a variety of paradigms when thinking about mental disorder, often separating these into biological, psychological, and social aspects.

- Many psychiatric disorders run in families and have a genetic contribution to their aetiology. For some, molecular genetic studies are of increasing relevance.

- Brain scanning has demonstrated changes in the structure and function of the brain, and biochemical investigations have shown changes in neurotransmitter function.

- Psychological approaches to understanding and treating mental disorder include behavioural models based on learning theory, cognitive models, and psychodynamic theory.

- Key psychiatric symptoms include disturbances of consciousness disturbance of memory, abnormalities of perception, abnormalities of thought, abnormalities of mood, and impaired insight.

- Psychiatrists use operationally defined criteria to improve the reliability of clinical diagnoses.

FURTHER READING

American Psychiatric Association. *Diagnostic and statistical manual*, 4th edn, text revision. Washington, DC: American Psychiatric Association, 1994.
This is the APA's classification of mental disorder (DSM-IV), commonly used in both clinical practice and clinical research.

D. Brown, J. Pedder, and A. Bateman. *Introduction to psychotherapy; an outline of psychodynamic principles and practice.* London: Routledge, 2000.
A good, easy-to-read introduction to dynamic psychotherapy.

M. G. Gelder, J. J. Lopez-Ibor, and N. C. Andreasen. *New Oxford textbook of psychiatry.* Oxford: University Press, 2000.
A major psychiatric reference book.

B. J. Saddock and V. A. Saddock. *Synopsis of psychiatry.* Philadelphia: Lippincott, Williams & Wilkins, 2003.
Another major psychiatric textbook.

A. Sims. *Symptoms in the mind*, 3rd edn. London: W. B. Saunders/Elsevier, 2003.
This excellent book is an introduction to psychopathology and phenomenology, and provides excellent explanations of common psychiatric symptoms.

E. Smith, S. Nolen-Hoeksema and B. Fredrickson. *Atkinson and Hilgard's introduction to psychology.* Belmont, CA: Wadsworth, 2002.
A standard basic psychology textbook.

World Health Organization. *The ICD-10 classification of mental and behavioural disorders.* Geneva, World Health Organization, 1992.
An alternative classification to the DSM-IV, more commonly used in clinical practice in the UK.

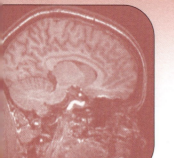

CHAPTER FIVE

Cerebrovascular diseases

Carl Clarke

Traumatic damage to the cerebral blood vessels leading to extradural and subdural haemorrhage is considered in section 12.2.1 on page 251.

INTRODUCTION

Damage to the blood supply to the brain due to cerebrovascular diseases is a major cause of death and disability. In this chapter we consider the main types of cerebrovascular disease: **stroke** and **subarachnoid haemorrhage**. Some people continue to classify subarachnoid haemorrhage as a form of stroke, but it is clinically and pathologically distinct and so is considered separately here.

5.1 Stroke

Definitions

A stroke is defined as a sudden loss of brain function lasting for more than 24 hours resulting from perturbation of its blood supply. The term cerebrovascular accident (CVA) has been used in place of stroke in the past. However, since stroke is not 'accidental', this term is no longer used.

Another pertinent term is **transient ischaemic attack** (TIA), which is a cerebral ischaemic event with all symptoms and signs disappearing within 24 hours. **Ischaemia** refers to any reduction in blood flow to an organ.

> A stroke is a sudden loss of brain function lasting for more than 24 hours resulting from perturbation of its blood supply.

> A transient ischaemic attack is a cerebral ischaemic event with all symptoms and signs disappearing within 24 hours.

Cerebral blood supply

It is crucial to understand the blood supply to the brain before considering the clinical effects of stroke. You will already be aware that blood is pumped from the heart to the major organs through arteries. After delivering nutrients and oxygen to the tissues, waste products, including carbon dioxide, are taken by the blood back to the heart via the veins. The blood is then pumped to the lungs to be re-oxygenated and for the carbon dioxide to be removed before it is re-circulated once more.

Blood is supplied to the brain through four large arteries. There are two carotid and two vertebral arteries, one on each side of the body. The carotid arteries each divide into the external and the internal carotid arteries. The internal carotid arteries pass through the skull base in two holes (foramen lacerum) and the vertebral arteries through the larger foramen magnum.

> Blood reaches specific areas of the brain through the two carotid and the two vertebral arteries.

As we see in Figure 5.1, once inside the skull, each internal carotid artery divides into an anterior and a middle cerebral artery. In contrast, the vertebral arteries fuse together to form the basilar artery which runs along the anterior surface of the brain stem supplying small branches to it. At the top of the brain stem, the basilar artery divides into the two posterior cerebral arteries. The two anterior cerebral arteries are connected by the anterior communicating artery and the posterior cerebral arteries are connected to each middle cerebral artery by the posterior communicating arteries. These connections form the **circle of Willis** which, in some circumstances, can allow blood to bypass a blocked artery.

We can see which parts of the brain are supplied by the carotid (or anterior) arteries and the vertebrobasilar (or posterior) arteries by looking at the simplified diagram in Figure 5.2.

SELF-CHECK 5.1

Which arteries supply blood to the different areas of the cerebral cortex, the brain stem and the cerebellum?

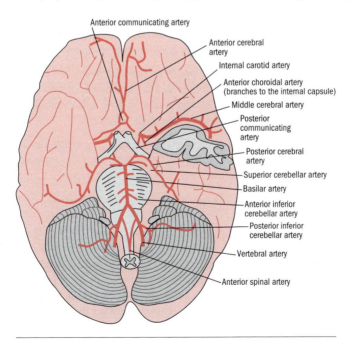

Anterior communicating artery

Anterior cerebral artery

Internal carotid artery

Anterior choroidal artery (branches to the internal capsule)

Middle cerebral artery

Posterior communicating artery

Posterior cerebral artery

Superior cerebellar artery

Basilar artery

Anterior inferior cerebellar artery

Posterior inferior cerebellar artery

Vertebral artery

Anterior spinal artery

Figure 5.1 Base of brain showing blood vessels forming the circle of Willis.

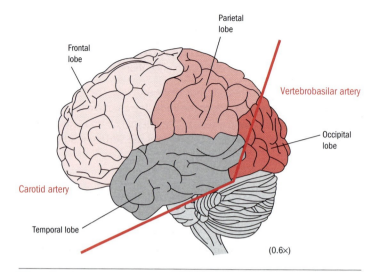

Figure 5.2 Simplified diagram showing the distribution of blood from the carotid and vertebrobasilar arteries.

5.1.1 How common are strokes and who are most at risk?

- Stroke is the third most common cause of death worldwide after ischaemic heart disease (blocked arteries to the heart) and all forms of cancer combined.

- Stroke is a disease of older people, with three-quarters occurring in those over 65 years of age. With the ageing of the population, stroke deaths will double by 2020.

- Stroke is the main cause of long-term neurological disability in adults, with over half of stroke survivors dependent on other people for their everyday activities.

The good news is that stroke **mortality** has been falling in developed countries, thanks to a combination of reduced risk factors (e.g. smoking) and improved medical care of stroke patients. The bad news is that stroke deaths have been increasing in eastern Europe and Russia, probably as a result of increased smoking.

Precise data on the numbers of stroke victims are beset by difficulties in the pathological classification of stroke and inaccurate death certification. However, it seems likely that all ethnic types are at the same risk of stroke if exposed to the same risk factors.

5.1.2 What are the likely causes of stroke?

The **aetiology** or cause of stroke largely depends on its pathological type, which will be considered in the next section. So, cerebral **haemorrhage** (see below) is more frequently caused by **hypertension** (high blood pressure), whereas cerebral **infarction** (see below) can be caused by hypertension, **diabetes**, smoking, obesity (but, unexpectedly, not a high cholesterol level), and cardiac **embolism** (clots from the heart). Some patients may have only one risk factor for stroke, whereas others may have many. Rarely, people suffer stroke with no risk factors; research is ongoing into why this occurs.

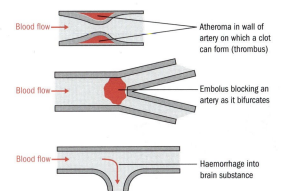

Blood flow → Atheroma in wall of artery on which a clot can form (thrombus)

Blood flow → Embolus blocking an artery as it bifurcates

Blood flow → Haemorrhage into brain substance

Figure 5.3 Pathological mechanisms of stroke.

Cerebral haemorrhage is caused by hypertension, whereas cerebral infarction is caused by hypertension, diabetes, smoking, obesity, and/or cardiac embolism.

5.1.3 What tissue changes are caused by stroke?

Around 80% of strokes are caused by cerebral infarction. Infarction occurs when an artery supplying blood to the brain is blocked.

Arteries can slowly fur up, like lime scale in a kettle. The substance narrowing the artery is called **atheroma** and the process is called **atherosclerosis** (look at the top of Figure 5.3). Atheroma is made up of fatty deposits, but how this stems from the vascular risk factors discussed above is not known in detail.

Alternatively, arteries can suddenly become blocked. This happens when a blood clot forms on a deposit or plaque of atheroma, so-called **thrombosis**. Sudden occlusion of an artery can occur if a clot of blood from an atheromatous plaque breaks loose and floats further down the narrowing vessel, eventually becoming lodged as shown in the middle diagram of Figure 5.3. This clot is called an **embolism**.

Emboli can also develop in the heart and travel to the brain, causing cerebral infarction. The cardiac conditions predisposing to this are irregular heart beating (especially **atrial fibrillation**) and recent **myocardial infarction** ('heart attack').

Around 50% of cerebral infarcts are caused by atherothromboembolism in medium to large arteries, 25% by damage to small intracranial arteries, 20% are due to cardiac embolism, and 5% to rare causes.

In 20% of strokes the cause is an intracerebral haemorrhage (as can be seen in Figure 5.4). In this condition an artery in the brain ruptures (look at the lower diagram in Figure 5.3), often as a result of high blood pressure, causing a leakage of blood into the brain substance (parenchyma) which in turn causes neurological damage.

5.1.4 What are the symptoms and signs of a stroke?

Interruption of the blood supply to part of the brain leads to immediate clinical effects. This is true whether the symptoms and signs are ultimately reversible, as in a transient

SELF-CHECK 5.2

What pathological processes cause stroke?

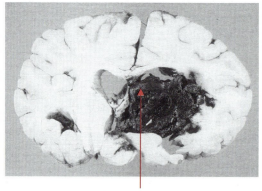

Haemorrhage into brain substance

Figure 5.4 Brain slice showing massive intracerebral haemorrhage.

ischaemic attack, or permanent, as in a 'completed' stroke. So patients complain of symptoms from vascular disorders as soon as they occur, unlike patients with cerebral tumours and neurodegenerative conditions in which the symptoms develop gradually and deteriorate over a period of time. This sudden or acute onset of symptoms in vascular disorders is very useful in differentiating them from these alternative chronic conditions.

➡ The anatomical organization of the brain is considered in section 1.4 on page 6.

To understand the symptoms and physical signs that people develop when they have a stroke, you must have some knowledge of the anatomy of the main motor, sensory, visual, and language pathways of the brain.

The most useful way to learn about the clinical features of stroke is to work through the Oxfordshire Community Stroke Project Classification (Table 5.1), which we will see later has useful prognostic value.

The classification has two categories for **total** and **partial anterior or carotid circulation syndromes** (TACS and PACS; see the case study in Box 5.1). For simplicity, the 'partial' category can be thought of as a minor version of the 'total' category. Usually, these syndromes are caused by occlusion of one of the carotid or middle cerebral arteries or a major haemorrhage into the frontal and parietal lobes.

Table 5.1 Oxfordshire Community Stroke Project Classification of stroke

Type	Abbreviation	Proportion of strokes (%)	Clinical features
Total anterior circulation syndrome	TACS	17	Hemi-motor loss; hemi-sensory loss; hemianopia; cortical dysfunction (dysphasia)
Partial anterior circulation syndrome	PACS	34	Any two of above or cortical dysfunction only
Lacunar syndrome	LACS	25	Pure hemi-motor; pure hemi-sensory; mixed hemi-motor and hemi-sensory; clumsy-hand dysarthria syndrome; or ataxic hemiparesis
Posterior circulation syndrome	POCS	24	Brain stem dysfunction (e.g. cranial nerve palsies; cerebellar signs); hemi-motor loss; hemi-sensory loss

In a TACS stroke, the patient loses strength in the side of the body opposite to the lesion because the corticospinal motor pathway crosses in the medulla of the brain stem. This loss of strength is called **hemiparesis**. Because the brunt of the damage affects the arm area of the cortex, the arm will be weaker than the leg and face. There will also be loss of sensation in the opposite side of the body as the damaged sensory pathways are also crossed. The patient loses vision to the side opposite the stroke, so-called **hemianopia**. The final feature is damage to higher cortical centres which can lead to **dysphasia** (language dysfunction) if the lesion is in the dominant hemisphere where the speech centres are situated.

The motor homunculus is considered in section 1.4.2 and in Figure 1.6 on page 10.

A **lacunar circulation syndrome** (LACS; see the case study in Box 5.2) stroke is usually caused by blockage of a small perforating artery from either the carotid or vertebrobasilar systems or a small haemorrhage deep within the brain. This leads to weakness and/or sensory loss of the opposite side of the body. Since the damage affects all of the corticospinal fibres where they are closely packed together, the weakness affects the face, arm and leg equally. Lacunar syndromes also produce the very rare presentations of clumsy-hand **dysarthria** syndrome and ataxic hemiparesis, which are beyond the scope of this book.

case study: Posterior circulation stroke (POCS)   BOX 5.3

- A 59-year-old man with no vascular risk factors was admitted after the sudden onset of left-sided weakness and double vision (**diplopia**).

- On examination, he had **ptosis** (drooping) of the right eye with a dilated right pupil and the right eye could not look inward and upward (i.e. third cranial nerve palsy). There was a severe left-sided weakness with face, arm, and leg equally affected.

- A CT brain scan was normal. A subsequent MRI scan showed low signal in the right midbrain at the level of the third nerve nucleus.

- Over the following 6 weeks, the diplopia settled and the weakness recovered by 70%. He was discharged on aspirin and dipyridamole retard as antiplatelet agents to prevent platelets clotting on atheromatous plaques. No cause was found for the stroke in spite of detailed investigations.

- When discharged from clinic 6 months later, he was left with only a mild weakness which did not interfere with activities of daily living.

SELF-CHECK 5.3

What are the four clinical types of stroke, and how are they differentiated clinically?

Posterior circulation syndrome (POCS; see the case study in Box 5.3) strokes are caused by occlusion of the vertebral or basilar arteries or their smaller branches or haemorrhage into the brain stem. They can lead to **contralateral** weakness and sensory loss, but this is usually combined with brain stem signs such as cranial nerve palsies or cerebellar signs.

5.1.5 What tests can we use to diagnose stroke?

Patients who have suffered a stroke or TIA require a battery of investigations or tests to confirm that their neurological problem was vascular in origin and, if so, what caused it. Many patients with severe strokes will be admitted to hospital, so these tests will be done during the admission. For minor strokes and TIAs, investigations are usually done on an outpatient basis.

There is a standard series of investigations which all such patients require, then a smaller list of optional tests depending on the clinical circumstances and what has been found on the initial tests.

Mandatory tests

SELF-CHECK 5.4

Why is CT imaging done after stroke?

If we look at Table 5.2, we can see details of the investigations which all stroke and TIA patients require, why they are needed, and the likelihood that they will change the patient's treatment.

One of the most important investigations that patients must have is a **CT scan** of the brain. The principles of this technique are described in more detail in Box 5.4.

Optional tests

Depending on the clinical features and the results of the mandatory investigations, further optional tests may be necessary. Many of these are based on ultrasound techniques, which are explained in Box 5.5.

Table 5.2 Mandatory investigations for all stroke and TIA patients

Investigation	Reason	Likelihood of changing patient's treatment (%)
Full blood count	Disorders of blood clotting as cause of stroke	1
Erythrocyte sedimentation rate (ESR)	Temporal arteritis (rare cause of stroke in the elderly)	2
Urea and electrolytes	Metabolic upset due to antihypertensive drugs	3
Plasma glucose	Diabetes as cause of stroke	5
Plasma cholesterol and other lipids	High lipid/cholesterol with obesity as cause of stroke	45
Electrocardiogram	Heart rhythm disturbance as cause of stroke	17
CT brain scan	Differentiation of cerebral infarction from haemorrhage; ensure not alternative diagnosis such as haemorrhage into a tumour or subarachnoid haemorrhage	20

extension: CT scanning

BOX 5.4

- CT scanning is an X-ray-based technique which produces cross-sectional images of the body: in this case, the brain.

- X-rays are produced by bombarding materials such as tungsten with electrons in a cathode ray tube. In conventional radiographs, the radiation is directed (collimated) at an area of the body. Different tissues within the organ then absorb (attenuate) the beam differently depending on their density (bone attenuates more than soft tissues). The remaining radiation goes through to a radiosensitive plate which is developed to reveal a 'negative' of the area in question.

- CT uses a complicated two-dimensional approach called **tomography**. In this, the X-ray tube and the detector rotate around the patient. Sophisticated mathematics resolves the multiple pieces of data for each small area of the subject (pixel). A two-dimensional X-ray picture of the subject is built up by the computer which can be displayed on a monitor or printed on to radiographic film. CT is an abbreviation for computed tomography.

- An intravenous injection of iodine containing **contrast medium** is sometimes used in CT to highlight certain lesions (e.g. arteriovenous malformations). Contrast media have high atomic number and so they absorb more radiation.

- Modern CT scanners move around the patient in a spiral or helix for faster acquisition, and can be used to create three-dimensional images.

- The greatest value of CT is in the emergency imaging of the brain. Most district general hospitals in the UK now have a CT scanner.

- The commonest acute neurological lesions are cerebral haemorrhages, which look white on CT, or cerebral infarction, which looks dark. The shape of the white lesion gives the nature of the haemorrhage. Other lesions may need contrast injection to be shown clearly, and some lesions are not shown at all. In the latter case, MRI scanning may be more valuable.

- CT is used in suspected stroke and TIA patients to exclude other diagnoses. Tumours in the brain can have a fragile blood supply which can rupture causing a large haemorrhage into the substance of the tumour. This can present suddenly, just like a stroke. Similarly, as we will see later, subarachnoid haemorrhage can lead to spasm in the cerebral arteries which can look like a stroke.

- CT is also invaluable in differentiating cerebral infarction (as can be seen in Figure 5.5) from haemorrhage (compare

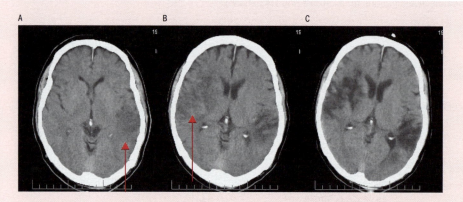

Figure 5.5 CT scans of the brain showing evolution of bihemispheric cerebral infarcts. Scan A was performed on the day of admission and shows low attenuation in the left parietal region (arrow). Scan B shows more extensive low attenuation in the left parietal region and now the right frontoparietal regions (arrow). Scan C was taken 6 weeks after admission and shows well-established extensive areas of cerebral infarction. Courtesy of Dr S. Sturman.

the CT scan in Figure 5.6). This cannot be done reliably with clinical examination. Since the treatment of infarction and haemorrhage can be very different, it is crucial to be able to define them correctly. For example, after an embolic infarction due to atrial fibrillation (see below), the patient might be anticoagulated, but this would be contra-indicated in cerebral haemorrhage as it would make the haemorrhage worse.

- CT imaging should be done within the first 24 hours for people with severe strokes, to ensure the diagnosis is correct and to exclude haemorrhage. However, within 24 hours of onset, the stroke itself may not show that well (take a look again at scan A in Figure 5.5) or not at all in about 50% of cases. Around 5–7 days after stroke, haemorrhages may have been reabsorbed and so it may be impossible to differentiate infarction from haemorrhage at this late stage with CT.

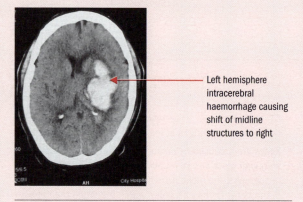

Left hemisphere intracerebral haemorrhage causing shift of midline structures to right

Figure 5.6 CT scan of the brain showing a large cerebral haemorrhage.

The most common cause of cardiac emboli is **atrial fibrillation**. In this condition, the atria beat too fast and ineffectually, leading to turbulence and thus clotting of the blood. These clots can pass through to the left ventricle which pumps them out to the cerebral arteries where they lodge, blocking the vessel and causing stroke or TIA. Atrial fibrillation in such patients is usually caused by ischaemic damage to the heart itself from vascular disease. It can also be caused by cardiac valve disorders such as mitral stenosis, due to previous rheumatic fever, or an overactive thyroid gland (hyperthyroidism or thyrotoxicosis).

Other causes of cardiac emboli include myocardial infarction ('heart attack') in which the arteries to the heart become blocked by vascular disease. This process is the equivalent of a stroke in the brain, so much so that some experts suggest that we should now call suspected stroke 'brain attack'. After myocardial infarction, the lining of the left ventricle can become damaged and sticky leading to thrombosis, clotting of blood, on

extension: Ultrasound-based investigations—carotid ultrasound and echocardiography

BOX 5.5

In ultrasound techniques, high-frequency sound waves are used to outline a part of the body. The waves are emitted from a probe which is held against the skin overlying the area of interest. The two are connected by a jelly which improves transmission of the impulses between the probe and the skin. Some structures reflect the waves better than others. The reflected waves are picked up by a sensor alongside the emitting part of the probe. These are then displayed as a two-dimensional, or more recently a three-dimensional, image of the structure on a monitor, or printed out.

Carotid ultrasound provides data on the visual appearance of the carotid artery in the neck and the flow within it. Blockages of greater than 70% may require removal by endarterectomy.

There are several types of echocardiography but they all provide images of the heart and its valves.

- **Carotid ultrasound** is used to assess the degree of narrowing (stenosis) in the carotid artery in the neck. It is applicable in patients with carotid (anterior) circulation strokes caused by infarction or patients who have had TIAs in the carotid territory. Previous trials have shown that such patients with a greater than 70% carotid stenosis benefit from unblocking of the artery by **carotid endarterectomy**, which is considered in more detail later in this chapter. However, such patients must be fit for major surgery; many may not be because of vascular disease in other organs (e.g. myocardial infarction, heart failure).

- Examining the heart with **echocardiography** is necessary when cardiac abnormalities have been found on clinical examination of the heart or on an electrocardiograph (ECG). The details of these techniques are beyond the scope of this book. However, they both suggest that the stroke or TIA is due to a source of emboli in the heart.

its surface. Fragments of this can break off, becoming emboli which travel to the brain and lead to stroke.

The final optional test that some patients may require is cerebral **angiography**. This is an X-ray-based technique, like CT imaging, but the X-rays are taken after an injection of contrast or dye into the artery being examined. This outlines the inside of the vessel and shows up any blockages. The contrast is injected from the end of a thin tube or catheter. The catheter is inserted via a needle puncture of the femoral artery in the groin under local anaesthetic. The catheter is then pushed up through other arteries to the carotid or vertebral arteries using X-ray guidance.

Figure 5.7 shows a carotid angiogram of a patient following stroke. It shows that the common carotid artery and its two branches, the external and the internal (which supplies blood to the brain) carotid arteries, are badly narrowed by atheroma (see where the arrow is pointing). Angiography is often done to confirm the results of carotid ultrasound which has suggested a greater than 70% narrowing or stenosis of the vessel. In such cases the patient may be a candidate for carotid endarterectomy.

Patients who have suffered a stroke or TIA require a battery of investigations including blood tests, an ECG, and a CT brain scan.

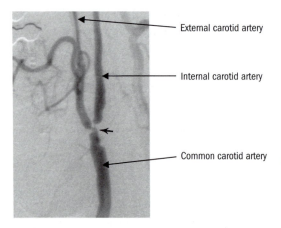

External carotid artery

Internal carotid artery

Common carotid artery

Figure 5.7 Carotid angiogram outlining major stenoses at the bifurcation of the common into the internal and external carotid arteries (arrow).

5.1.6 What treatments are available for stroke?

The treatment of patients after stroke can be divided into three types, largely according to the temporal order in which the treatment required.

- On the admission of patients with moderate to severe stroke, **immediate measures** are necessary to support the patient.
- After the acute phase of the first few days after stroke, **rehabilitation** commences with various techniques such as physiotherapy and speech and language therapy.
- Around the same time, the results of investigations should be known so that **secondary prevention** measures can be taken to treat the cause or causes of the stroke or TIA to try to stop it happening again.

Immediate treatment

The immediate treatment of patients with moderate to severe strokes requires hospital admission. The emergency department team will initiate the standard ABC of care:

- **Airway**—ensure air can get to the lungs through the nose or mouth, if necessary using nasal or mouth airway tube or by inserting an endotracheal tube.
- **Breathing**—ensure the lungs can work properly to exchange gases.
- **Circulation**—ensure the heart is beating properly and that blood is circulating at a normal blood pressure.

The patient will usually be given oxygen via a face mask to increase the amount of oxygen being carried to the brain. Although the neurons in the middle of the stroke area are destined to die, some neurons at the edge of the stroke, in the so-called **ischaemic penumbra**, may not die if they are well cared for. Oxygen may help such cells.

Immediate care will also include inserting an intravenous drip to ensure the patient does not become dehydrated. Dehydration might lead to a drop in blood pressure and further damage in the ischaemic penumbra.

Stroke patients who are confused or unconscious will have a urinary catheter inserted into the bladder. This prevents urinary incontinence which can lead to pressure sores (skin damage due to lying in one position for too long).

Many drugs have undergone clinical trials in the acute phase of stroke in the hope that they might reduce the severity of the damage to the brain. However, only two types of drug have been shown to be effective in this situation:

- A single dose of aspirin immediately on presentation has been shown to reduce the risk of early recurrent stroke and increases the chance of survival free of disability.

- **Thrombolytic therapy** given by intravenous injection dissolves the clot which is blocking the artery. So called 'clot busting' drugs include tissue plasminogen activator (tPA). This activates anti-clotting mechanisms in the blood which help to break the clot up. However, clinical trials have shown that tPA is only effective if given within 3 hours of cerebral infarction. Very few patients reach hospital within this time. This treatment also requires that the patient has had an immediate CT scan to exclude a haemorrhage and to show early subtle signs of infarction. Very few hospitals in the UK have the facilities to provide such a service. Further trials are ongoing to determine whether later thrombolysis can be effective with new types of thrombolytic.

Rehabilitation

Once the patient has overcome the acute effects of the stroke, rehabilitation can begin. This aims to improve function, where possible, and minimize the effects of loss of function on patient's every day life.

- **Physiotherapy** concentrates on improving strength and adaptation to deficits in gait, posture, balance, and transfers (moving from one area to another, e.g. bed to chair, chair to wheelchair).

- **Speech and language therapy** is appropriate for patients with dysphasia (language disturbance), dysarthria (slurred speech), and also **dysphagia** (difficulty in swallowing).

- **Occupational therapy** helps the patient to adapt their life and its occupations to any residual deficit using problem-solving approaches. This is likely to include the provision of aids and adaptations such as aids for walking (e.g. sticks, frames, wheelchairs) or for eating (e.g. non-slip mats, large-handled cutlery).

If the patient has difficulty eating then a **nutritionalist** (dietitian) will be involved with their care. Bladder dysfunction will require the input of a **continence nurse** who can provide advice on approaches such as permanent urinary catheterization, intermittent self-catheterization, urinary sheaths, and continence pads. A **neuropsychologist** may be required to address aspects of cognitive dysfunction after stroke.

Clinical trials have shown that rehabilitation is best done in a dedicated stroke unit. This reduces both final disability levels and mortality from stroke. Although the precise details of what comprises a stroke unit is not clearly understood from these trials, it is likely to include a multidisciplinary team of doctors and the therapists detailed above.

Secondary prevention

Secondary prevention measures following stroke and TIA include treatment of the risk factors which have caused the problem in each case. This may include treatment

extension: Secondary prevention measures following stroke and TIA

BOX 5.6

- **Treat hypertension**—reduce salt intake, increase exercise, medication (e.g. bendro-flumethiazide; beta blockers—atenolol).
- **Treat diabetes**—diet, weight reduction, oral hypoglycaemics (e.g. metformin), subcutaneous injections of insulin.
- **Treat hyperlipidaemia**—diet, weight reduction, medication (i.e. statins—simvastatin).
- **Smoking cessation**—willpower, short-term nicotine replacement (e.g. patches).
- **Antiplatelet agents** to prevent the risk of clots forming on atheromatous plaques—e.g. aspirin, dipyridamole retard, clopidogril.
- **Anticoagulation** (warfarin)—for patients with established cardiac emboli.
- **Carotid endarterectomy** (see text).

of hypertension, diabetes, hyperlipidaemia, and smoking as detailed in Box 5.6. Most patients will also be given antiplatelet agents such as aspirin and dipyridamole retard. These agents reduce the ability of platelets to stimulate blood clotting, thereby reducing the risks of thrombosis and embolism.

In a very small number of patients following carotid stroke or TIA, it may be necessary to remove the atheromatous plaque causing a severe (>70%) blockage of a carotid artery surgically. This operation is called **carotid endarterectomy**. It is done only in people who have suffered carotid TIAs or a partial anterior (carotid) circulation syndrome stroke which is due to infarction not haemorrhage. The danger is that by leaving the plaque, further thrombosis and embolism may occur leading to a devastating stroke.

Figure 5.8 shows the details of carotid endarterectomy. Under a general anaesthetic, the affected carotid artery is exposed, then clamped above and below the plaque. A shunt is previously inserted above and below the locations of the clamps to allow blood to continue to flow to the brain. The artery is then opened longitudinally and the atheromatous plaque on the surface of the vessel is physically stripped out. The vessel is then sewn up and the clamps and the shunt tube removed.

Carotid endarterectomy is not without its risks. Strokes may actually be caused by the operation because, the shunt may not allow sufficient blood flow to the brain during the operation and clots may form on the rough surface of the vessel left after surgery. Clinical trials are now attempting to refine which patients are likely to suffer strokes as a result of the operation, so that it can be avoided.

SELF-CHECK 5.5

How is a severe stroke treated?

5.1.7 **What is the long-term outcome of a stroke?**

The outcome or **prognosis** following the different types of stroke is detailed in Table 5.3. From this we learn that TACS strokes have the worst prognosis, with 60% of patients being dead 12 months after the event and most of the rest left with major disability so that they are dependent on others in their activities of daily living.

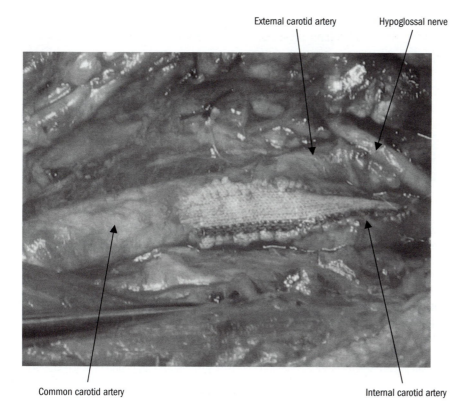

External carotid artery   Hypoglossal nerve

Common carotid artery   Internal carotid artery

Figure 5.8 Carotid endarterectomy. Note the patch over the previous incision at the bifurcation of the carotid artery. Courtesy of Mr S. Silverman. A full-colour version of this image is shown in the plates section.

Table 5.3 Prognosis at 12 months following stroke (from Oxfordshire Community Stroke Project)

Type	Dead (%)	Dependent (%)	Independent (%)
Total anterior circulation syndrome	60	36	4
Partial anterior circulation syndrome	16	30	54
Lacunar syndrome	11	28	61
Posterior circulation syndrome	20	20	60

5.1.8 Multiple cerebral infarction

In recent years, we have realized that some people do not just have single discrete strokes; they suffer multiple strokes, many of which may be clinically silent with no symptoms or signs to be seen. With the ageing of the population, many more people with vascular risk factors are being seen who go on to develop multiple cerebral infarcts. In view of this increasing problem, this condition deserves a separate section of this chapter.

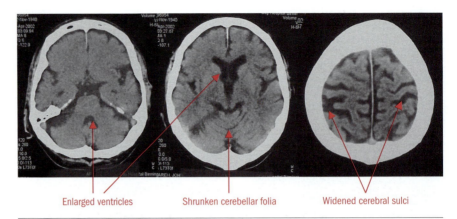

Enlarged ventricles   Shrunken cerebellar folia   Widened cerebral sulci

Figure 5.9 CT scan showing the features of marked cerebral shrinkage due to multiple cerebral infarction.

The main presentations of multiple infarcts include progressive cognitive decline (dementia), parkinsonism, and urinary incontinence. Since most of the strokes in this condition are small and many without any symptoms, they gradually build up over some years causing patients to develop severe problems by the time they present to clinic. In some patients, each stroke is large enough to be noticed and so the patient will have a stepwise decline in function. In others, though, each stroke is not obvious and the decline is more gradual, just like in neurodegenerative conditions such as Alzheimer's and Parkinson's diseases.

It can take expert judgement to differentiate a multiple infarct state from these neuro-degenerative conditions. Imaging in multiple cerebral infarction may show just shrinkage of the brain (as can be seen in Figure 5.9), but in other cases it can show large areas of cortical (grey matter) and subcortical (white matter) infarction.

We do not have any guidance from clinical trials on what secondary prevention measures are effective in this condition. It is assumed that most would work, although carotid endarterectomy is not appropriate without trial evidence in view of the dangers of causing a stroke.

5.2 Subarachnoid haemorrhage and intracranial aneurysms

The layered structuring of the meninges is described in section 1.2.3 on page 5.

Subarachnoid haemorrhage (SAH) occurs when blood leaks into the subarachnoid space. You should familiarize yourself with the three layers of the meninges and thus the subarachnoid space.

SAH can occur in several conditions, but in 90% it is due to ruptured intracranial **aneurysm**, so this is the focus for this part of the chapter.

5.2.1 How common is SAH and who are most at risk?

The incidence of SAH is around 10 per 100 000 of the population per year, so about 5000 people will have such a haemorrhage each year in the UK.

5.2.2 What are the likely causes of SAH?

Subarachnoid haemorrhage is caused by:

- ruptured intracranial aneurysm
- ruptured arteriovenous malformation
- other very rare conditions.

Why aneurysms form is unknown, but they are increased in those who smoke or abuse alcohol and in those with hypertension or a family history of the disorder.

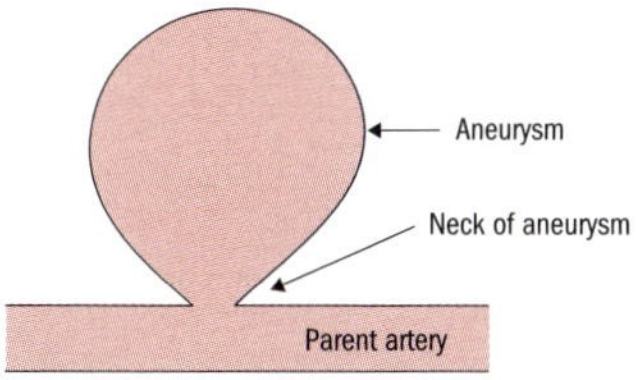

Figure 5.10 Schematic diagram of an aneurysm.

5.2.3 What tissue changes occur in SAH?

The reason or reasons why weakness develops in intracranial arteries leading to aneurysms is not known. We can imagine that the high pressure of the blood pressing on a weakened artery wall would lead to the vessel wall billowing outward like a balloon (as shown schematically in Figure 5.10). Once the aneurysm wall gets too thin, it bursts, also just like a balloon. Blood then leaks out into the subarachnoid space.

The other, rarer, cause of SAH is rupture of an **arteriovenous malformation** (AVM). In this condition, an abnormal connection between a set of intracranial arteries and veins forms, bypassing the capillary bed. The reason for this is not known in most cases. Because thin veins come under high arterial pressure, they develop weaknesses which can rupture leading to SAH.

More information on arteriovenous malformations and their treatment can be found in section 12.2.3 on page 259.

SELF-CHECK 5.6

What is subarachnoid haemorrhage and what causes it?

5.2.4 What are the symptoms and signs of SAH?

SAH most commonly presents with sudden, severe headache. Patients often give a graphic description of the suddenness and severity of the pain: 'as though I had been hit over the head with a cricket bat'. They can also complain of a stiff neck, which can be difficult to passively move on examination. Other symptoms include brief loss of consciousness, nausea, and vomiting.

> Subarachnoid haemorrhage most commonly presents with sudden, severe headache.

The blood in the subarachnoid space leads to irritation of other nearby arteries which have not ruptured. These arteries can go into **vasospasm**. This spasm narrows the lumen of the artery and thus reduces the blood supply to areas of the brain. This can give rise to symptoms and signs similar to that of stroke which is why, in the past, SAH has been included under the heading of stroke. Vasospasm eventually resolves, if the patient survives, and for many people its effects can be reversible.

Sometimes aneurysms are large enough to compress adjacent structures, even before they rupture in some cases. One classical presentation of an aneurysm of the posterior communicating artery is of SAH along with a third cranial nerve palsy, since the nerve lies very close to the artery (see the case study in Box 5.7).

The presenting symptoms and signs of SAH are not always typical. Clinicians seeing such patients in the emergency department must have a high index of suspicion for SAH otherwise it can be missed. 'If you don't think about it, you won't diagnose it!'

SELF-CHECK 5.7

How does subarachnoid haemorrhage present?

case study: Subarachnoid haemorrhage

BOX
5.7

- A 65-year-old woman presented to the emergency department after a sudden collapse. She quickly came round, but had the worst headache she had ever suffered. An hour later, she reported double vision (diplopia).

- On examination, she was mildly confused. She had drooping of the right eyelid (ptosis) with a dilated right pupil, and the right eye could not look inward and upward (i.e. third cranial nerve palsy).

- A CT scan confirmed blood in the subarachnoid space around the brain stem (see Figure 5.11).

- She was transferred to the care of her regional neurosurgical unit. One day after the event, she had an angiogram which confirmed the presence of a right posterior communicating artery aneurysm. The next day, after giving written informed consent, she underwent successful coiling of the aneurysm.

- Six months later, she had no residual deficit when reviewed in clinic.

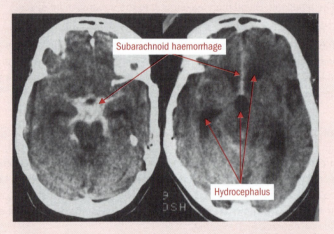

Figure 5.11 CT scan of patient with subarachnoid haemorrhage leading to obstructive hydrocephalus.

5.2.5 What tests can we use to diagnose SAH?

The main investigation for SAH is CT imaging. This not only shows the blood, but its distribution can suggest which vessel has ruptured. This is important to know since some patients have multiple aneurysms and treatment must be given to the one that has just bled.

> The first investigation in suspected subarachnoid haemorrhage is CT imaging.

If you look carefully at Figure 5.11, you can see large amounts of blood in the sub-arachnoid space deep around the brain stem which looks white compared with the rest

extension: Lumbar puncture (LP)   **BOX 5.8**

- Lumbar puncture is an invasive technique: a needle is inserted in the lumbar region of the back between the spinous processes of the vertebrae and pushed through into the subarachnoid space. It is done under local anaesthetic. Although it sounds barbaric, in fact it is not too uncomfortable if done by an experienced practitioner. Once the needle is in the subarachnoid space, drops of CSF drip from the end of the needle and are caught in sterile bottles.

- The CSF is sent to the laboratory for analysis of colour (spectrophotometry), cell counts, protein, and glucose. The needle is then removed and, after a short rest, the patient can get up. The only significant side effect is a post-LP headache.

- LP is used in the diagnosis of subarachnoid haemorrhage (presence of xanthochromia, breakdown product of red blood cells), meningitis and encephalitis (high white blood cell count), and multiple sclerosis (presence of oligoclonal bands).

- The red blood cells which leak into the subarachnoid space during a haemorrhage slowly break down. Since these breakdown products are yellow or xanthochromic, the CSF obtained at LP looks yellow. This may not be clear to the naked eye, but spectrophotometry in the laboratory can detect it. It takes at least 12 hours for enough blood to have broken down for the **xanthochromia** to be detectable. This means that the LP must be done 12 hours after the patient first noticed symptoms.

of the intracranial structures. The body tries to clear the subarachnoid blood through the normal CSF pathways. Since the arachnoid villi which absorb CSF can get blocked by this blood, continued production of CSF but blockage of its outflow leads to expansion of the CSF spaces. This is referred to as **hydrocephalus** (and can be seen where indicated in Figure 5.11).

Subarachnoid blood does not always show up on a CT brain scan. Presumably there is either not enough blood to show, particularly if the scan has been done too soon, or the scan has been done too late and the blood has been absorbed. In this situation, the patient has a **lumbar puncture**. Box 5.8 explains more about this technique.

Whether the SAH has been proven by CT or LP, the patient next has an **angiogram**.

Angiography is described in section 5.1.5 on page 93.

During angiography, all four of the main arteries to the brain are injected with contrast which outlines the lumen of the vessel and shows up any aneurysms.

Figure 5.12 shows the CT scan of a patient with an anterior communicating artery aneurysm which has caused SAH, much of which is between the frontal lobes of the brain (look at the top CT scans). The angiogram outlines a small bilobed aneurysm on this artery.

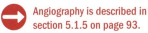

SELF-CHECK 5.8

What investigations should be done in a patient with suspected subarachnoid haemorrhage?

5.2.6 What treatments are available for SAH?

Until the last few years, the main treatment for intracranial aneurysms was surgical **clipping**. Under general anaesthetic, the skin and bone in the region of the aneurysm

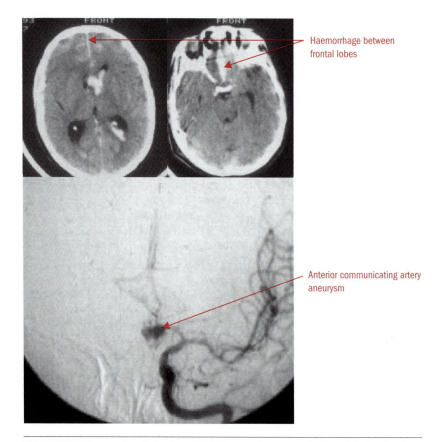

Haemorrhage between
frontal lobes

Anterior communicating artery
aneurysm

Figure 5.12 CT scan showing subarachnoid haemorrhage, much of which is localized
between the frontal lobes, due to an anterior communicating artery aneurysm which is
demonstrated by angiography.

were opened as a form of flap. Very carefully, the surgeon then retracted the brain to
uncover the aneurysm. A special clip was then placed across the neck of the aneurysm.
The blood in the aneurysm then clotted, so the risk of re-rupture was prevented. However, the risk of damage to the brain at the time of surgery can be high, so alternative
treatment methods have been sought.

A non-surgical technique has now replaced surgical clipping, at least for certain types
of aneurysm. Intra-arterial **coiling** of aneurysms seems to be safer, although there are
still concerns over its long-term effects. You can see from Figure 5.13 that coiling uses
an angiographic technique. A tiny catheter is passed up into the parent vessel right up
to the neck of the aneurysm. Then a thin titanium coil is released into the lumen of the
aneurysm. This is pre-formed to jump back into a coil shape once it leaves the catheter.
Several coils are released into the aneurysm until most of it is occluded. Titanium is
thrombogenic, so any tiny spaces left in the aneurysm between the wires clot off so that
further bleeding cannot occur.

SELF-CHECK 5.9

How can aneurysmal SAH be
treated?

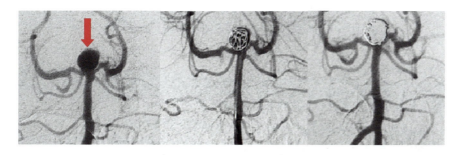

Figure 5.13 Intra-arterial coiling of an aneurysm. The left panel shows a basilar tip aneurysm (arrow) at angiography. In the middle panel, the aneurysm has been partially occluded by one coil. Several other coils have been added for almost complete occlusion in the right panel. Reproduced courtesy of Dr S. Chavda.

5.2.7 What is the likely long-term outcome of SAH?

Aneurysmal SAH is a dangerous condition. Around 40% of patients with SAH who are admitted to hospital die within one month. More than one third of those who survive will have severe physical and/or mental disability. Therefore, it is very important that a high index of suspicion is maintained for diagnosing the condition in emergency departments.

SUMMARY

- A stroke is a sudden loss of brain function lasting for more than 24 hours resulting from perturbation of its blood supply.

- A transient ischaemic attack (TIA) is a cerebral ischaemic event with all symptoms and signs disappearing within 24 hours.

- The two carotid and two vertebral arteries supply blood to the brain in a specific distribution.

- Stroke is the third most common cause of death worldwide.

- Cerebral haemorrhage is caused by hypertension, whereas cerebral infarction is caused by hypertension, diabetes, smoking, obesity, and/or cardiac embolism.

- The Oxfordshire Community Stroke Project Classification of stroke syndromes divides them into four categories: total anterior circulation syndrome (TACS); partial anterior circulation syndrome (PACS); lacunar circulation syndrome (LACS); posterior circulation syndrome (POCS).

- Patients who have suffered a stroke or TIA require a battery of investigations including blood tests, an ECG, and a CT brain scan.

- CT imaging should be done within 24 hours of severe stroke to ensure the diagnosis is correct and to exclude haemorrhage.

- Treatment of stroke includes immediate supportive measures, rehabilitation, and the institution of secondary prevention measures.

- Subarachnoid haemorrhage occurs when blood leaks into the subarachnoid space, most commonly from a ruptured intracranial aneurysm.

- SAH most commonly presents with sudden, severe headache.

- All patients with suspected SAH should have CT imaging followed by a lumbar puncture if the scan is normal.

- Radiological coiling of aneurysms is preferred to surgical clipping at present.

FURTHER READING

E. M. Manno. Subarachnoid haemorrhage. *Neurologic Clinics* 2004: **22**; 347–366.
A general overview of latest developments in the diagnosis and treatment of subarachnoid haemorrhage.

Neurology in practice: Issue 1—Stroke. *Journal of Neurology, Neurosurgery and Psychiatry* 2001; **70**(Suppl. 1).
More advanced discussion of current issues in stroke management.

C. Warlow, C. Sudlow, M. Dennis *et al.* Stroke. *Lancet* 2003; **362**: 1211–1224.
An excellent overview of all aspects of stroke.

CHAPTER SIX

Epilepsy

John Jefferys and John Fox

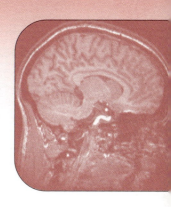

INTRODUCTION

Epilepsy is one of the most common serious brain disorders, with a prevalence of just under 1% of the population. In the UK about 50 new cases per 100 000 population are diagnosed each year. Although most people with epilepsy have their seizures controlled effectively by currently available drugs, a substantial minority do not and may require other treatments such as surgery. In this chapter we define epilepsy, describe the main kinds of epilepsy, say something of the underlying mechanisms, and finally discuss treatment.

6.1 What is epilepsy?

The diagnosis of epilepsy requires two or more seizures that cannot be explained by clinical problems originating outside the brain. The symptoms of seizures depend on which part of the brain is affected (as we shall see below), but they always result from sudden abnormal and excessively synchronized and intense activity in one or more populations of cortical neurons. This abnormal activity usually can be recorded with the **electroencephalogram** (EEG) which detects electrical signals produced by the brain (see Box 6.1 for more details). Epileptic seizures can be recorded through the thickness of the scalp, skull, and **meninges** because the synchronization of neural activity generates relatively large and rhythmic potentials.

> Epilepsy is a group of conditions exhibiting recurring seizures during which brain function is disrupted by excessively intense and/or synchronized activity of cortical neurons.

extension: The electroencephalogram (EEG)—recording brain waves

Neurons produce small electrical signals when they are active. These are the basis of cellular electrophysiological recording methods of the kinds discussed in Chapter 2. Although each neuron only produces a very small current, the cortex contains huge numbers of neurons organized with their **dendrites** roughly parallel.

As a consequence, if many of the neurons are doing the same thing at the same time, the currents they produce can become large enough to produce voltages that can be recorded from the scalp. These currents have to be large because the recording electrodes on the scalp are separated from the source of the electrical signals by the membranes around the brain, fluid-filled spaces, bone, fat, and skin, as we can see from the top part of Figure 6.1. During epileptic activity neurons become excessively synchronized—that is, they do the same thing at the same time—so that the EEG can be a very useful tool.

Figure 6.1 shows a cartoon of the electric current that flows when an excitatory **synapse** is active at the apical dendrites: it flows into the dendrite and spreads some distance along the inside of the neuron before leaking back out. The return path of the current sets up the voltage gradient which can be recorded from the surface as long as enough cells are active at the same time.

The activity recorded at each electrode depends on the overall activity of many thousands of neurons in the underlying cortex.

If the seizure is **focal**, it will only be seen at the electrode(s) closest to the focus. If the seizure is **generalized**, it will be seen simultaneously at electrodes across both hemispheres.

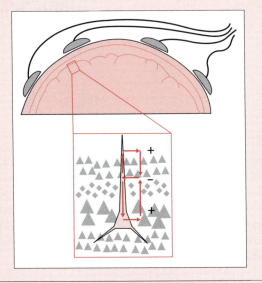

Figure 6.1 The recording of the EEG signal from the scalp.

6.2 What are the symptoms and signs of epilepsy?

Symptoms of epileptic seizures typically include:

- temporary changes in mental state or level of consciousness
- abnormal sensory experiences (such as numbness spreading across parts of the body, flashes of light, and strange feelings in the gut)
- characteristic abnormal movements, such as sustained (tonic) or rhythmic (clonic) muscle contractions.

Much more detail on the manifestations of the different types of epilepsy is given in section 6.4 below.

The precise symptoms observed during a seizure depend upon which part of the brain is involved.

It is important to realize that everyone can experience a seizure if sufficiently physically stressed. Circumstances which will precipitate a seizure include severe sleep deprivation; suddenly stopping drugs such as alcohol, barbiturates, or **benzodiazepines**; head injury; some kinds of poisoning; and various metabolic disturbances including uncontrolled diabetes and low levels of ions such as calcium, sodium, or magnesium. These are known as **symptomatic seizures** and are not epilepsy.

The most common cause of symptomatic seizures in children under 5 years old is fever; these **febrile seizures** occur in about 5% of the population, and are usually benign. Other symptomatic seizures also are common, with a lifetime prevalence of 2–5% of the population.

6.3 How do we diagnose epilepsy?

The crucial evidence in diagnosing epilepsy is the **history** taken from the patient and an eye-witness to the attack. Rarely will any useful information be gained from clinical examination.

All patients should have an EEG, but the chances are low that a seizure will occur during a routine EEG recording. Fortunately, the EEG does show some more limited abnormal activity between attacks. These are called **interictal** (between seizure) spikes and other brief epileptiform discharges. They usually are more localized and much briefer than seizures, and they help considerably with the diagnosis of epilepsy. The main use of the EEG is in helping to decide what type of epilepsy the patient is suffering from, as we can see from Figure 6.2. Panel (a) of this figure shows normal alpha-wave activity, recorded from the occipital region (that part of the **cortex** that processes visual information). Note the rhythmic 9 Hz (cycles per second) activity when the eyes are closed, which is then abolished when the eyes are opened (denoted by the arrow). The other panels in Figure 6.2 denote typical waveforms seen in different forms of epilepsy, and we will return to these later in this chapter.

Patients may also have **neuroimaging** to exclude a structural underlying cause for their condition (such as a brain **tumour**) and the most sensitive is **magnetic resonance imaging** (MRI), which is described in more detail in Box 6.2.

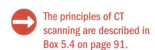

The principles of CT scanning are described in Box 5.4 on page 91.

The level of **prolactin** in the blood is increased for a short period following certain types of seizure (especially generalized tonic-clonic) and measurement of this hormone can be helpful in distinguishing between epilepsy and **pseudoseizures**.

The other important causes of transient loss of consciousness seen in clinic are conditions that cause a reduction in cerebral blood flow, such as **cardiac syncope** (heart rhythm disturbance such as heart block) and **vasovagal syncope** or a faint (loss of consciousness due to failure in the neural control of blood pressure). Reduced oxygenation of the brain may itself cause a brief seizure, further complicating the diagnosis.

Cardiac syncope is usually brief and associated with other cardiac symptoms such as palpitations. In vasovagal syncope, the person has warning symptoms such as feeling hot, dizzy, and faint for a few seconds or minutes before they lose consciousness. The latter often occur in characteristic situations such as prolonged standing, after a

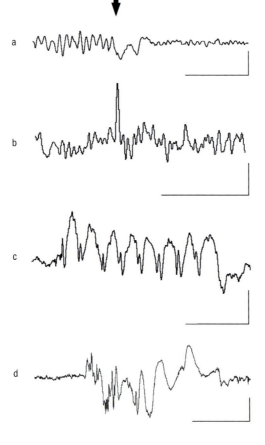

Figure 6.2 EEG waveforms, recorded using scalp electrodes. The horizontal calibration bars show 1 second in all traces; vertical calibration bars show 70 μV, 50 μV, 100 μV, and 100 μV for a, b, c, and d, respectively. The arrow in (a) indicates opening of the eyes.

extension: MRI   BOX 6.2

- MRI is an imaging technique based on the magnetic properties of a tissue. Like CT scanning, it produces cross-sectional images of the structure in question.

- MRI is a complex technique to explain. However, it is essentially based on the magnetic properties of the hydrogen atom. The hydrogen atom nucleus is a single proton which spins and so has a positive charge. This means that it has magnetic properties. In the first step of MRI, a large magnetic field is applied to the patient so that the hydrogen atoms align parallel or antiparallel with the external field. In this external magnetic field, hydrogen atoms 'spin' around the line of the magnetic field, which is called **precession**.

- The next step is to apply a second magnetic field at right angles to the original field. This is called a **radiofrequency pulse** and is given through a **coil**. The net magnetization vector of the hydrogen atoms turns towards the coil. This adds energy to the system.

- The final step is to stop the radiofrequency pulse so that the hydrogen atoms **relax** back to their previous vector. This releases energy in the form of a radiofrequency pulse and this pulse is picked up by the same coil, amplified, and converted into the image, using the tomography principles used in CT scanning.

- It is sometimes useful to use an intravenous contrast injection of a substance called gadolinium. This can highlight certain lesions such as the actively growing area of a tumour.

- MRI provides more detail of the substance of the brain than CT scanning. Although MRI scanners are expensive, most district general hospitals in the UK have one.

large meal, or on getting out of bed in the middle of the night (for example, micturition syncope).

Symptoms that appear to be seizures may in fact be pseudoseizures (non-epileptic attacks) which have behavioural rather than neurological causes.

The distinction between epilepsy, symptomatic seizures, pseudoseizures, and loss of consciousness due to reduced blood flow to the brain is important for decisions on the appropriate treatments. There is no point trying to treat epilepsy if the underlying problem is faints or cardiovascular disease. This is a significant problem: overlapping symptoms between epilepsy, cerebrovascular, and psychological disorders can lead to difficulties in diagnosis resulting in uncertain diagnoses in as many as 20% of cases.

The diagnosis of epilepsy is not made lightly because it still (and inappropriately) carries social stigma, and impacts on lifestyle—for instance the ability to hold a driving licence or to undertake certain jobs and pastimes.

> Symptomatic seizures may occur in people without epilepsy if exposed to certain conditions such as the taking or discontinuing of certain drugs, electrical stimulation, cardiovascular problems, or metabolic diseases.

SELF-CHECK 6.1

What investigations are carried out to help diagnosis in a patient whose history suggests a possible seizure?

6.4 How are the different types of epilepsy classified?

Epilepsy is a group of disorders rather than a single entity; the International League Against Epilepsy (ILAE, <*www.ilae-epilepsy.org*>), for example, recognizes 30 self-limited seizure types and 36 epilepsy syndromes.

The most important distinction, however, is between **generalized seizures** (in which the abnormal activity begins simultaneously over a wide area of both cerebral cortices, at least within the time resolution of the EEG) and **focal seizures** (in which the abnormal activity starts, and may remain, in one localized region of the brain).

6.4.1 Generalized seizures

Generalized seizures result in loss of consciousness, which perhaps is not surprising given the extent of the disruption of normal brain function. They fall into several classes and we will list some of them here:

Tonic-clonic seizures

This is the kind of epilepsy that most people would recognize. They are often called **grand mal** seizures. The patient becomes rigid and may fall during the tonic phase, which is followed by the clonic phase when their muscles rhythmically relax and contract. The patient will often bite their tongue and, during the clonic phase, may be **incontinent**. Following the seizure, there is usually a period of confusion and tiredness. A case study of this seizure type is described in Box 6.3.

case study: Idiopathic generalized epilepsy   BOX 6.3

A 25-year-old man had experienced two episodes of loss of consciousness. Both had occurred without warning. On the first occasion, he had been alone and, when he regained consciousness, he was aware that his muscles ached and that he had bitten his tongue. On the second occasion, he had been with his mother who said that he had suddenly collapsed, become rigid, and his face had turned blue. After a few moments, he started to make rhythmic jerking movements of his arms and legs and this continued for about a minute. An ambulance was called, and when paramedics arrived the patient was conscious but confused.

Routine medical examination showed no abnormalities and an MRI head scan was normal. His EEG, however, showed brief irregular complex discharges which contained spikes and slow waves; this activity could be seen in both hemispheres and there was no consistently localized abnormality.

A diagnosis of idiopathic generalized epilepsy was made: the seizure type was tonic-clonic (grand mal).

Treatment was started with sodium valproate. At follow-up, 1 year later, he reported no further attacks.

Absence epilepsy

This is a very different kind of generalized epilepsy and is often described as **petit mal** epilepsy. During an absence seizure, patients lose consciousness for just a few seconds. These seizures are not associated with loss of posture or other changes in muscular activity (apart, sometimes, from rhythmic movements of the eyelids or other minor facial movements). Absence seizures are most common in children and can be mistaken for day-dreaming. A description of an absence epilepsy patient is given in Box 6.4, and if

case study: Absence epilepsy   BOX 6.4

A 10-year-old boy had repeated brief episodes during which he appeared to 'switch off'. His parents said that, in these episodes, he stared straight ahead, looked blank for a few seconds, but then carried on as if nothing had happened. He was of average intelligence, but one of his teachers had thought he was prone to daydreaming.

A routine medical examination showed no abnormalities. An EEG recording, however, showed that during these episodes, normal brain activity was interrupted by 3/s spike and slow wave discharges which occurred synchronously through both hemispheres and lasted for about 4 sec.

A diagnosis of absence (petit mal) epilepsy was made and he was treated with ethosuximide, which successfully controlled his attacks.

we look at the EEG waveform in panel (c) of Figure 6.2, we can see the 3 Hz spike and wave activity that is characteristic of this form of generalized epilepsy.

Tonic seizures

These have a widespread steady, or tonic, muscular contraction, usually leading to falling. Although rapid recovery occurs, there is a significant risk of injury from falls.

Atonic seizures or drop attacks

These are characterized by a sudden loss of muscle tone. There is, again, a rapid recovery but a significant risk of injury.

Myoclonic seizures

These are brief, sudden jerking of one or more limbs or trunk.

6.4.2 Focal seizures

The focal epilepsies start in some specific brain region. This can be seen as localized synchronous EEG activity, so-called spikes and sharp waves between seizures (interictal), and as localized onsets of seizures (although this is not likely to be recorded in most patients because their seizures are relatively infrequent).

Focal seizures have symptoms that depend on where the focus is located. As a group they are more common than the generalized epilepsies, at least in adults. In a simple focal seizure, there is no loss of consciousness; if consciousness is impaired, the seizure is often described as complex.

We will consider here three types of focal seizure:

- **Focal sensory seizures**—In these, the patient experiences sensory symptoms, the nature of which depends on the location of the focus. A focus in the occipital cortex, for example generates visual symptoms, whereas one in the somatosensory strip creates symptoms that appear to come from the opposite side of the body surface.

- **Focal motor seizures**—These have motor symptoms. If restricted to the motor strip, these may consist of simple, localized tonic or clonic contractions on the side of the body opposite to the affected hemisphere. More bizarre movements or posturing may be seen, however, if the focus is in the frontal lobe.

- **Temporal lobe epilepsy**—This is the most frequently encountered form of adult focal epilepsy. The temporal lobe is an association area of the cortex, closely related to the limbic system; seizures in this region may therefore give rise to a mixture of motor, sensory and emotional symptoms. Panel (b) of Figure 6.2 illustrates the interictal spike discharge, recorded from the temporal region, that is typically seen in this form of focal epilepsy. Patients frequently describe an **aura** at the onset of their seizure; this may consist of an odour, taste, abdominal sensation, feelings of *déjà vu*, or irrational fear. This may progress to a period of a few minutes during which the patients lose contact with reality and may stare, fail to respond to questions, and perhaps make complex, stereotyped movements such as fumbling with clothes, chewing, or lip smacking. These movements are often described as **automatisms**. A case study of temporal lobe epilepsy is described in Box 6.5.

The lobes of the cortex associated with sensory systems are described in section 1.4.2 on page 8.

The cortical components of the motor system are discussed in more detail in section 1.4.2 on page 8.

SELF-CHECK 6.2

How does a generalized seizure differ from a focal seizure?

case study: Temporal lobe epilepsy

BOX 6.5

A 30-year-old woman suffered from repeated episodes in which she experienced a sensation of churning in her stomach, and this was frequently followed by periods of a minute or so during which she felt 'unreal'. In addition, friends had told her that, on occasions, she would break off conversation and stare blankly in front of her; sometimes she would also make chewing movements, before returning to normality after a minute or so.

Routine examination showed no abnormality, and standard MRI examination of her head was also within normal limits. An EEG showed spike discharges which were generated independently in both temporal regions.

A diagnosis of temporal lobe epilepsy was made and she was treated with carbamazepine, which reduced the frequency of her attacks.

6.4.3 Secondary generalization

Although a seizure may start at a localized focus, the abnormal activity sometimes spreads. The classical example of seizure spread is called **Jacksonian march**, which is the spread of seizure activity through contiguous parts of the cortex, producing symptoms in the associated parts of the body, such as spreading from the hand region to the forearm, upper arm, and shoulder. It is most obvious in the motor system, but also occurs in other cortical areas.

When a focal seizure extends to the whole cortex, it can cause loss of consciousness and a generalized tonic-clonic seizure; this is termed **secondary generalization**. If an EEG is being recorded during such a seizure, it shows repeated, rhythmic spikes at the focus during the early part of the seizure, but there is a gradual, progressive spread of activity as increasing numbers of neurons are recruited into the discharges which eventually include both hemispheres.

6.4.4 Reflex epilepsy

Some epilepsies have seizures that can be triggered by sensory stimuli of various kinds. The commonest trigger is a flickering light, and stroboscopic lights are routinely used to try to trigger diagnostic abnormalities in the EEG. If seizures only occur following specific stimuli then the condition is called **reflex epilepsy**, and is classified by the kind of stimulus (light or photic, music, reading, startle, and so on). An example of the complex EEG waveforms that can be evoked by photic stimulation in patients suffering from **juvenile myoclonic epilepsy**, can be seen in panel (d) of Figure 6.2.

Reflex epilepsies can be either focal or generalized.

6.4.5 Status epilepticus

Most seizures are transient events, lasting, at most, a few minutes. On occasions, however, they fail to stop spontaneously and the patient enters **status epilepticus**. This is a serious medical emergency which can lead to death unless treated quickly.

> The classification of the epilepsies is a complex task, but is important both for the treatment and for predicting the course of the disease.

6.5 What are the underlying causes of epilepsy?

Epilepsies may have no discernible cause by way of a structural **lesion** in the brain or a gene mutation, but sufferers may exhibit just a low seizure threshold in an otherwise normal brain. These are called **idiopathic** epilepsies and they are common. Fortunately they usually have a good response to drugs and are rarely associated with other disabilities.

Other epilepsies may be secondary to structural lesions in the brain that can be seen with neuroimaging or by examination of post-mortem tissue histologically; these are called **symptomatic epilepsies**. We will consider these in more detail below.

A third group of epilepsies are thought to be symptomatic, but no pathology has been identified and may never be. These used to be called **cryptogenic**, but the term is being phased out in favour of the more precise '**probably symptomatic**'.

> Idiopathic epilepsies are those in which there is no obvious cause in the form of a structural lesion or a genetic abnormality.

The kinds of pathology that can be associated with symptomatic epilepsies include neuronal migration disorders, head injury, brain tumours, neuronal loss and gliosis, and gene mutations.

6.5.1 Neuronal migration disorders

These are increasingly frequently recognized as imaging and pathology improve. They can be caused by gene mutations that interfere with the complex process of organizing the circuitry of the brain. These disorders include some drastic structural changes in the brain: a second layer of **grey matter** contained within the **white matter** of the cortex (so-called **double cortex**); a very smooth cortex, lacking the normal **gyri** and **sulci** (so-called **lissencephaly**); and lots of very small gyri in place of the normal-sized ones (**polymicrogyria**).

There is further discussion of the incidence of epilepsy following traumatic brain injury in section 12.2.1 on page 255.

6.5.2 Head injury

Injuries that penetrate the skull are particularly linked with the subsequent development of epilepsy. Lesions may be visible on MRI. Breakdown products from blood, particularly ferric and ferrous ions, may act as an irritant that leads to seizures.

6.5.3 Brain tumours

Tumours often trigger seizures, at least partly because they release glutamate into the extracellular space. A typical presentation of such a case is described in Box 6.6.

A further case study of focal epilepsy associated with a brain tumour is described in Box 12.5 on page 257.

> **case study: Seizures triggered by a brain tumour**   **BOX 6.6**
>
> A 35-year-old man presented following a single, generalized tonic-clonic seizure. He gave a 1-month history of headaches, which were diffuse and more marked when awaking in the morning. Over a period of several months, he had also experienced numerous episodes in which he had a strong sensation that he had previously been in the place and situation in which he now found himself (*déjà vu*); these episodes lasted no more than a few seconds.
>
> Routine medical examination showed no abnormalities. An EEG, however, showed spike discharges (and slow waves) in the left temporal region and an MRI scan showed a glioma in the same region.
>
> The tumour was surgically removed.

6.5.4 Neuronal loss and gliosis

Neuronal loss and **gliosis** are commonly associated with epilepsy. Temporal lobe epilepsy, in particular, is often associated with hippocampal **sclerosis** which can be detected by MRI (as we can see from the image in Figure 6.3).

Hippocampal sclerosis can also be demonstrated using **histology**. If we look at the top part of Figure 6.4, we can see a stained section of a normal hippocampus. Below this is a section of a sclerotic hippocampus surgically removed from a patient with temporal lobe epilepsy. Although the dentate gyrus is preserved in the temporal lobe epilepsy case, the CA1 and CA3 regions of the hippocampus are severely shrunk and have lost most of their neurons. The subiculum has also shrunk in this case.

There is some debate on whether hippocampal sclerosis is the cause or consequence of epileptic seizures. What is clear is that neurons in general, and hippocampal neurons in particular, are susceptible to damage if they are exposed to high concentrations of the neurotransmitter glutamate. Focal seizures are linked with a considerable release of glutamate (this is discussed further in section 6.6.1 on mechanisms of focal seizures below), and if it stays at high levels long enough, it triggers a process called **excitotoxicity**, in which the prolonged depolarization leads to accumulation of calcium ions (Ca^{2+}) inside the neurons.

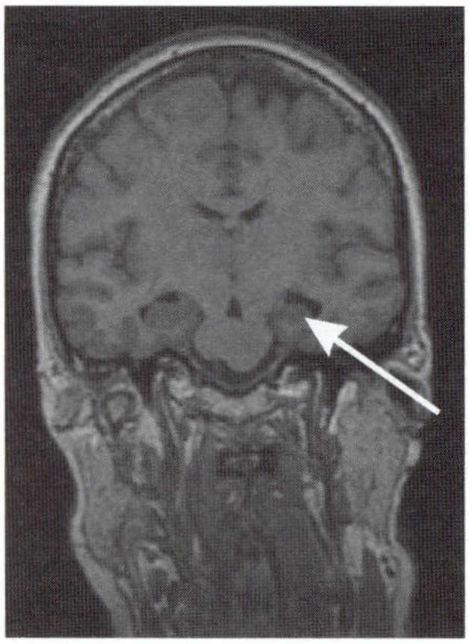

Figure 6.3 A T1 weighted MRI scan showing severe left hippocampal atrophy (as indicated by the arrow). Figure courtesy of Dr Richard Roberts.

(a)

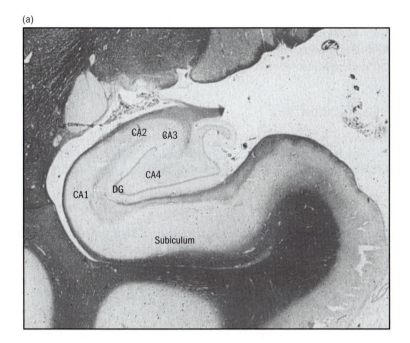

(b)

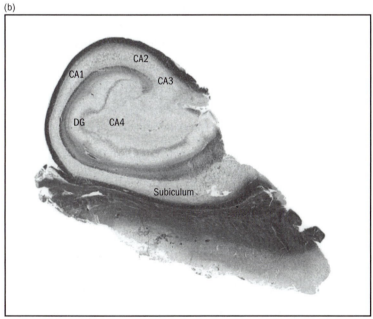

Figure 6.4 Histology of hippocampal sclerosis. A section of a normal hippocampus (a), and a sclerotic hippocampus surgically removed from a patient with temporal lobe epilepsy (b). (DG = dentate gyrus; CA1–4 are subregions of the hippocampus; subiculum is a group of regions next to the hippocampus). Pictures courtesy of Dr A. Princivalle. A full-colour version of this image is shown in the plates section.

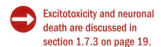

Excitotoxicity and neuronal death are discussed in section 1.7.3 on page 19.

High concentrations of intracellular Ca²⁺ in turn trigger a sequence of intracellular reactions that result in neuronal death. The tissue that is left is mostly composed of glia, resulting in a relatively dense and white mass that is described as sclerotic (because of its dense white appearance).

6.5.5 Gene mutations

Our understanding of the genetics of the epilepsies has advanced rapidly in recent years. At the moment the field is too fluid for gene mutations to be included as symptomatic epilepsies in the formal ILAE classification, but they are recognized as specific syndromes.

Fragile X syndrome is discussed in more detail in section 3.4.2 on page 51.

Some mutations, such as the fragile X and Rett syndromes, are primarily linked with intellectual disability, with seizures being an added complication.

Others are more specifically associated with epilepsy. Several of these are mutations of **ion channels**, known as **channelopathies**, which makes sense in terms of what we know about basic mechanisms of epileptic activity. A list of some of the genetic forms of epilepsy can be seen in Table 6.1, and these genetic epilepsies can be divided into the monogenic and polygenic syndromes.

- **Monogenic epilepsies** are those that have straightforward **Mendelian inheritance**. They include mutations of: **GABA_A receptor** genes (for example, *alpha-1A322D*) responsible for 'autosomal dominant juvenile myoclonic epilepsy', and **potassium (K⁺) channel** genes (*KCNQ2* and *KCNQ3*) responsible for 'benign familial neonatal convulsions'. Both of these examples impair inhibitory mechanisms, providing an explanation of the disease.

- Complex **polygenic epilepsies** include childhood absence epilepsy, where a mutation of the low threshold T-type Ca²⁺ channel gene (*CACNA1H*) is one susceptibility factor among several that determine the occurrence of the disease. This Ca²⁺ channel is thought to play a key role in generating the very rhythmic EEG 'spike and wave' pattern that characterizes this form of epilepsy, as we shall see in section 6.6.2.

Table 6.1 Genetic forms of epilepsy

Gene product	Gene	Epilepsy
Sodium channel	SCN1A, 1B	GEFS+
Sodium channel	SCN2A	Benign familial neonatal epilepsy channel
Potassium channel	KCNQ2/3	Benign familial neonatal epilepsy
	KCNA1	Partial epilepsy/episodic ataxia
Calcium (T-type) channel	CACNA1H	Childhood absence epilepsy
GABA_A receptor	GABRG2	GEFS+; Childhood absence epilepsy
	GABRA1	Juvenile myoclonic epilepsy
Nicotinic cholinergic receptor	CHRNA4, CHRNB2	Autosomal dominant nocturnal frontal lobe epilepsy
Unknown	LGI1	Autosomal dominant lateral temporal epilepsy with auditory features

Advances in our understanding of the genetics of epilepsy have led to the identification of new syndromes. One example is **generalized epilepsy with febrile seizures plus** (GEFS+), which is associated, in different families, with mutations of genes for subunits of either sodium (Na^+) channels or $GABA_A$ receptors. The genetic analysis was difficult because the mutation leads to several different kinds of epilepsy within each family, so that they were considered as completely different conditions until the mutations were discovered.

The epilepsies that have a simple Mendelian inheritance are a very small minority; more frequently, epilepsies are complex diseases with multiple genetic and other risk factors, such as the *CACNA1H* mutation for childhood absence epilepsy. Even in those with a single well-defined mutation, the relationship between the mutation and the disease is far from straightforward. We should also remember that mutations for inherited epilepsies do not necessarily encode ion channels; for instance, the *LGI1* gene is linked to lateral temporal lobe epilepsy, but so far has no clear potential mechanisms.

 There is further discussion of genetic factors in epilepsy in section 3.5.1 on page 53.

There is further discussion of genetic factors in epilepsy in section 3.5.1 on page 53.

SELF-CHECK 6.3

What are the main causes of epilepsy?

6.6 What are the cellular and molecular mechanisms that underlie epilepsy?

The underlying pathophysiological mechanisms of some kinds of epilepsy are now understood in detail. This is the case for focal epilepsy in the cortex and for absence seizures. Much of this progress has come from animal models which allow us to examine the cellular and molecular changes that result in epilepsy.

6.6.1 Experimental focal epilepsy

Experimental models of focal epilepsy fall into two broad groups; **acute** and **chronic**. Acute models use convulsant drugs or other treatments to trigger epileptic activity in normal brain tissue, so in reality they model symptomatic seizures rather than epilepsy. More details of such convulsant drugs are given in Box 6.7.

Chronic models of focal epilepsy, on the other hand, depend on brain tissue that has been changed in some way to make it generate epileptic activity without the presence of a convulsant treatment. These changes can be produced by selective breeding, targeted genetic manipulation, or treatment with some epilepsy-causing agent.

Acute focal epilepsy

Acute models of focal epilepsy can be used *in vivo* (in a living animal) or *in vitro* (using tissue from an animal). The *in vivo* models are often used for screening potential antiepileptic drugs, and usually involve inducing seizures either by injection of a drug called pentylenetetrazole (also known as metrazol), or by electrical stimulation.

The *in vitro* forms of these models have been used extensively in basic research on mechanisms. In these, the brain slice (see Box 6.8) plays a key role because it provides a good compromise between being thick enough to preserve enough brain circuitry and thin enough to allow easy access to the tissue for drugs and ions.

extension: Convulsant drugs

BOX
6.7

The kinds of treatment that can make normal brain tissue produce epileptic discharges are those that:

1. Block inhibitory synapses, either using $GABA_A$ receptor antagonists such as penicillin, bicuculline, and picrotoxin, or replacing chloride ions (Cl^-) with larger negatively charged ions that will not go through the $GABA_A$ receptor channel.

2. Increase excitability, for instance by increasing extracellular levels of K^+ (although this also interferes with synaptic inhibition because it alters the amount of Cl^- inside the neurons).

3. Potentiate excitatory synapses, either by unblocking the NMDA class of glutamate receptors by removing magnesium ions, or by blocking some kinds of K^+ channel found in presynaptic axons with 4-aminopyridine, dendrotoxin (from the venom of the green mamba snake) or mast cell degranulating peptide (MCD), isolated from bee venom. These K^+ channel blockers tend to boost both EPSPs and IPSPs, which is something of a warning against thinking of epilepsy as a simple algebraic sum of excitation minus inhibition.

extension: Brain slices

BOX
6.8

The brain slice preparation *in vitro* has been a crucial tool in helping us understand epilepsy, as well as many other aspects of neuronal function.

Brain slices are cut from the brains of animals that have been humanely killed, or occasionally from tissue removed from patients during brain surgery. Typically the slices are 0.4 mm thick, which turns out to be a reasonable compromise between the need to preserve the neuronal circuitry in brain tissue, and the need to allow enough oxygen and other nutrients to diffuse throughout the tissue. The diffusion properties of oxygen, and its consumption by the metabolism of the tissue at near-physiological temperatures (often around 35 °C), produce a critical thickness of around 0.4 mm.

The advantages of the brain slice include: the stability of the tissue for recording, particularly for intracellular or patch recording; the visibility of anatomical landmarks such as cell layers or, with suitable microscopes, of individual living neurons; and accessibility for drugs and ions with the blood–brain barrier.

A photograph of a rat brain slice showing the major cell layers of the hippocampus is shown in Figure 6.5.

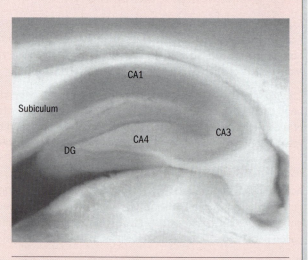

Figure 6.5 The brain slice. A hippocampal slice from a rat brain showing the major cell layers (abbreviations are as in Figure 6.4).

Chain reaction model

The epileptic discharges produced by these kinds of treatment result from a chain reaction. We know from both anatomical and physiological research that the excitatory pyramidal cells in hippocampus and **neocortex** can excite other pyramidal cells in the same population as well as their more distant targets. If these local recurrent synapses are strong enough, or common enough, they can lead to excitation spreading through the whole neuronal population.

Small degrees of connectivity can result in very rapid recruitment of a population of neurons. If we imagine a population of 1000 neurons with a probability of just 1% that any pair is directly connected, one neuron can excite its 10 targets, which together can excite their 100 targets minus those already active (probably 1), which can excite their 990 (1000–10) targets minus those already active, so recruiting the whole population within 4–5 synapses.

This rapid spread of excitation is illustrated in Figure 6.6, which shows that even when connectivity is low (just two randomly selected postsynaptic targets per neuron), the whole population of 100 neurons is soon recruited. In practice the probability of one cell exciting its targets is indeed low—a few per cent is a typical value in the CA3 region of the hippocampus, where the synapses are relatively strong.

This probability can be increased substantially if, as often is the case, the pyramidal cells generate a burst of action potentials which allow the synaptic potentials to add up, so-called **temporal** (or time-dependent) **summation**. These bursts of action potentials depend upon the neurons' membrane potentials remaining depolarized for longer, for instance because of the presence of other kinds of voltage-dependent channels carrying either Na^+ or Ca^{2+}, which stay open much longer than the Na^+ channel responsible for the typical action potential.

The ability to fire action potentials rapidly is important for epilepsy. We will see below that many **anticonvulsants** work by preventing rapid bursts of action potentials, and we saw in Table 6.1 that mutations of Na^+ channels can be responsible for epilepsy; such mutations mostly increase the open time of those channels.

Of course, these recurrent connections are not there to make us epileptic. Rather they are there to perform the computations required in that part of the brain for learning associations between stimuli, recognizing objects, perception, and so on.

Normally the chain reaction that can be sustained by these connections is held in check by the presence of several forms of inhibition. The most obvious is in the form of inhibitory interneurons which use GABA as their neurotransmitter. Although these neurons are much less common (10–20% of the total) in the neocortex and hippocampus than the excitatory, glutamate-releasing principal neurons, they are placed strategically to prevent overexcitation of the tissue.

In fact, there are many classes of inhibitory interneuron. The most relevant here are those that receive excitatory inputs from the pyramidal (principal) cells in the region. When enough of the pyramidal cells fire, these inhibitory interneurons become very active and damp down the activity before it gets out of hand, as is illustrated in Figure 6.7. In this figure, we can see that the GABAergic basket cell receives excitatory synaptic inputs from many of the pyramidal cells in the region, so that it detects the

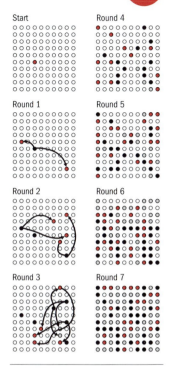

Figure 6.6 Focal epilepsy; the chain reaction. This cartoon illustrates how excitation can spread throughout a population of neurons (here it is 100), even when the connectivity seems low (here two randomly chosen postsynaptic targets per neuron).

 Temporal summation of synaptic potentials is explained in more detail in section 2.2.5 on page 31.

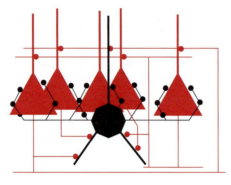

Figure 6.7 The role of inhibitory neurons in damping down over-excitation. The majority of neurons in the cortex and related structures are excitatory (shown as red pyramids). The GABA-containing inhibitory basket cell shown here (black) reduces pyramidal cell excitability.

overall level of excitation of the local population of neurons, and in turn makes inhibitory synaptic connections on many of these pyramidal cells. This allows basket cells, and similar inhibitory neurons, to detect the build up of excitation and stop it getting out of control.

This explains why drugs that interfere with GABA-mediated inhibition are so effective in triggering epileptic activity, and why drugs that enhance inhibition can be useful anti-convulsants (see section 6.7.2).

> The mechanisms responsible for focal epilepsies have been extensively studied using experimental models and involve a chain reaction of excitation.

Chronic focal epilepsy

As we have seen, epilepsy is a chronic disease in which the brain's structure and/or function are abnormal in ways that result in seizures without an obvious cause, such as a convulsant drug or a metabolic disturbance.

Chronic models make some change in the brains of experimental animals to make them prone to epileptic seizures. In some cases it is possible to find close parallels between chronic experimental epilepsies and specific epilepsies within the clinical classification, but this is not essential for them to be valuable. The main role of these experimental models is to reveal basic principles of the **pathophysiology** of epilepsy.

Chronic experimental focal epilepsies can, in principle, be produced either by genetic modification or by some experimental manipulation (termed **epileptogenic treatment**) of normal animals.

One exciting development is the insertion of genes containing mutations that are known to result in epilepsy in humans. This work is in its early stages, and there is no clear general picture yet: the gap between the molecular biology of a mutated gene and the physical expression of the disease is massive, and presents a major challenge.

There also exist rats and mice that spontaneously developed focal epilepsy and that have been bred on to utilize their epileptic traits. Some examples include:

- the **tottering mouse**, which is named after its characteristic gait, and which has both focal and absence seizures

- **Frings mouse** with audiogenic or sound-induced seizures, which turns out to have a similar mutation to that in human *LGI1* which results in an epilepsy with auditory features (as seen in Table 6.1)
- the **genetic epilepsy prone rat** (GEPR), which has focal and both primary and secondary generalized tonic clonic seizures.

Some chronic focal epilepsy models depend on injecting substances such as kainate (obtained from a kind of Japanese seaweed) or pilocarpine (a drug that acts on acetyl-choline receptors) either into the brain or into the body as a whole. These model the focal epilepsies. The details are beyond the scope of this chapter, but these and other similar models produce multiple changes, many of which are also seen in brain tissue from humans with epilepsy, and include:

- Changes in voltage-gated ion channels, also called **acquired channelopathies**.
- Changes in synaptic inhibition: for instance, there is evidence of selective loss of particular kinds of inhibitory neuron.
- Changes in synaptic excitation.
- Changes in connectivity. The most well-known is the sprouting of new mossy fibres in the dentate gyrus; increasing numbers of excitatory connections within a population of excitatory neurons should increase the likelihood of positive feedback, and hence of a chain reaction.
- Neuronal loss. Large numbers of neurons can be lost, for instance in the hippocampus in temporal lobe epilepsy. This probably can largely be blamed on excitotoxicity with excessive levels of the neurotransmitter glutamate triggering a cascade of enzymes that ultimately kill neurons.
- Glia may change their properties, altering their ability to take up neurotransmitters after they have been released, and their ability to control key extracellular ions such as K⁺.

The range of changes known to occur in epileptic tissue can be bewildering. What makes the story more complex is that some of the changes appear to promote epileptic activity while others restrain it, and conceivably could be the brain's in-built antiepileptic treatment.

> **SELF-CHECK 6.4**
>
> What is the significance of the chain reaction model of epilepsy?

6.6.2 Experimental absence epilepsy

The main primary generalized epilepsy that has proved amenable to experimental invest-igation is absence epilepsy. Absence epilepsy has both acute and chronic models. The acute models date back to the mid-twentieth century when treatment with penicillin pro-duced the classic spike and wave discharge of absence seizures, at least in cats.

Rats and mice can have absence-like spike and wave activity spontaneously. Some of these rodents have been bred for this trait, such as the genetic absence epilepsy rats of Strasbourg (GAERS), WAG/Rij rats, and many lines of mice, usually first recognized by unusual behaviours (hence names like tottering, stargazer, and lethargic).

The earliest work on acute models showed that the synchronous spike and wave dis-charges of absence seizures depended on both the **thalamus** and the neocortex. Chronic models have largely reinforced that idea. Figure 6.8 this illustrates the relationship between the main components in this circuit.

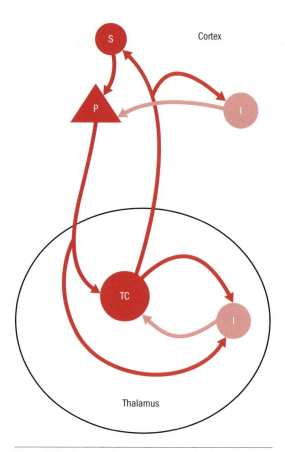

Cortex

Thalamus

Figure 6.8 Diagram of thalamocortical circuits involved in absence seizures. Red cells are excitatory and pink ones are inhibitory. In the cortex, P indicates pyramidal cells, S stellate, and I inhibitory cells. In the thalamus, TC indicates thalamocortical or relay neurons, I inhibitory cells, mainly in the nucleus reticularis thalami, which consists of inhibitory neurons only, and surrounds the relay nuclei which transmit sensory information up to the cortex.

The level of synchronization across the thalamus and neocortex varies in normal non-epileptic brains. During alert consciousness, and during rapid eye movement (REM) sleep, the EEG is desynchronized and the various parts of the pathways between thalamus and cortex and back are kept distinct. During slow wave sleep, the EEG becomes much more synchronized with slow delta waves (at around 1 cycle/second).

The EEG becomes more synchronous even when a subject rests with their eyes closed, when alpha waves (around 10 cycles/second) appear in the occipital region, as we saw in panel (a) of Figure 6.2. We can imagine that it may be a relatively small step for the pathology of absence epilepsy to subvert the normal flexibility in the degree of synchronization of the thalamocortical system to the widespread pathological synchronization of the spike and wave discharges.

The theory is that during absence seizures the thalamocortical system develops a degree of **synchrony** not normally found when people are awake, at a rhythm—3 cycles/second

—which is not normally seen. Thalamic neurons have the ability to generate action potentials on the rebound from an IPSP. The widespread synchrony of the EEG during absence seizures is due to synchronous IPSPs followed by rebound excitation of the thalamic neurons that project to the cortex and generate the spike part of the epileptic waveform; the slower wave then is generated by the subsequent wave of inhibition in the cortex. The synchronization of the IPSPs results from both divergence (individual neurons making synapses on many neurons) and convergence (each neuron receiving synapses from many neurons).

Absence epilepsy is quite different from many others because it depends on inhibition, which is why most antiepileptic drugs that enhance GABA receptor function are not useful. The T-type Ca^{2+} channel mentioned in Table 6.1 plays a critical role because it produces rebound excitation after periods of strong hyperpolarization by IPSPs. It has the strange property of needing this hyperpolarization to allow it to open, at a threshold below normal resting membrane potential, and thus excite the neuron.

> Absence epilepsy arises from excessive oscillations of excitation and inhibition in the thalamocortical system.

SELF-CHECK 6.5

How is the 3/second spike and wave activity, that is characteristically seen in absence or petit mal epilepsy, generated?

6.7 How is epilepsy treated?

6.7.1 First aid

If you come across someone having a seizure, there are a few simple things you can do:

- Stay calm.
- Prevent people crowding round the patient.
- Time the duration of the seizure—if it lasts longer than a couple of minutes, it is status epilepticus and needs emergency medical care.
- Prevent the patient's head hitting hard surfaces. Only try to move the patient if they are in a dangerous position (for example, near traffic, stairs, or open water).
- Do not restrain movements, and never try to put anything into the mouth.

When the seizure stops, put the person into the recovery position (as seen in Figure 6.9) and check that respiration is not obstructed. Remain with them until they recover fully or until medical staff take over. Remember that a period of confusion often follows a seizure; offer reassurance and try to minimize any embarrassment that may occur, especially if there has been incontinence.

6.7.2 Antiepileptic drugs

Many drugs are available to control epilepsy; the choice of treatment depends on seizure type and on the side effects experienced by individual patients.

Simple absence seizures (petit mal epilepsy) usually respond to ethosuximide. Patients with primary generalized tonic clonic seizures are often treated with sodium valproate,

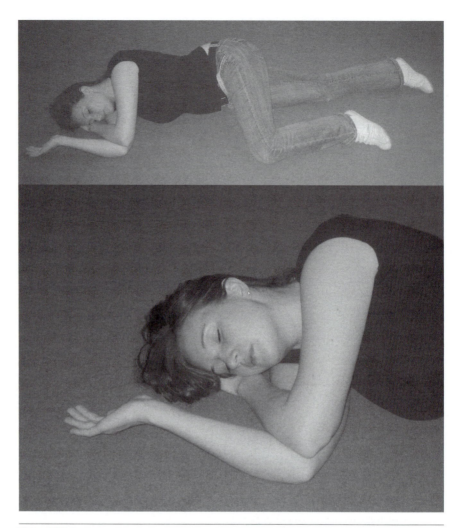

Figure 6.9 The recovery position.

lamotrigine, topiramate, or phenytoin; phenobarbitone is also effective, but may cause unacceptable sedation. Carbamazepine is usually considered the drug of choice for partial epilepsy (with or without secondary generalization), but lamotrigine and topiramate can also be effective.

Although benzodiazepines are not used in the long-term treatment of epilepsy, intravenous lorazepam is the drug of choice for the emergency treatment of status epilepticus. If this is unsuccessful, the patient may require admission to an intensive care unit where they may be paralysed, ventilated, and treated with intravenous thiopentone or other anaesthetic agents.

Anticonvulsant or antiepileptic drugs (AEDs) target a variety of neuronal properties and usually have more than one mechanism of action. In broad terms we can consider the major functional targets as GABAergic inhibition, glutamate receptors, Na^+ channels, and Ca^{2+} channels.

Most epilepsies are treated with drugs, most of which fall into one or more of the following functional groups: GABA enhancement, Na$^+$ channel depression, Ca^{2+} channel depression, and glutamate depression.

 Ion channels and their role in normal neuronal function are described in section 2.1 on page 21.

Drugs acting at GABA synapses

The first effective antiepileptic drug was bromide, which increases currents through the GABA$_A$ receptor because bromide ions (Br$^-$) can pass through the ion channel faster than the chemically related, but larger, Cl$^-$ ion. This makes inhibition stronger and thus more effective at opposing the build-up of excitation required for a seizure. Bromide is not normally used to treat humans any more because of undesirable side effects.

 Glutamatergic and GABAergic neurotransmission are considered in section 2.2.4 on page 29.

The benzodiazepines such as clobazam and clonazepam are relatively clean and well-understood drugs. They have specific binding sites on the GABA$_A$ receptor, which is more fully described in Box 6.9, and enhance the currents that flow when GABA binds to the receptor. Unfortunately GABA$_A$ receptors are important in many aspects of brain function and these kinds of drug can produce undesirable side effects on cognition and mood. In addition, their long-term use leads to tolerance and physical dependence, mostly due to downregulation of receptors, and abrupt withdrawal of these drugs can provoke seizures.

As mentioned above, benzodiazepines are important in the treatment of status epilepticus. The preferred drug is now lorazepam, which is longer acting than diazepam, but both are administered intravenously.

The use of benzodiazepines in the treatment of anxiety is discussed in section 13.5.1 on page 278.

Barbiturates also have specific binding sites on GABA$_A$ receptors and enhance inhibitory synaptic currents. The antiepileptic drug phenobarbitone also depresses voltage-gated Na$^+$ and Ca^{2+} currents. It is rarely used today in the UK because of its sedative properties.

---

extension: The GABA$_A$ receptor

BOX 6.9

GABA$_A$ receptors are located postsynaptically and have a channel that is selectively permeable to Cl$^-$. Increased conductance of Cl$^-$ through this channel hyperpolarizes the postsynaptic cell, thus reducing the likelihood of it firing an action potential. GABA$_A$ receptors are therefore inhibitory.

Similarly to the NMDA receptor (see Box 6.10 below), the GABA$_A$ receptor has a number of binding or modulatory sites. Apart from the GABA binding site itself, many important drug groups, such as benzodiazepines, barbiturates, and neurosteroids, act at sites that potentiate the effects of GABA on this receptor. In contrast, the convulsant drug, picrotoxin, blocks the Cl$^-$ channel, thus preventing the postsynaptic inhibitory effects of GABA.

Structurally, GABA$_A$ receptors are pentamers; that is, they consist of five subunits. The most common of these are the alpha, beta, and gamma subunits, each of which can exist in up to six molecular subtypes. This gives many possible different permutations, of which relatively few are functional.

Interestingly, modern molecular techniques have indicated that specific subunits are required to confer sensitivity to particular drugs. For instance, both the alpha-2 and alpha-3 subunits contribute to the anxiolytic effects of benzodiazepines. This finding offers the prospect of developing more selectively targeted drugs for GABA$_A$ receptors in the future.

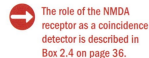
Inhibiting neurotransmitter reuptake mechanisms has proved a useful strategy in treating other conditions, as described in Box 2.3 on page 30. Most notable is the use of serotonin selective reuptake inhibitors (SSRIs) in depression, as described in section 14.7.1 on page 300.

Other drugs acting at GABA-ergic synapses have rather different modes of action. Vigabatrin blocks the enzyme that degrades GABA. Its use is limited to specific epilepsies (infantile spasms, and occasionally partial seizures in adults). Vigabatrin can damage the retina, where GABA also is an important transmitter, so that vision needs to be checked regularly as a precaution. Gabapentin has less clear mechanisms but may increase levels of intracellular GABA by altering amino acid uptake into the brain. Tiagabine blocks GABA uptake into glia and neurons by binding to the GABA transporter, GAT-1. This has the effect of leaving GABA in the synaptic cleft longer than normal, so prolonging and amplifying the effect of the naturally released transmitter.

Glutamate receptors

The importance of excitatory synaptic transmission in the generation of focal seizures suggested that glutamatergic synapses may be good targets for AEDs. Unfortunately this approach has not yet been as successful as was hoped.

The NMDA class of glutamate receptor proved a very effective target in experimental models, but unfortunately drugs that target this receptor had adverse effects on cognitive function when tested in humans. However, more subtle pharmacological modulation of NMDA receptors may yet prove effective, and more detailed information on the function and some structural features of this type of receptor is provided in Box 6.10.

In fact, felbamate binds to the glycine site on NMDA receptors and weakens their activity. Felbamate is one of the antiepileptic drugs with multiple actions and also depresses Na^+ channels, and high-voltage activated Ca^{2+} channels and potentiates $GABA_A$ receptors.

Topiramate blocks the AMPA-kainate class of glutamate receptor, in addition to its effects on both transient and persistent Na^+ currents, high-voltage activated Ca^{2+} currents and $GABA_A$ receptors. Topiramate also weakly inhibits **carbonic anhydrase**.

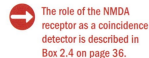
The role of the NMDA receptor as a coincidence detector is described in Box 2.4 on page 36.

extension: The NMDA receptor **BOX 6.10**

NMDA receptors are a specific class of glutamate receptor with special properties that make them important both in learning and memory, and in epilepsy. At resting potentials they normally are blocked by a magnesium ion which needs to be dislodged by depolarization of the membrane before current can flow through the ion channel. The current is carried by Na^+, K^+, and Ca^{2+} ions (the Ca^{2+} ions are important in synaptic plasticity, and in the excess that can occur during prolonged seizures that can trigger neuronal death).

The combination of depolarization and extracellular glutamate, that occurs during epileptic seizures, means that NMDA receptors are strongly activated during epileptic seizures. They add to the synaptic currents through AMPA or kainic acid type glutamate receptors, and because they stay open longer they add substantially to epileptic depolarizations, which presumably is why NMDA receptor antagonists are effective in many experimental epilepsy models.

The NMDA receptor has multiple binding sites, like most synaptic receptors, but in this case it needs both glutamate and glycine to bind before it will open. This second amino acid binding site is an attractive target for antiepileptic drugs, and is one part of the cellular action of felbamate.

Sodium channel drugs

Several useful AEDs prevent Na^+ channels opening too often or for too long, so that they reduce the maximum firing rates of neurons. Interestingly the opposite seems to be the case with some of the epilepsies based on channelopathies, both genetic and acquired.

Major examples of antiepileptic drugs acting at Na^+ channels include phenytoin, carbamazepine, oxcarbazepine, and lamotrigine. Lamotrigine also has actions on high-threshold Ca^{2+} channels. Two other drugs, topiramate and felbamate, have reasonably well-established actions on Na^+ channels along with other effects listed below, and there are suggestions that valproate and ethosuximide also affect Na^+ channels.

Calcium channel drugs

Ethosuximide is the drug of choice for absence epilepsy. Its ability to depress a low-threshold type of voltage-dependent Ca^{2+} current (carried by the T channel) has raised considerable interest in the light of theories on the mechanism of absence seizures. However, it does have effects on some other ion channels too.

Several other drugs depress high-threshold Ca^{2+} currents (not through T-type channels) along with their other cellular effects. These include: felbamate, topiramate, gabapentin, levetiracetam, and phenobarbital.

SELF-CHECK 6.6

What are the main targets of antiepileptic drugs?

6.7.3 Non-drug treatments

A substantial minority, perhaps up to 30%, of patients with epilepsy do not have their seizures well controlled by antiepileptic drugs, either because of drug resistance (as described in Box 6.11) or because of severe side effects. There are some alternatives for such people.

---

extension: Drug resistance   **BOX 6.11**

Drug resistance is a problem found in several areas of medicine. It is perhaps best known in cancer treatment, but also is a significant problem in epilepsy.

Epilepsy probably shares one mechanism with cancer: that is, the expression of multiple drug transporter proteins. These proteins bind many different kinds of drug, and presumably other foreign substances, to remove them. They are present in glia and on blood vessels: astrocytes have so-called **foot processes** which are close to blood vessels and which are responsible for exchanging materials between the brain and blood. These locations are ideal for keeping the drugs away from neurons.

There appear to be more of these multidrug transporters in patients with drug resistance. Genetic studies have shown that certain polymorphisms of the genes for these proteins are associated with drug resistance, suggesting that the problem may be genetic in some cases. One research goal is to interfere with the working of these transporters to prevent them removing the antiepileptic drugs from the extracellular space in the brain.

Surgery

If the epileptic focus is well localized, it can be removed surgically. Obviously it is crucial that the part of the brain responsible for the seizures has been identified unambiguously. It also must not be too close to eloquent cortex, such as the speech areas, which will cause substantial disability if damaged. As long as these and other criteria are met, then epilepsy surgery can be very effective.

Finding exactly which bit of the brain needs to be removed uses several kinds of investigation. Clinical symptoms always are the starting point, but then more intensive methods confirm and refine the localization. Non-invasive imaging investigations are increasingly important. Hippocampal sclerosis, where hippocampal neurons have died and been replaced by glia, is a good marker for temporal lobe epilepsy (as shown in Figures 6.3 and 6.4). Other local malformations in the cortex can also indicate sources of seizures that can be amenable to surgery.

Electrical recording is important too, using EEG recordings from the scalp and, in some cases, recordings from the surface of the brain or from inside the brain tissue itself. In the end the final measure of whether the surgeon has removed the correct piece of brain is that the patient stops having seizures.

Stimulation

Electrical stimulation has been used with good results in the treatment of Parkinson's disease. Brain stimulation methods are under investigation for the treatment of epilepsy, both using deep brain stimulation that is broadly similar to the approach used in Parkinson's disease, and also stimulation of the epileptic focus itself. Although there are some encouraging case reports, neither method has so far been fully validated by controlled clinical trials, so both remain experimental treatments.

In contrast, vagal nerve stimulation has been studied extensively and does seem to reduce seizure frequency and severity to a useful degree. The vagal nerve is one of the cranial nerves emerging from the brain stem. It is mainly involved in controlling heart rate and other autonomic and visceral functions. The stimulation is applied to the left vagus in the neck; this side is chosen to avoid side effects. Its mechanism is not clear, but is thought to depend on a diffuse reduction in cortical excitability. The **afferent axons** in the vagus connect directly or indirectly widely throughout the brain, including the structures most directly involved in epilepsy such as the neocortex, hippocampus, thalamus, and so on.

Ketogenic diet

This treatment is based on an old observation that fasting suppresses seizures. The ketogenic diet is high in fat, has adequate levels of protein, and is low in carbohydrate. The low levels of carbohydrate alter the body's metabolism so that it uses fats rather than carbohydrates for most of its energy production. Chemicals called ketones, including acetone, are produced as part of this process. The ketogenic diet can be useful in children with severe epilepsy, reducing seizure frequency by about one half in about one half of patients. How it suppresses seizures remains something of a mystery.

Future directions

Better targeted and better tolerated treatments remain important goals.

- More precise and less invasive surgical methods are being developed, paralleling improvements in imaging and other methods for localizing brain regions responsible for triggering seizures.

- Drugs can always be improved. In part, this will continue through chemists making small changes to structures of existing drugs, and then testing to see whether this improves effectiveness and reduces side effects. Perhaps more exciting is the search for completely new classes of compound, either by serendipity, as in the case of levetiracetam, or by basic research. One interesting approach is to make inactive compounds of known antiepileptic drugs that are converted into their active form by some intrinsic property of epileptic seizures. The idea is that this targets the active drugs at the earliest stages of the seizure and stops it. One example is a drug called DP-valproate, which is converted to valproate by an enzyme that is released from cells during seizures, but not at other times.

- Gene and cell therapies have been a major interest in many aspects of medical research in recent years. Gene therapies use attenuated viruses or other vectors to introduce genes into brain cells to try to depress epileptic activity. Several attempts to boost GABA release or receptor function, or to depress glutamate function have had limited success. Perhaps more promising is the production of peptides which are often released with other transmitters, particularly GABA, and which modulate neuronal excitability. Examples include neuropeptide Y and galanin. Both work well in experimental models, but they are a long way from clinical applications.

- Cell-based therapies implant cells that release substances that might be therapeutic. Perhaps the best known is the introduction of cells that release dopamine into the striatum of patients with Parkinson's disease. In the case of epilepsy, cells that make and release seizure-suppressing compounds (GABA, noradrenaline, serotonin, acetylcholine) have been implanted in the brain. This works in experimental models, but the grafted cells die within a few weeks, which is a serious problem for developing treatments. Both approaches need much more development before they can be used clinically.

SUMMARY

- Epilepsy is a group of conditions that all share a tendency to recurring seizures in which brain function is abruptly disrupted by excessively intense and/or excessively synchronized activity of cortical neurons.

- The precise symptoms depend on which part of the brain is involved.

- Classifying the epilepsies is a complex task which is important for treatment and for predicting the course of the disease.

- The causes of the epilepsies, where they can be determined, include stroke, trauma, tumours, problems in cortical development, and gene mutations.

- Symptomatic seizures can occur in people without epilepsy if they are exposed to the appropriate conditions, such as taking or discontinuing certain drugs, electrical stimulation, cardiovascular problems, and metabolic diseases.

- The mechanisms responsible for epileptic seizures are fairly well understood in some cases: a chain reaction of excitation in the case of focal epilepsies, and excessive oscillations of excitation and inhibition in the thalamocortical system in the case of absence seizures.

- Most epilepsies are treated with drugs, most of which fall into one or more of the following functional groups: GABA enhancement, Na^+ channel depression, Ca^+ channel depression, and glutamate depression.

FURTHER READING

Web sites

Several of the major epilepsy organizations maintain very informative sites. These include:

American Epilepsy Society

International League Against Epilepsy

National Institute of Neurological Disorders and Stroke (US) <www.ninds.nih.gov/disorders/epilepsy/epilepsy.htm>

National Society for Epilepsy (UK) has a specialized site which has a useful library of articles at <www.e-epilepsy.org.uk/pages/articles/>

Review articles

In addition, the following may be of interest to those interested in learning more about the mechanisms underlying epilepsy:

G. Avanzini and S. Franceschetti. Cellular biology of epileptogenesis. *Lancet Neurology* 2003; **2**: 33–42.
A review of epileptogenic mechanisms focusing on genetically determined alterations in ion channels and changes in glutamate, GABA, and acetylcholine receptor function.

R. Guerrini, G. Casari, and C. Marini. The genetic and molecular basis of epilepsy. *Trends in Molecular Medicine* 2003; **9**: 300–306.
A brief review of the genetics of idiopathic epilepsies.

H. Lerche, Y.G. Weber, K. Jurkat-Rott, and F. Lehmann-Horn. Ion channel defects in idiopathic epilepsies. *Current Pharmaceutical Design* 2005; **11**: 2737–2752.
This review focuses on mutations in genes encoding ion channels that have been linked to idiopathic epilepsy syndromes.

CHAPTER SEVEN

Alzheimer's disease and related disorders

Zsuzsanna Nagy

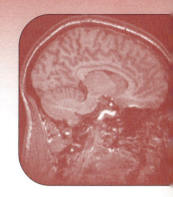

INTRODUCTION

Dementia is an acquired global impairment of intellect, memory, and personality, without impairment of consciousness. It is a disease of old age, so its prevalence increases with age, as we can see by looking at the graph in Figure 7.1.

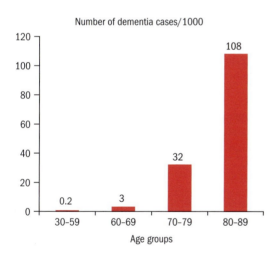

Number of dementia cases/1000

Figure 7.1 The prevalence of dementia in Europe. Based on data from W. A. Rocca *et al.*, *Annals of Neurology*, 1991; **30**: 381.

7.1 How common is Alzheimer's disease?

Alzheimer's disease (AD) is an irreversible progressive dementia of long duration which is named after the German psychiatrist Alois Alzheimer (see Box 7.1). Around one half of the people with dementia have AD, which makes it the most common degenerative disease of the brain. It also means that AD is the third most common cause of death in the Western world, after heart disease and cancer.

extension: Alois Alzheimer and the first patient   **BOX 7.1**

Alois Alzheimer (1864–1915) was a German psychiatrist. Although he worked on several diseases, including epilepsy, he is best known for the disease that bears his name. He first presented his historical case report at a conference in 1906, then published it as a journal article in 1907.

His patient, Auguste D, was admitted to a mental asylum at the age of 51. She was suffering from severe cognitive deficit and was aggressive. She also had hallucinations, delusions, and paranoia. At her death in 1906 her brain was sent to Alois Alzheimer, who had moved to another hospital. Using the Bielshowsky silver impregnation technique, he found amyloid plaques and neurofibrillary tangles in her brain.

AD was not, however, first discovered by Alzheimer. Neither did he claim to have discovered a new disease. It was Kraepelin, his close friend and colleague, who first suggested that the disease should be named after Alzheimer. The suggestion was not unequivocally popular in its time, and its legitimacy is still a matter of debate.

Kraepelin omitted to acknowledge that the pathology associated with the clinical symptoms of AD were known and discussed as early as 1887 (Beljahow). The disease was studied by many pathologists and psychiatrists, such as Fuller, Redlich, Leri, and Oskar Fischer and authorities in the field were not happy that 'this was hurriedly baptized as Alzheimer's disease'.

In retrospect, Kraepelin's announcement looks even worse, because he allegedly omitted/ modified certain facts of the original scientific description of the case, to make it look novel.

The personal, social, and economic consequences are made more severe by the long duration of the disease (10–15 years from the appearance of symptoms) and the lack of any means of prevention.

The gradually increasing age of the population in developed countries indicates that the number of AD patients will increase sharply in the future. Without a useful treatment strategy, it is predicted that the worldwide number of AD sufferers will increase from 12 million in 2000 to 50 million by 2050.

SELF-CHECK 7.1

How large is the Alzheimer's problem worldwide?

> AD is the most common neurodegenerative disease.

7.2 What are the symptoms and signs of Alzheimer's disease?

7.2.1 The early stages of Alzheimer's disease

As we see in Box 7.2, the early stages of AD appear as simple forgetfulness which is very often confused with age-related memory problems. People do not remember recent events, such as things they have done the day before. The long-term memory is not affected at this stage; patients remember events long past. Family members can

case study: The early stages of AD

BOX 7.2

A 69-year-old retired accountant was referred to the psychiatrist by her GP because of poor memory. She had a previous long history of depression that followed her divorce 23 years earlier.

Her daughter informs the doctor that recently her mother has become apathetic and started to ignore housework and gardening, a hobby she very much enjoyed before. Following her move to a new house, she has not even bothered to unpack. The daughter also recounts that her mother has recently spent £16 000 on double glazing, expenditure very uncharacteristic of her.

The standard cognitive tests were carried out by the psychiatrist. She scored maximum on all tests.

The psychiatrist diagnosed depression and prescribed an antidepressant.

usually recall the stage when the patient started to retell old stories again and again, remembering the story but not remembering that they have told it already.

As the disease progresses, the forgetfulness starts to affect routine activities that were performed without a problem before. Everyday chores, such as cooking, become difficult, especially if unexpected interruptions occur. Patients get lost in their own neighbourhood. Solving simple mathematical problems, such as the household accounts, is not possible any more.

Patients also suffer personality changes. They behave in a manner that would have been uncharacteristic of them. Financially astute people start to overspend, and active people lose interest in their hobbies and life in general. Assertive personalities stop talking to avoid making mistakes. Self-neglect appears at this stage; previously prim old ladies forget to bathe or comb their hair.

The patients are aware of memory problems, so they try to compensate for their difficulties by either using reminders or letting someone else talk and take decisions for them. Aggressive behaviour might appear as a result of anxiety and frustration.

> The initial clinical features of AD are forgetfulness, especially for recent events, and behavioural changes that can resemble depression.

7.2.2 Later symptoms and clinical signs

As the disease progresses (see Box 7.3), changes in memory and behaviour become more noticeable. Patients are incapable of organizing their thoughts or covering up memory lapses with written notes to themselves. They are not able to follow instructions written by other people, and the memory gaps are filled with stories that they make up. They also become more and more confused and they do not recognize their own family members and friends. The repetition of old stories degenerates into repeating just words or statements. The repetitive behaviour also extends to pointless movements, such as fingering buttons or pacing restlessly.

case study: The later stages of AD

BOX 7.3

Three years later, the patient described in Box 7.2 was referred to a memory clinic by her GP after her daughter found her lying naked on the kitchen floor.

The daughter recounted that her mother had become muddled, stubborn, irritable, and angry. She was incontinent of urine and refused to dress on her own. She had also been lost several times lately on her way home from town.

In the memory clinic the nurse administered standard cognitive tests. During the test she was asked about her date of birth. Although she could accurately recall the day and month, she did not remember the year. At the insistence of the nurse about the year she was born she replied, 'I haven't decided yet'. To the question whether she could remember when World War II started she answered: 'haven't been out to see what is going on'. She was also unable to read the clock. The nurse noted that during the test she kept repeating: 'my dad might be coming home today' and 'my dad would answer your questions'.

The nurse also noted that the patient was restless during the interview, lacked insight, and had problems concentrating.

She scored 38 out of the possible 107 points in the test.

At the clinic a full neurological examination was difficult because she was uncooperative. She kept giggling, a sign of disinhibition. There were no focal neurological signs, but the patient had a mildly raised blood pressure.

A CT brain scan showed moderate generalized brain atrophy, with disproportionate temporal lobe atrophy. Some periventricular low attenuation was also noted due to small strokes. The diagnosis of the clinician was possible AD with a vascular component.

The patient died 4 years later. In the final year, she was mute and bedridden. The post-mortem revealed fully developed AD and very mild vascular disease of the brain.

Loss of insight and judgement may lead to safety problems, such as setting light to the carpet to warm the room. Antisocial behavioural patterns can develop, such as cursing or attacking people without reason. Inappropriate sexual behaviour can also develop, with risqué remarks in public and sexual advances.

Paranoid behaviour (jealousy or accusations of theft) is common, together with delusions and visual hallucinations (seeing people who are not there). Patients become more and more dependent on their carer as they require constant help to eat, dress, or take their medicine.

7.2.3 Severe Alzheimer's disease

In the most advanced stages of AD (see Box 7.3), the patient is unable to recognize even close family or themself. Their speech is completely incomprehensible and they often become **mute**. They are also increasingly difficult to manage, because they often refuse to cooperate, refusing to eat, or get out of bed, or go to the bathroom. Weight loss leads to an emaciated appearance. Their gait is unsteady and falls are common. Often patients are too weak to stand alone. **Incontinence** of urine and bowels appears as the patients become bedridden. The general deterioration is associated with frequent infections and sometimes **seizures**. At this stage of the disease patients require constant full-time care.

> AD leads to complications such as falls and infections. Around half of AD patients eventually die of bronchopneumonia.

SELF-CHECK 7.2

What are the main clinical features of AD?

7.3 What tests can we use to diagnose Alzheimer's disease?

The definite diagnosis of AD can only be made at post-mortem examination. While the patient is alive the clinical diagnosis always carries a degree of uncertainty.

The clinical picture of a gradually worsening dementia in a patient with no other neurological disorder responsible for dementia strongly suggests the diagnosis of AD. If evidence of another neurological disorder is discovered, such as multiple strokes, AD is still possible as long as the extent of the other disease does not explain the severity of the clinical symptoms.

The diagnosis of **probable AD** requires a higher degree of certainty and can usually be made only after detailed clinical and laboratory investigations. This requires that the patient is referred for cognitive and neuropsychological tests and neuroimaging. Any other brain disorder that could account for the dementia and alterations of consciousness must be excluded, and the disease must start after the age of 40 years (early-onset AD) and usually after 65 years (late-onset AD).

The diagnosis is further supported by finding of progressive worsening of specific cognitive function (i.e. **dysphasia**, **dyspraxia** (see Box 7.4), **agnosia**), altered behaviour, family history of AD, and normal blood test results. Usually brain **atrophy** is seen on CT scanning, and SPECT scanning can show reduced temporal lobe blood flow as is described more fully in Box 7.5).

A description of the principles of CT scanning is given in Box 5.4 on page 91. SPECT scanning is described in more detail in Box 8.3 on page 159.

---

extension: Dyspraxia

BOX 7.4

Dyspraxia is the impairment of the planning, executing, and sequencing of motor movements. Dyspraxia is a relatively late sign in AD and its appearance usually signals the beginning of an accelerated decline. The most often used cognitive tests available include tasks that allow the testing of praxis.

The praxis tests included in the CAMDEX (Cambridge Mental Disorders of the Elderly Examination) are the pentagon, spiral, house, and clock drawing tasks. Healthy elderly people usually perform consistently well on these praxis tests.

The performance of AD patients progressively deteriorates as the disease progresses, as we can see in Figure 7.2, which compares the results of the praxis test in a healthy elderly person and an AD patient tested for 5 consecutive years.

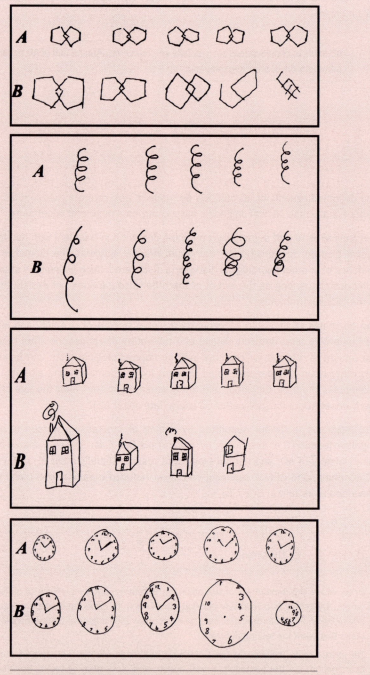

Figure 7.2 The results of the praxis tests in five consecutive years (from left to right). Comparison between a healthy elderly person (A) and an Alzheimer's disease patient (B). Reproduced with permission from M. Z. Smith *et al.*, *Dementia and Geriatric Cognitive Disorders*, 2001; **12**: 281–288. Copyright Karger, 2001.

extension: Use of CT and SPECT in the diagnosis of AD

BOX 7.5

Researchers from Oxford (OPTIMA) discovered that by tilting the axis of cross-sectional CT imaging, they could produce images of the entire medial temporal lobe, the structure affected very early in AD. This can be seen by comparing the two images in Figure 7.3.

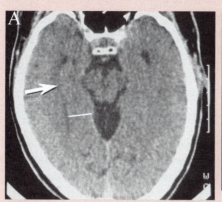
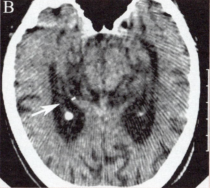

Figure 7.3 CT images using the Oxford Medial temporal lobe angle in a healthy elderly individual (A) and an age-matched AD patient (B). Reproduced with permission from J. H. Morris and Zs. Nagy, 'Alzheimer's disease' in *The Neuropathology of Dementia* (eds M. M. Esiri, V. M-Y. Lee, J. Q. Trojanowski), pp. 161–206. Copyright Cambridge University Press, 2004.

In the healthy elderly individual (A) the medial temporal lobe retains its normal thickness (dotted white line) and the lateral ventricle appears only as a thin black line on the CT scans (arrow). In the AD patient (of the same age) (B) the medial temporal lobe is shrunken (tissue thickness indicated by the white line) and the ventricle appears as an enlarged black cavity (arrow).

SPECT imaging in AD is used to map the changes in the blood flow in the brain. The early reduction of blood flow in the parietotemporal region is a specific sign that can appear in AD. If we look at the two SPECT images in Figure 7.4, we can clearly see the much-reduced blood flow in the AD patient.

(a) (b)

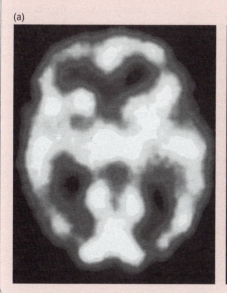
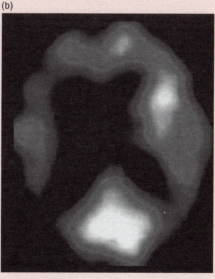

Figure 7.4 SPECT images showing the difference in brain blood flow between a healthy elderly individual (a) and an age-matched AD patient (b). Reproduced with permission from J. H. Morris and Zs. Nagy, 'Alzheimer's disease' in *The Neuropathology of Dementia* (eds M. M. Esiri, V. M-Y. Lee, J. Q. Trojanowski) pp. 161–206. Copyright Cambridge University Press, 2004. A full-colour version of this image is shown in the plates section.

The appearance of psychiatric symptoms (such as depression; insomnia; delusions; illusions; hallucinations; catastrophic verbal, emotional and physical outbursts; and sexual disorders), incontinence, and weight loss are also consistent with the diagnosis. Other neurological abnormalities (such as motor signs, increased muscle tone, myoclonus (jerky limb movements), gait disorders, and seizures) may appear in advanced disease.

The diagnosis of AD is excluded if the dementia had a sudden apoplectic onset, or seizures or gait disorders appear early. Similarly the finding of focal neurological signs (hemiparesis, sensory loss, visual field deficits, and early incoordination) are all incompatible with the diagnosis of probable AD.

7.3.1 How can Alzheimer's disease be differentiated from other dementias?

AD can be difficult to diagnose in the early stages, as mild memory problems are indistinguishable from those commonly associated with normal ageing or mild depression. The early personality changes are easily put down to depression in the elderly.

Later on, when the cognitive deficits worsen and dementia is diagnosed, the differential diagnosis from other organic disease is imperative as some can be treated or slowed by medical intervention.

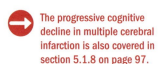

The progressive cognitive decline in multiple cerebral infarction is also covered in section 5.1.8 on page 97.

The second most common cause of dementia (15%) in the elderly is cerebrovascular disease.

The differential diagnosis of **multi-infarct dementia** relies partly on clinical signs and partly on neuroimaging. Multi-infarct dementia may show sudden deterioration if the patient has a stroke, but this is not universal. CT shows patchy lesions often localized in the white matter. Clinical differentiation is difficult because 20–40% of AD patients also have cerebrovascular disease of varying severity, so the slowly progressing AD-type dementia can be punctuated by sudden deterioration that makes the cognitive deficit abruptly worse.

Metabolic diseases such as **hypothyroidism** and vitamin deficiencies (vitamin B_{12}) account for another 10% of all dementia cases. Blood tests to exclude these diseases are mandatory in the evaluation of all demented patients.

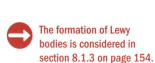

The formation of Lewy bodies is considered in section 8.1.3 on page 154.

Lewy body dementia can be difficult to diagnose unless the patient develops early Parkinsonian signs. A fluctuating course and visual hallucinations are a clue to the diagnosis. In around 30% of cases, patients have signs of both Lewy body dementia and AD.

Rarer causes of dementia are considered in Box 7.6.

SELF-CHECK 7.3

What other conditions can look like AD?

The differential diagnosis of AD can be difficult especially in early stages of the disease. In the later stages the presence of multiple pathologies makes differential diagnosis complicated.

7.4 What tissue changes are caused by Alzheimer's disease?

The most striking change in the post-mortem AD brain is shrinkage or atrophy of the brain which is most apparent in the temporal lobe (an example of the post-mortem appearance of an AD brain is shown in Figure 7.5).

From this we can see that the loss of brain tissue (atrophy) is easy to appreciate from the wide sulci (the grooves indicated by the stars) in the middle section of the brain, comprising the temporal pole (bottom star) and parietal lobe (top star). The frontal

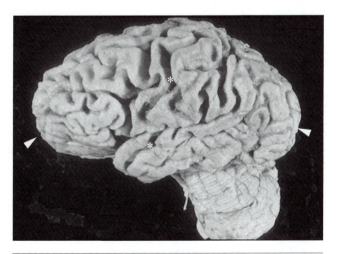

Figure 7.5 The post-mortem appearance of the brain in Alzheimer's disease. Reproduced with permission from J. H. Morris and Zs. Nagy, 'Alzheimer's disease' in *The Neuropathology of Dementia* (eds M. M. Esiri, V. M-Y. Lee, J. Q. Trojanowski) pp. 161–206. Copyright Cambridge University Press, 2004.

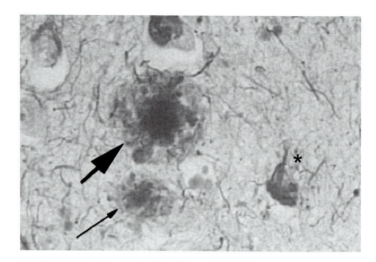

Figure 7.6 Amyloid plaques (arrows) and neurofibrillary tangle (star) stained by the Bielshowsky silver impregnation method. A full-colour version of this image is shown in the plates section.

lobe (arrowhead at the front of the brain) is relatively spared, while the occipital lobe (arrowhead at the back of the brain) is not affected by the disease.

Brain atrophy is associated with the appearance of specific pathological features in the brain. Using the silver impregnation method developed by Bielshowsky (see Box 7.1), Alois Alzheimer described **miliary deposits** in the brain. These are called the **amyloid plaques** and are found outside nerve cells.

He also identified the flame-shaped intracellular fibrils called **neurofibrillary tangles**. Even today the diagnosis of AD relies on the identification of these two pathological hallmarks using the same silver staining technique as Alzheimer used almost 100 years ago. If we look at Figure 7.6, we can see amyloid plaques (identified by arrows) and a neurofibrillary tangle (identified by a star) in a brain section from an AD patient.

7.4.1 Amyloid plaques

Chemical analysis of plaques revealed that they consisted of deposits of an insoluble short fragment (**beta-amyloid**) peptide, of a much larger protein called **amyloid precursor protein (APP)**. APP is a transmembrane protein and its functions are still to be elucidated. Its localization led to speculation that APP might be a cell-surface receptor. Alternative theories postulated that it has a role in the development of synaptic connections and the learning associated neuronal remodelling process.

Looking at the top part of Figure 7.7, we can see that in normal circumstances APP is cleaved or cut in such a fashion that the two-step process (pink arrow step 1, black arrow step 2) leads to the formation of short soluble fragments which are thought to have **neuroprotective** properties. However, in AD the first step is altered (processing site indicated by red arrow). This alteration results in the formation of beta-amyloid at the end of the two-step process (red arrow step 1, black arrow step 2). Beta-amyloid

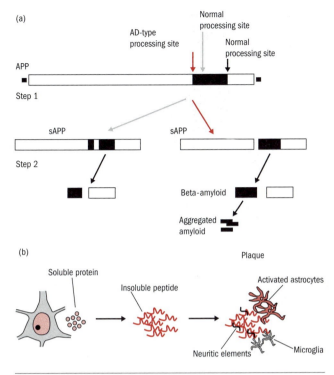

Figure 7.7 The generation of the beta-amyloid fragment from APP (a) and the maturation process of the plaques (b). Reproduced with permission from J. H. Morris and Zs. Nagy, 'Alzheimer's disease' in The Neuropathology of Dementia (eds M. M. Esiri, V. M-Y. Lee, J. Q. Trojanowski) pp. 161–206, Copyright Cambridge University Press, 2004.

has a strong tendency to aggregate, and the insoluble aggregates accumulate over time outside nerve cells leading to the formation of plaques.

7.4.2 Neurofibrillary tangles

Tangles are almost exclusively made of an abnormal form of the **tau protein**. Tau is a long intracellular protein that has the role of holding together **microtubules**. Microtubules are rather like the bars of a scaffold, and are responsible for the transport mechanisms in neurons, so they are pivotal to the survival of the cell. They also provide the **cytoskeleton** of the nerve cells, giving stability to its connections and contributing to the synaptic remodelling essential for the learning process. Since the microtubules are dynamic structures (they constantly change), the tau protein has the ability to detach and reattach.

In AD, tau protein is detached from microtubules and undergoes chemical modifications (**phosphorylation**) that prevent its reattachment. This process leads to the accumulation of the hyperphosphorylated tau in the cell and the decay of the microtubules. The hyper-phosphorylated tau has a strong affinity to form paired helical filaments (PHFs) with itself, thereby becoming insoluble. As the microtubules disintegrate the PHFs start to accumulate in the cell body of the nerve cells forming the classical tangles, as we can see

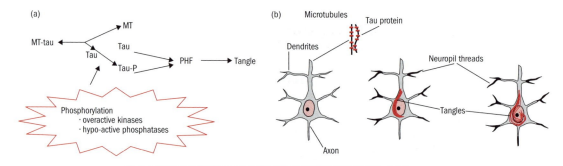

Figure 7.8 The changes of the tau protein in AD (a) and the gradual formation of the tangles inside nerve cells (b). Reproduced with permission from J. H. Morris and Zs. Nagy, 'Alzheimer's disease' in *The Neuropathology of Dementia* (eds M. M. Esiri, V. M-Y. Lee, J. Q. Trojanowski) pp. 161–206, Copyright Cambridge University Press, 2004.

in Figure 7.8. The accumulation of similar PHFs in the axons and dendrites of the neurons are called neuropil threads, because of their appearance under the microscope.

The destruction of microtubules and the filling of the cell with this amorphous material lead to cell death. The tangles are so indestructible that they remain in the tissue long after the neuron has died ('tombstone tangle').

The distribution of plaques and tangles in the AD brain is described in more detail in Box 7.7.

---

extension: Distribution of plaques and tangles in the brain   **BOX 7.7**

The accumulation of the two pathological hallmarks of AD does not affect every brain region equally.

Amyloid plaques tend to appear mainly in the association cortical regions of the brain. They invade the hippocampus and other medial temporal lobe structures very late in the disease process. In contrast, neurofibrillary tangles appear first in the medial temporal lobe regions and then spread to the association cortical areas of the brain.

The easiest way to see the differential distribution of tangles in the brain is to look at very thin sections (0.15 mm) across the whole brain (white line in inset (a) indicates the plane of the section) as we can see in Figure 7.9.

The section obtained was stained with a special silver stain (called the Gallyas impregnation) to visualize only the tangles (black). The darker the staining appears, the more tangles there are in the region. The medial temporal lobe (arrowhead at bottom left) is the first to be affected by tangle formation; therefore it contains more tangles than any other region. The tangles then spread to the lateral temporal lobe (arrowhead at

bottom right) and finally to the association cortical regions (arrowhead at top right), which are the regions least affected.

The development of the tangles appears to parallel the evolution of the clinical symptoms. As we can see in Figure 7.9, this starts with memory deficit (related to the function of the medial temporal lobe) and leads on to other cognitive dysfunction (related to the function of the association cortex). The primary motor and sensory areas remain spared by the disease.

The observation that tangle development follows a strict pathway led to the development of a staging system. This is called **Braak staging** after the pathologist who described it. It allows the precise pathological description of the brain pathology in AD. The staging system has become part of the routine diagnostic procedure and is invaluable as a research tool.

The association between the tangles and clinical symptoms, and the lack of relationship between plaque formation and cognitive deficit, indicates that the feature responsible for the functional consequences of AD is the tangle formation; amyloid deposition appears to be only a by-product of the disease.

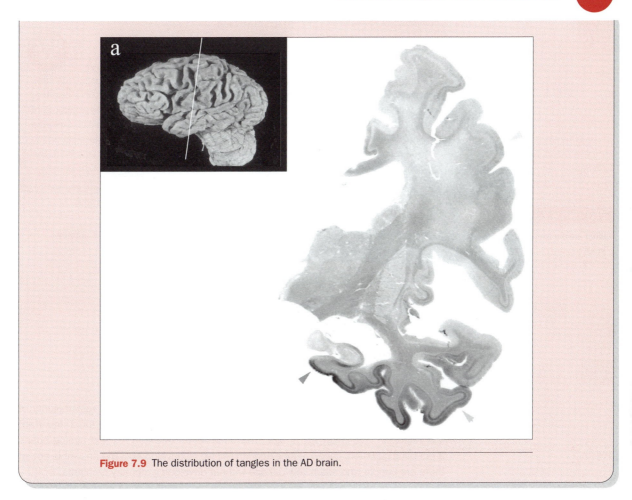

Figure 7.9 The distribution of tangles in the AD brain.

7.4.3 Other pathological changes

The accumulation of plaques and tangles is a diagnostic prerequisite for AD. However, this does not mean that these are the only two pathological changes that appear in the brain. Parallel to the formation of mainly the tangle pathology, there is an excessive loss of neurons in brain regions severely affected by AD. Synaptic loss is also typical as well as the loss of neurotransmitters. The reduction of acetylcholine in AD appears relatively early and correlates well with the loss of function.

Amyloid deposits are not restricted to plaques. They can appear in the wall of blood vessels leading to what is called **amyloid angiopathy**. Although the accumulation of this vascular amyloid is impressive in some patients, it does not seem to lead to any functional consequences.

Post-mortem analysis in many cases shows that other diseases can coexist with AD, and more details of these are given in Box 7.8.

Even when the pathological diagnosis of AD is clear cut, post-mortem examination commonly shows that other pathologies, such as vascular disease or Parkinson's disease, are coexistent. In the case of such mixed pathologies the brain has a smaller amount of each pathology (e.g. fewer plaques and tangles and fewer infarcts) than would be expected from the severity of the clinical symptoms. It appears that the effect of coexisting pathologies in the brain is cumulative, leading to more severe and rapidly evolving dementia. The presence of multiple pathologies also makes the clinical picture very difficult to identify.

SELF-CHECK 7.4

What are the main pathologies in AD?

> The main pathologies in AD are the development of extracellular amyloid plaques and intracellular neurofibrillary tangles.

7.5 What are the likely causes of Alzheimer's disease?

7.5.1 Risk factors

A small proportion of AD cases are genetically determined, but the vast majority of patients suffer from the late-onset, sporadic form of the disease. The most important risk factor for late-onset AD is age. The association between AD and ageing poses a troubling question: if we live long enough will we all develop AD? The answer is no, as there are people who reach very old age without developing memory problems.

Epidemiological studies show gender is also important in the genesis of AD, with women tending to develop the condition after the menopause. **Diabetes**, **hypertension**, and **atherosclerosis** predispose to AD, and dementia induced by repetitive head injury is associated with the development of AD-type pathology in the brain.

The role of poor education and reduced physical activity in AD causation are also well documented. More recent studies indicate that vitamin deficiencies, especially folate and the B vitamins, can also contribute to the development of AD.

Although no clear genetic cause has been identified for late-onset AD, the fact that the disease tends to accumulate in families does point to inherited risk factors. So far, the only identified genetic factor associated with late onset AD is a variant of the **apolipoprotein E** (*ApoE*) gene. ApoE is a lipoprotein, and its variant ApoE4 was found to be associated with atherosclerosis. Research indicates that the same variant is associated with an elevated risk of AD. However, having this variant of the *ApoE* gene does not invariably mean that the person will develop AD; it only means that if the disease does appear, it will begin earlier, will develop faster, and that the brain will have more plaques and tangles.

As described above many factors increase the risk of developing AD. Over the years many theories have developed in trying to understand what causes this devastating brain disorder, and how the risk factors might affect its development and evolution.

Ultimately, every attempt to explain the course of events leading to the destruction of entire neuronal populations has aimed to develop new therapies, and new diagnostic methods that would be more accurate, and could identify the patients well before the clinical symptoms fully develop.

7.5.2 Is Alzheimer's disease genetic?

As discussed above, the observation that AD can run in families indicated that there might be a genetic component to its origin. This is also suggested by Down's syndrome patients, with three copies of chromosomes 21 instead of two, invariably developing AD by the time they reach their 40s.

 The genetic basis of Down's syndrome, and its association with AD, is discussed in section 3.3.1 on page 47.

In the 1980s, a large family was identified in which several members suffered from early-onset AD. Genetic analysis indicated that the disease was inherited in an autosomal dominant Mendelian fashion.

Pioneering genetic research identified a mutation in the APP protein, the precursor for beta-amyloid, as discussed in section 7.4.1, in this large AD family. The gene for APP is located on chromosome 21, the same chromosome responsible for Down's syndrome. Mutations on the APP gene have been identified in other large families, but the search for genetic alterations in APP in the more common (95%) late-onset AD cases was unsuccessful.

The 1990s brought another promising discovery. Mutations in another two genes, the **presenilins**, were identified as the causative factor in familial forms of AD. Researchers had high hopes of finding the ultimate genetic culprit, but it transpired that these mutations were also very rare and had no association with late-onset AD.

The associations between these genetic mutations and the incidence of these in the early- and late-onset forms of AD are summarized in Table 7.1. The mutations discovered on the *APP*, *PS-1*, and *PS-2* genes are found in a very small proportion of AD patients. However, when these mutations are present, they have a very strong effect: almost all people with any of these mutations develop AD.

7.5.3 Amyloid cascade hypothesis

The finding of the APP mutations associated with early-onset AD, and the localization of the APP gene to chromosome 21, led to the development of the **amyloid cascade hypothesis**.

Table 7.1 Genetic causes of AD

Gene	Age of onset (years; range)	Penetrance	% of familial AD	% of all cases of AD
APP	50s (30–60)	100	Approx. 5	Less than 1
PS-1	50s (20–62)	100	Approx. 50	Approx. 5
PS-2	60s (30–86)	98	Less than 5	Less than 1

APP, amyloid precursor protein; *PS-1*, presenilin-1, *PS-2*: presenilin-2.

Penetrance: the percentage of people who get the disease if they have the genetic risk factor.

This hypothesis postulates that the deposition of beta-amyloid in the form of plaques (see section 7.3.1), either due to a mutation of APP or the overproduction of APP in Down's syndrome, is the cause of AD.

Hundreds of studies in the following decades concentrated on proving that the accumulation of beta-amyloid is the primary triggering event that leads to nerve cell death, the formation of tangles, loss of synapses, and ultimately dementia. The hypothesis, and the research that has followed since, has left a lot of questions unanswered, and arguments for and against the amyloid cascade hypothesis are set out in Table 7.2.

Table 7.2 Arguments for and against the amyloid cascade hypothesis

For	Against
Mutations in the amyloid precursor protein can lead to the development of early-onset AD	There are only around 20 families in the whole world where this is the case, representing around 0.15% of all AD sufferers
	Any possible mechanism by which these mutations may cause AD has been demonstrated in one single family
	There are several mutations on the APP protein that do not cause AD or any other disease
	There are no abnormalities in the APP gene in the large majority of AD patients
Down's syndrome patients, with three copies of the *APP* gene instead of two, invariably develop AD	*APP* is not the only gene on the fragment of chromosome 21 necessary for Down's syndrome
	The brain pathology in Down's syndrome is there well before beta-amyloid is deposited in the form of plaques
	The development of the AD-type neuritic pathology does not appear to be a direct consequence of the beta-amyloid deposition in these patients
The mouse models for beta-amyloid mutations develop plaques in their brain and suffer some damage to brain function	These animals carry 32–64 copies of a human gene in their nerve cells and there is no control model to illustrate that any species-alien protein in this quantity is not harmful
	These animals never develop the neuritic pathology specific for AD
	They show only mild cognitive impairment
	They are only a model for brain amyloidosis and not for AD
Beta-amyloid is toxic to neurons in culture and initiates processes that may lead to the formation of the neuritic pathology	Toxicity studies use 10 000 times higher doses of beta-amyloid that that found in the human brain
	There is no apparent toxic effect of amyloid deposits in AD brains
	The possible link between amyloid and tangles is only hypothetical and was never actually proven
Beta-amyloid is the cause of AD-type pathology in the brain and its deposition leads to dementia	There are no signs of any brain dysfunction in people who have only beta-amyloid deposits in their brain
	Nerve cell dysfunction and dementia are related to the development of tangles, with or without plaques

Alternative theories are also proving more accurate in describing the events that cause this disease. However, the amyloid cascade hypothesis is still the dominating theory of AD. There has been considerable investment in research to reduce the burden of beta-amyloid in AD patients with the hope of curing the disease, as described in section 7.6.3 below.

7.5.4 The role of tau

As discussed in section 7.4.2, the pathological feature responsible for the clinical symptoms of AD is the neurofibrillary tangle. We have seen that these flame-shaped intraneuronal inclusions consist of the hyperphosphorylated form of the microtubule associated protein, tau.

The chemical changes (phosphorylation) that increase the ability of tau to form the PHFs of the tangles have attracted much attention. It is well documented that enzymes that encourage this transformation (**kinases**) are more active in the brain of AD patients. Additionally, the enzymes that would counteract this process (**phosphatases**) are reduced.

As we can see by looking again at the top part of Figure 7.8, a consequence of this is that the balance between phosphorylation (attachment of phospho groups) and dephosphorylation (detachment of phospho groups) is shifted towards phosphorylation.

Although the nature of the chemical imbalance is well understood, we still have no understanding of what causes this imbalance between the two opposing chemical reactions. We also have no indications as to what links the tau pathology to the beta-amyloid production. Why is the chemistry of these two, seemingly unrelated, proteins altered at the same time? Why is their distribution in the brain so different?

The search for the causes and processes involved in the formation of AD pathology, and associated nerve cell death, is ongoing. New hypotheses are formulated, studied, argued over again and again. The discovery of the true nature of the pathogenic process, which will allow the development of effective therapies and early detection, will be one of the most important discoveries of medical science in the future.

> **SELF-CHECK 7.5**
>
> What are the possible causes of AD?

7.6 What treatments are available for Alzheimer's disease?

At present, we do not have a treatment that can slow or halt the progression of AD. Similarly, we have no means of preventing the disease. The available drugs offer only short-term symptomatic relief for some, but not all, AD patients. Preventive interventions are aimed at reducing risk factors rather than stopping the disease process itself.

7.6.1 Preventive measures

Table 7.3 lists some of the preventive measures which are aimed at reducing some of the known risk factors for AD. Most of these interventions have some scientific support and clinical following, but their true efficacy remains to be proven.

Table 7.3 Preventive measures for AD

Risk factor	Preventive intervention
Vascular disease	Treat high blood pressure, avoid smoking and high fat diets
Low education	Retain intellectual activities, written memory aids
Low physical activity	Maintained physical exercise, especially those requiring manual skill (knitting)
High cholesterol	Low-fat diet, cholesterol-lowering drugs
Vitamin deficiencies	Maintain a healthy diet, vitamin supplements
Ageing	Protect against age-related oxidative damage—vitamin supplements
Menopause	Hormone replacement therapy (but increases the risk of certain cancers)

The use of food supplements that are thought to enhance memory, such as lecithin and ginko biloba, is advocated by some, but their therapeutic value is supported only by anecdotal evidence or speculation.

7.6.2 Symptomatic treatments

Early studies indicated that the development of the plaques and tangles is paralleled by the reduction of neurotransmitters, especially acetylcholine, in the brain regions affected by AD. This discovery led to the hypothesis that drugs that could boost the activity of acetylcholine might reduce the functional consequences of the disease. There were hopes that such treatment might even halt the progression of the disease.

The **cholinesterase inhibitors** donepezil, rivastigmine, and galantamine slow down the metabolism of acetylcholine. This increases the effect of the neurotransmitter even when its production is reduced. Although early clinical trials in AD showed promising results, the latest large-scale studies indicate that these drugs help only a fraction of patients. It is also evident that the beneficial effects of the drug are limited to reducing the effect of the condition on memory.

7.6.3 Neuroprotective treatments

The amyloid cascade hypothesis postulated that the accumulation of beta-amyloid is the primary pathology of AD, leading to cell death and the formation of the tangle pathology. Although the hypothesis was never actually proven, and the toxicity of beta-amyloid is highly questionable, a lot of effort has been put into reducing and reversing the deposition of this insoluble protein in the brain.

Early approaches attempted to manipulate the chemical processes involved in the processing of APP into beta-amyloid. These drugs (called gamma-secretase inhibitors) proved to be too toxic, producing too many harmful side effects.

A more recent approach has attempted to mobilize the patient's own immune system against beta-amyloid. A vaccine was developed which was supposed to trigger an immune response in order to break down and clear away the plaques. Although vaccination was successful in removing plaques from the brain of animals, clinical studies in humans had to be abandoned because of unexpected severe side effects.

7.6.4 Future strategies

The search for an effective preventive measure for AD is ongoing. Currently several strategies are being investigated.

Cholesterol-lowering drugs (**statins**), by reducing one of the risk factors for AD, could prove useful, but the results of large clinical trials are still awaited.

Also, since some anti-inflammatory drugs appear to prevent the development of AD, current research is aimed at understanding the mechanisms by which these drugs have a beneficial effect in an attempt to translate this empirical observation into treatment.

> Currently there is no treatment for AD. The available drugs only provide symptomatic relief for a small number of patients.

SELF-CHECK 7.6

What treatments are available for AD?

7.7 What does the future hold for patients with Alzheimer's disease?

At present, the diagnosis of AD means only the prospect of long-term suffering for both patients and relatives, without the hope of a curative treatment or lasting symptomatic relief. Over the 10–15 years of disease progression patients lose their memories and personality; in other words everything that makes them who they are. Eventually they lose their life.

For the relatives, the grieving over the loss of their loved one is a prolonged agony, as they have to watch the person they knew and loved slowly fade away. The increasing social and economic problem that AD represents fuels research efforts by both government agencies and the pharmaceutical industry.

As several therapeutic strategies are being investigated the hope for more effective drugs in the next 10 years appears realistic.

SUMMARY

- AD is the most common neurodegenerative disease.
- The main pathologies in AD are the development of extracellular amyloid plaques and intracellular neurofibrillary tangles.
- The initial clinical features of AD are forgetfulness especially for recent events and behavioural changes that can resemble depression.
- AD leads to complications such as falls and infections.
- Around one half of AD patients eventually die of bronchopneumonia.

- The differential diagnosis of AD can be difficult, especially in early stages of the disease.
- In the later stages the presence of multiple pathologies makes differential diagnosis complicated.
- There is no treatment that slows the progression of AD.
- The cholinesterase inhibitors only provide symptomatic relief for a small number of patients.

FURTHER READING

Reference books

R. Jacoby and C. Oppenheimer. *Psychiatry in the elderly*, 3rd edn. New York: Oxford University Press, 2002.

M. M. Esiri, J. H. Morris, and J. Trojanowski (eds). *The neuropathology of dementia.* New York: Cambridge University Press, 2004.

Review articles

K. Herrup, R. Neve, S. L. Ackerman, and A. Copani. Divide and die: cell cycle events as triggers of nerve cell death. *Journal of Neuroscience* 2004; **24**: 9232–9239.
Discusses the most novel and most controversial hypothesis for the origin and development of Alzheimer's disease.

S. Lovestone and D. M. McLoughlin. Protein aggregates and dementia: is there a common toxicity? *Journal of Neurology, Neurosurgery and Psychiatry* 2002; **72**: 152–161.
A thorough and detailed discussion of all dementias characterized by protein deposits, and the common links between them.

A. Mudher and S. Lovestone. AD—do tauists and baptists finally shake hands? *Trends in Neurosciences* 2002; **25**: 22–26.
Discussion of two opposing theories about the primary event in Alzheimer's disease.

Z. Nagy. The last neuronal division: a unifying hypothesis for the pathogenesis of AD. *Journal of Cellular and Molecular Medicine* 2005; **9**: 531–541.
Detailed discussion of the most novel hypothesis regarding the origin and development of Alzheimer's disease.

R. L. Neve and N. K. Robakis. AD: a re-examination of the amyloid hypothesis. *Trends in Neurosciences* 1998; **21**: 15–19.
Re-examines the scientific validity of the amyloid cascade hypothesis.

D. R. Thal, K. Del Tredici, and H. Braak. Neurodegeneration in normal brain aging and disease. *Science of Aging Knowledge Environment* 2004; 23: 26.
Creates an elegant link between ageing and dementia.

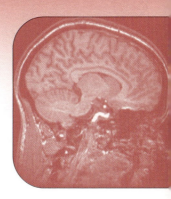

CHAPTER EIGHT

Other neurodegenerative conditions

Carl Clarke and Karen Morrison

INTRODUCTION

Neurodegenerative diseases are those in which neurons die over some years, leading to a slowly progressive clinical course. This process is distinct from, for example, vascular disorders in which there is a specific problem with the blood supply to the brain leading to the sudden onset of symptoms and clinical signs.

The most common neurodegenerative diseases are:

- Alzheimer's disease
- Huntington's disease
- Motor neuron disease
- Parkinson's disease

We have described Alzheimer's disease in the previous chapter, so here we concentrate on the three other major neurodegenerative diseases.

8.1 Parkinson's disease

Parkinson's disease (PD) is the second most common neurodegenerative disease after Alzheimer's disease. In common with Alzheimer's disease, people with PD live with the condition for many years, so it causes significant long-term disability and is costly to health-care systems.

8.1.1 How common is Parkinson's disease and who are at most risk?

PD affects around 120 people per 100 000, so there are about 100 000 patients with PD in the UK with 8000 new cases presenting each year. Its frequency increases with age; 2% of the population over the age of 65 years develop PD. The age structure of the whole UK population will age over the next 20 years, which will lead to a doubling or trebling in the number of cases of PD.

> Parkinson's disease is the second most common neurodegenerative disease after Alzheimer's disease.

8.1.2 What are the likely causes of Parkinson's disease?

We do not know what causes PD in most cases. There are two possible types of causative factor: something in the environment, and internal genetic factors.

Environmental causes

Table 8.1 shows us some of the environmental factors which have caused clinical problems similar to PD in the past. One of the most interesting is the neurotoxin 1-methyl-4-phenyl-1,2,3,6-tetrahydropyridine (MPTP), the structure of which is shown in Figure 8.1. In the early 1980s, a chemist in San Francisco was synthesizing an illicit pethidine analogue for intravenous drug abusers, but he used too high a reaction temperature, which led to the manufacture of MPTP. Those who took large amounts of this drug developed a severe **parkinsonian syndrome**. MPTP is not present in sufficient quantities in the environment to be a cause of PD, but its structure is similar to that of some pesticides. Observational studies have shown a small increased risk of PD in those exposed to pesticides, rural residence, farming, and drinking well water.

Genetic causes

We see in Table 8.2 the list of genetic forms of PD. These are rare, probably accounting for no more than 5% of cases attending PD clinics in the UK. One of the most important discoveries is that some of these genetic forms of PD may have a common pathway leading to neurodegeneration involving the organelle that removes unwanted proteins from the **dopamine** cell, called the **proteasome**.

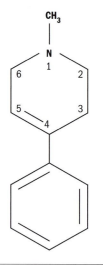

Figure 8.1 Chemical structure of 1-methyl-4-phenyl-1,2,3,6-tetrahydropyridine.

SELF-CHECK 8.1

What are the possible causes of Parkinson's disease?

Table 8.1 Environmental causes of parkinsonism

Increased risk	Decreased risk
Pesticides	Cigarette smoking
Rural residence, farming, drinking well water	Caffeine (coffee)
1-methyl-4-phenyl-1,2,3,6-tetrahydropyridine	
Manganese and copper	
Encephalitis lethargica	
Influenza	
Head injury	

Table 8.2 Genetic forms of Parkinson's disease

Name	Gene	Inheritance
Park 1	*a synuclein*	AD
Park 2	*Parkin*	AR
Park 3	*?*	AD
Park 4	*?*	AD
Park 5	*UCH-L1*	AD
Park 6	*PINK-1*	AR
Park 7	*DJ-1*	AR
Park 8	*LRRK2*	AD
Park 9	*?*	AR
Park 10	*?*	?Iceland
Park 11	*?*	?US
FTDP-17	*Tau*	AD

LRRK2, leucine-rich repeat kinase 2; *PINK-1*, phosphatase and tensin homologue deleted on chromosome 10 (PTEN) induced kinase 1; *UCH-L1*, ubiquitin carboxy-terminal hydrolase L1.

8.1.3 What tissue changes occur in Parkinson's disease?

Pathological changes

The main pathological processes in PD are the death of the dopamine releasing neurons between the **substantia nigra** and the **striatum**, and the formation of **Lewy bodies**.

Figure 8.2A shows a cross section of the midbrain of a normal person at post-mortem. If we compare this to Figure 8.2B, which shows the equivalent section in someone with

The structure of the basal ganglia, which includes the substantia nigra and striatum, is described in section 1.4.3 on page 14 and shown in Figure 1.9.

(a)

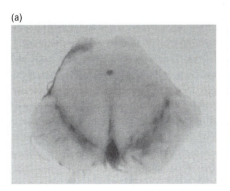

(b)

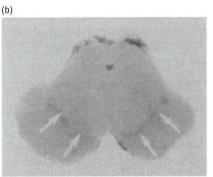

Figure 8.2 Post-mortem section through the midbrain of a normal person (a) and someone with Parkinson's disease, showing the loss of melanin pigment (b). Reproduced with permission from C. E. Clarke, *Parkinson's disease in practice*. Royal Society of Medicine Press, London. Copyright Royal Society of Medicine, 2001. A full-colour version of this image is shown in the plates section.

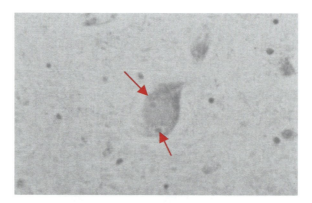

Figure 8.3 High-power magnification of a section of the substantia nigra showing a dopaminergic neuron containing Lewy bodies (arrows). Reproduced with permission from C. E. Clarke, *Parkinson's disease in practice*. Royal Society of Medicine Press, London. Copyright Royal Society of Medicine, 2001. A full-colour version of this image is shown in the plates section.

PD, the loss of the pigment melanin, which is a by-product of dopamine metabolism, is clear to see.

Examination of the substantia nigra under high-power magnification reveals the loss of individual dopaminergic cells and the accumulation of intraneuronal inclusions called **Lewy bodies** after the German neuropathologist who originally described them. You will note from Figure 8.3 that Lewy bodies take up eosin stain, producing a dense red staining of their core surrounded by a paler halo. The mechanism by which Lewy bodies form is still unknown, but they are likely to be an end-product of the pathophysiological process that has caused PD.

> Death of the dopamine-releasing neurons between the substantia nigra and the striatum, and formation of Lewy bodies, are the principal pathological processes in Parkinson's disease.

Biochemical changes

Around 80% of the nigral dopamine must be lost before patients develop symptoms of PD, which shows that there are considerable compensation mechanisms. These include increased turnover of dopamine in the remaining neurons and a postsynaptic increase in dopamine receptor sensitivity.

> 80% of the nigral dopamine is lost before the symptoms and signs of Parkinson's disease develop.

Other biochemical changes have been found in the substantia nigra in PD. These include increased production of oxidative free radicals, increased iron accumulation, and a deficiency in mitochondria of respiratory chain complex 1 activity. It is not known whether these are primary causative changes or secondary to some other process.

Considerable strides have been made in recent years in elucidating the functional organization of the basal ganglia structures involved in PD, many using the MPTP model of PD in non-human primates. The details of the connectivity of these nuclei and what happens in PD and other movement disorders are beyond the scope of this book, but readers who are interested should refer to one of the more detailed sources in the further reading section.

8.1.4 What are the symptoms and signs of Parkinson's disease?

Initial symptoms and clinical signs

As we see in the case study in Box 8.1, people with early PD present with three sets of symptoms and signs:

- tremor
- rigidity
- bradykinesia and hypokinesia.

> The initial clinical features of Parkinson's disease are rest tremor, rigidity, bradykinesia, and hypokinesia.

The most common is **tremor**. This is an involuntary, rhythmical, alternating movement of the fingers when the patient is relaxed or at rest. The thumb and index finger often rub together as though they were rolling a pill between them, so this is called a **pill-rolling tremor**.

Patients complain of stiffness of their limbs. On examination, we can detect this by passively moving the patient's wrist up and down. The resistance felt when doing this in PD is called **rigidity**.

---

case study: Early Parkinson's disease
BOX
8.1

A 72-year-old retired accountant presents to his GP with shaking of his right hand for 6 months. He has also noticed that his right shoulder is stiff and occasionally painful.

His GP thinks that he has lost facial expression and wonders whether this is Parkinson's disease.

In the neurology clinic, he is found to have right pill-rolling rest tremor and rigidity in the right wrist. He is generally slow and has lost arm swing on the right when he walks. He does not smile as much as one would expect.

He was commenced on levodopa as co-careldopa and, when seen in clinic 2 months later, he was much improved with no stiffness and only mild tremor.

case study: Later Parkinson's disease

A 76-year-old woman had had Parkinson's disease for 14 years. She lived alone and was mobile around the house with the help of the furniture, but used a walking stick when walking outside the house. She was taking levodopa, ropinirole, and entacapone which kept her switched on for most of the waking day. She had suffered from imbalance for several years and had suffered several minor falls with no injuries.

She was admitted acutely to the emergency department after falling when out doing her shopping. She was trying to turn round to reach something from a supermarket shelf but overbalanced backwards and fell heavily on her right side.

The emergency department staff found that she had a very painful right hip which she would not let them move. An X-ray confirmed that she had a fractured neck of femur (hip bone). The orthopaedic team took her to theatre to replace the hip with a prosthesis.

Over the next week, she mobilized well with the aid of the physiotherapists and a walking frame. Three weeks after the accident, she was discharged home with a care package which included meals-on-wheels and a home help.

The terms **bradykinesia** (slowness of movement) and **hypokinesia** (poverty or loss of movement) are used very loosely. Patients rarely complain of slowing down; they usually notice it, but attribute it to old age! Hypokinesia is manifest as loss of facial expression and loss of the normal swinging of the arms which we do when we walk.

All of these symptoms and signs are worse down one side of the body in PD.

Later symptoms and clinical signs

As PD progresses, the clinical features outlined above deteriorate and new problems develop.

As the case study in Box 8.2 demonstrates, one of the most frequent of these later problems is impairment of balance, which leads to falls. The patient's gait tends to be slow and shuffling, with imbalance usually on turning. Falls can, in turn, lead to fractures which can even prove fatal. Balance problems do not respond to medication like the other symptoms of PD, so it has a major impact on patient's quality of life.

The other common debilitating aspect of the later stages of PD is **dementia**. Progressive cognitive decline can be helped a little by the anticholinesterase drugs which were originally developed for Alzheimer's disease. However, it continues to progress and is a frequent cause for residential home placement.

PD patients with dementia often develop psychotic symptoms, but these can occur in isolation, often as a result of changes in medication. The most common are hallucinations and confusion. The hallucinations tend to be visual and of people or animals. The confusion is typically intermittent, so sometimes the patient is clear thinking but very quickly they can become confused.

Depression is common in PD but this usually responds to standard antidepressant medication.

Table 8.3 Other clinical features of the later stages of Parkinson's disease

Feature	Description of common symptoms
Speech disorders	Low volume; fast with a tendency to stumble over words
Sleep disorders	Restlessness of legs; vivid dreams; acting out dreams
Difficulty swallowing	Choking; coughing; chest infections
Constipation	
Low blood pressure	Light headedness on standing
Bladder problems	Passing urine frequently; having to go to the toilet quickly
Pain	Frozen shoulder
Oedema	Swelling of legs due to fluid accumulation
Saliva	Excess leading to drooling
Sweating	

A problem unique to later PD is the development of **motor complications**. These are comprised of:

- **dyskinesia**—involuntary writhing movements of the limbs, trunk, or face
- **dystonia**—most commonly painful calf cramps in the early morning off-period
- **response fluctuations**—both wearing off of the effects of medication at the end-of-dose and unpredictable on/off fluctuations in which the patient switches rapidly from the mobile 'on' phase and the immobile 'off' phase, like a light being switched on and off.

Motor complications are related to levodopa therapy and to progression of the disease, as they rarely develop before levodopa is used or in the early stages of the condition.

As we see in Table 8.3, there are many other features seen in the later stages of PD which lead to accumulating disability over the 15–20 years of the condition.

> Parkinson's disease leads to a large number of complications in its later stages including imbalance and falls, dementia, depression, psychosis, and motor complications.

SELF-CHECK 8.2

What are the main clinical features of Parkinson's disease?

How can Parkinson's disease be differentiated clinically from similar conditions?

We will now explore the large number of conditions that can look like Parkinson's disease.

Essential tremor is also a condition of older people in which they develop a tremor of the hand and arms when they are doing things. This leads to mild disabilities such as shaking and rattling of tea cups and spoons, and difficulty using a screwdriver. No other signs develop, unlike in PD. However, without sufficient experience in differentiating these conditions, they can easily be confused.

> It can be difficult to differentiate Parkinson's disease from essential tremor.

Table 8.4 Causes of a parkinsonian syndrome

Parkinson's disease

Drugs, e.g. phenothiazines

Multiple cerebral infarcts

Trauma (pugilistic encephalopathy or punch drunk syndrome)

Toxin-induced, e.g. MPTP, CO, Mn, Cu

Parkinson's plus syndromes, e.g. progressive supranuclear palsy (PSP) and multiple system atrophy (MSA)

As you can see from Table 8.4, many other diseases cause a parkinsonian syndrome, i.e. tremor, rigidity, and bradykinesia/hypokinesia. It can be extremely difficult to sort these out, so all patients with suspected PD should be referred to an expert clinician in the field.

SELF-CHECK 8.3

What other conditions can look like Parkinson's disease?

> It can be difficult to differentiate Parkinson's disease from other causes of a parkinsonian syndrome.

8.1.5 What tests can we use to diagnose Parkinson's disease?

Many people find it hard to believe that the diagnosis of PD still remains a clinical one. A clinician with expert training and experience in diagnosing this group of conditions will be able to reach an accurate diagnosis in most cases.

In the last few years, a new imaging modality has become available to help in the differentiation of essential tremor from a parkinsonian syndrome. This is explained in Box 8.3. It is only required in a very small proportion of cases attending a movement disorders clinic.

8.1.6 What treatments are available for Parkinson's disease?

Neuroprotective treatments

PD is a slowly progressive condition and, at the moment, all of the therapies we have aim to improve the patient's symptoms and signs; we do not have any treatment that will slow or halt the underlying degenerative process of PD. Such a **neuroprotective therapy** is one of the main goals of research in PD.

Many compounds have been shown to protect dopaminergic neurons from various insults in tissue culture and experimental models of PD. The next step is to test these substances in clinical trials in patients with PD. There have been some encouraging clinical trials with selegiline and the dopamine agonists ropinirole and pramipexole. However, these results are now considered unreliable. Unfortunately, there is considerable debate about how neuroprotection trials should be done in PD.

A systematic programme of neuroprotection trials in PD is ongoing in the US (NetPD), but these have encountered significant design problems.

extension: Use of single photon emission CT (SPECT) in differentiating essential tremor from Parkinson's disease

BOX 8.3

In SPECT imaging, a gamma ray emitting radioactive isotope is tagged to a molecule of interest called a **tracer**. This tracer is given to the patient by intravenous injection. The labelled cocaine derivative ^{123}I-FP-CIT (*N*-ω-fluoropropyl-2β-carboxymethoxy-3β-{4-iodophenyl}tropane) is most commonly used for tremor diagnosis in the UK. This labels the presynaptic dopamine reuptake site and thus the presynaptic neuron which can be visualized in two-dimensional images by the gamma-ray detecting 'camera'. We see an example of these in Figure 8.4.

These demonstrate normal uptake in the caudate and putamen in normal people, patients with essential tremor, neuroleptic-induced parkinsonism, and psychogenic parkinsonism. However, there is reduced uptake in those with PD, PD with dementia, MSA, and PSP.

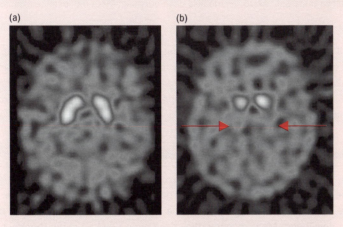

(a) (b)

Figure 8.4 Single photon emission computed tomography (SPECT) using the tracer ^{123}I-FP-CIT (see text for details). (a) shows normal uptake in the caudate and putamen (like inverted commas). (b) shows reduced uptake in the putamen in a parkinsonian syndrome (like full stops; arrows). Courtesy of Dr A Notgi. A full-colour version of this image is shown in the plates section.

Symptomatic treatments

The main treatment for PD is **levodopa**. As we see in Figure 8.5, this is metabolized in the brain into dopamine. We cannot administer dopamine itself as it does not cross the blood–brain barrier.

Levodopa is given orally, along with an amino acid decarboxylase (AADC) inhibitor to reduce its metabolism in the rest of the body so that more gets to the brain. The combination of levodopa and the AADC inhibitor carbidopa is called co-careldopa and the combination with benserazide is called co-beneldopa.

The blood–brain barrier is described in section 1.2.3 on page 5.

Levodopa preparations are still the best treatment for the motor symptoms of PD. However, levodopa can cause short- and long-term side effects. These short-term problems

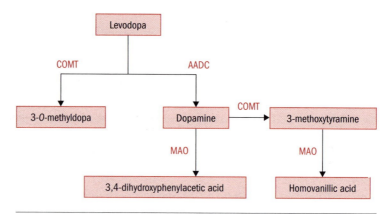

Figure 8.5 Metabolism of levodopa. Enzymes: COMT, catechol-*O*-methytransferase; AADC, amino acid decarboxylase; MAO, monoamine oxidase.

consist of loss of appetite, nausea, vomiting, and **postural hypotension** (drop in blood pressure on standing), but they are usually mild and can be blocked by the antiemetic domperidone. The long-term motor complications of levodopa have been described in section 8.1.4. To avoid the latter, a new approach of starting patients on a dopamine agonist has been proposed.

> Levodopa remains the mainstay of the treatment for Parkinson's disease.

Dopamine agonists bind directly with the postsynaptic dopamine receptors. Initially, they were developed as a treatment for the later stages of PD once motor complications had developed. More recently, they have been used as initial therapy to reduce the development of motor complications in the first place. However, they are not as effective in treating the physical impairments caused by PD, so there continues to be much debate about which should be the initial therapy. This may be resolved by a large clinical study which is ongoing in the UK called the PD MED trial.

As we see in Table 8.5, there are other treatments for PD, but these are beyond the scope of this book.

8.1.7 What is the long-term outcome of Parkinson's disease?

In spite of the development of effective **symptomatic treatments** for PD, patients still die in excess of their peers without the condition. The duration of PD is highly variable, with patients who develop it at a young age having it for up to 30 or 40 years compared with people in their 70s who may only have it for 10–15 years.

SELF-CHECK 8.4

How does levodopa treatment work in Parkinson's disease?

Table 8.5 Treatments for Parkinson's disease

Medical	
Drug class	Generic drug name
Levodopa and AADC	Co-careldopa, co-beneldopa
Dopamine agonists	Bromocriptine, cabergoline, lisuride, pergolide, pramipexole, ropinirole
Catechol-O-methyl transferase inhibitors	Entacapone, tolcapone
Monoamine oxidase inhibitors	Selegiline, rasagiline
Beta-adrenergic receptor antagonists	Propranolol
Adamantamines	Amantadine
Muscarinic acetylcholine receptor antagonists	Trihexyphenidyl, orphenadrine
Nursing and allied health professionals	
Parkinson's disease nurse specialist	
Physiotherapy	
Occupational therapy	
Speech and language therapy	
Surgical	
Bilateral subthalamic nucleus stimulation	

8.2 Motor neuron disease

Motor neuron disease (MND), also known in the USA as amyotrophic lateral sclerosis (ALS), is the most common disease affecting motor nerves in adults. It progresses rapidly, with most people affected dying within a few years of the onset of symptoms. Death in MND is usually due to respiratory muscles being weak, but the disease also causes weakness in limb muscles and in those involved with speech and swallowing. MND is one of the diseases in which the issue of assisted suicide is sometimes raised.

8.2.1 How common is motor neuron disease and who are at most risk?

Although MND is the most common disease affecting motor neurons, it is fortunately quite rare, affecting only about 10 people per 100 000. This means that the average GP in the UK will only see one person with MND in their lifetime of practice. Most patients present between the ages of 50 and 70 years. The disease is more common in men (male:female ratio 1.6:1) and increases in incidence with age. As the population as a whole increases in age, the number of people with MND is going to increase.

MND is a rare disease but increasing in incidence as the population ages.

8.2.2 What are the likely causes of motor neuron disease?

The causes of MND are not known. As in PD, the neurodegeneration is thought to occur as a result of a combination of environmental and genetic factors.

Environmental causes

Table 8.6 lists the main environmental factors that have been linked to MND. Of these, only smoking consistently comes up in different studies. In the past it was thought that high-level sustained exercise, such as that experienced by long-distance runners and cyclists, might be a risk factor for the disease, but recent large studies have not consistently shown this.

Controversy surrounds reports of increased incidence of MND in military personnel, particularly those who served in the first Gulf War. Possible causative agents that have been implicated in military personnel include exposure to toxins such as the insect repellent DEET, or aerosolized lead generated by firing weapons, or exposure to certain viruses in vaccinations. It is not clear if there really is an increased incidence in MND here, or if it reflects a bias in the reporting of the disease.

Another report intriguingly shows a sixfold higher incidence of MND in footballers who have played in the top divisions of the Italian football league compared to that expected from the background incidence of MND in Italy. Many possible reasons have been put forward to explain this increase, including intensive physical exercise, frequent trauma such as sustained when heading the ball, frequent air travel, exposure to illegal drugs, or contact with high levels of toxic herbicides or fertilizers applied to the pitches. Another possibility is that the finding is a chance association. If you investigate many possible causes, **spurious associations** will by chance crop up.

MND occurs worldwide and at similar frequency in Europe, Africa, and the Americas. There are a few places where the disease is much more frequent, such as the Kii peninsula in Japan and on the island of Guam, where an incidence more than 100 times higher than elsewhere has been reported. Many factors have been investigated as being possibly responsible for this, including the theory that the toxic amino acid beta-methylamino-L-alanine (BMAA) found in cycad nuts is key. The Chamorro people of Guam ingest cycad nuts, but in insufficient amounts to cause nerve damage. Recent work has shown that the flying fox ingests large quantities of the nuts and concentrates the toxic BMAA in its body. Such flying foxes are considered a delicacy in Guam, and the proposal is that it is ingestion of the foxes, with their high concentrations of BMAA, that has caused the

Table 8.6 Environmental factors in MND

Smoking	Probable risk factor
Sustained physical exercise	Unproven suggested risk factor
Exposure to metals, e.g. iron, mercury, manganese	Unproven suggested risk factor
Military service	Unproven suggested risk factor
Certain occupations e.g. aircraft pilots	Unproven suggested risk factor
History of trauma or electric shock	Probably not a risk factor
Alcohol consumption	Probably not a risk factor

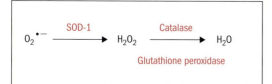

Figure 8.6 Actions of Cu/Zn superoxide dismutase, SOD-1.

MND-like disease. In support of the theory, the incidence of MND in Guam has declined in recent years, mirroring a decline in the number of flying foxes.

Infection with the polio virus results in a disease affecting just motor nerves, so another theory is that MND is due to infection by a polio-like virus. However, there is not much evidence to link polio, or a similar virus, to MND, with many studies having sought and not found markers of virus infection in the disease.

Genetic causes

Most people with MND do not have any family history of the disease. Only 5–10% of people with MND have such a family history, usually compatible with **autosomal dominant inheritance**. In 20% of these familial MND cases, mutations are found in the gene encoding the cytosolic enzyme Cu/Zn superoxide dismutase (*SOD-1*). Figure 8.6 shows that the action of this enzyme is to detoxify oxygen free radicals and protect cells against excess oxidation. Mutated SOD-1 enzyme in familial MND gains a new toxic function, causing it to damage motor neurons, but the exact mechanism for the selective motor neuron damage remains unknown. No genetic defects have been found as yet in the 80% of familial cases without *SOD-1* mutations. The search for such genes is hampered by the lack of large families with MND suitable for **genetic linkage studies**.

8.2.3 What tissue changes occur in motor neuron disease?

Figure 8.7 shows an outline of the human motor system. Central motor neurons, with cell bodies in the motor cortex, project axons to form the **corticospinal tracts**. These then form synapses with lower motor neurons in the spinal cord. Axons project from

SELF-CHECK 8.5

What are some of the environmental factors that may increase the risk of MND?

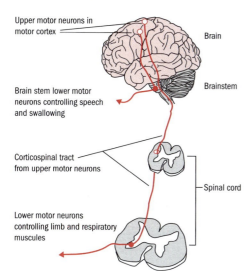

Upper motor neurons in motor cortex

Brain

Brain stem lower motor neurons controlling speech and swallowing

Brainstem

Corticospinal tract from upper motor neurons

Spinal cord

Lower motor neurons controlling limb and respiratory muscles

Figure 8.7 Outline of the human motor system.

(a)   (b)

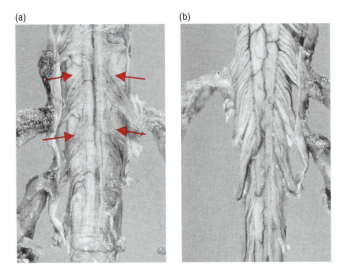

Figure 8.8 Spinal cord showing loss of motor nerve roots in MND.
(a) Spinal cord from a patient who died from MND. The anterior motor
nerve roots (indicated by arrows) are severely atrophied. A normal
post-mortem spinal cord is shown in (b) for comparison. Photographs
courtesy of Dr Martyn Carey.

the lower motor neurons via peripheral nerves and connect with muscle fibres at the
neuromuscular junction.

The characteristic pathological feature of MND is loss of upper and lower motor neurons.
The arrows in Figure 8.8a indicate the atrophy of the lower motor neuron nerve roots as
they leave the spinal cord in a post-mortem spinal cord of a patient who died with MND.
The normal appearance of these nerve roots is shown in Figure 8.8b.

The cell bodies of the motor nuclei in the brainstem are also affected, which gives rise
to the symptoms of impaired speech and swallowing in the disease.

As with Alzheimer's and Parkinson's diseases, abnormal intraneuronal inclusions are
seen in MND in the cell bodies of the remaining motor neurons. We can see an example
of this in Figure 8.9. The inclusions in MND characteristically stain heavily with dyes
which detect ubiquitin, a protein that is often added to other proteins before they are
degraded in the proteasome.

Biochemical pathways

Disruption of many intracellular pathways is thought to occur in MND, as shown in
Figure 8.10. Key pathways involved include **excitotoxicity**, mediated via glutamate, the
brain's major excitatory neurotransmitter, excess oxidative damage to proteins and DNA,
impaired cellular transport by **neurofilaments**, and abnormalities in mitochondrial function.

SELF-CHECK 8.6

What biochemical pathways are
thought to be involved in MND?

Ultimately intracellular regulation of calcium is disrupted and the affected motor neurons
are thought to die by **apoptosis**. It is not known why the disorder is so selective for the
motor system. Even in familial disease caused by *SOD-1* mutations, although mutated
SOD-1 is present in many cell types throughout the body, only motor neurons are affected.

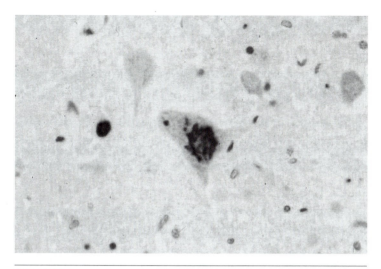

Figure 8.9 High-power view of motor neurons in MND showing ubiquitinated inclusions. Photograph courtesy of Dr Martyn Carey.

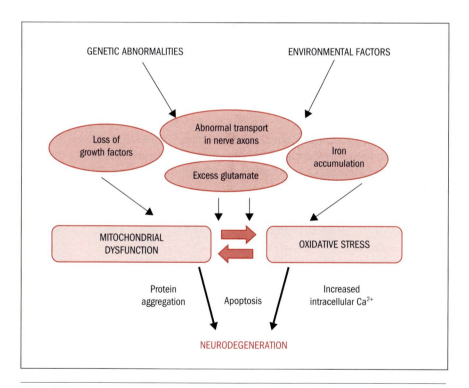

Figure 8.10 Some of the pathways considered key to motor neuron death in MND.

case study: Limb presentation of MND

BOX
8.4

A 52-year-old man has noticed thinning of his hands for the last 4 months. He has difficulty turning his door key in the lock, and unscrewing jars. He has developed stiffness around his shoulders and in his forearms and is generally very tired.

When seen in neurology clinic 6 weeks later, his hands and arms are noticeably weak and wasted. Fasciculation is evident in the muscles of his arms and forearms and, despite his muscle wasting, the reflexes in his arms are brisk. His speech is mildly slurred but he has no difficulty swallowing. He has no numbness or tingling anywhere and his vision is fine. Routine blood tests are normal and a cervical spine MRI scan does not show any disease of the spine or nerve roots.

Electrophysiological tests confirm a disease of motor nerves, with normal sensory conduction and with widespread denervation in the muscles of upper and lower limbs.

8.2.4 What are the symptoms and signs of motor neuron disease?

The most common way for people with MND to present is with weakness and wasting in their limbs, as illustrated in the case study in Box 8.4.

Some people present with **fasciculations** and features suggesting mainly lower motor neuron involvement, others with mainly upper motor neuron signs. The clinical features that may differentiate these are shown in Figure 8.11. As the disease progresses, upper and lower motor neuron features develop. About a quarter of people present with speech or swallowing problems, as illustrated in the case study in Box 8.5. Eventually people with these symptoms usually develop symptoms in the limbs, and likewise people who begin with limb involvement will eventually develop speech and swallowing difficulties. Clinical features that are not seen in MND are listed in Table 8.7.

Table 8.7 Clinical features not seen in MND

Sensory symptoms and signs

Autonomic nerve disease

Abnormal eye movements

Bladder or bowel symptoms

Marked changes in memory, personality, and intellect

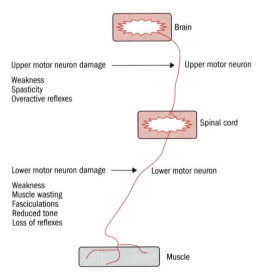

Figure 8.11 Clinical features arising from upper and lower motor neuron cell damage.

> **case study:** **Bulbar presentation of MND**
>
> **BOX 8.5**
>
> --
>
> A 66-year-old woman was initially seen in the ear, nose, and throat clinic because of a 6 month history of progressively slurred speech. An MRI scan of her brain failed to reveal any lesion in the brain stem. When seen in the neurology clinic some 3 months later she had marked slurring of her speech, but was still intelligible if she spoke slowly. She didn't feel that her tongue was moving properly and had difficulty chewing meat. She had to drink slowly, otherwise she coughed and spluttered, but had no problem swallowing soft food.
>
> On examination her tongue was wasted and fasciculating, with slowed movements. Her neck was weak, tending to fall forward. Although her limbs were strong electrophysiological tests confirmed denervation in her arm muscles.
>
> On review 4 months later her speech was sufficiently unclear that she communicated with the doctor in writing. She could no longer swallow food and requested that a feeding tube be inserted.
>
> Over the next 6 months strength in her arms and then in her legs decreased. She became increasingly breathless, first on exertion, then at rest. She found assisted ventilation via a nasal mask uncomfortable and could not tolerate this. She died as the result of a chest infection 20 months after the onset of slurred speech.

> MND affects upper and lower motor neurons. Sensory function and cognition remain intact.

8.2.5 What tests can we use to diagnose motor neuron disease?

MND is diagnosed on the basis of the history of the symptoms and signs pointing to a disorder of motor neurons. There is no specific blood test or brain imaging tool that allows MND to be distinguished from other disorders. Investigations are carried out to exclude other diseases that may mimic MND, such as those listed in Table 8.8. Electrophysiological tests are used to confirm that the disease is one of degeneration of motor rather than sensory neurons and to confirm that muscles are weak because of interruption of their nerve supply rather than due to a **myopathy**.

Table 8.8 Disorders that can mimic MND

Degenerative disease of the spine
Syringomyelia—a cavitating disorder of the spinal cord
Damage to the spinal cord following radiotherapy
Various inherited diseases, e.g. spinal muscular atrophy
Endocrine diseases, e.g. overactive thyroid or parathyroid glands
Multifocal motor neuropathy—a rare immune disorder
Lead or mercury poisoning
Lymphoma—cancer of the lymphatic system

8.2.6 What treatments are available for motor neuron disease?

Unfortunately there are no treatments that halt or reverse the progressive motor neuron damage in MND. On the basis of some of the proposed mechanisms in the disease, such as those shown in Figure 8.10, various therapies have been tested in clinical trials. These include antioxidants such as vitamin E and *N*-acetylcysteine; creatine, an agent thought to increase the function of mitochondria; and various factors that promote nerve growth such as brain-derived neurotrophic factor and insulin-like growth factor.

The only agent in clinical use that has shown an effect in prolonging survival in MND is riluzole, an agent that has many effects including reducing glutamate release pre-synaptically and also reducing glutamate's postsynaptic effects. Oral riluzole therapy improves survival for about 3 months if the drug is taken for 18 months. It does not make patients feel stronger, and some question the value of an agent with such modest benefit on survival in this relentlessly progressive disease.

Research on treatments has until recently been hampered by the lack of any good animal or cellular models of the disease. The discovery of *SOD-1* mutations in some familial MND patients has led to the development of a mouse model for MND, with copies of mutant forms of human *SOD-1* introduced into mice via genetic engineering (see Box 8.6).

Studies in the *SOD-1* mouse model have led to several new theories of the cause of MND and allowed many compounds to be screened for therapeutic effect.

One such compound is vascular endothelial growth factor (VEGF; Box 8.7). When VEGF is given intravenously to patients, it generates an intense immunological reaction,

---

extension: Development of *SOD-1* mouse model of MND
BOX 8.6

In 1993 it was discovered that mutations in the *SOD-1* gene are found in some people with inherited MND. As a step towards determining how *SOD-1* mutations might cause MND, researchers investigated the *SOD-1* gene in mice. First, mice were made by genetic engineering with copies of the mouse *SOD-1* gene deleted. The mice seemed normal. Another strategy was then followed, adding into mice copies of the human *SOD-1* gene with the same mutations that had been identified in inherited MND. This time the mice did develop disease, with muscle wasting and weakness. These features were first noticeable when the mice were a few months old, the equivalent to human middle age. The weakness and wasting then progressed, similar to human MND.

Pathological examination of the mice showed them to have many of the same features that are seen in human MND, with loss of cell bodies of motor neurons and inclusions in remaining motor neurons.

Several strains of human mutant *SOD-1* mice have since been produced, each with a different human *SOD-1* mutation added. The human mutant *SOD-1* mouse provides for the first time a good model for human MND. No naturally occurring mice with a disease so similar to MND have previously been found. Many potential therapies have been screened in this mouse model of MND over the last 10 years. Unfortunately none of them has as yet shown great benefit in humans, but screening continues.

extension: Vascular endothelial growth factor (VEGF) is linked to MND

BOX 8.7

VEGF is a protein with many essential functions, including promoting growth of blood vessels during normal growth and development, and increasing blood vessel permeability. The level of VEGF is highly regulated in the body, and is tightly controlled by levels of oxygen in the tissues. When the level of oxygen falls, this is sensed by cells and VEGF production is increased.

In 2001 researchers in Belgium were investigating the role of VEGF in developing tumours. They used genetic engineering in a laboratory mouse to specifically remove the controlling element of the VEGF gene that allows the gene to be turned on when oxygen levels are low. To the researchers' surprise, mice with the deletion of this oxygen-control element of VEGF developed a disorder with similarities to human MND. The mice were normal at birth but then developed weakness and wasting in their muscles when a few months old. Neuropathological examination subsequently confirmed that the muscle wasting and weakness was because of damage to the motor neurons, with pathological changes similar to those seen in human MND.

The hypothesis was put forward that an inability to increase VEGF levels when motor neurons are low in oxygen may be relevant to human MND. VEGF has since been shown to have effects to increase blood supply to nerves and also to directly promote nerve growth. Work is now progressing to develop a form of VEGF that can be directly tested as a therapy in MND patients.

resulting in many side effects and limiting its usefulness. Ongoing work is exploring further using **neurotropic** viruses which track along peripheral nerves into the CNS. The gene encoding VEGF is tagged to these viruses which are then injected into muscle and in this way VEGF protein is delivered to the CNS where it can exert its maximum effect without causing unwanted side effects.

Stem cell therapy is also being explored as a possibility for MND treatment, but the hurdles to this approach are huge. A source of motor neuron stem cells needs to be identified. The stem cells will have to be delivered to the CNS in sufficient numbers and then coaxed to form the correct synaptic connections to reconstitute the damage motor pathways. It may be more realistic to target neural cell stem cells already present in the adult CNS and manipulate these to develop into new motor neurons, or to use **exogenous** stem cells as a source of neurotrophic factors to be delivered to sites in the CNS.

SELF-CHECK 8.7

What are some of the therapies being tested in MND?

8.2.7 What is the long-term outcome of motor neuron disease?

As MND progresses muscle weakness increases and marked muscle atrophy occurs. All **striated muscle** is involved, except the muscles that are involved in maintaining bladder and bowel continence and the eye muscles. In late stages some people are only able to communicate by moving their eyes, spelling out words letter by letter on a special board by directing a laser attached to their eyeball. When speech is lost,

(a)

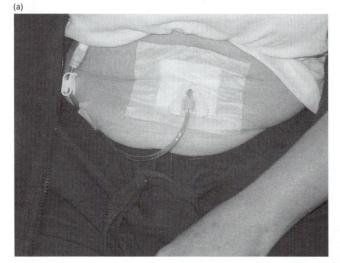

(b)

(c)

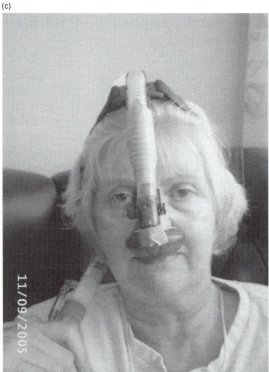

Figure 8.12 (a) A feeding tube directly placed in the stomach for use when swallowing is impaired. (b) A device for communicating when speech is lost (Lightwriter). (c) MND patient using nasal ventilation mask.

comunication may be maintained using a lap-held keyboard with a synthetic voice (as seen in Figure 8.12b). When swallowing is no longer possible, people can be fed via a tube placed directly into the stomach (Figure 8.12a). Some people with respiratory impairment can be helped by assisting ventilation with continuous positive pressure air supplied via a tightly fitting nasal mask (Figure 8.12c). People with MND usually die as a result of respiratory failure and consequent pneumonia. Choking to death is a very rare terminal event.

As communication can be very difficult in late-stage MND, many patients write **advance directives**, legal documents indicating their choice for treatment in the later stages when they may be unable to make their wishes known. Some patients opt for assisted suicide in this disease, travelling abroad to countries where this is legal. In the UK, assisted suicide for the terminally ill is currently illegal. Legislation is being considered by parliament and this situation may change in the future.

Survival in MND has increased over recent years. This has been attributed to better clinical management in multidisciplinary teams, the use of riluzole, and the use of feeding tubes and assisted ventilation. Much media attention in MND focuses on the 'right to die' in MND. People involved with MND patients are becoming more proactive in championing the 'right to live' with MND, raising awareness and encouraging more research into treatments for this dreaded disease.

8.3 Huntington's disease

Huntington's disease (HD) is an uncommon neurodegenerative disease. Unlike the other neurodegenerative conditions we have examined in this chapter, HD has a clear genetic causation.

8.3.1 How common is Huntington's disease and who are at most risk?

HD affects 7 per 100 000 of the UK population, so there are around 4000 people with the condition at any one time. The peak age of onset is 35−45 years of age.

One of the most fascinating aspects of HD is that the high frequency of the condition in the UK is mirrored in countries which were colonized by white settlers in the seventeenth and eighteenth centuries. This suggests a genetic **founder effect**, with immigrants with the HD gene who went to these 'new' countries 'founding' the condition in their new homelands.

8.3.2 What is the likely cause of Huntington's disease?

HD is an inherited condition with an autosomal dominant inheritance pattern. It is caused by a genetic mutation on chromosome 4 leading to an abnormality in a protein called **huntingtin**. The function of this protein is currently unknown.

 More information on the genetic defect associated with Huntington's disease can be found in section 3.4.1 on page 51.

8.3.3 What tissue changes occur in Huntington's disease?

The genetic abnormality we see in HD leads to death of **GABAergic cells** in the striatum of the brain. With our better understanding of the connectivity of basal ganglia structures over the last 10 years has come an appreciation of why the death of these GABAminergic cells leads to the involuntary movements described in the next section, but the details of this are beyond the scope of this book.

SELF-CHECK *8.8*

What is the cause of Huntington's disease?

8.3.4 What are the symptoms and signs of Huntington's disease?

As we see from the case study in Box 8.8, the most prominent clinical feature we see in HD is progressive cognitive decline (dementia). This can be accompanied by changes

case study: Huntington's disease

BOX 8.8

A 37-year-old man was brought to the movement disorders clinic by his wife. She thought he had been behaving oddly over the last year: he had forgotten several important meetings at work and her recent birthday. He had made reasonable excuses on all these occasions, but it was happening too often for just stress or overwork. The patient himself was not aware of any problems at all. His wife also reported that he was getting a little fidgety and could not sit still when watching television.

He denied any family history of neurological disorder, although his paternal aunt had been admitted to hospital for a psychiatric condition.

On examination, he had very mild choreiform movements of the trunk and distally in the limbs.

The neurologist raised the possibility of Huntington's disease, but the patient and his wife did not recall any other family history of the condition. The consultant sent them away to ask about the condition in the family and to locate death certificates of the patient's parents and aunts and uncles.

The patient's wife telephoned the neurologist's secretary a few days later in a distraught state. She had telephoned her mother-in-law who informed her that the patient's aunt had died of Huntington's disease several years ago. To make things worse, the patient's father was currently under investigation for what was suspected to be a dementia.

The neurologist arranged to counsel the couple in the next clinic and referred them on to the local neurogeneticist. The latter arranged for the Huntington's disease gene assay which confirmed the diagnosis.

The neurologist also informed the specialist caring for the patient's father about the possibility of Huntington's disease. Subsequently, the father's gene assay also proved to be positive.

in mood (e.g. depression), psychosis (e.g. paranoid delusions, auditory hallucinations), and behavioural disturbance (e.g. increased sexual drive).

Many different types of movement disorder can be seen in HD but the most common is **chorea**. Choreiform movements are brief, twitchy movements of the limbs, trunk, or face. Late in the condition, patients can become parkinsonian; there is also a childhood variant of the condition which causes parkinsonism. Balance problems are common as HD progresses and falls become commonplace. One of the major problems encountered in the terminal stage of the illness is dysphagia (difficulty swallowing).

> The key clinical features of Huntington's disease are family history, dementia, and chorea.

8.3.5 What tests can we use to diagnose Huntington's disease?

In most new cases of HD, there is a family history of the disorder, so the clinician already has a high index of suspicion for the diagnosis. The triad of autosomal dominant inheritance, cognitive problems, and a movement disorder strongly suggest the diagnosis. It is now possible to refer such patients to clinical neurogeneticists for further counselling, then a blood test to confirm that they have the genetic mutation of HD.

8.3.6 What treatments are available for Huntington's disease?

There is no neuroprotective therapy for HD. All that can be done at present is to treat the symptoms of the disorder and support the patient and their family.

There is no treatment for the dementia in HD, but the behavioural problems can respond to dopamine antagonists (e.g. typical and atypical antipsychotics). These agents can also reduce chorea.

8.3.7 What is the long-term outcome of Huntington's disease?

The rate of progression of HD depends on the size of the genetic mutation. In general, we find that most patients progress to death over 10–20 years. In contrast, those with an age of onset in their 60s and 70s usually have just a mild dementia, because they only have a small gene abnormality. This group can survive for 30–40 years.

SUMMARY

- Parkinson's disease is the second most common neurodegenerative disease after Alzheimer's disease.

- Although the cause(s) of Parkinson's disease are unknown, various genetic and environmental precipitants have been suggested.

- 80% of the nigral dopamine is lost before the symptoms and signs of Parkinson's disease develop.

- The initial clinical features of Parkinson's disease are rest tremor, rigidity, bradykinesia and hypokinesia.

- Parkinson's disease leads to a large number of complications in its later stages including imbalance and falls, dementia, depression, psychosis, and motor complications.

- Levodopa remains the main stay of the treatment for Parkinson's disease.

- MND is rare but important and is increasingly highlighted in the media because of the issue of assisted suicide.

- MND affects upper and lower motor neurons. Sensory function and cognition are intact.

- Average survival with MND is about 2 years from diagnosis. There is still no cure or treatment that significantly alters prognosis.

- Riluzole, an antiglutamate agent, prolongs survival in MND on average for 3 months if taken for 18 months.

- The key clinical features of Huntington's disease are family history, dementia and chorea.

FURTHER READING

General

R. L. Watts and W. C. Koller. *Movement disorders. Neurologic principles and practice*, 2nd edn. New York: McGraw-Hill, 2004.
Detailed reviews of all types of movement disorders.

Parkinson's disease

C. E. Clarke. *Parkinson's disease in practice*, 2nd edn. London: Royal Society of Medicine, 2007.
A short overview of all aspects of Parkinson's disease.

J. R. Playfer and J. V. Hindle. *Parkinson's disease in the older patient.* London: Arnold, 2001.
A more detailed text on Parkinson's disease.

Motor neuron disease

R. H. Brown, V. Meininger and M. Swash. *Amyotrophic lateral sclerosis.* London: Martin Dunitz, 2000.
A detailed textbook covering all aspects of MND.

D. W. Cleveland and J. D. Rothstein—From Charcot to Lou Gehrig: deciphering selective motor neuron death in ALS. *Nature Reviews, Neuroscience* 2001; **2**: 806–808.
A short review outlining some of the mechanisms in MND.

K. E. Morrison. Therapies in ALS—beyond riluzole. *Current Opinion in Pharmacology* 2002; **2**: 302–309.
A review on mechanisms in MND and potential treatments.

CHAPTER NINE

Brain infections

Karen Morrison and John Jefferys

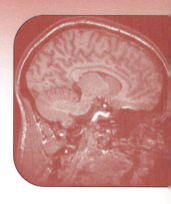

INTRODUCTION

Infection can occur both in the membranes covering the brain and in the substance of the brain itself. In this chapter we consider various causes of such infections and the resulting symptoms, signs and available treatments. We also discuss brain abscesses, localized areas of infection within the brain, and the recently described disease of variant Creutzfeldt–Jakob disease, vCJD, an example of a very rare brain infection caused by an abnormal protein.

Definitions

The Greek suffix for infection is *-itis*, and thus **meningitis** is the term given to describe infection of the meninges, the pia and arachnoid membranes covering the brain. Infection in these membranes quickly spreads to involve the subarachnoid space and the cerebral ventricles. Infection of the brain substance itself is known as **encephalitis**. Often meningitis and encephalitis occur together.

> Meningitis and encephalitis often occur together.

9.1 How do microorganisms cause brain infections?

The main organisms that infect the brain are similar to those that can infect other parts of the body, namely **bacteria**, **viruses**, **parasites**, and **fungi** (some of the more common of these are listed in Table 9.1). The infectious organisms most often enter the central nervous system (CNS) directly through an open wound such as sustained in head trauma, or from tooth or sinus infection, or travel into the brain via the bloodstream, a process known as **haematogenous spread**. More rarely, infections can reach the brain

Table 9.1 Organisms that can cause brain infections

Type of organism	Examples
Bacteria	*Pneumococcus*
	Neisseria meningitidis
	Haemophilus influenzae
	Staphylococcus
	Listeria
Viruses	Herpes simplex
	Enteroviruses
	Varicella-zoster
	Mumps
	Rubella
Fungi	*Candida*
	Aspergillus
	Cryptococcus
Parasites	Malaria
	Toxoplasma
	Toxocara
	Hydatid
	Schistosomiasis

by travelling into the CNS along peripheral nerves. This is the way that viruses such as the **herpes** simplex virus, which causes cold sores, or the herpes zoster virus, which causes chickenpox, enter the CNS.

Microorganisms bring about harmful effects to the body's tissues by various means. Many bacteria produce soluble toxins, which travel in the bloodstream, causing inflammation and killing cells either directly or via a series of chemical reactions. **Exotoxins** are toxins which are excreted by living bacteria, such as botulinum toxin or tetanus toxin. Botulinum toxin interferes with the secretion of acetylcholine at cholinergic synapses in the peripheral nervous system to cause paralysis, whereas tetanus toxin affects synapses in the CNS resulting in widespread muscular spasms. **Endotoxins** are structural elements of the cell wall of bacteria and are released only when the bacterium dies. When endotoxins enter the bloodstream they cause fever, inflammatory reactions, and cell **necrosis** in various organs. Viruses enter the cells of the body and rely on nuclear factors in these host cells to allow them to replicate their DNA. They invade the body's tissues and damage cells either directly or by effects on the **immune system**.

9.1.1 What defensive mechanisms might limit the spread of infection?

When infectious organisms enter the tissue of the body, there are three main defensive mechanisms to limit their multiplication and spread and bring about their destruction.

These are inflammation, phagocytosis, and activation of the immune response. **Inflammation** involves an increase in the blood flow to the site of infection with leakage of protein-rich fluid from the blood vessels into the surrounding tissues. Subsets of white blood cells termed **polymorphs** and **macrophages** migrate from the blood vessels into the tissues where they ingest the invading organisms by process known as **phagocytosis**.

Activation of the **immune system** also involves the **lymphocyte** subset of white blood cells. On contact with foreign **pathogens**, B lymphocytes become activated and synthesize **antibodies** to specifically neutralize the pathogen. Another subset of lymphocytes, the T lymphocytes, are crucially important in the immune response. Cytotoxic T cells, or **killer T cells**, destroy infected target cells while **helper T cells** proliferate and become activated to synthesize **cytokines**, soluble chemicals that also act against the invader. Another subset of T cells termed **suppressor T cells** suppress activation of the immune system and are particularly important in protecting the body against **autoimmune disease** in which cells of the immune system damage healthy body cells.

> The main defence mechanisms to limit multiplication and spread of infectious organisms in the tissues of the body are inflammation, phagocytosis, and activation of the immune response.

These mechanisms to protect the body against infection have many beneficial effects, but they can also generate harmful effects. For example, the swelling of infected brain that occurs with inflammation may cause damage as the brain is confined within the restricted space of the skull. Brain swelling can result in a rise in tissue pressure which may impair function directly or interfere with blood flow and cause ischaemic injury. Harmful effects can also result from over-activation or inappropriate activation of components of the immune system to cause autoimmune disease, as mentioned above.

9.1.2 Opportunistic infections

There are many organisms that rarely cause disease in normal individuals but may cause overwhelming infections in individuals with impaired immune responses. These are known as **opportunistic infections**. Impaired immune responses may occur as a consequence of diseases which primarily affect the function of cells of the immune system such as in the acquired immunodeficiency syndrome (AIDS), or as a side effect of drugs given to reduce inflammation, e.g. corticosteroid therapy. Another common cause of impaired immunity is the administration of **immunosuppressant drugs**, which are designed specifically to reduce unwanted immune responses to foreign **antigens**, such as those introduced when an individual undergoes organ transplantation.

> Organisms that rarely cause disease in normal individuals may cause overwhelming infections in people with impaired immune responses. Such infections are known as opportunistic infections.

9.2 Bacterial meningitis

9.2.1 How common is bacterial meningitis and who is most at risk?

Bacterial meningitis occurs worldwide with an annual **incidence** of about 5 per 100 000. Meningitis, and specifically meningitis caused by the pneumococcus, is a notifiable disease in the UK, meaning that when a case is diagnosed the relevant public health authority needs to be notified. This allows outbreaks of the disease to be promptly identified and managed, with contacts of suspected cases treated with appropriate **prophylactic** medication.

Bacterial meningitis can affect individuals of all ages, although the organism likely to be responsible for the infection varies depending on age, as we shall see below (see section 9.2.2). As with other infections, bacterial meningitis is more frequently seen in individuals with impaired immune responses caused by the presence of other diseases, e.g. AIDS, or due to administration of immunosuppressant drugs. Figure 9.1 shows the post-mortem brain from an individual who has died from bacterial meningitis, with a thick purulent discharge covering the meninges clearly evident.

9.2.2 What are the likely causes of bacterial meningitis?

The main bacteria that cause meningitis, and the age ranges at which they are most prevalent, are listed in Table 9.2. Most cases are due to infection with the pneumococcus. Group B streptococci, *Escherichia coli*, and *Listeria* are causes of the infection in children younger than 3 months. *Neisseria meningitides*, *Pneumococcus*, and *Haemophilus* are common causes in children aged 3 months to 17 years. Pneumococcal and neisserial meningitides are the most common causes in those aged 18–50 years, whereas the

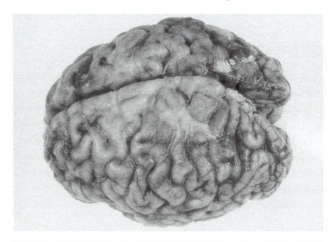

Figure 9.1 Post-mortem brain from a patient who died from meningitis. Notice the thick purulent discharge covering the brain surface. Figure courtesy of Dr Martyn Carey. A full-colour version of this image is shown in the plates section.

Table 9.2 Main causes of bacterial meningitis in the UK

Age	Organism
Newborn	Group B streptococcus
	Escherichia coli
	Listeria
	Proteus mirabilis
3 months–17 years	*Neisseria meningitidis*
	Pneumococcus
	Haemophilus influenzae
17–50 years	*Pneumococcus*
	Neisseria meningitidis
Over 50 years	*Pneumococcus*
	Listeria
	Gram-negative bacilli

Pneumococcus, *Listeria*, and gram-negative bacilli are common causes in those over 50 years old. The disease is usually caused by haematogenous spread from infection elsewhere in the body such as the lungs, or by local spread from infection of the nasal sinuses, middle ear, teeth, or penetrating head injury. Sometimes the infection follows a neurosurgical procedure and rarely follows **lumbar puncture** or epidural anaesthesia.

SELF-CHECK 9.1

What organisms are likely to cause bacterial meningitis at different ages?

9.2.3 What are the symptoms and clinical signs of bacterial meningitis?

The typical features of bacterial meningitis are rapid onset of generalized headache, fever, photophobia, and **meningism**, developing over a day or two as illustrated by the case history in Box 9.1. Additional symptoms include irritability and confusion, decreased consciousness, **myalgia**, anorexia, tachycardia, and nausea and vomiting. Children may develop severe neck stiffness resulting in an arched posture known as **opisthotonos**. Infection with the meningococcus in the bloodstream may be accompanied by a characteristic skin rash caused by bleeding into the skin (this can be seen in Figure 9.2). The rash is typical of a **purpuric rash**, meaning that the red/purple skin lesions do not lose their colour when pressure is applied e.g. by pressing a glass on to the skin. Non-specific skin rashes are frequently seen with various viral infections and can also occur as a side effect of antibiotic therapy in sensitive people, so the mere presence of a skin rash does not imply meningococcal septicaemia.

Bacterial meningitis does not usually result in any specific patterns of weakness, sensory disturbance, or movement disorder. Sometimes children will have an epileptic seizure in association with the infection, but this is rare in adults. If the infection is very severe the pressure inside the brain rises, resulting in the sign of **papilloedema**. This appearance is due to swelling of the optic nerve head as it joins the retina, and is visible by looking into the back of the eye with an ophthalmoscope. Figure 11.1 on

---

case study: Acute bacterial meningitis/encephalitis

BOX 9.1

A 20-year-old university student felt non-specifically unwell one evening and went to bed early. The next morning she woke with a stiff neck, fever, and generalized headache. By lunchtime her headache had increased in severity despite her taking oral paracetamol, and she had photophobia. By late afternoon she had become drowsy and her flatmates found her difficult to rouse. An ambulance was called and she was given intravenous antibiotics by the paramedics when they arrived 20 minutes later.

On arrival in casualty she was barely conscious. She received further intravenous antibiotics and intravenous aciclovir. Subsequently a lumbar puncture was performed which showed a raised opening pressure of CSF, and turbid fluid was tapped. It contained over 2000 polymorphs per mL, no detectable glucose and a protein level of 1.8 g/L. Staining of the CSF showed gram-positive cocci with the characteristics of pneumococci.

Despite treatment with appropriate antibiotics she required intensive care for many days, was hospitalized for several weeks, and was left with residual poor memory and concentration, and poor vision.

(a)

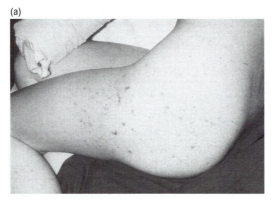

(b)

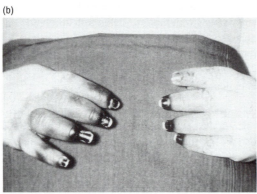

Figure 9.2 (a) The typical purpuric skin rash of meningococcal infection. The skin lesions do not lose their colour when pressure is applied, such as by pressing a glass on to the skin. (b) The fingers of a patient that have become gangrenous due to overwhelming meningococcal infection in the blood. The infection caused a profound drop in the patient's blood pressure and the blood supply to the fingers was severely impaired causing necrosis and death of the tissues. Photographs courtesy of T. S. J. Elliott. A full-colour version of this image is shown in the plates section.

page 230 shows the difference between a normal optic disc and the swollen disc margins typical of papilloedema. If the pressure rise inside the brain is severe, coma may occur.

The diagnosis of bacterial meningitis is usually not difficult to make, although sometimes other disorders can present with similar features. For example **subarachnoid haemorrhage** can be mistaken for bacterial meningitis in an unconscious patient when there is no history available of the very sudden onset typical of haemorrhage.

Subarachnoid haemorrhage is covered in section 5.2 on page 98.

Localized areas of brain infection, brain abscesses (we shall cover these in section 9.7 below), or a subdural **empyema**, a collection of pus beneath the dural meninges, can also sometimes mimic meningitis.

SELF-CHECK 9.2

What are the key features of bacterial meningitis?

9.2.4 What tests can be done to diagnose bacterial meningitis?

The aim of these tests is to confirm the clinical diagnosis and to identify the microbial cause so that appropriate specific treatment can be given. Investigations also aim to find out the source of the infection so that can be treated too. The key test is examination of the CSF obtained by lumbar puncture.

A description of the lumbar puncture procedure is given in Box 5.8 on page 101.

> A key test in confirming the diagnosis of bacterial meningitis is examining a sample of CSF obtained by lumbar puncture.

If there is evidence of raised intracranial pressure, such as the presence of papilloedema, or there are any abnormal neurological signs that suggest that a **cerebral abscess** may be present, a **CT brain scan** should be obtained prior before the lumbar puncture.

CT brain scans are described in Box 5.4 on page 91.

Bacterial meningitis is a medical emergency, and appropriate intravenous antibiotics need to be given promptly. If there is going to be any delay in carrying out the lumbar puncture or in obtaining the CT brain scan, antibiotics that are active against the range of the common causative organisms should be given intravenously straight away.

What might we find in the CSF in acute bacterial meningitis?

Table 9.3 lists the main features of the CSF in bacterial and viral meningitis compared to normal. We will consider viral meningitis later in this chapter. Normal CSF looks clear to the naked eye; in bacterial meningitis the fluid looks cloudy or turbid. Normally there are no white blood cells in the CSF, but in bacterial meningitis there are many white blood cells in the fluid, usually more than 1000/mL, and most of these cells are **polymorphonuclear leukocytes**, the type of white cells most active in phagocytosing bacteria.

In infants, and if the infection is very severe, paradoxically the white blood cell count in the CSF may be much lower or even normal. Sometimes if the patient has already received antibiotics, the white blood count will be raised, but this time with lymphocytes rather than polymorphs present. The message is that the CSF findings have to be interpreted along with the clinical signs and history of each individual patient. In viral and fungal meningitis the lymphocyte count is increased rather than any increase in polymorphs. In infection due to parasites another subset of white blood cells, the **eosinophils**, are increased.

Table 9.3 Contents of normal CSF and the CSF in meningitis

	Normal	Bacterial meningitis	Viral meningitis
Appearance	Clear	Cloudy, yellow	Clear, or slightly turbid
Opening pressure	approx10 cm H_2O	>18 cm H_2O	Normal or only mildly elevated
White cell count (cells/mL)	<5	>1000 and can be much higher	10–2000
Type of cells present	Lymphocytes	Mainly neutrophils	Mainly lymphocytes
Glucose level	2.8–4.2 mmol/L	Decreased	Normal
Protein level	0.15–0.45g/L	Increased, often to >1 g/L	Normal or mildly elevated
Staining for organisms	None seen	Organisms seen in >50% of untreated cases	None seen
Culture for bacteria	Negative	Usually positive	Negative

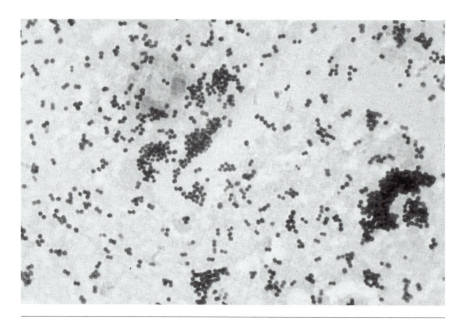

Figure 9.3 A CSF sample that has been stained with specific dyes to reveal numerous pneumococci, seen here as dark blue spherical organisms tending to clump together. Photograph courtesy of T. S. J. Elliott. A full-colour version of this image is shown in the plates section.

SELF-CHECK 9.3

What are the typical cellular and biochemical findings in normal CSF compared to those in bacterial and viral meningitis?

The protein content of the CSF is raised in bacterial meningitis (normal is between 0.15 and 0.45 g/L) and the glucose content is usually low, sometimes very low. (The normal CSF glucose is 2.8–4.2 mmol/L, and is 0.5–0.6 times the blood glucose concentration.) The CSF is then centrifuged and the cellular deposit is stained with dyes specifically chosen to stain various species of bacteria. Figure 9.3 shows an example of CSF stained with a dye that reveals numerous pneumococci as darkly stained, spherical organisms. Other organisms, such as meningococci and *Haemophilus influenzae*, have similar specific staining and morphological features that allow their identification. Samples of the fluid are then cultured and the sensitivities of the specific organisms for particular antibiotics are determined.

What other investigations are carried out in bacterial meningitis?

Normally the peripheral venous blood is sampled, and will also show an increased number of white blood cells. The **erythrocyte sedimentation rate** (ESR) is also raised, a measure of the increase in viscosity of the blood due to the presence of inflammation.

Samples of blood are also injected into culture media to try to grow and isolate the specific causative organisms in the blood, in addition to culturing the CSF. Such **blood cultures** are particularly important if they have been taken before administration of intravenous antibiotics when CSF cultures have been taken after such treatment. Samples for culture to try to identify the causative organism are also taken from any sites where infection is considered likely, such as the throat, nose, urine, skin lesions, etc.

Other investigations depend on the likely source and type of infection determined from the specific clinical history and examination in an individual patient. For example, a chest radiograph may reveal the lung as the source of infection in tuberculosis or pneumococcal disease.

SELF-CHECK 9.4

How can bacterial meningitis be diagnosed?

9.2.5 What treatments are available for bacterial meningitis?

The key feature of bacterial meningitis is that it requires treatment with antibiotics without delay. The antibiotics most likely to be effective are chosen empirically, and the choice can then be refined in hours or days depending on the results of staining of the CSF and sensitivity tests. Antibiotics need to be given in high dosages and intravenously. Table 9.4 lists the current recommendations for choice of antibiotics in the UK. The

Table 9.4 Suggested treatments for bacterial meningitis

Organism	Treatment
Pneumococcus	Penicillin G
	OR ceftriaxone or cefotaxime
Neisseria meningitidis	Penicillin G
Haemophilus influenzae	Ceftriaxone or cefotaxime
	AND steroids in children*
Listeria	Ampicillin and gentamicin
Group B streptococcus	Penicillin G
If allergic to penicillin:	
Haemophilus influenzae	Chloramphenicol
Neisseria meningitidis	Chloramphenicol
Pneumococcus	Vancomycin
Listeria	Trimethoprim
In acutely ill patient give intravenous antibiotics before organism is identified. Adjust regime once lumbar puncture results and sensitivities known	Ceftriaxone or cefotaxime
	AND vancomycin
	AND ampicillin (if suspect listeria)
	AND gentamicin (in newborn)

* There is reasonable evidence that intravenous dexamethasone, a steroid, reduces the incidence of neurological sequelae in children with *Haemophilus* meningitis.

extension: Mechanism of action of penicillins and cephalosporins

BOX 9.2

The cornerstone of treatment of bacterial meningitis is with members of the penicillin or cephalosporin drug families. Both of these types of drug are based on a beta-lactam structure. They act to inhibit synthesis of the cell wall of bacteria, specifically by inhibiting cross-linking of peptides on mucopolysaccharides, specific sugar structures in the bacterial cell wall.

Mammalian cells do not have this outer cell wall, so the drugs selectively target the bacterial cells. Once the bacterial cell wall is disrupted the organism cannot control the flow of ions and water across the wall; the cell swells and eventually bursts. Both penicillin and cephalosporins need to be given intravenously in meningitis as their absorption from the gut into the bloodstream is too slow after oral administration and they are broken down by acid in the stomach.

Some bacteria have developed resistance to penicillin by synthesizing enzymes termed beta-lactamases that break down the beta-lactam structure, rendering it useless. Ceftriaxone and cefotaxime are so-called third-generation cephalosporins. They have been specifically developed because they penetrate well into the CSF and they are not usually susceptible to bacterial beta-lactamases. They are each effective against a broad range of bacteria.

mechanism of action of the widely used penicillin and cephalosporin antibiotics is briefly outlined in Box 9.2.

There is conflicting advice about the use of corticosteroid therapy in acute bacterial meningitis. Steroids are potent anti-inflammatory drugs, and are very effective in reducing brain swelling due to oedema. However, these drugs are also known to have effects on white blood cells, rendering them less effective in fighting infections. Recent trials have suggested that steroids should be used in bacterial meningitis due to *Haemophilus influenzae* type B infection in children, and in adults when the meningitis is due to tuberculosis, but in other instances probably should not be routinely used.

SELF-CHECK 9.5

How is bacterial meningitis treated?

Headaches should be treated with appropriate analgesic agents such as oral dihydro-codeine or co-proxamol, or intramuscular opiates. If seizures occur they should be treated with standard antiepileptic drugs such as phenytoin or sodium valproate.

Treatment of contacts

Some forms of bacterial meningitis, e.g. pneumococcal disease, can be very rapidly spread between individuals. For this reason it is recommended that household contacts and individuals with close contact with people affected with meningococcal meningitis receive prophylactic antibiotics to avoid becoming infected themselves.

How can bacterial meningitis be prevented?

In recent years vaccines have been developed which can help prevent certain forms of bacterial meningitis. *Haemophilus* vaccine (HiB) is now offered routinely to all children in the UK and is very effective at preventing *Haemophilus influenzae* meningitis which can be a serious infection in the very young. The pneumococcal conjugate vaccine is also now a routine childhood immunization and is very effective at preventing pneumococcal meningitis. As pneumococcal meningitis can spread quickly between contacts of affected individuals. It is recommended that individuals living in close proximity to others, such as military recruits or students, should also be offered vaccination.

SELF-CHECK 9.6

What steps can be taken to prevent bacterial meningitis?

9.2.6 What is the long-term outlook for bacterial meningitis?

Many complications can follow acute bacterial infection in the brain. The normal resorption of CSF may be impaired by the presence of the high-protein inflammatory exudate in meningitis. **Hydrocephalus** may result, requiring the use of neurosurgical shunt procedures to relieve the high pressures. This is illustrated in Figure 9.4, showing the position of a shunt taking fluid from the cerebral ventricles into the abdomen.

Further information on the use of neurosurgical shunts for the treatment of hydrocephalus can be found in section 12.2.4 on page 262.

Various nerves within the brain may be damaged by scarring as the infection in the meninges takes hold, resulting in double vision, deafness, facial paralysis, vertigo, and blindness. Infection may spread to the cerebral vessels to cause **vasculitis**, with resultant infarction, seizures, and mental impairment. A cerebral abscess or subdural empyema (see section 9.7) may follow. Infection of the substance of the brain, **encephalitis**, may result, or infection of the spinal cord, **myelitis**.

Bacterial meningitis is a serious disease with an overall **mortality** of about 10%. The fatality rate is even higher in young children, in people who are **immunocompromised**, and if infection is with the pneumococcus. Recovery may be complete, or survivors may be left with residual disability due to blindness, deafness, epilepsy, or mental handicap.

> Bacterial meningitis is a serious disease with an overall mortality of about 10%. It requires prompt treatment with the appropriate intravenous antibiotic without delay.

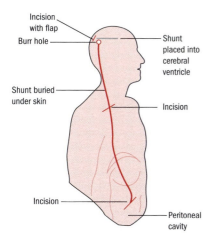

Figure 9.4 The position of a ventriculo-peritoneal shunt, draining CSF from the cerebral ventricles into the peritoneal cavity in the abdomen.

9.3 Viral meningitis

9.3.1 How common is viral meningitis and who are most at risk?

Mild degrees of neck stiffness, drowsiness, and sometimes even confusion are common in a wide range of illnesses with fever caused by viruses. This probably represents a mild form of meningitis and encephalitis. However, it is usually only when the neurological features are pronounced that a diagnosis of viral meningitis or encephalitis is made. Viral meningitis is probably more common than bacterial meningitis, with some studies reporting an incidence of 10 cases per 100 000 people per year. Sometimes the disease is very mild, with only minor symptoms, so it is likely that the incidence figures are really much higher. Viral meningitis can occur at any age, but like bacterial infections, the disease is usually more serious in the very young, the very old, and immunocompromised individuals.

The major causative agents of viral meningitis are listed in Table 9.5.

9.3.2 What are the symptoms and signs of viral meningitis?

The main features of viral meningitis are fever, headache, and neck stiffness. Other symptoms and signs depend on the specific virus involved.

Table 9.5 Causes of viral meningitis

Most common	Enterovirus	Account for 50–80% of all cases
		Over 80 types recognized
		Commonest are coxsackie and echoviruses
	Arbovirus	e.g. West Nile virus
	Herpes simplex virus type 2	
	Human immunodeficiency virus	
Less common	Herpes simplex virus type 1	
	Lymphocytic choriomeningitis	
	Mumps	
Rare	Adenovirus	
	Cytomegalovirus	
	Epstein–Barr virus	
	Measles	
	Rubella	
	Varicella-zoster	
	Influenzae	
	Parainfluenzae	

For example, **chickenpox** causes an itchy red rash that starts on the trunk and face and then spreads to the limbs, scalp, and mucous membranes. Red spots on the skin develop into blisters over a few hours and scab over in a few days. Chickenpox can be complicated by meningitis and encephalitis. Sometimes the virus causes an infection specifically of the cerebellum, and patients develop acute ataxia and unsteadiness. Once an individual has been infected with chickenpox, the varicella virus may remain latent in sensory nerves within the CNS. The virus may then reappear many years later to give a vesicular rash and pain in the segment of skin supplied by the sensory nerve, causing shingles, also known as herpes zoster.

Glandular fever is caused by the **Epstein–Barr virus**. The main symptoms are fever, sore throat, tiredness, and generalized aches. There is tender enlargement of lymph glands throughout the body and there may be a faint red rash which can be made worse if antibiotics are inadvertently given for this viral infection. Jaundice can occur if the liver is inflamed, and meningitis occurs in about 1% of cases.

Infection with the **mumps virus** causes fever, headache, and typical enlargement of the salivary glands. It is complicated by inflammation of the testicles in about 20% of cases, particularly if the infection occurs after puberty. Deafness occurs in about 1 case in 15, and usually resolves completely. Meningitis and encephalitis occur in about 1 case in 1000.

Measles can be complicated by both meningitis and encephalitis. Infection with the virus is also associated with the very rare disorder of subacute sclerosing panencephalitis, a disorder in which there is persistent infection of the brain with the virus. Years after the first infection with measles, the patient gradually develops dementia and muscle jerking and spasticity. This rare complication is invariably fatal within a few years.

Polio is caused by an **enterovirus**, and usually just causes fever, headache, and neck stiffness. Rarely, however, paralytic polio may follow, as a result of viral infection of the cell bodies of lower motor neurons in the spinal cord. Weakness and limb pain can occur, usually asymmetrically. Most patients recover completely after a few weeks, but some are left with mild weakness and rarely patients are left severely paralysed.

> **SELF-CHECK 9.7**
>
> What are the key features of viral meningitis?

9.3.3 What tests can be done to diagnose viral meningitis?

Most cases of viral meningitis are diagnosed clinically, with no specific tests carried out to confirm the diagnosis. In ill individuals, if there are features to suggest encephalitis or if bacterial meningitis needs to be excluded, the CSF should be examined by means of a lumbar puncture. The typical CSF findings in viral meningitis are listed in Table 9.3 and include a raised lymphocyte count, a normal or slightly raised protein content, and a normal or only slightly reduced glucose content. It is usually not possible to culture the causative virus from the CSF. However, specific antibodies may be detected in the CSF indicating recent or current infection with the particular virus. In recent years it has become possible to amplify some specific viral DNAs from CSF using the **polymerase chain reaction** (PCR). This has allowed many cases of herpes simplex meningitis (and encephalitis, as we shall see in section 9.6) to be specifically diagnosed. Box 9.3 explains PCR in more detail.

> **SELF-CHECK 9.8**
>
> What tests can be carried out to diagnose viral meningitis?

---

extension: Polymerase chain reaction (PCR)

BOX 9.3

This is a laboratory technique that was developed in 1987 by an American scientist, Kary Mullis, and for which he received the Nobel prize. The technique involves a method of amplifying specific regions of DNA templates many thousands of times. It relies on knowing the sequence of the DNA region to be amplified.

Small synthetic primers of known DNA sequence flanking the DNA region to be amplified are added to the template along with a DNA polymerase, an enzyme that specifically allows a new strand of DNA to be synthesized according to the template of the original DNA sequence. The procedure involves heating the DNA to denature the double-stranded helical structure, cooling the reaction to allow the small primers to bind to the template strand, and then heating the reaction again to allow the DNA polymerase enzyme to work efficiently. Thermal cycling machines are programmed to allow these sequential heating and cooling cycles to repeat between 30 and 40 times.

If primers are used that specifically bind to and flank regions of DNA sequence from a specific organism, such as the herpes simplex virus, and a sample of CSF is used as the DNA template, the reaction can be used to determine if any specific viral DNA is present in the CSF. In addition to allowing genetic diagnoses, PCR is widely used widely in DNA cloning procedures, in DNA sequencing and in many forensic applications where only very small amounts of DNA are available.

9.3.4 What treatments are available for viral meningitis and what is the long-term outlook?

Viral meningitis is usually a benign condition, and most patients recover completely within a few days without any specific treatment. Some infections can cause long-term deficits, for example deafness following measles or mumps, and paralysis following acute polio.

If patients are ill, and if encephalitis is present, the standard treatment is with the antiviral agent aciclovir. Aciclovir is really a pro-drug. To become effective it needs to be converted to aciclovir monophosphate by an enzyme, thymidine kinase, that is only found in viruses. It is then further converted to its active triphosphate form by enzymes found in human cells. This active form reduces production of viral DNA by competing with deoxyguanosine triphosphate in the cell for the main DNA polymerase enzyme that synthesizes viral DNA. Once aciclovir triphosphate is incorporated into the viral DNA no new DNA can be synthesized and the virus cannot replicate.

> Viral meningitis is usually a mild condition from which patients recover fully within a few days with no specific treatment.

9.4 Fungal and yeast infections of the brain

Fungi and yeast are rare causes of brain infection. They are, however, becoming more frequent as they tend to occur in immunocompromised individuals, such as those on steroids or other immunosuppressant drugs, in patients taking **cytotoxic drugs**, for example for cancer chemotherapy, or in people with AIDS. The most common causes of such infections in the UK are cryptococcus, candidiasis, and mucormycosis.

The symptoms are those of subacute or chronic meningitis, often accompanied by signs of raised intracranial pressure and cranial nerve palsies. The organisms can also cause encephalitis. Brain abscesses or localized areas of inflammation known as **granulomata** may form and the organisms may cause infection of the blood vessels, **vasculitis**, causing ischaemic or haemorrhagic strokes.

The diagnosis is made by either biopsy of an abscess or granuloma or by finding specific fungal antigens in the CSF or blood. Often the cell count, protein content, and glucose content of the CSF will be normal and the CSF may need to be repeatedly examined and tested before a definite diagnosis can be made.

Treatment of fungal disease is with intravenous amphotericin. This agent binds to ergosterol, a chemical in the membrane of fungi, and forms a pore in the cell wall. This leads to leakage of vital intracellular ions such as potassium, resulting in fungal cell death. The drug causes many side effects including renal damage, which can limit effective doses being used. Flucytosine is another antifungal drug in widespread use that specifically inhibits fungal DNA synthesis. Treatment of brain fungal infections must be maintained for at least 4–6 weeks.

> Fungal and yeast infections in the brain are rare but increasing in frequency. They most often occur in immunocompromised individuals.

9.5 Protozoal brain infection

Malaria is the most important parasitic disease in the world, with 40% of the world's population living in **endemic** areas. Between 300 and 500 million people in the world are affected each year, with around 1 million deaths annually; 90% of deaths occur in sub-Saharan Africa, many of them in young children who are particularly susceptible to the infection. There are about 1800 cases of malaria in the UK each year, and 1% of these are fatal. All of the people in the UK with malaria are thought to have acquired the disease abroad, mainly from Africa and south Asia.

The signs and symptoms of malaria are associated with the asexual development of the parasite in red blood cells. The various stages of the life cycle of the malaria parasite can be seen in Figure 9.5. Sexual stages of the malaria parasite are ingested when a female anopheles mosquito feeds on an individual who has, or has recently recovered from, malaria (see stage 1). The male and female stages fuse in the mosquito's gut and

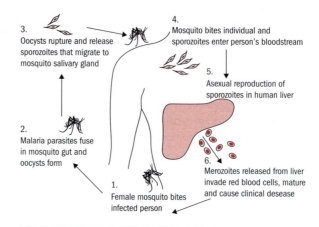

3.
Oocysts rupture and release
sporozoites that migrate to
mosquito salivary gland

4.
Mosquito bites individual and
sporozoites enter person's bloodstream

5.
Asexual reproduction of
sporozoites in human liver

2.
Malaria parasites fuse
in mosquito gut and
oocysts form

6.
Merozoites released from liver
invade red blood cells, mature
and cause clinical desease

1.
Female mosquito bites
infected person

Figure 9.5 Outline of the life cycle of the malaria parasite.

SELF-CHECK 9.9

Outline the life cycle of the
malaria parasite. At what stage do
clinical symptoms occur?

the resulting oocysts penetrate the gut wall (stage 2). Daughter parasites known as sporozoites grow within the cyst and eventually burst through the wall and migrate to the salivary glands (stage 3). When the mosquito feeds on its next human victim (stage 4) the sporozoites travel in the bloodstream to the individual's liver, where they undergo intracellular asexual reproduction (stage 5). After 1–3 weeks the resulting merozoites eventually burst through the liver cells and invade red blood cells where they mature and cause clinical disease (stage 6).

There are various forms of malaria caused by infection with different species of *Plasmodium—falciparum, vivax, malariae,* and *ovale*. All cause acute febrile illnesses characterized by paroxysms of fever occurring every 48 or 72 hours, with afebrile intervals and a tendency to relapse and remit over months or even years. The severity of infection is determined by the species and strain of the infecting parasite, the age, genetic make-up, state of immunity, and general health of the patient, and their use of anti-malarial drugs.

Cerebral malaria is the most serious form and is caused by infection with *Plasmodium falciparum*. As with the other forms, symptoms appear when the merozoites are in the red blood cells, with fever, chills, rigors, headache, and general malaise. The onset of cerebral malaria is then heralded by confusion, and in severe infections the patient may lapse into unconsciousness. Seizures may occur, particularly in children.

Many mechanisms are proposed to account for the confusion and unconsciousness. Large numbers of parasites are found in the red blood cells in the cerebral circulation and can interfere with the way the cells squeeze through the brain capillaries, causing ischaemic damage. Brain levels of oxygen and glucose are reduced, and tissue damage is also thought to occur because of excess oxidation, excitotoxicity, and the increased production of inflammatory cytokines and nitric oxide. The **blood–brain barrier** is disrupted and intracranial pressure is raised. Seizures, both clinically apparent and subclinical, also contribute to the mechanism of coma.

Diagnosis is made by examination of the blood for parasites within red blood cells. This may have to be repeated several times to obtain a positive result. Treatment is with intravenous quinine or quinidine. These drugs act by specifically inhibiting haem polymerase, a key enzyme in the *Plasmodium falciparum* parasite. About one fifth of cases of cerebral malaria are fatal, with children particularly susceptible to severe infection. Adult survivors tend to make a full recovery, but around 10% of children who survive an episode of cerebral malaria tend to suffer sequelae such as hemiplegia, epilepsy, ataxia, or mental retardation.

> Malaria is rare in the UK but very common worldwide as 40% of the world's population live in endemic areas. Malaria needs to be considered as the diagnosis in anyone entering the UK from an endemic area who has fever.

9.6 Encephalitis

Encephalitis means 'inflammation of the brain' and is most commonly taken to imply viral infection of the brain. Almost always there is associated meningitis in addition to encephalitis. It is fortunately a rare condition. Although many different viruses can cause the condition, often no specific viral cause can be identified. In the UK the most commonly identified virus is herpes simplex; other viruses that may cause encephalitis are listed in Table 9.6.

Table 9.6 Viral causes of encephalitis

Herpes simplex virus
Arbovirus, e.g. West Nile virus, Japanese encephalitis virus
Enterovirus
Epstein–Barr virus
Mumps
Measles
Rubella
Human immunodeficiency virus

9.6.1 What are the symptoms and signs of encephalitis?

Encephalitis usually develops subacutely over a few days. Patients usually have fever and general malaise. They then develop a generalized headache, become drowsy, and may have seizures. As the disease progresses the patient may become confused and aggressive or may lapse into coma as intracranial pressure rises. Usually there are no symptoms and signs to suggest a single focus of infection. However, herpes simplex infection particularly infects the temporal lobes, so in conscious patients there may be signs of impaired memory or **aphasia**. There may be a widespread skin rash, for example if the encephalitis is due to measles or herpes zoster.

> **SELF-CHECK 9.10**
>
> What is meant by encephalitis, and what organisms cause it?

9.6.2 What tests are done to diagnose encephalitis?

The investigations to diagnose encephalitis are essentially the same as those used to diagnose meningitis. Examination of the CSF is important and reveals a modest rise in the lymphocyte count and slight rise in the protein content, with a normal or only slightly reduced glucose content. These findings are similar to those seen in viral meningitis, as can be seen in Table 9.3, or meningitis due to tuberculosis or to fungal infection. As in viral meningitis, it is usually not possible to culture the causative virus from the CSF although specific viral antibodies may be detected in the CSF indicating recent or current infection. The presence of specific viral DNA, particularly herpes simplex DNA, should be sought using PCR on samples of the CSF (see Box 9.3 above).

A patient with suspected encephalitis will usually undergo EEG investigation. This usually shows widespread slowing of the normal brain wave pattern, as can be seen in Figure 9.6. Sometimes the particular brain wave pattern of a sharp wave followed by a slow wave is seen in herpes simplex encephalitis, but this is not diagnostic of this

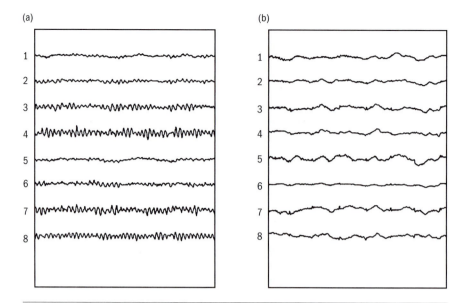

Figure 9.6 EEG traces from (a) a normal individual and (b) a patient with encephalitis. Traces numbered 1–4 are recorded over the right side of the skull from the frontal to the occipital region and traces 5–8 are the equivalent recordings on the left. Panel (a) shows the recording from a normal individual, with rhythmic waves present in both hemispheres, most marked in the posterior recordings. Panel (b) shows the equivalent EEG trace from a patient with encephalitis, with loss of these normal rhythms and a generalized slowing of the rhythmic brain waves. Images courtesy of Dr J. Fox.

disease as similar changes are also seen in other disorders such as Creutzfeldt–Jakob disease (as we shall see in section 9.8).

SELF-CHECK 9.11

How would you investigate someone with encephalitis?

9.6.3 **Treatment and outcome of encephalitis**

The various forms of herpes encephalitis are treated with the antiviral agent aciclovir (see section 9.3.4). Other than this, no specific treatments are available and thus treatment consists of general supportive measures, ensuring adequate nutrition and hydration, and preventing seizures. As there is no reliable way to diagnose herpes simplex encephalitis on clinical grounds, all patients with encephalitis tend to be given aciclovir routinely until the diagnosis of herpes simplex encephalitis has been excluded by CSF testing. Corticosteroids are not usually given unless patients are critically ill.

Most patients with encephalitis recover completely within days. However, in those with herpes simplex encephalitis the infection is usually more severe, and there is a high mortality of 40%. Severe memory impairment, aphasia, and behavioural problems can persist in survivors.

> Most patients with encephalitis recover completely within days. However, herpes simplex encephalitis usually causes a severe infection, with a high mortality rate of 40%, despite treatment with the antiviral agent aciclovir.

9.7 Intracranial abscess

An abscess is the term used to denote a localized collection of pus. Thus an intracranial abscess is a localized collection of pus within the brain. The abscess is caused by localized bacterial infection which can arise as a result of direct invasion of the brain from infection elsewhere in the head, such as from the ear canal, the nasal sinuses, or a bad tooth; or it can arise from distant sites within the body and be carried into the brain via the bloodstream. Often there are several types of bacteria within the abscess, including organisms that need oxygen to survive and those that are capable of **anaerobic metabolism**. The most common organisms found in brain abscesses are *Streptococcus milleri*, *Pneumococcus*, *Bacteroides*, and *Staphylococcus aureus*. Amoebae and fungi are rare causes of brain abscesses. Sometimes a collection of pus forms over the surface of the brain and spreads between the layers of the dura and arachnoid membranes. This is known as an **empyema**.

> **SELF-CHECK 9.12**
>
> **What organisms are typically found in brain abscesses?**

9.7.1 What are the clinical features of a brain abscess?

As the abscess forms at a specific site within the brain, the features are those of a space-occupying lesion at that site. The abscess can cause motor symptoms, sensory symptoms, or disturbances of vision, hearing, or speech for example. The abscess may irritate the surrounding cerebral cortex and epileptic seizures may result. It may cause the pressure inside the skull to rise, giving the characteristic features of headache, papilloedema, drowsiness, meningism, and nausea typical of raised intracranial pressure. The cause for the abscess, for example dental sepsis, may be evident. Often the patient is generally unwell as a result of septicaemia with bacteria in the bloodstream. A subdural empyema often causes a severe headache and will cause other signs depending on its size and site. The post-mortem appearance of a large brain abscess is shown in Figure 9.7.

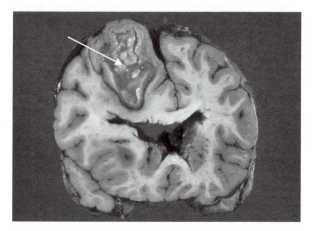

Figure 9.7 Post-mortem appearance of a brain abscess. Note how well demarcated the abscess is from the surrounding brain tissue. The brain tissue in the centre of the abscess, denoted by an arrow, has lost all of its structure and begun to liquefy. Image courtesy of Dr Martyn Carey. A full-colour version of this image is shown in the plates section.

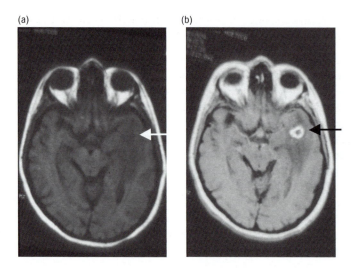

(a)   (b)

Figure 9.8 MRI of the head showing a brain abscess. Images both without (a) and with (b) intravenous contrast agent are shown. The abscess is evident on panel (a) as an area of low signal intensity, denoted by the white arrow, but is much more clearly seen in panel (b) where it enhances brightly, shown by the black arrow. Images courtesy of Dr David Yates.

9.7.2 What tests are done to diagnose a brain abscess?

If one has a clinical suspicion that a brain abscess may be the diagnosis, the most important investigation is to adequately image the brain, with either CT or MRI. The abscess is evident on scanning as a mass lesion, usually of low density with surrounding oedema (as can be seen in Figure 9.8a). Characteristically a ring of enhancement is seen surrounding the abscess following administration of an intravenous contrast agent (as indicated in Figure 9.8b). A lumbar puncture is contraindicated if a cerebral abscess is present. This is because introduction of the spinal needle may so reduce the pressure in the spinal cord that the relatively higher pressure within the brain forces the base of the brain through the narrow opening at the base of the skull. This can lead to excessive pressure on vital centres within the brain stem and risk of death.

> Lumbar puncture is contraindicated if a cerebral abscess is present, as reducing spinal pressure may cause raised pressure on vital brain structures.

9.7.3 How can a brain abscess be treated?

The organisms within an abscess generate an intense inflammatory reaction that can result in a thick wall of inflammatory tissue separating the abscess from the surrounding tissue. Often the blood supply penetrates poorly into the abscess so that antibiotics, even if administered intravenously, cannot adequately penetrate the infected centre. Hence the treatment for an intracranial abscess is to excise the abscess and aspirate the pus. Sometimes such aspiration can be done through a burr hole drilled through the skull. More usually adequate removal requires a formal craniotomy to remove the pus, followed by appropriate intravenous antibiotic therapy.

The prognosis for full recovery from an intracranial abscess is not good. About 20% of cases are fatal, and many of the survivors have residual neurological deficits and seizures.

> Intracranial abscesses usually require surgical excision and aspiration of the pus. Treatment with intravenous antibiotics is insufficient as the drugs cannot penetrate through the thick abscess wall.

SELF-CHECK 9.13
What are the clinical features of a brain abscess? How is it diagnosed?

9.8 Transmissible spongiform encephalopathies or prion diseases

All the infections we have described so far are caused by organisms that are familiar to biology. Recently, a group of transmissible diseases has become newsworthy. These are the **transmissible spongiform encephalopathies** (TSEs). They are 'transmissible' because they can be transmitted from one animal to another by exposure to infected brain tissue.

As we will see below, the disease-causing agent is a rogue protein, and may take years, or even decades, before it causes any symptoms. Fortunately these diseases cannot be transmitted by normal contact. Where they have been transmitted it is has been by accident: contaminated instruments and tissues used in neurosurgery, contaminated growth hormone from **pituitary glands** from corpses, and exposure to human brain during funeral rites by the Foré tribe in Papua New Guinea (which had stopped by 1960).

9.8.1 What are the symptoms of prion diseases and how are they diagnosed?

As we see in the case report in Box 9.4, the symptoms of prion diseases typically include dementia and movement disorders (ataxia and myoclonus). Some prion diseases have other specific symptoms, such as chronic pain, anxiety, and insomnia (see below). Prion diseases tend to be diagnosed when alternative causes of these symptoms have been excluded. The definitive diagnosis is often made post-mortem: the 'spongiform' in TSE refers to the characteristic appearance of affected brain tissue seen through a microscope—there are large vacuoles or holes in the tissue, which in fact are large swellings in neurons, as we can see by comparing the two images of post-mortem brain in Figure 9.9. In addition, microscopic deposits of the pathogenic form of **prion protein** may be detectable by either **histology** or **molecular biology**.

Although **incubation periods** can be very long, over 40 years in some Foré cases, the progression of the disease from diagnosis to death usually takes from a few months to a few years, depending on the specific disease.

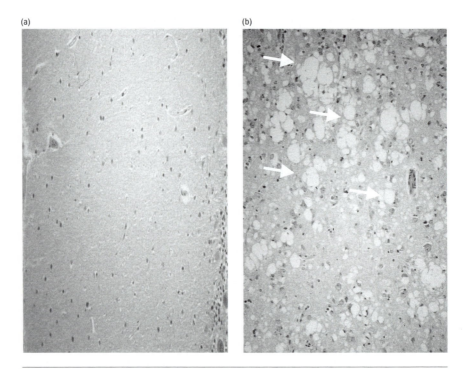

(a)   (b)

Figure 9.9 Sections of stained brain tissue to show the structure: (a) Tissue from a normal brain. (b) A section from a similar brain region from a patient who died with CJD. In this section multiple white 'holes' are evident, denoted by arrows, which is why this pathological finding is termed 'spongiform' change. Images courtesy of Dr Martyn Carey. A full-colour version of this image is shown in the plates section.

9.8.2 How common are prion diseases?

These unusual diseases remain extremely rare. The most prominent of them are listed in Table 9.7 along with the equivalent disorders in other animals. The most common human prion disease is sporadic Creutzfeldt–Jakob disease, CJD, which occurs in about 1 person per million per year, so it is not a common disease.

The other human forms are even less common; for instance, the form associated with bovine spongiform encephalopathy (BSE) or mad cow disease killed about 150 people in the UK between 1996 and 2005, out of a total population of almost 60 million. It is even rarer in other countries. Just under 600 people died of sporadic CJD during the same period in the UK. Gerstmann–Sträussler–Scheinker disease (GSS) is the most common of the familial prion diseases and killed just under 20 people during the same 10-year period in the UK; the other familial forms totalled 33 and the **iatrogenic** forms 34.

9.8.3 What is the infectious agent in prion diseases?

The TSEs used to be classified as slow viral diseases, but the infectious material seems to lack **nucleic acids**. Instead, they depend on an abnormal form of a normal protein

Table 9.7 Prion diseases (transmissible spongiform encephalopathies)

Disease	Cause	Comment
Human		
Creutzfeldt–Jakob Disease (CJD)	Sporadic	Incidence 1 per million per year
Variant CJD (vCJD)	Ingestion of BSE-contaminated material	Peaked at about 1 per 2 million per year in UK
Gerstmann–Sträussler–Scheinker disease (GSS), fatal familial insomnia (FFI) + ~10 other diseases	Genetic—mutation of prion protein gene (Prnp)	Incidence of GSS (the most common) 1 per 15 million
Accidental ('iatrogenic')	Brain surgery, corneal and dural grafts, human growth hormone injections	Very rare
Kuru	Exposure to infected human brain during funeral rites in Foré region of Papua New Guinea	Now ended
Other animals		
	Species	
Scrapie	Sheep and goats	Known since 1732. Appears to have an environmental reservoir
BSE	Cattle and related species	Identified in 1985. Amplified by high protein feeds. Now declining
Feline spongiform encephalopathy	Cats	Probably BSE contamination of feed. Now rare
Transmissible mink encephalopathy	Mink	Identified in 1947, mainly US
Chronic wasting disease	Elk, deer	Identified in 1967. Theoretical risk of transmission to human; cause for concern in US

known as **prion protein**. This 'protein-only' hypothesis was a revolutionary concept because proteins depend on production by nucleic acids—DNA and RNA. It now is fairly clear that the disease-causing prion protein replicates by changing the shape of the normal prion protein that occurs in all our brains.

The idea is that the abnormal form (PrP^{Sc}) is produced from the normal form (PrP^{C}). The 'Sc' superscript refers to scrapie, which is the sheep version of this disease—the first to be recognized as a distinct disease. The original idea was that PrP^{Sc} interacted with PrP^{C} to change its shape to make it into PrP^{Sc}, but now it seems more likely that small amounts of PrP normally exist in a more rigid shape (a structure with more **beta-pleated sheet** than in PrP^{C}), and that the disease process starts when that beta form clumps into small clusters.

This process is shown schematically in Figure 9.10, from which we can see that the normal 'cellular' or 'constitutive' PrP molecules normally have a shape rich in alpha-helix, shown in the figure as a green circle. They are thought to unravel into an unfolded, flexible structure which can refold into PrP^{C} or, more rarely, into beta-PrP (red square), which is rich in the relatively rigid beta-pleated sheet structure. All of these forms are normal and harmless. The risk of prion disease starts when several beta-PrP molecules stick together to form a stable cluster of molecules (an oligomer) and then recruit more

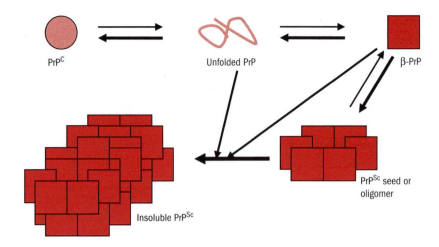

Figure 9.10 Possible mechanism for the replication and accumulation of PrP^{Sc}, the pathogenic form of the normal prion protein, PrP^{C}. The normal 'cellular' or 'constitutive' PrP molecules normally have a shape rich in alpha-helix, shown as a pink circle. They are thought to unravel into an unfolded, flexible structure which can refold into PrP^{C} or, more rarely, into beta-PrP (red square), which is rich in the relatively rigid beta-pleated sheet structure. All of these forms are normal and harmless. The risk of prion disease starts when several beta-PrP molecules stick together to form a stable oligomer or multi-molecular cluster and then recruit more PrP molecules (unfolded- or beta-PrP) to make the large, protease-resistant, insoluble PrP^{Sc}, accumulation, which is large enough to be seen with the light microscope.

PrP molecules (unfolded or beta-PrP) to make the large, protease-resistant, insoluble PrP^{Sc} molecules, which are large enough to be seen with the light microscope.

Whatever the mechanism of formation of PrP^{Sc}, replication depends on a continuous source of PrP^{C}. Compelling evidence for this comes from the finding that genetically modified mice that do not make normal prion protein cannot contract prion disease. PrP^{Sc} binds into aggregates that ultimately can become large enough to be seen with a light microscope. It was once thought that these large clumps of PrP^{Sc} were responsible for killing neurons, but it now looks as though the small oligomers, of around six PrP^{Sc} molecules, may be the culprit.

9.8.4 How do you 'catch' prion diseases?

This question really asks 'how does the PrP^{Sc} seed get into the brain?' This depends on the specific disease (see Table 9.7). In the most common human prion disease, sporadic CJD, this probably is a very rare (and extremely unlucky) random production of too much PrP^{Sc}. In the case of the inherited forms of prion disease, it appears that mutations in the prion protein gene cause instability in the structure of PrP^{C}: GSS and fatal familial insomnia (FFI) are two examples of the dozen or so rare inherited versions of these diseases. Finally, the acquired prion diseases depend on infection with PrP^{Sc} either through food or through contaminated instruments or tissues (iatrogenic disease).

The kind of prion disease that recently caused considerable anxiety, and financial damage, is a new variant of CJD (now called vCJD). It was discovered during the mid-1990s. It differs from other prion diseases, in that it affects younger people than does sporadic

case study: Variant CJD

BOX 9.4

A 28-year-old woman presented to her GP with a 2 month history of painful tingling in the soles of both feet. She also mentioned that she felt that her memory had been deteriorating for the previous 6 months. She was feeling depressed and her family reported that she was becoming withdrawn and introverted compared to her previous outgoing personality.

When she was reviewed some 2 months later her memory was markedly impaired and she had difficulty maintaining a normal conversation. Over the next few months she developed incoordination and became unsteady walking. Her memory and intellect deteriorated further and she became demented. She developed widespread involuntary jerking of the muscles of her limbs and trunk and died 16 months after the onset of the burning sensations in her feet.

Neuropathological examination of her brain post-mortem showed widespread spongiform changes and PrP plaques, confirming the diagnosis of vCJD.

CJD, and it often presents with psychiatric symptoms and/or pains in the extremities. By far the most likely source of vCJD is exposure of humans to cattle products contaminated with BSE. The details remain very unclear because of the difficulty in finding out, decades after the event, both what patients ate and what were the precise ingredients in most food products. Curiously, scrapie has been known in sheep for at least two centuries, but has not been linked with human disease in spite of the use of sheep brain in several food products and as a delicacy in its own right.

BSE was first recognized in cattle in the UK in 1986 and reached a peak of 36 000 confirmed cases during 1992. Where BSE came from is far from clear, although the two most likely explanations are scrapie crossing the species barrier from sheep to cattle, or the amplification of a very rare cattle disease by the intensive feeding methods used at the time.

Whatever its origin, BSE has now fallen to very low levels, to <100 cases in 2004, following the prohibition of mammalian protein in animal feed, and an active surveillance and culling programme. The control of BSE seems to have led to a considerable reduction in the incidence of vCJD, which is encouraging, although whether this is the end of vCJD remains in doubt because of uncertainties over the range of incubation times and susceptibilities in the population as a whole.

Prion disease has been transmitted to humans through surgical instruments, despite the use of normal decontamination methods. Unfortunately PrP^{Sc} sticks very firmly to metal surfaces, and is remarkably resistant to many disinfectants and conventional autoclaving. Higher temperatures (137 °C instead of 121 °C) and chemicals such as relatively strong sodium hydroxide (caustic soda) or sodium hypochlorite (bleach) are needed, and there is an argument for using disposable instruments wherever possible.

Transplantation of corneas and the dura mater (the outer membrane covering the brain) has resulted in transmission of sporadic CJD, as has the use of human growth hormone extracted from the pituitaries of cadavers. The evidence on blood transfusions leading to transmission of prion disease is less clear, but removal of the white blood cells (or leucodepletion) and restrictions on blood donors are prudent precautions.

9.8.5 How can prion diseases be treated?

Unfortunately there are no cures for any of the prion diseases at present. Death follows diagnosis of sporadic CJD within about 6 months; GSS and vCJD can take several years. Treatments remain experimental and controversial.

Some have proved effective in animal models of prion diseases either *in vitro* or in culture. Quinacrine is licensed for use in treating malaria and other protozoal injections, and is in clinical trial in the UK. Sporadic reports of its use have shown limited benefit, but without a full clinical trial it is difficult to draw any conclusions. Pentosan polyphosphate has also been used in isolated cases where it may have slowed the course of the disease. This drug is related to heparin, and is an anticoagulant. It does not cross the blood–brain barrier and needs to be injected into the ventricles, an invasive procedure. In general the small numbers of cases make clinical trials extremely difficult in these diseases, but they could be crucially important if an epidemic were to develop in future.

SELF-CHECK 9.14

What is the infectious agent in CJD? How is it treated?

> Prion diseases are caused by infection with an abnormal protein. The incubation period of variant CJD is unknown and there are no definitely effective therapies.

SUMMARY

- The body's main defence mechanisms to limit multiplication and spread of infectious organisms are inflammation, phagocytosis, and activation of the immune response.

- Bacteria, viruses, fungi, and protozoa can all cause infections of the brain and meninges.

- Meningitis and encephalitis often occur together.

- Organisms that rarely cause disease in normal individuals may cause overwhelming infections in people with impaired immune responses. Such infections are known as opportunistic infections.

- Bacterial meningitis is a serious disease with an overall mortality of about 10%. It requires prompt treatment with the appropriate intravenous antibiotic.

- A key test in confirming the diagnosis of bacterial meningitis is examining a sample of CSF obtained via a lumbar puncture.

- Viral meningitis is usually a mild condition from which patients fully recover within a few days with no specific treatment.

- Fungal and yeast infections in the brain are rare but increasing in frequency. They most often occur in immunocompromised individuals.

- Malaria is rare in the UK but very common worldwide as 40% of the world's population live in endemic areas. Malaria needs to be considered as the diagnosis in anyone entering the UK from an endemic area who has fever.

- Most patients with encephalitis recover completely within days. However herpes simplex encephalitis usually causes a severe infection, with a high mortality rate of 40%, despite treatment with the antiviral agent aciclovir.

- Lumbar puncture is contraindicated if a cerebral abscess is present, as reducing spinal pressure may caused raised pressure on vital brain structures.

- Intracranial abscesses usually require surgical excision and aspiration of the pus. Treatment with intravenous antibiotics is insufficient as the drugs cannot penetrate through the thick abscess wall.

- Prion diseases are caused by infection with an abnormal protein. The incubation period of vCJD is unknown and there are no definitely effective therapies.

FURTHER READING

General

A. Verma. Infections of the nervous system. Chapter 59 in *Neurology in clinical practice*, 4th edn, eds W. G. Bradley, R. B. Daroff, G. Fenichel and J. Jankovic. Oxford: Butterworth Heinemann, 2004.
A detailed chapter in a large textbook covering many aspects of brain infection.

Meningitis

There are many good websites with information on meningitis, for example:

Meningitis Research Foundation of Canada
  <www.meningitis.ca/whatismeningitis>

Health Protection Agency <www.phls.co.uk>.
Gives up-to-date epidemiological information from the UK on various infectious diseases and contains lots of useful information about CNS diseases.

Encephalitis

A. Caudhuri and P. G. Kennedy. Diagnosis and treatment of viral encephalitis. *Postgraduate Medical Journal* 2002; **78**(924): 575–483.
A detailed review of treatment of this disorder.

Prion diseases

R. S. G. Knight and R. G. Will. Prion diseases. Neurology in practice. Supplement to *Journal of Neurology Neurosurgery and Psychiatry* 2004; **75**: 36–42.
A well-illustrated review of several prion diseases.

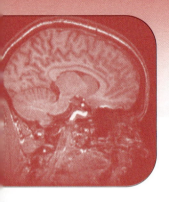

CHAPTER TEN

Multiple sclerosis

Karen Morrison

INTRODUCTION

Multiple sclerosis (MS) is the most common cause of severe physical disability in young adults in the UK. Although the exact mechanism of disease is unknown, we think that MS arises because of a disturbance of the immune system within the central nervous system. Areas of inflammation form around the myelin sheath of nerves within the brain and eventually there is loss of nerve axons and scarring. A major feature of MS is that symptoms initially come and go, giving a characteristic relapsing and remitting pattern of disease.

10.1 How common is multiple sclerosis and who are most at risk?

There is a wide geographic variation in the **incidence** of MS. Looking at the world map in Figure 10.1, we can see that MS is more common in temperate zones in the northern and southern hemispheres and very rare in equatorial regions. This variation is also seen over quite short distances. For example, the **prevalence** of the disease in the south of England is around 60 per 100 000, while that in the Orkney Islands off the north coast of Scotland is nearly 300 per 100 000. The symptoms of MS usually begin between the ages of 20 and 40 years with a peak at the age of 25 years. The disease is more common in women (female: male ratio 1.7:1), similar to other disorders such as rheumatoid arthritis in which an underlying disorder of the immune system is considered key.

> Multiple sclerosis is the most common cause of severe physical disability in young adults in the UK.

Figure 10.1 Prevalence of MS in different regions. Numbers are prevalence per 10^5 population. The chequerboard pattern in South Africa reflects the high incidence in English-speaking whites migrating as adults to South Africa versus the low incidence in the indigenous Cape population. Data obtained from 'The distribution of multiple sclerosis', Chapter 2 in *McAlpine's multiple sclerosis*, 4th edn, eds D. A. Compston *et al.*, Churchill Livingstone, 2006.

10.2 What are the likely causes of multiple sclerosis?

The cause of MS is unknown. There is good evidence for both environmental and genetic factors being involved. It is thought that the disease is triggered in childhood by an environmental factor in individuals who are genetically susceptible, and that the inflammation and neurological disability results from abnormal reactions in an individual's immune system.

10.2.1 Environmental factors

The increased incidence of MS in regions of the world with a temperate climate is very suggestive of environmental factors being important. There are exceptions to this, however, which need an explanation. For example, Japan is a low-risk area for MS, yet is at the same latitude as areas of high prevalence in Europe. Part of the explanation seems to be that race is an additional determinant of MS risk, with white populations from northern Europe being the most susceptible and Asians, Africans, and American Indians having the lowest risk.

One factor that has been widely studied is that certain viruses which are found in temperate regions are important in triggering MS. Many attempts to culture viruses from autopsy or biopsy derived material have given no consistent results. Tests to recover specific viral **genomes** from people with MS have proved negative. Studies of **Epstein–Barr virus**, measles, and various **herpesviruses**, along with the bacterium *Chlamydia pneumoniae*, have yielded varying results. Overall there is still no firm evidence that virus infection is a trigger in MS.

Migration data has been used to support the theory that an infectious agent is involved in MS. People migrating from an area of high risk to one of low risk after the age of puberty carry their former high risk with them. If migration occurs in childhood, the risk is that of the new area to which the person has migrated.

10.2.2 Genetic factors

There is good evidence that genetic factors are important in causing MS. One way of looking for genetic factors in diseases is to look at how the disease occurs in twins. If a disease is more frequently seen in both **identical twins** than in both **non-identical twins**, this is considered good evidence that the disease has a strong genetic component. MS is found in both identical twins in 30% of cases, compared with occurring in both non-identical twins in only 3–5% of cases.

Many studies have looked at the risk of developing MS in families of people with the disease. Take a closer look at the data in Table 10.1. There is a risk of a sibling of an MS patient developing the disease of 3–5%, some 30–50 times higher than the background risk in the population. The increased risk decreases progressively for children, aunts, uncles, and cousins. An interesting, and unexplained, observation is that it is rarer for a father and son both to have MS, than for a mother and her son or daughter to have the disease. A few studies have looked at the risk in adopted children of people with MS and found no increased risk. This suggests that genetic factors, rather than environmental factors, are important in causing the increased risk in families.

Table 10.1 Risk of multiple sclerosis within families

Parent with MS	Son	Daughter
Mother	3.8%	3.7%
Father	0.8%	2%
Sibling with MS	Sister	Brother
Female	5.6%	2.2%
Male	3.5%	4%
Twin with MS	Either sex	
Identical	35%	
Non-identical	4%	

Data from A. D. Sadovnick , P. A. Baird, and R. H. Ward, Multiple sclerosis: updated risks for relatives. *American Journal of Medical Genetics* 1988; **29**: 533–541.

Despite the evidence pointing to major genetic factors in MS, no **genetic linkage studies** have identified any specific genes that cause MS, but genetic studies consistently point to genes in the **HLA region** on chromosome 6 as being involved in the disease. This is not surprising, as the HLA region encodes many of the genes important in the immune response.

SELF-CHECK 10.1

What are the likely causes of MS?

10.3 What tissue changes occur in multiple sclerosis?

The primary pathology of multiple sclerosis is found in the central nervous system (CNS), in the white-matter regions of the brain where myelinated axons run.

10.3.1 MS is an immune disease

In health, our immune system protects the body against bacteria, viruses, and toxins. When any foreign **antigen** enters the body, for example through the gut or a cut in the skin, white blood cells known as **lymphocytes** are stimulated to divide and act as a defence. There are two basic types of lymphocytes, termed B cells and T cells.

T cells become activated when they encounter foreign antigens, and release soluble factors known as **cytokines** which have many cellular effects. There are two broad categories of T cell: T1 cells increase inflammation and T2 cells suppress inflammation. Normally the balance between the two is tightly controlled.

B cells are also activated when they encounter foreign antigens, and when stimulated they produce **antibodies** which can destroy invading bacteria, viruses or toxins. In health, stimulated B and T cells are prevented from crossing into the brain via the **blood–brain barrier**, a specialized system of connections between the cells of the brain endothelium, preventing free flow of blood constituents from the rest of the body into the brain.

 The blood–brain barrier is described in section 1.2.3 on page 6.

In MS we think one of the earliest features is damage occurring to the blood–brain barrier by a process not yet understood. Activated lymphocytes are then able to cross the barrier and enter the CNS. There they release many cytokines such as the proteins interleukin-2, interferon gamma, and tumour necrosis factor beta. A chain of reactions is triggered that results in damage to the myelin sheath surrounding nerve axons and the formation of localized regions of inflammation known as **plaques**.

We can see this sequence of events in Figure 10.2. **Macrophages**, other specialized blood cells, are also important in forming plaques, attacking the myelin directly and killing the oligodendrocyte cells. The presence of inflammatory plaques prevents the normal transmission of electrical impulses along the nerve, interfering with **saltatory conduction**, as we can see in Figure 10.3.

 The transmission of an action potential is described in detail in section 2.2.2 on page 27.

Symptoms and signs develop depending on where in the CNS the demyelinating plaque occurs (we will learn more about this in section 10.4). Individual plaques are usually about 1 cm in diameter but they may join up to form larger lesions.

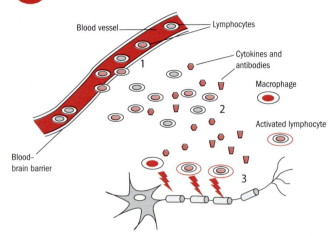

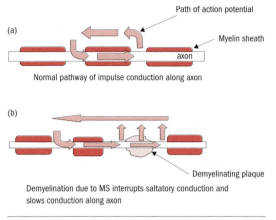

Figure 10.2 Proposed pathways in MS: 1. The first event in MS is thought to be damage occurring to the blood brain barrier that allows lymphocytes to cross into the CNS. 2. Lymphocytes become activated in the CNS and release cytokines and antibodies. 3. The activated lymphocytes recruit macrophages and together they attack the myelin sheath and trigger reactions that result in damage of the myelin and localized areas of inflammation known as plaques.

Figure 10.3 Saltatory conduction is disrupted in MS: (a) The normal pathway of impulse conduction along a n axon. (b) How the normal conduction pathway is disrupted when demyelination occurs. Current leaks from the axon and conduction is slowed.

In the early stages of MS the underlying oligodendrocyte damage is such that recovery of the cells is possible and, in time, remyelination of the axons travelling through the plaque can occur. This process takes several weeks and corresponds to the presence of symptoms of the disease during a relapse and then recovery from those symptoms.

With repeated relapses of the disease, the process of remyelination is imperfect and nerve impulse transmission along the axon does not fully recover. In time individual axons die and scar tissue forms at the site of the inflammatory plaque. Impulse transmission along the nerve does not return. This corresponds to the progressive stage of MS, when disability accumulates.

> MS arises because of damage to the blood–brain barrier and activation of the immune system within the CNS.

10.3.2 What might be the initial trigger?

It is not known what triggers the initial breakdown of the blood–brain barrier in MS. One possibility is that certain bacteria or viruses share structural similarities with key proteins in myelin and infection with them causes activation of T lymphocytes which can cross-react with myelin. Myelin basic protein (MBP) accounts for 30% of the protein in myelin and is considered a prime candidate for the initial immune attack in MS. T cells responding to MBP are found in peripheral blood in normal individuals and in higher levels in people with active MS.

10.4 What are the symptoms and clinical signs of multiple sclerosis?

10.4.1 Patterns of clinical disease

There are several patterns of clinical disease, and some of these are illustrated in Figure 10.4. The most common form is the 'relapsing and remitting' form, in which symptoms occur for about 4–5 weeks, corresponding to disruption of neuronal conduction because of an inflammatory plaque forming at a particular place in the CNS. As the inflammation resolves and the myelin sheath re-forms, conduction is restored and the symptoms wear off and eventually disappear. At the end of this time function is fully back to normal and the person is left with no disability. Further episodes of relapse and remission occur over the years, with the patient making a full recovery each time, as illustrated in the case study in Box 10.1.

After years of the disease coming and going many patients will enter the 'secondary progressive' phase of illness (see the middle diagram in Figure 10.4).

In this phase symptoms build up due to plaques forming, but recovery of nerve transmission through the plaques is incomplete and individuals are left with residual symptoms and signs. The incomplete recovery in symptoms reflects incomplete resolution of the inflammatory plaque in the myelin sheath and scarring and loss of the underlying axons. In time the cumulative disability due to several incomplete recoveries can be very great.

---

case study: Relapsing and remitting MS

BOX 10.1

A 24-year-old student awakes one morning to find she is very unsteady on standing and tends to fall over when walking. Over the next few days the feeling of imbalance increases; she notices double vision on looking to the right. She goes to the hospital emergency department.

When examined in hospital she has abnormal eye movements compatible with a lesion in the nerves to muscles controlling her right eye. She also has reduced vision in her right eye. She is unsteady, with increased tone and reflexes in her arms and legs, and impaired perception of sensation in both legs and feet. A brain MR scan shows high signal lesions compatible with MS plaques in the periventricular regions of both cerebral hemispheres and in the brain stem.

When she was 20 years old she had experienced an episode of reduced vision in her right eye, described as if she were looking at objects through a layer of gauze, along with pain in her eye when she looked around. She had gone to her GP who suggested that there might be some inflammation in the nerve to the eye and her symptoms were likely to resolve. No investigations were done. The visual disturbance lasted about 4 weeks and then her vision recovered to normal.

Aged 22 years she had noticed odd tingling sensations in her right arm which lasted about 6 weeks and then disappeared. She did not seek medical advice during that episode.

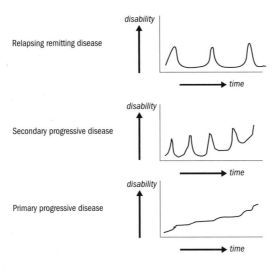

Figure 10.4 Patterns of disease seen in MS.

Another pattern of disease is known as 'primary progressive disease', illustrated in Box 10.2 and in the lower diagram of Figure 10.4. In such cases the patient never makes a full recovery, even after the first attack of the disease, and is left with residual disability from the onset which gradually worsens. Fortunately this form of MS is less frequent than the other types.

> MS is most commonly a relapsing and remitting disease at the onset of symptoms.

case study: Primary progressive multiple sclerosis

BOX 10.2

A 33-year-old woman has a month's history of clumsiness and a feeling of heaviness in her left leg. Over the next few months she notices more marked weakness in the leg and has to walk with the aid of a stick. The symptoms in her leg then stay fairly constant for about 4 months before the leg then becomes increasingly stiff, with painful spasms in the muscles of her thigh. In addition she notices stiffness and clumsiness in her left arm and is aware of a band of altered sensation, described as 'tightness', around her abdomen.

Over the next year the weakness in her limbs increases along with the painful stiffness. She also develops an odd feeling of partial numbness in her right thigh and outer leg, and double vision, noticed particularly when she looks down. Over the next 3 years her symptoms steadily worsen and she loses the ability to walk independently. She is also troubled by urinary frequency and urgency and becomes very depressed.

She is all too aware of the nature of progressive MS, as she had cared for her disabled mother who also had MS, with symptoms beginning in her late thirties and gradually progressing until her death from pneumonia aged 58 years.

Plate section

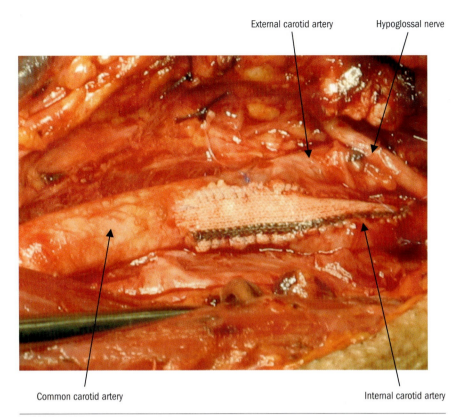

External carotid artery

Hypoglossal nerve

Common carotid artery

Internal carotid artery

Figure 5.8 Carotid endarterectomy. Note the patch over the previous incision at the bifurcation of the carotid artery. Courtesy of Mr S. Silverman.

(a)

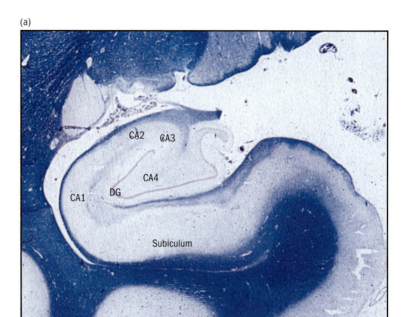

(b)

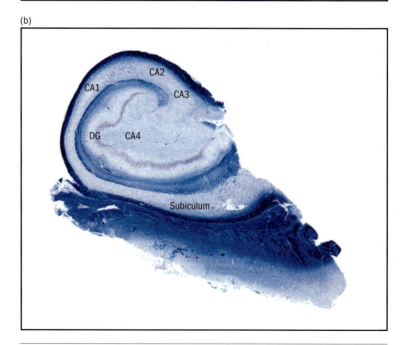

Figure 6.4 Histology of hippocampal sclerosis. A section of a normal hippocampus (a), and a sclerotic hippocampus surgically removed from a patient with temporal lobe epilepsy (b). (DG = dentate gyrus; CA1–4 are subregions of the hippocampus; subiculum is a group of regions next to the hippocampus). Pictures courtesy of Dr A. Princivalle.

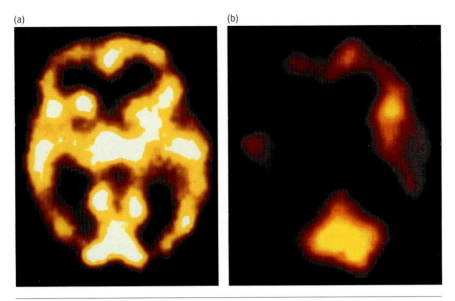

Figure 7.4 SPECT images showing the difference in brain blood flow between a healthy elderly individual (a) and an age-matched AD patient (b). Reproduced with permission from J. H. Morris and Zs. Nagy, 'Alzheimer's disease' in *The Neuropathology of Dementia* (eds M. M. Esiri, V. M-Y. Lee, J. Q. Trojanowski) pp. 161–206. Copyright Cambridge University Press, 2004.

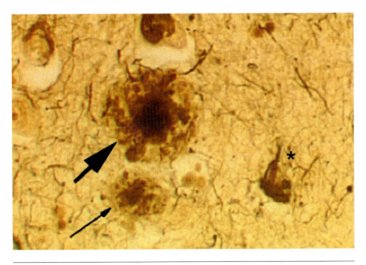

Figure 7.6 Amyloid plaques (arrows) and neurofibrillary tangle (star) stained by the Bielshowsky silver impregnation method.

(a)

(b)

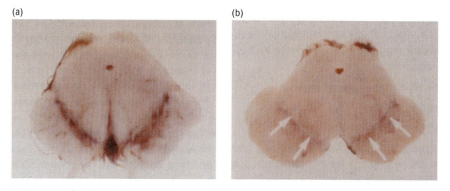

Figure 8.2 Post-mortem section through the midbrain of a normal person (a) and someone with Parkinson's disease, showing the loss of melanin pigment (b). Reproduced with permission from C. E. Clarke, *Parkinson's disease in practice*. Royal Society of Medicine Press, London. Copyright Royal Society of Medicine, 2001.

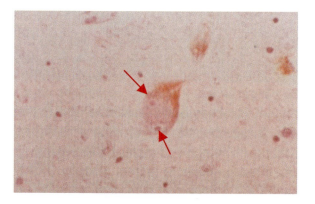

Figure 8.3 High-power magnification of a section of the substantia nigra showing a dopaminergic neuron containing Lewy bodies (arrows). Reproduced with permission from C. E. Clarke, *Parkinson's disease in practice*. Royal Society of Medicine Press, London. Copyright Royal Society of Medicine, 2001.

(a) (b)

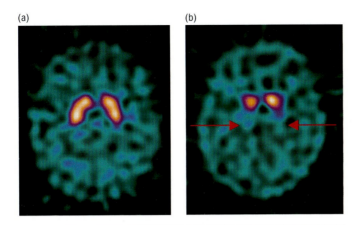

Figure 8.4 Single photon emission computed tomography (SPECT) using the tracer ^{123}I-FP-CIT (DaTScan). (a) shows normal uptake in the caudate and putamen (like inverted commas). (b) shows reduced uptake in the putamen in a parkinsonian syndrome (like full stops; arrows). Courtesy of Dr A Notgi.

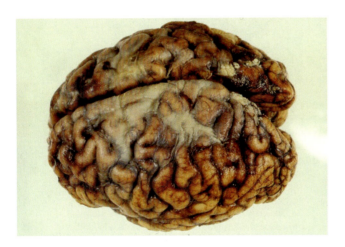

Figure 9.1 Post-mortem brain from a patient who died from meningitis. Notice the thick purulent discharge covering the brain surface. Figure courtesy of Dr Martyn Carey.

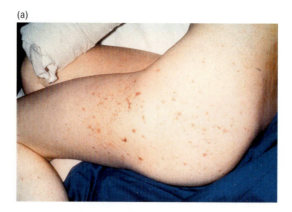

(a)

(b)

Figure 9.2 (a) The typical purpuric skin rash of meningococcal infection. The skin lesions do not lose their colour when pressure is applied, such as by pressing a glass on to the skin. (b) The fingers of a patient that have become gangrenous due to overwhelming meningococcal infection in the blood. The infection caused a profound drop in the patient's blood pressure and the blood supply to the fingers was severely impaired causing necrosis and death of the tissues. Photographs courtesy of T. S. J. Elliott.

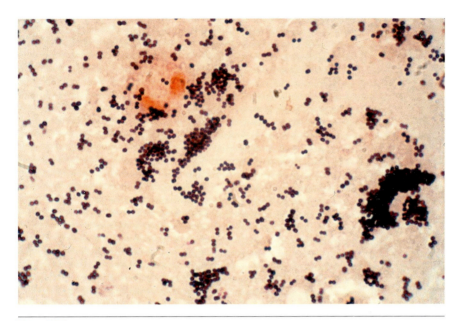

Figure 9.3 A CSF sample that has been stained with specific dyes to reveal numerous pneumococci, seen here as dark blue spherical organisms tending to clump together. Photograph courtesy of T. S. J. Elliott.

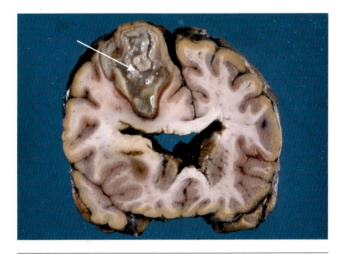

Figure 9.7 Post-mortem appearance of a brain abscess. Note how well demarcated the abscess is from the surrounding brain tissue. The brain tissue in the centre of the abscess, denoted by an arrow, has lost all of its structure and begun to liquefy. Image courtesy of Dr Martyn Carey.

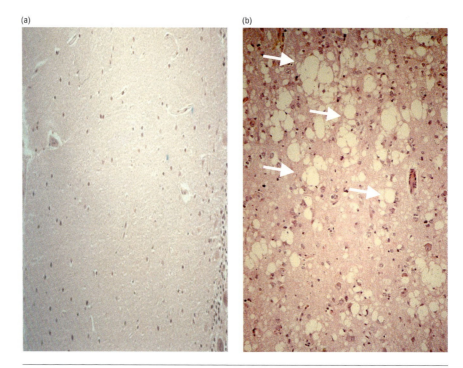

Figure 9.9 Sections of stained brain tissue to show the structure: (a) Tissue from a normal brain. (b) A section from a similar brain region from a patient who died with CJD. In this section multiple white 'holes' are evident, denoted by arrows, which is why this pathological finding is termed 'spongiform' change. Images courtesy of Dr Martyn Carey.

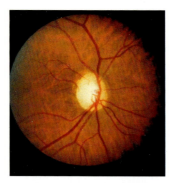

Figure 10.5 Optic atrophy. The figure shows the appearance of the retina at the back of the eye in a patient with optic atrophy secondary to MS. The atrophied optic disc appears as a white, well-demarcated disc. Vision in the eye has been lost.

(a)

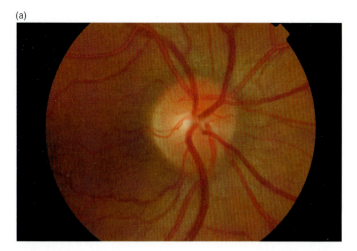

(b)

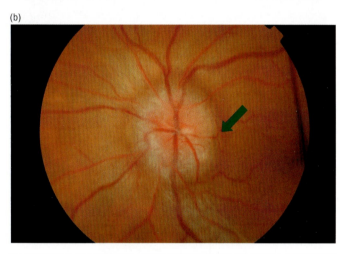

Figure 11.1 (a) A normal optic disc viewed through an ophthalmoscope.
(b) Papilloedema. Note the swelling of the edge of the disc margins
(arrow). Image courtesy of Dr A Ball.

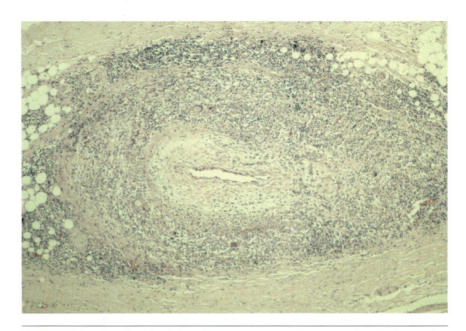

Figure 11.2 Cross-section of an inflamed temporal artery in temporal arteritis. The lumen of the vessel, where blood flows, is surrounded by large numbers of inflammatory cells which stain blue. Image courtesy of Dr P. Barber.

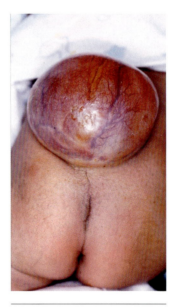

Figure 12.1 Myelomeningocele on the back of a newborn girl. The yellow-red area in the centre of the cystic malformation is the malformed spinal cord which is split in two parts and exposed to the environment. This was repaired on the first day of life to prevent meningitis and to protect the exposed spinal cord from further deterioration.

10.4.2 **Triggers of relapse**

We do not know what triggers relapses in the relapsing-remitting forms of the disease. Data from many studies suggests that relapses occur on average 0.6 times per year. It seems that relapses are more likely to occur following a viral infection. Controversy exists about a link between relapses and other possible precipitants including stressful life events, trauma, and vaccinations.

10.4.3 **Symptoms**

The inflammatory plaques which form in MS can arise in any myelinated nerves within the CNS and thus there is great variability in the symptoms of MS. Some sites are more prone to developing plaques than others such as the optic nerves, the myelin of nerves as they run close to the cerebral ventricles, and nerve axons within the spinal cord. Table 10.2 lists some of the common sites for MS plaques and the corresponding symptoms that may be associated with them.

Characteristically there will be several different symptoms in MS at any time, reflecting the presence of plaques in different places within the CNS. Some of the symptoms are made worse by an increase in temperature, such as when in a hot bath, in hot weather, or on exercise. This is known as **Uhthoff's phenomenon**.

Optic neuritis

This is one of the most frequent ways in which MS presents. An inflammatory plaque forms on one of the optic nerves, to give the symptom of progressive blurring of vision in the eye. The blurred vision increases over the course of a week or so, sometimes resulting in complete blindness in the eye, and is usually accompanied by pain in the eye that is worse on movement. The pain usually resolves within a week and the vision recovers within a month or so. Even when vision has recovered, examination of the eye may show **optic atrophy**, reflecting loss of some myelinated nerve fibres, as can be seen in Figure 10.5. Optic neuritis may occur in both eyes, either simultaneously or sequentially, and can sometimes be recurrent.

Sensory features

When the inflammatory plaques form in the myelin of sensory neurons, various sensory symptoms may result. These include numbness, tingling, itching, or tightness in the

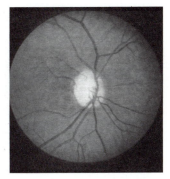

Figure 10.5 Optic atrophy. The figure shows the appearance of the retina at the back of the eye in a patient with optic atrophy secondary to MS. The atrophied optic disc appears as a white, well-demarcated disc. Vision in the eye has been lost. A full-colour version of this image is shown in the plates section.

Table 10.2 Sites of MS plaques and corresponding symptoms

Site of plaque	Symptoms
Motor pathways	Weakness, stiffness
Sensory pathways	Tingling, numbness, burning, itching
Cerebellum	Unsteadiness, incoordination, slurred speech
Brain stem	Double vision, vertigo, nausea, vomiting
Spinal cord	Weakness, stiffness, sensory disturbance below the spinal level
	Bladder and bowel disturbance

area of skin supplied by the particular sensory neurons affected. Intense burning pain may occur. The limbs, the trunk, and the face may be involved. The symptoms tend to spread and intensify over several days and may come and go over many years.

Often patients have difficulty describing the odd sensations, and sometimes these symptoms are misinterpreted by medical professionals as being hysterical and having no physical cause. **Lhermitte's symptom** is the term used to describe an unpleasant electric-shock-like sensation in the back and radiating into the legs and sometimes the arms that occurs on flexing the neck. It can occur with any lesion in the cervical spinal cord, but is most frequently seen with cervical spine MS plaques.

Motor features

If the inflammatory plaques occur on myelinated upper motor neurons (as shown in Figure 8.11 on page 166), motor symptoms of weakness and spasticity will result. The legs are affected more frequently than the arms, and usually affected asymmetrically. Eventually spastic **paraparesis** and then **paraplegia** will result. Spasms can be troublesome, particularly at night.

Sphincter involvement

When plaques occur in the descending pathways that contain the nerves controlling continence, bladder and bowel symptoms can result. Urinary frequency and urgency are common symptoms. The bladder may become small and spastic, and empty involuntarily when only small volumes of urine are present. Urinary infections are frequent. Constipation is often present in advanced MS. Impotence is also common.

Brain stem and cerebellum

If plagues occur in the brainstem and cerebellum, nausea, vomiting, and unsteadiness may occur. Patients may also develop double vision and problems with speech and swallowing. Unwanted tremor may occur.

Other features

Tiredness is a major symptom in MS, particularly during an acute relapse. Cognitive impairment and depression occur in about half of MS patients with advanced disease. Seizures in MS are rare.

SELF-CHECK 10.3

What are the symptoms of optic neuritis? Why do they arise?

> MS causes very varied symptoms depending on where in the CNS the demyelinating plaques form.

10.5 What tests can we use to diagnose multiple sclerosis?

There is no specific blood or laboratory test that allows a diagnosis of MS to be made. Diagnosis is based on the clinical features suggesting 'multiple lesions in time and space', i.e. plaques occurring at different times and at multiple sites within the CNS.

Table 10.3 Diseases that may cause similar symptoms to MS

Cerebral infarction

Intracranial tumours

Inflammation of cerebral blood vessels—cerebral vasculitis

Intracranial vascular abnormalities

Spinal cord compression from tumour

Motor neuron disease

Infection, either acute or chronic

Other inflammatory disorders, e.g. sarcoidosis

Hereditary degenerative diseases, e.g. cerebellar ataxia

Investigations such as brain MRI and examination of the CSF are used to provide additional information that, along with the clinical features, help in making the diagnosis. Other diseases that may cause similar features need to be excluded, particularly those disorders for which specific treatments are available. Diseases that may cause symptoms similar to MS are listed in Table 10.3.

> The diagnosis of MS is based on clinical features in keeping with multiple plaques in various places in the CNS occurring at different times.

10.5.1 MRI

The MRI scans in Figure 10.6 show us the inflammatory plaques within the CNS due to MS. Discrete, hyperintense lesions are evident within the white matter. Typically several lesions will be identified on imaging, more than those that can be clearly linked to discrete symptoms. Lesions are typically seen in the **periventricular** areas, and may occur in the cervical spinal cord and the brainstem. The appearance alone of the lesions does not allow them to be reliably distinguished from multiple infarcts, but their distribution solely within white matter and the clinical context usually allows the distinction to be made.

Sometimes gadolinium-diethylenetriaminepentaacetic acid is given to patients before scanning. This paramagnetic contrast agent only crosses disrupted blood–brain barrier, and thus only highlights new or newly active plaques. It is used to give an idea of how active the disease is at a given time. Gadolinium enhancement usually lasts less than 4 weeks after the appearance of a plaque, and is reduced or disappears after treatment with steroids.

Much research has focused on techniques to assess the total volume of plaques in people with MS on MRI, as a measure which could be used to follow the progression of the disease. Unfortunately the total plaque volume does not seem to correlate well with the degree of clinical disability.

CT scanning is not usually sufficiently sensitive to detect MS plaques.

(a)

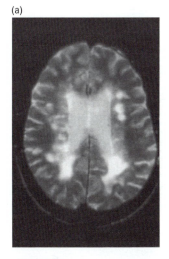

(b)

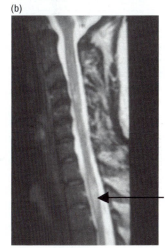

Figure 10.6 MRI scans showing lesions in the white matter typical of those seen in MS. The lesions show as bright white signals in these images. (a) Lesions around the ventricles. (b) Lesions in the cervical spinal cord. The lowest lesion (arrowed) can be seen to be expanding the spinal cord. Images courtesy of Dr David Yates.

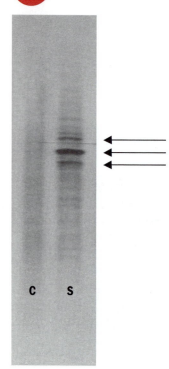

Figure 10.7 Electrophoresis of CSF sample from a patient with MS (denoted s) and from a normal individual (denoted c). Oligoclonal bands are indicated by arrows in the sample from the MS patient. Image courtesy of Dr Abid Karim.

10.5.2 **CSF examination**

Most patients in whom the diagnosis of MS is being queried will undergo examination of the CSF in addition to brain MRI. The main CSF feature in keeping with a diagnosis of MS is the presence of **oligoclonal bands** in the fluid which are not present in a serum sample taken from the patient at the same time. An example of this is shown in Figure 10.7. These bands represent a number of specific **immunoglobulins** which have been synthesized within the CNS, rather than being made in the peripheral circulation and thus present in serum too. Much research has focused on these specific immuno-globulins present in MS patients. They represent a mixture of proteins, and differ from patient to patient. Their presence gives weight to the theory that the immune system is involved in the mechanism of MS, but their analysis has not as yet allowed the specific trigger for the immune activation in the disease to be identified.

It is important to note that the presence of oligoclonal bands in the CSF is not specific to MS. These bands are also are found in other diseases including neurosyphilis, meningitis and encephalitis, cerebral infarction, intracranial tumours, and other inflammatory dis-eases. The intensity of the bands does not seem to correlate well with the activity of MS, and some patients with MS will not show oligoclonal bands. Thus the CSF changes are used to support the diagnosis of MS in clinically appropriate circumstances rather than to provide proof of the diagnosis.

10.5.3 **Evoked potential studies**

These studies involve measuring the electrical response on the scalp to various sensory inputs such as visual stimulation (flickering lights shone into one eye), auditory stimulation (applying a clicking sound to one ear), or electrical stimulation of a peri-pheral nerve. The electrical response is picked up by electrodes applied to the scalp, similar to those used to record the EEG. Responses from each eye, ear, or limb are compared with the response from the other eye, ear, or limb, recording the time taken to pick up the response in the scalp. Any delay in the response may reflect the presence of a lesion in the sensory pathway on that side, such as an MS inflammatory plaque.

In the past evoked potential studies were used to confirm a clinically equivocal lesion or to pick up additional asymptomatic lesions, and thus confirm the 'multiple' lesions required for diagnosis. MRI has largely overtaken evoked potential studies in this role, and they are now used less often.

10.5.4 **Investigating the first clinical episode of MS**

A particular issue arises when an individual presents with a symptom that may represent the first episode of what might eventually develop into MS, such as a single episode of optic neuritis. Various studies have followed up such individuals for many years to determine if there are any ways of identifying those who will go on to experience further episodes and thus develop 'multiple' sclerosis. Investigations such as brain and spine MRI, evaluation of CSF, and evoked potential studies can help determine the likelihood of the patient developing MS. Looking at the data shown in Table 10.4 we can see that if both the brain MRI scan and CSF examination are normal in a person who presents

Table 10.4 Investigations at first presentation and subsequent risk of developing MS

Feature at first clinical presentation	Percentage of patients progressing to MS at 5 years
Brain MRI showing plaques	65
Normal brain MRI scan	18
Oligoclonal bands in CSF	60
CSF contents normal	16

SELF-CHECK 10.4

How would you investigate and advise someone who has a single episode of optic neuritis?

with isolated optic neuritis, there is only a 15–20% chance that they will go on to develop MS. This is in comparison to a 60–70% chance if both the MRI brain scan and CSF findings are abnormal and compatible with MS.

10.6 What treatments are available for multiple sclerosis?

As with other neurological disorders, therapies can be divided into those that treat symptoms of the disease and those targeted against the primary mechanism of the disease.

10.6.1 Symptomatic treatments

Corticosteroids are the main symptomatic therapy in MS. They are given in high doses intravenously for short periods of time and hasten remission from acute relapses. Their exact mechanism of action is unknown. It is thought that they help restore the integrity of the blood–brain barrier, preventing further activated lymphocytes from entering the CNS, they suppress the activity of toxic cytokines produced by activated T cells, and they suppress inflammation. Corticosteroids are also useful in relieving the pain associated with optic neuritis. Corticosteroids do not affect the long-term course of the disease and should not be given for long periods because of the many unwanted side effects which are listed in Table 10.5.

Muscle spasms can be treated by regular therapy with oral baclofen, a GABA agonist which acts at the level of the spinal cord. Care needs to be taken with the dose given, as an unwanted side effect of baclofen therapy is weakness. Other agents to reduce spasm are benzodiazepines, acting within the CNS, and tizanidine, a centrally active alpha$_2$-noradrenergic agonist. Sometimes botulinum toxin is used to relieve severe spasm by injection into specific sites. It acts by preventing release of acetylcholine at the **neuromuscular junction**.

Urinary frequency and urgency can sometimes be helped by giving anticholinergic drugs which inhibit bladder muscle contractions. Urinary infections can be treated with antibiotics. Constipation can be avoided by having a high-fibre diet, or treated with laxatives or enemas.

Table 10.5 Some side effects of corticosteroid treatment

Truncal obesity and weight gain
Thinning of the skin
Bruising
Hirsutism
Myopathy
Hypertension
Diabetes
Insomnia
Anxiety
Depression
Psychosis
Osteoporosis
Glaucoma
Cataracts
Increased risk of infection
Exacerbation of peptic ulcer disease

extension: Use of cannabis in treating MS symptoms

BOX 10.3

Many patients with MS have experimented with alternative therapies (see website <*www.nationalmssociety.org/spotlight-cam.asp*>).

There are anecdotal reports that cannabis is beneficial and it is suggested that up to 8% of people with MS regularly use the drug to relieve symptoms such as pain, nausea, muscle spasms, bladder symptoms, and tremor.

The plant *Cannabis sativa* contains many proteins, including more than 60 oxygen-containing aromatic hydrocarbon compounds collectively known as **cannabinoids**. Ethanol extracts of whole cannabis are available to take orally, as are tablets containing the active ingredients Δ-9-tetrahydrocannabinol and cannabidiol.

Alternatively the plant can be smoked, which seems to give more rapid and reproducible blood concentrations of cannabinoids than oral administration. The mechanism of action of cannabis has been proposed to involve antioxidant and anti-inflammatory activities, with effects on intracellular calcium homeostasis.

Since 2003 there have been a number of reports of randomized, placebo-controlled clinical trials of oral cannabis extracts in MS. One study involving 160 patients showed a reduction in the total symptoms of spasticity, spasms, tremor, and bladder symptoms as reported by the patients using a visual scale. Another large UK study treated 630 patients with either oral cannabis extract, tetrahydrocannabinol, or placebo and followed the change in spasticity over a period of 15 weeks. This study did not find any improvement in the spasticity score in those taking the drug but did report that patients' mobility increased and pain decreased, suggesting cannabinoids may be clinically useful.

Tremor in MS can be very disabling and difficult to treat. Various anticonvulsants can be tried including carbamazepine, gabapentin, and clonazapam. Some patients are successfully treated by surgical **thalamotomy** or **deep brain stimulation**.

Pain in MS is often paroxysmal, occurring in spasms at frequent intervals. Sometimes the antiepileptic drugs carbamazepine or phenytoin are useful. Tricyclic antidepressant drugs may also be effective, acting via anticholinergic mechanisms. The pain due to immobility in joints can be eased with non-steroidal anti-inflammatory drugs. Some patients report that cannabis can relieve paroxysmal pain, spasms, and other symptoms in MS and further detail of this is given in Box 10.3. Supplying the drug is currently illegal in the UK. It is anticipated that this will be challenged should the drug be shown to be effective in future clinical trials.

SELF-CHECK 10.5

What therapies are available to control symptoms in MS?

Overwhelming tiredness is a frequent symptom in MS and one that it is very difficult to treat. Recent studies with modafinil, an agent developed to treat the excessive sleepiness of **narcolepsy**, have shown some success. **Selective serotonin reuptake inhibitors** (SSRIs) can sometimes help in treating fatigue, in addition to the depression which is commonly seen.

Clinical trials

Trials of new therapies in MS require careful design as the natural history of the disease is to relapse and remit and the disease course is very variable. Large numbers of patients must be included and followed over several years to take account of the normal variation in disease course between patients.

Table 10.6 Kurtzke expanded disability status scale (EDSS). The EDSS quantifies disability in eight functional systems (FS). A functional system score (FSS) is given in each of these systems. The functional systems are: pyramidal, cerebellar, brainstem, sensory, bowel and bladder, visual, cerebral and other. EDSS steps 1.0–4.5 refer to people with MS who are fully ambulatory. EDSS steps 5.0–9.5 are defined by the impairment to ambulation

0.0	Normal neurological examination
1.0	No disability, minimal signs in one FS
1.5	No disability, minimal signs in more than one FS
2.0	Minimal disability in one FS
2.5	Mild disability in one FS or minimal disability in two FS
3.0	Moderate disability in one FS, or mild disability in three or four FS. Fully ambulatory
3.5	Fully ambulatory but with moderate disability in one FS and more than minimal disability in several others
4.0	Fully ambulatory without aid, self-sufficient, up and about some 12 hours a day despite relatively severe disability; able to walk without aid or rest some 500 m
4.5	Fully ambulatory without aid, up and about much of the day, able to work a full day, may otherwise have some limitation of full activity or require minimal assistance; characterized by relatively severe disability; able to walk without aid or rest some 300 m
5.0	Ambulatory without aid or rest for about 200 m; disability severe enough to impair full daily activities (work a full day without special provisions)
5.5	Ambulatory without aid or rest for about 100 m; disability severe enough to preclude full daily activities
6.0	Intermittent or unilateral constant assistance (cane, crutch, brace) required to walk about 100 m with or without resting
6.5	Constant bilateral assistance (canes, crutches, braces) required to walk about 20 m without resting
7.0	Unable to walk beyond approximately five meters even with aid, essentially restricted to wheelchair; wheels self in standard wheelchair and transfers alone; up and about in wheelchair some 12 hours a day
7.5	Unable to take more than a few steps; restricted to wheelchair; may need aid in transfer; wheels self but cannot carry on in standard wheelchair a full day; may require motorized wheelchair
8.0	Essentially restricted to bed or chair or perambulated in wheelchair, but may be out of bed itself much of the day; retains many self-care functions; generally has effective use of arms
8.5	Essentially restricted to bed much of day; has some effective use of arms retains some self-care functions
9.0	Confined to bed; can still communicate and eat
9.5	Totally helpless bed patient; unable to communicate effectively or eat/swallow
10.0	Death due to MS

From: Kurtzke JF, Rating neurologic impairment in multiple sclerosis: an expanded disability status scale (EDSS). *Neurology* 1983, **33**: 1444–1452.

Various rating scales have been developed to give standard measures of the degree of disability in MS, such as the Kurtzke Expanded Disability Status Scale, which is described more fully in Table 10.6. Such scales can be used to monitor patients in trials over time and provide a measure of the effectiveness of a given therapy.

Repeated brain MRI, with and without gadolinium enhancement, is also often used to provide another measure of the effect of new drugs on the underlying disease. As mentioned earlier however, the number of plaques seen on MRI does not seem to correlate well with the degree of physical disability from the disease.

10.6.2 Mechanistic treatments aimed at preventing relapses and progression of long-term disability

Since the mid-1990s various treatments have become available which aim to lessen the underlying immune activation in MS and slow or halt the progressive phase of the disease. These drugs are expensive and have only been convincingly shown to be of benefit in reducing the rate of relapses in the disease rather than altering the long-term course. Overall they reduce the number of relapses by 30%. Government guidelines exist for the prescription of these drugs in the UK prescribed through the National Health Service (<*www.nice.org.uk/page.aspx?o=38119*>).

> Several drugs are now available that alter the immune response in MS. These drugs are more effective in reducing the frequency of relapses in MS rather than influencing the course of the progressive phase of the disease.

Interferon beta

Interferons are proteins naturally produced by the body which are normally active in preventing infections by viruses. Early MS research showed that one of the interferons, interferon gamma, was involved in the formation of demyelinating plaques in MS.

Interferon beta, a synthetic compound, damps down the production of interferon gamma in the nervous system. Other actions of interferon beta include reducing the migration of T lymphocytes across the blood–brain barrier, suppressing T1 lymphocyte activity and increasing T2 lymphocyte suppressor cell activity. Three types of interferon beta are available, all with similar efficacy and all requiring to be injected. The dosage schedules vary, from daily to once per week.

Glatiramer acetate

This is a synthetic compound containing a mixture of **polypeptides** made from the **amino acids** tyrosine, glutamate, alanine, and lysine. It is thought that this synthetic mixture resembles MBP, a major constituent of normal myelin. Glatiramer actetate is thought to act in MS by blocking the interaction of activated T cells with myelin and by altering the balance of pro-inflammatory T1 cells and suppressor T2 cells. The drug is given by daily subcutaneous injection.

SELF-CHECK 10.6

What therapies are available to prevent relapses and progression of disability in MS?

With repeated use over months interferon beta and glatiramer acetate themselves generate an immune response, with antibodies forming against these synthetic compounds. The effectiveness of the drugs is lessened when such antibodies are present.

Other agents aimed at preventing long-term disability include the **immunosuppressant drugs** azathioprine, mitoxantrone, and cyclophosphamide, but lack of efficacy and unwanted side effects have limited their use.

10.7 What is the long-term outcome?

There is great variability in the course of disease between individuals with MS and in the overall prognosis. Table 10.7 lists some of the factors, both good and bad, that may give a guide to the likely course of the disease. MS is a chronic disease, and people tend to have symptoms for many years. It has been estimated that half of MS patients will die as a direct result of their disease, and half from unrelated causes. On average people with MS live for 82% of the normal lifespan.

> About half of all people with MS die as a result of their disease. Average lifespan is around 80% of normal.

10.7.1 New therapies targeted to the immune response

Much research is currently focused on developing therapies that will be effective both in preventing relapses, and in slowing or stopping the disability in progressive disease. Many of these therapies are directed against aspects of the immune response, targeting processes such as the migration of lymphocytes across the blood–brain barrier, cytokine release from activated lymphocytes, or the inflammatory reactions that eventually result in plaque formation and loss of axons.

Another approach has been to use monoclonal antibodies generated specifically to bind to various proteins on lymphocytes and thus block their effects.

Some of these new therapies that have shown beneficial effects in early trials are listed in Table 10.8, along with their proposed mode of action.

Experiments have also suggested that suppression of the immune system followed by transplantation of **stem cells** from the bone marrow can induce remission in severe MS. Stem cells can enter the CNS and differentiate into glia and possibly neurons, and may therefore be able to produce remyelination and axonal repair at the site of MS plaques.

Table 10.7 Predictors of disease course in MS

Better prognosis	Worse prognosis
Female	Male
Relapsing-remitting course at onset	Incomplete recovery after first episode
Long interval to second relapse	Short inter-attack interval
Low frequency of attacks early in disease course	High relapse rate in first few years
Normal brain MRI at presentation	Abnormal brain MRI with large lesion load
No disability after 5 years	Substantial disability after 5 years
Presentation at younger age	Advanced age at presentation

Table 10.8 Some of the newer therapies being tested in MS

Therapy	Proposed mode of action
Intravenous immunoglobulin	Modifies balance between T1 and T2 lymphocyte subtypes. May neutralize circulating antibodies against myelin
Plasma exchange	Removal of pathogenic antibodies
Monoclonal antibodies, e.g. Campath1H, daclizumab, rituximab, natalizumab	Act against specific antigens on subset of lymphocytes. Some prevent lymphocytes sticking to blood vessel and migrating across blood–brain barrier
Pentoxifylline	Suppresses inflammatory cytokine production
Statins	Lipid lowering drugs which also have effects on the immune system
Oestrogens	May decrease inflammatory cytokine production by activated T cells
T cell vaccination	Reduces myelin-specific immune responses

Major disadvantages of the stem cell therapy tried to date include the limited effectiveness and the high level of side effects and increased **mortality** compared to conventional MS therapies. Refinements in the future may however lead to more effective cell based therapies.

SUMMARY

- MS is the most common cause of severe physical disability in young adults in the UK.

- MS arises because of damage to the blood–brain barrier and activation of the immune system within the CNS.

- MS is most commonly a relapsing and remitting disease at the onset of symptoms.

- MS causes very varied symptoms depending on where in the CNS the demyelinating plaques form.

- The diagnosis of MS is based on clinical features in keeping with multiple plaques in various places in the CNS occurring at different times.

- Several drugs are now available that alter the immune response in MS. These drugs are more effective in reducing the frequency of relapses in MS rather than influencing the course of the progressive phase of the disease.

- About half of all people with MS die as a result of their disease. Average lifespan is around 80% of normal.

FURTHER READING

M. J. Olek and D. M. Dawson. Multiple sclerosis and other demyelinating diseases of the central nervous system. In *Neurology in Clinical Practice*, 4th edn,. eds W. G. Bradley, R. B. Daroff, G. Fenichel and J. Jankovic, pp. 1631–1664. Oxford: Butterworth Heinemann, 2004.
A detailed chapter covering clinical and pathological aspects of MS.

A. J. Thompson and W. I. McDonald. Multiple sclerosis and its pathophysiology. In *Diseases of the nervous system: clinical neurobiology*, 2nd edn, ed. W. I. McDonald, A. K. Asbury, and G. M. McKhann, pp. 1209–1228. Philadelphia: W. B. Saunders, 1992.
Concise chapter with focus on underlying mechanisms of disease in MS in addition to covering clinical aspects.

Review papers

The following two short reviews detail steps in the diagnosis and management of MS and a consideration of disease-modifying therapies:

S. M. Leary, B. Porter and A. J. Thompson. Multiple sclerosis: diagnosis and the management of acute relapses. *Postgraduate Medical Journal* 2005; **81**; 302–308.

J. Zajicek. Diagnosis and disease modifying treatments in multiple sclerosis. *Postgraduate Medical Journal* 2005; **81**; 556–561.

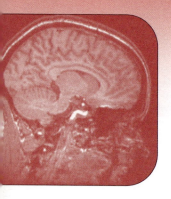

Headache and chronic pain

Carl Clarke and Barbara Hoggart

> **INTRODUCTION**
> Headache (**cephalgia**) is one of the most common of all medical symptoms. Chronic pain syndromes are also common and lead to considerable disability and suffering.

11.1 Headache

We will use the International Headache Society Classification of the various types of headache disorder, which is outlined in Table 11.1. As you will see from this, there are many different types of headache disorder but only a small number of these are common.

> Tension-type headache and migraine are extremely common.

11.1.1 Tension-type headache

Tension-type headache (TTH) is the most common of all the headache disorders. It is artificially divided into episodic and chronic TTH depending on whether the headache is present on less or more than 15 days per month.

How common are tension-type headaches and who are most at risk?

Episodic TTH is extremely common in the population; in fact, you have probably had this yourself. Studies show that episodic TTH occurs in 24–74% of people over a 12-month period. This compares with 2% of people who suffer chronic TTH over 12 months.

Table 11.1 2003 International Headache Society classification of headache disorders

IHS classification	Name	Frequency of diagnoses in author's department (%)
1	Migraine	39
2	Tension-type headache	46
3	Cluster headache and other trigeminal autonomic cephalgias	2
4	Other primary headache disorders	2
5	Headache due to head and/or neck trauma	2
6	Headache due to cranial or cervical disorder	<1
7	Headache due to non-vascular disorder	<1
8	Headache due to substance or its withdrawal	3
9	Headache due to infection	<1
10	Headache due to disorder of homeostasis (e.g. hypertensive encephalopathy, sleep apnoea)	<1
11	Headache due to other cranial disorder	<1
12	Headache due to psychiatric disorder	<1
13	Cranial neuralgias	<1
14	Other and unclassified headache disorders	<1

What are the likely causes of tension-type headaches?

TTH is probably caused by a number of different underlying problems, but little is known about these. The most common relationship is with symptoms of anxiety and depression.

What tissue changes occur in tension-type headaches?

Since little is known of the causes of TTH, the precise **pathophysiology** of the condition is unknown. However, in those with anxiety and depression, it is likely that tension develops in the muscles of the head and neck which in some way leads to headache.

What are the symptoms and clinical signs of tension-type headaches?

TTH is described as a mild to moderate pressing or tightening feeling which is felt all over the head. As we see in Box 11.1, patients often describe TTH as though 'my head will explode' or as though 'there is a tight band around my head'. This usually does not stop everyday activities. Some patients suffer mild nausea and **photophobia** (aversion to light) or **phonophobia** (aversion to noise) during the headaches.

In episodic TTH, the headache occurs on less than 15 days in a month. These are the type of headaches you have probably suffered yourself when under pressure, with exams for example. If the headaches become more frequent than 15 days in a month, then they are classified as chronic TTH.

> Tension-type headache is described as a mild to moderate pressing or tightening feeling which is felt all over the head.

> **case study:** Tension-type headache   **BOX 11.1**
>
> ---
>
> A 44-year-old man attended his GP's surgery with a 3-month history of headaches. These were felt in the occipital and frontal regions; at other times he said the top of his head felt as if it was going to blow off. The headaches had been continuous since their onset and unrelieved by occasional analgesics. He complained that the headaches were of increasing severity and becoming more troublesome.
>
> His GP found neurological examination was normal. A diagnosis of chronic tension-type headache was made.
>
> On further exploration, his GP discovered that the patient had been under enormous stress at work with a large project to supervise over the last 6 months. The GP gave advice on stress management, including more delegation at work. No medication was prescribed.
>
> When the GP reviewed the situation 3 weeks later, there had already been considerable improvement and by 12 weeks, the headaches had disappeared.

In addition to TTH, some patients may have more severe symptoms of anxiety such as **palpitations** (fast heart beat), **hyperventilation** (overbreathing), distal **paraesthesiae** (fingertip and toe pins and needles), hand **tremor** (shaking), and/or **panic attacks** (most of the previous symptoms in a short space of time). They may also suffer from symptoms of depression such as low mood, **anhedonia** (loss of enjoyment in life), **insomnia** (poor sleep), and loss of appetite and weight.

> People with tension-type headache may suffer from symptoms of anxiety and depression.

What tests can we use to diagnose tension-type headache?

In patients with a typical history of TTH and normal examination, there is no need to pursue further investigations to look for an underlying secondary cause.

Recent research has shown that the chance of finding a serious underlying lesion in the brain by imaging with CT or MRI in patients with typical TTH is 6 per 1000. In another study in normal volunteers, the chance of finding serious intracranial pathology on CT scanning was also 6 per 1000. So imaging people with TTH is like screening the normal population, which detects too few lesions to be cost-effective.

We can see in Table 11.2 the symptoms and signs that would alert a doctor to the possibility of more serious pathology in any patient with headache. These so-called **red flags** are looked for in every headache patient when they are evaluated. If such a warning symptom or sign is found, then further investigations such as neuroimaging and blood tests may be required. This will be discussed further when we consider secondary causes of headache in section 11.1.4.

SELF-CHECK 11.1

What are the warning symptoms and clinical signs in patients with headaches which suggest a serious cause?

> Patients with tension-type headaches do not usually require any investigations.

Table 11.2 Warning symptoms and signs (red flags) in patients with headache disorders.

Symptom or sign	Possible lesion
Headache wakes the patient in the early hours of the morning	Tumour
Twitching of the face, arm, or leg (epilepsy)	Tumour
Loss of consciousness (epilepsy)	Tumour
Progressive weakness or sensory loss of the face, arm, or leg	Tumour
Swollen optic disc (papilloedema)	Tumour or idiopathic intracranial hypertension
Sudden severe headache	Subarachnoid haemorrhage
Scalp tenderness	Temporal arteritis
Clusters of short-lived attacks with watering of eye or nose	Cluster headache

What treatments are available for tension-type headache?

Many patients with mild TTH require only firm reassurance from their GP and advice about lifestyle measures to reduce stress. In some people, their anxiety and/or depressive disorder is more severe, so advice from a counsellor and even a psychiatrist may be needed. Such people may also need antidepressant medication. Some antidepressants can be useful in treating the symptoms of anxiety.

 The pharmacological treatments of anxiety and depressive disorders are considered in sections 13.5.1 (page 278) and 14.7.1 (page 300) respectively.

> Most patients with tension-type headaches will respond to reassurance and lifestyle advice to reduce stress.

What is the long-term outcome of tension-type headache?

Although TTH is not a life-threatening condition, it is very common and leads to considerable debility in the population and, as a result, time off work. Most patients with episodic TTH will settle with conservative treatment such as reassurance and lifestyle measures. The much smaller group of patients with chronic TTH can suffer for many years, in spite of aggressive psychological and psychiatric input.

SELF-CHECK 11.2

How does tension-type headache present and how should it be investigated?

11.1.2 Migraine

Migraine is almost as common as TTH in the population. Since migrainous headaches can be more severe than TTH, this condition causes more disruption to patient's lives, so they consult for medical advice more frequently.

How common is migraine and who are at most risk?

The frequency of migraine is very different for men and women: 15–20% of women have migraine compared with 5–7% of men. The reasons for this are not known. The peak in the frequency for both sexes is in the 25–55 year old age group, when people are at their most productive from society's perspective. So migraine can lead to a lot of absenteeism.

What are the likely causes of migraine?

The causes of migraine remain unknown. It can be triggered by a number of well-known precipitants including stress, oral contraceptive, diet (e.g. chocolate, cheese, coffee, tea, red wine), exercise, altered sleep pattern, and travelling.

What tissue changes occur in migraine?

We do not know the precise pathophysiology of migraine. However, there are two theories of how migraine may occur:

- The **neural theory** is based on the phenomenon of **cortical spreading depression**. The latter has been investigated in animals but has yet to be confirmed in humans. Cortical spreading depression is a wave of depolarization which propagates across the cerebral cortex at the rate of 2–3 mm/min. Transient depression of spontaneous and evoked neuronal activity occurs, lasting for several minutes. This is preceded by brief neuronal activation. Since the visual **aura** of a migraine attack spreads across the cortex at the rate of 3 mm/min, it is likely that this is due in some way to cortical spreading depression.

- The **vascular theory** of migraine possibly explains the headache phase of the condition. **Afferent** neurons from the trigeminal cranial nerve innervate the proximal parts of the larger cerebral vessels and the dura. These fibres carry pain sensation to the trigeminal nucleus in the brain stem, which is then relayed to the thalamus and thus the cortex. Depolarization in the trigeminal ganglion leads to central transmission of pain and also the retrograde release of vasoactive peptides which cause vasodilatation in the dura. In experimental models, cortical spreading depression can stimulate the trigeminovascular system, so migraine may be caused by spreading depression triggering the trigeminal nucleus.

What are the symptoms and clinical signs of migraine?

Around 60% of patients with migraine have a **premonitory phase**. This warning before the main attack can occur for 48 hours before the onset, in which case the symptoms usually remain stable, or it can arise around 6 hours before the attack and evolve gradually into the attack. Premonitory symptoms can be psychological (for example, fatigue, depression, euphoria, and irritability), neurological (such as photophobia, dysphasia, or yawning) and/or more general (such as neck stiffness, coldness, thirst, and food cravings).

Many, but not all migraineurs, have an aura phase before the headache develops. This usually evolves over 20–30 minutes and in most cases settles within 60 minutes of onset. The most common aura is visual in nature. The patient sees flashing lights (**photopsia**), zigzag lines (synonymous with fortification spectra and **teichopsia**; like an old map of a walled city), loss of a small part of vision near to centre of the visual field (**paracentral scotoma**), and/or **hemianopia**. A much smaller proportion of patients report sensory symptoms such as paraesthesiae or numbness. **Dysphasia**, **hemiparesis**, sensation of spinning (**vertigo**), and **ophthalmoparesis** (eye movement disorder) are rare. Extremely rarely, migraine can cause confusion and even coma.

> The aura of a migraine attack is comprised of sensory, motor and/or cortical dysfunction which evolves over 20–30 minutes and usually lasts less than 60 minutes.

> ## case study: Migraine with aura
>
> BOX 11.2
>
> ---
>
> A 24-year-old right-handed secretary had a stressful day at work and had to miss lunch. In the afternoon she developed tingling of the right hand which slowly extended up the arm. Ten minutes later, she developed numbness of the right face and of the right side of the tongue. The hand began to improve but she became aware of loss of vision on the right. After 20 minutes, she tried to telephone her mother but she could not put words together (dysphasia). Her mother collected her and brought her to her GP's surgery. By this time, her original symptoms had resolved, but she then had a severe left-sided headache and vomited in the waiting room. Her mother was worried that she might have had a stroke or a brain haemorrhage.
>
> Her GP found neurological examination to be normal.
>
> The GP reassured the patient and her mother that this was a typical migraine attack and that further investigations were not required. He gave her anti-emetic and analgesic injections and advised her to go home to bed.
>
> The following morning she felt well and returned to work.

The final feature of a migraine attack is the headache phase. Patients develop a severe, throbbing, unilateral headache. This is often associated with photophobia, phonophobia, nausea, and vomiting.

Box 11.2 provides you with a classical case study of someone suffering a migraine attack.

> Migraine causes moderate to severe unilateral, throbbing headache, often with nausea and photophobia.

Not all patients suffer an aura before a migraine attack. These are referred to as **migraine without aura**. Similarly, in some migraine attacks the aura is not followed by headache, a so-called **migraine equivalent**.

> Not everyone has an aura with their migraine.

> Not everyone has a headache with their migraine aura.

What tests can we use to diagnose migraine?

Most patients with migraine do not need any further investigations. If the history is typical and neurological examination normal, then the detection rate for neuroimaging is similar to that in the normal population.

We have already discussed the red flags outlined in Table 11.2. If any of these are present in a patient with migraine, then CT or MRI will be necessary.

A common clinical problem is to differentiate a stroke from a migraine attack in a middle-aged patient who has suffered visual, somatosensory, or motor loss. The crucial point is that the aura of a migraine attack evolves over 20–30 minutes then goes within 60 minutes in most cases. In contrast, the deficit of a stroke comes on suddenly and often stays for more than 60 minutes.

> Most patients with migraine do not need investigations.

What treatments are available for migraine?

After full reassurance and providing an explanation of the diagnosis, the treatment of migraine should include consideration of any precipitating factors. This will include reducing stress levels and removing any dietary or medication triggers. Patients may also be helped by suggesting that they keep to regular mealtimes, have reasonable amounts of sleep, and take regular exercise.

Those who have fewer than 2–4 migraine attacks per month should be given an **acute** treatment regime only, since prophylactic medication will not be effective. The initial treatment should be simple analgesics such as aspirin, paracetamol, or ibuprofen. It is likely that many patients will have tried these over-the-counter remedies before seeking medical attention. However, it should be checked that they were taking adequate doses.

The next step is to add to the analgesic an anti-sickness (antiemetic) agent such as domperidone or metoclopramide. These can be beneficial for all aspects of a migraine, not just vomiting. If this fails, or if the patient has severe attacks from the outset, then one of the triptan class of **5-hydroxytryptamine** (5-HT, **serotonin**) receptor antagonists should be prescribed.

Patients with migraine who suffer more than 2–4 attacks per month should receive the acute treatment outlined above at the time of the attack along with a **prophylactic** treatment regime to reduce the frequency of the attacks. Such drugs are not very efficacious: the best response is a 50% reduction in frequency of migraine attacks in 50% of patients.

The current list of prophylactic drugs includes beta-adrenergic antagonists (synonymous with beta-blockers; for example atenolol or propranolol), antiepileptic drugs (topiramate, sodium valproate), and antidepressants (amitriptyline). Usually, patients will be given one of these agents to take continuously at a low dose for 2–3 months. If this does not reduce the frequency of the attacks then the dose will be increased and the patient reviewed again in 2–3 months. If a maximally tolerated dose of one drug fails, then this is stopped and another one commenced at a low dose and so on.

What is the long-term outcome of migraine?

SELF-CHECK 11.3

What are the symptoms and clinical signs of migraine?

Like TTH headache, migraine is not a life-threatening condition. However, the severity and frequency of the headache leads to many sufferers losing considerable time off work during their most productive years. Therefore, migraine has a major impact on society and better acute and prophylactic treatments are required.

11.1.3 **Cluster headache**

Cluster headache is a rare form of primary headache disorder, but it causes particularly severe pain and requires specific medication.

How common is cluster headache and who are most at risk?

Cluster headache is rare, accounting for only 2% of diagnoses in the author's neurology clinic. Its frequency in the general population is around 0.1%, with more men being affected than women.

What are the likely causes of cluster headache?

The cause of the condition is unknown.

What tissue changes are caused by cluster headache?

The precise pathophysiological mechanism of cluster headache is unknown. However, it is one of a small group of conditions which share similar clinical features: pain in the trigeminal nerve territory and **autonomic dysfunction**. These conditions are now being grouped together as **trigeminal autonomic cephalgias**. The names of these conditions as listed in Table 11.3.

We saw that the pathophysiology of migraine somehow involves the trigeminal nerve and its nucleus, as here in cluster headache, but migraine rarely leads to autonomic disturbance which always occurs in these conditions.

What are the symptoms and clinical signs of cluster headache?

The case study in Box 11.3 provides a typical description of cluster headache. This condition causes severe unilateral, ocular, and/or frontal headache. The duration of the attacks is short compared with migraine; each lasts for around 30–90 minutes. The pain can be excruciating, with patients banging their head on a wall or even committing suicide.

The diagnostic feature is the autonomic dysfunction; most commonly watering of an eye and unilateral nasal discharge due to overactivity of the parasympathetic nervous system. Rarely, patients suffer a **Horner's syndrome** (**ptosis**, **miosis**, reduced sweating on face) due to underactivity of the sympathetic nervous system.

> Cluster headache leads to short-lasting severe, unilateral, frontal, or ocular pain associated with autonomic dysfunction such as watering of the eye.

Table 11.3 The trigeminal autonomic cephalgias

Cluster headache
Paroxysmal hemicrania, hemicrania continuans
Short-lasting unilateral neuralgiform headache with conjunctival injection and tearing (SUNCT)

case study: Cluster headache

BOX 11.3

A 44-year-old man presents to the neurology clinic with an 8-week history of daytime attacks of severe pain behind the right eye. During the attacks, his right eye waters. These attacks occur five or six times a week, rarely more than once in a day, each one lasting around an hour. More recently, a persistent mild headache has developed over the right side of the head. He recalls something similar lasting a few weeks several years ago, but then the attacks occurred at night.

Neurological examination and head MRI are normal.

He was treated with a tapering course of prednisolone and regular verapamil. On his return to clinic 2 weeks later, the attacks had halved in frequency and he had not suffered any side effects from the medication. A further 2 weeks later, the attacks had stopped and the patient was extremely grateful. The prednisolone was withdrawn after 6 weeks and the verapamil after 4 months with no recurrence of the attacks.

Eight months later, he presented again with further attacks. The combination of prednisolone and verapamil was again effective.

Although the attacks are short-lived, they can be repeated several times in the day. Often the attacks occur at the same time of day, commonly in the night. The condition is called 'cluster' headache as the attacks usually come in clusters lasting for a month or two, with a gap then for several months before another bout. Occasionally, this pattern of episodic cluster headache deteriorates to a chronic condition in which no remissions occur or the remissions last for less than 2 weeks.

What tests can we use to diagnose cluster headache?

Very rarely, the symptoms of cluster headache occur as a result of an underlying cranial tumour, infection, or vascular malformation. Since these conditions cannot be reliably diagnosed clinically, it is suggested that all patients with cluster headache are referred for cranial MRI.

What treatments are available for cluster headache?

The treatment of cluster headache is very different from other headache disorders. Effective acute treatment at the time of the attack requires a rapidly administered triptan (for example, intranasal or subcutaneous sumatriptan) or, for reasons that are obscure, inhaled oxygen.

Patients must also have prophylactic treatment. Although prednisolone (a steroid drug) is effective in aborting a cluster, relapses are common unless another agent is combined with it. Verapamil (a calcium-channel blocker) is the most commonly used prophylactic, followed by methysergide and lithium.

SELF-CHECK 11.4

How do the symptoms and clinical signs of cluster headache differ from those of migraine?

What is the long-term outcome of cluster headache?

Regrettably, cluster headache is a lifelong condition, although there is a tendency for the remissions between clusters to get longer with age.

11.1.4 Secondary headache disorders

As we saw in Table 11.1, many other conditions affecting the head and neck area lead to headache. We cannot consider all of these here, but the next section describes in brief the most important secondary headache disorders.

Medication overuse headache

The most common cause of headache after TTH and migraine is **medication overuse headache**. Perhaps after a run of episodic TTH, people begin to take headache medication several times every day. The headaches get worse, so they take more medication. They then present to their GP or the neurology clinic with chronic daily headache: continuous generalized headache with no other specific diagnostic features. Although this is identical to chronic TTH, the use of medication regularly makes medication overuse headache the most likely diagnosis.

This type of headache can be caused by simple analgesics (aspirin, paracetamol, ibuprofen) but is particularly common with codeine-based analgesics. It also occurs with triptans and ergotamine. The treatment of choice is to withdraw such medication immediately. This can result in withdrawal symptoms like those seen with narcotics, so short courses of sedatives are sometimes required to help the patient get over this.

> Medication overuse headache is a common cause of chronic daily headache.

Intracranial tumour

It is uncommon for **intracranial tumours** to present with headache alone, and no other symptoms more suggestive of a tumour. As we have already noted, the red flags in Table 11.2 consider the warning signs that suggest the possibility of a tumour. The case study in Box 11.4 gives an example of such a patient.

 Intracranial tumours are considered in more detail in section 12.2.2 on page 255.

---

case study: Intracranial tumour   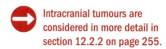 **BOX 11.4**

A 65-year-old man visited his GP's surgery complaining of slurred speech and headache. Over the last month, he had noticed slurred speech followed by spasm of his face which lasted a few seconds to be followed by increasing weakness of his left arm. During this period, he had constant right frontotemporal headaches which woke him from sleep in the early hours of the morning.

Neurological examination showed mild left facial and upper limb weakness. At fundoscopy, the discs were normal with no papilloedema.

He was referred urgently to his local neurology unit where an urgent MRI scan showed a large mass in the right frontoparietal cortex.

He was transferred to the care of the regional neurosurgical centre. A biopsy of the lesion showed that it was a high-grade (rapidly growing) astrocytoma. He was referred for radiotherapy, which he declined. He died 3 months later.

(a)

(b)

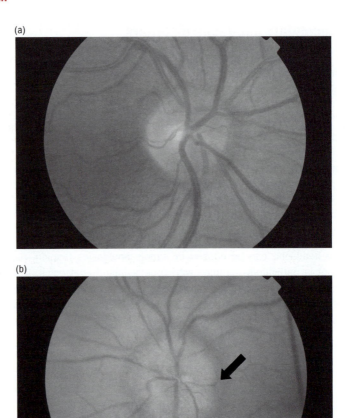

Figure 11.1 (a) A normal optic disc viewed through an ophthalmoscope. (b) Papilloedema. Note the swelling of the edge of the disc margins (arrow). Image courtesy of Dr A Ball. A full-colour version of this image is shown in the plates section.

Idiopathic intracranial hypertension

An uncommon cause of headache is **idiopathic intracranial hypertension** (IIH). It was previously called 'benign' intracranial hypertension, but because it can have serious consequences, as we shall see later, it is now referred to as 'idiopathic'. This means that we do not know what causes the condition.

As we see from the case report in Box 11.5, patients present with a non-specific generalized headache but, on examination, they are found to have a swollen optic disc (**papilloedema**). Figure 11.1 shows what papilloedema looks like when the back of the eye is looked at with an **ophthalmoscope**.

> Idiopathic intracranial hypertension leads to headache and papilloedema.

case study: Idiopathic intracranial hypertension

BOX 11.5

A 16-year-old obese young woman who had been taking the contraceptive pill for 9 months went to see her GP because she had developed headaches. These occurred at various times of the day and were all over her head. She also noticed that, when she bent over, her vision became blurred. Her vision also went black for a few seconds on getting out of bed in the morning.

Her GP found that she had bilateral papilloedema and referred her urgently to her local neurology unit.

An MRI scan was normal but, at lumbar puncture, she had a CSF pressure of 40 cm of H_2O (normal < 25).

A diagnosis of idiopathic intracranial hypertension was made. The contraceptive pill was stopped and she was placed on a strict diet. She was also given acetazolamide.

When reviewed in clinic 2 weeks later, the visual obscurations had gone and her headaches were a little better. She had lost 1.5 kg in weight. By 6 months after presentation, the headaches had gone and she had lost 16 kg. The diuretic was gradually withdrawn.

These patients usually have an urgent CT scan which is normal, thereby excluding the other main cause of papilloedema—an intracranial tumour. They then have a lumbar puncture at which the intracranial pressure is measured with a manometer tube attached to the end of the needle, and this is found to be high.

IIH is particularly common in obese young women, those on the oral contraceptive pill, and in pregnancy. The reason(s) for this are unknown, but it suggests that the condition may be caused by hormonal changes.

Some patients also have so much pressure on their optic nerves that they have **visual obscurations**. When they stand up after bending over or on getting out of bed, their vision goes completely for a few seconds and they are effectively blind. In severe cases, the pressure is so high that the patient loses vision all the time. This can improve slowly with treatment, but the danger of the condition is that some people can go blind.

People with IIH are treated with a water tablet or **diuretic**, often one called acetazolamide. This reduces the intracranial pressure. The cause of the condition is then rectified. So, obese patients must lose weight. If pregnancy is the cause, diuretics can generally hold the condition until after the child is delivered. If these measures are insufficient and the intracranial pressure continues to rise, then occasional IIH patients need the pressure relieving by a shunt tube inserted into a lateral ventricle which is tunnelled under the skin to the abdominal cavity (**ventriculo-peritoneal shunt**).

Figure 9.4 on page 185 shows the positioning of a ventriculo-peritoneal shunt.

Temporal arteritis

Temporal arteritis occurs in elderly people, but its cause is unknown. Figure 11.2 shows a cross-section of one of the temporal arteries from such a patient which has been **biopsied** surgically and examined under the microscope. This shows marked inflammation in the artery with numerous white blood cells showing up blue because of staining of their nuclei by the stain that has been added to the section.

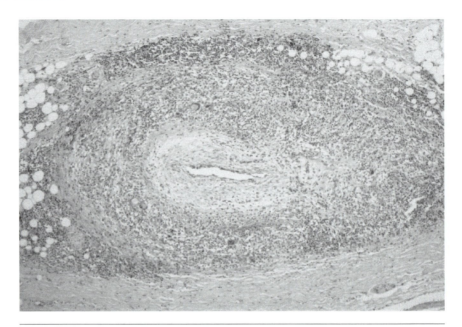

Figure 11.2 Cross-section of an inflamed temporal artery in temporal arteritis. The lumen of the vessel, where blood flows, is surrounded by large numbers of inflammatory cells which stain blue. Image courtesy of Dr P. Barber. A full-colour version of this image is shown in the plates section.

As we see from the case study in Box 11.6, temporal arteritis presents with headaches that are often felt in the temples where the superficial temporal arteries are inflamed. This can lead to tenderness of the scalp when the hair is combed or brushed.

There can be other mild symptoms, such as general weakness and loss of weight. The concern about this condition is that it can lead to inflammation in the arteries supplying the brain and the eye, thereby leading to stroke or blindness.

---

case study: Temporal arteritis

BOX 11.6

A 67-year-old woman went to her GP with right-sided headaches which she had had for several weeks. She had also felt rather unwell in a non-specific way over the last few months and had lost some weight. She wanted a 'tonic'.

On direct questioning, her GP discovered that her scalp was tender on the right when she brushed it.

On examination, there was objective scalp tenderness on the right but no other abnormalities.

The GP arranged an urgent ESR, which was very high at 110 mm.

He started her on a tapering course of prednisolone tablets for her temporal arteritis.

When she was reviewed 4 days later, the headache had gone and she felt 'wonderful'. The GP kept her on a small dose of prednisolone for 2 years then slowly withdrew it without any recurrence.

In suspected cases, a blood test called the **erythrocyte sedimentation rate** (ESR) is done and the result is usually very high. This is not specific for temporal arteritis, though. Occasionally, the diagnosis must be confirmed by taking a biopsy sample of the temporal artery surgically, as in Figure 11.2.

> Temporal arteritis presents with headaches and, in some cases, scalp tenderness.

The treatment of temporal arteritis is steroid therapy with prednisolone. This suppresses the inflammation in the whole body, so the headaches and the other manifestations of the condition rapidly disappear. This rapid improvement helps to confirm the diagnosis.

> The key investigations for temporal arteritis are the ESR and the response to prednisolone therapy.

11.2 Chronic pain

11.2.1 How common is chronic pain and who are most at risk?

Long-term pain is a common condition. A European survey of 46 000 people found that one in five people suffered from chronic pain. The highest incidence was in the working population, with 45–60 year olds representing 43% of sufferers.

> One in five people in Europe suffer from chronic pain.

11.2.2 How is pain defined?

The International Association for the Study of Pain (IASP) has defined pain as: 'An unpleasant sensory and emotional experience associated with actual or potential tissue damage and expressed in terms of such damage'.

11.2.3 What is the difference between acute and chronic pain?

Chronic pain has been defined as pain lasting for more than 3 months. In reality the margins between acute pain and chronic pain are arbitrary. Chronic pain is acute pain that has not stopped hurting because differences in causation and mechanism develop. These changes require different treatments. As you can see in Table 11.4, the features of acute and chronic pain are different.

SELF-CHECK 11.5

How do acute and chronic pain differ?

Table 11.4 Features of acute and chronic pain

Acute pain	Chronic pain
Predictable	Unpredictable
Associated with tissue damage	Tissue damage often unclear
Nerve pathway well defined	Neuronal connections complex
Self limiting	Resolution not predictable
Treatment analgesia	Treatment multidisciplinary
Useful warning function	Often no obvious function

11.2.4 How is pain perceived?

Peripheral activation

We know that acute tissue damage activates sensory nerve fibres that respond to painful stimuli in the periphery. Sherrington first proposed the existence of the **nociceptor** in 1906. The nociceptor is a primary sensory neuron activated by stimuli resulting from tissue damage.

> The nociceptor is a primary sensory neuron activated by stimuli resulting from tissue damage.

The two key receptor classes are A-delta primary sensory fibres, which respond to intense mechanical stimuli, and C-fibres, which respond to noxious thermal, mechanical, and chemical stimuli. The cell bodies of these afferent fibres lie in the dorsal root ganglia, and the fibres then project into the grey matter of the dorsal horn of the spinal cord, as we can see illustrated in Figure 11.3. In addition, A-beta primary sensory fibres also respond to mechanical stimuli and make inhibitory connections within the dorsal horn of the spinal cord. These A-beta fibres are not directly involved in the pain pathway but are the gatekeepers; that is, stimulating them, such as by rubbing a painful area, can reduce the sensation of pain.

This **gate control theory of pain** was first described in 1962 by pioneers of pain research, Wall and Melzack, and is explained in more detail in Box 11.7. This theory proposes that

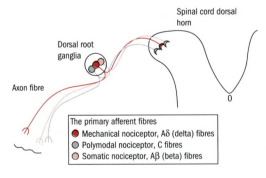

Spinal cord dorsal horn

Dorsal root ganglia

Axon fibre

0

The primary afferent fibres
- Mechanical nociceptor, Aδ (delta) fibres
- Polymodal nociceptor, C fibres
- Somatic nociceptor, Aβ (beta) fibres

Figure 11.3 Primary sensory neurons and synaptic connections in the dorsal horn of the spinal cord, showing the three types of primary afferent fibres. Red, mechanical noticeptor A-delta fibres; pink, polymodal receptor C fibres; dotted, somatic nociceptor A-beta fibres. Drawing courtesy of Dr K. Whitehead.

extension: The gate control theory of pain

BOX 11.7

Looking at the diagram in Figure 11.4, we can see that wide dynamic range (WDR) neurons in the spinal cord receive projections from sensory fibres and project this information to higher brain centres.

Inhibitory interneurons (IN) are able to modulate the information received by the WDR by the projections they receive from innocuous A-beta fibres and noxious A-delta and C fibres.

The gate control theory proposes that large diameter, non-nociceptive fibres (A-beta) are able to indirectly inhibit the effects of the pain fibres (A-delta/C) by forming an excitatory (+) connection with IN. In turn, this decreases the chance of the WDR transmitting the pain stimuli, thus 'closing a gate'.

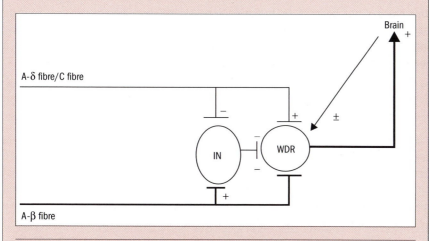

Figure 11.4 A schematic representation of the gate control theory of pain transmission. WDR, wide dynamic range neuron; IN, inhibitory interneuron; (+) represents an excitatory synapse; (−) represents an inhibitory synapse.

there is a neuronal 'gate' in the spinal cord that can modulate incoming pain signals, and that this gate can also be opened or closed by messages from the brain.

The peripheral release of certain neurotransmitters in response to pain, particularly tachykinins (for example, substance P and calcitonin-gene-related peptide (CGRP)), is known as the **axon reflex** or **neurogenic inflammation**. Neurogenic inflammation increases the sensitivity of the nociceptor. This peripheral sensitization lowers the threshold of the nociceptor so that it responds more readily to noxious stimuli (**hyperalgesia**) and also can be activated by innocuous stimuli (**allodynia**).

The spinal cord relay

As we saw in Figure 11.3, nerve impulses pass from the periphery to the dorsal horn of the spinal cord. The neurons of the dorsal horn of the spinal cord can become sensitized to pain impulses and the patient becomes hypersensitive to noxious stimuli.

Nociceptors make synaptic connections with neurons in the dorsal horn of the spinal cord. In the outer layers (laminae) of the dorsal horn, the activity of the small-diameter sensory fibres (C-fibres) is thought to be faithfully transmitted to projection neurons, and then to higher brain centres, to produce the perception of localized pain and temperature sensation.

In the deeper laminae of the dorsal horn, however, the terminals of the primary afferent fibres have more complex connections to spinal interneurons and projection neurons. As we have seen in Box 11.7, WDR neurons receive input from sensory fibres that are stimulated by innocuous stimuli (A-beta fibres) as well as those that convey noxious stimuli (C-fibres). The properties of WDR neurons are not fixed. Repeated and high-intensity input into the WDR neurons results in an increase in their receptive field and a decrease in their threshold.

The role and function of the NMDA receptor are considered in more detail in Box 2.4 on page 36, and also in Box 6.10 on page 126.

This process has been linked to the neurophysiologic condition of **wind-up**. Wind-up has been described as a cellular model of learning and memory produced by unblocking of the *N*-methyl-D-aspartate (NMDA) receptor, which is normally blocked by a magnesium ion.

Activation of this receptor leads to the production of nitric oxide and prostaglandins, which when released into the nerve synapse stimulate the production of more presynaptically released neurotransmitters. The result of this is an amplification of pain signals.

Clinically, wind-up produces a situation where the patient may develop both **hyperalgesia** and **allodynia**. This process is a normal consequence of an acute pain episode and serves to encourage protection of the injured area while healing takes place. In normal circumstances, when an episode of acute pain resolves, so does central sensitization because the input from the nociceptors has ceased.

The risk of the neuroplastic changes of wind-up becoming permanent increases the longer the nociceptive input to the dorsal horn continues. Clinically this is characterized by exaggerated responses to innocuous and noxious stimulation, and enlarged cutaneous receptive fields.

Onward transmission of pain signals to higher centres in the brain

Pain is transmitted to the brain along the spinothalamic tract. The message is forwarded to the periaquaductal grey (PAG) matter, the reticular formation, thalamus, cerebral cortex, and limbic system. These structures discriminate pain and can activate the release of endogenous modulators of pain control.

The release of the opiate beta-endorphin **serotonin** and **noradrenaline** acts as a feedback control and alters the sensation of pain, mental state (for example, stress or depression) can also influence the perception of pain by stimulating the production of the same neurotransmitters.

Functional magnetic resonance imaging (fMRI) has helped in the investigation of the influence of the anticipation of pain. This research has shown that anticipation of pain activates sites close to, yet distinct from pain pathways, and alters the sensation of pain.

As you can now appreciate, much is known about the mechanism of pain production, but the way in which all of these pathways are integrated is still unclear.

SELF-CHECK 11.6

What are the mechanisms by which pain sensation is modulated before it reaches the cerebral cortex?

11.2.5 How do we measure pain intensity?

We only measure pain intensity in order to assess the effect of treatment or the progress of a disease or condition. There are three main ways of recording pain intensity in clinical practice:

- **visual analogue scale (VAS)**—rated by the patient by marking a point on a 100-mm line to indicate the intensity of their pain

- **numerical rating scale (NRS)**—the patient selects a number between 1 and 10 to indicate the severity of their pain

- **verbal rating scale (VRS)**—the patient selects a descriptor from a list of 4–15 words to indicate their pain (for example, 0 = no pain, 1 = mild pain, 2 = moderate pain, 3 = severe pain).

A comprehensive pain assessment addresses behaviour, psychology, and other influences on pain in addition to intensity.

> The measurement of change in pain is essential to monitor effectiveness of treatment.

11.2.6 What different types of chronic pain are there?

There are two types of chronic pain:

- In **nociceptive pain**, nerve endings (nociceptors) are activated by inflammation or damage to tissues in the body, thereby transmitting pain signals via the peripheral nerves and the spinal cord to the brain.

- In **neuropathic pain**, nociceptive activity causes changes to occur in the peripheral or central nervous system, often without obvious associated tissue damage. In reality many pains have a mixed picture, such as sciatica in association with back pain.

Nociceptive chronic pain

A European survey in 2002 and 2003 showed that nociceptive chronic pain was due to osteoarthritis (34%), low back pain (15%), trauma (12%), rheumatoid arthritis (9%), and headache (7%).

The management of nociceptive pain includes analgesia and rehabilitation. Amelioration of the pain rather than cure is a more achievable goal. Non-pharmacological treatments include physiotherapy, acupuncture, and transcutaneous electrical nerve stimulation (TENS). Psychological support for coping with the impact of chronic pain must always be considered.

The World Health Organization (WHO) has developed a system called the WHO analgesic ladder which is outlined in Table 11.5. The ladder describes an escalation in analgesia as the rungs of the ladder are ascended. The rise up the ladder is in response to untreated pain.

It is essential in the pharmacological management of pain that the medication is taken regularly, in the correct dosage, and for an adequate period of time to assess efficacy. Only then should consideration be given to changing the medication because of lack of effectiveness.

Table 11.5 The WHO analgesic ladder

Step	Treatment
1	Paracetamol ± adjuvant therapy[a]
2	Weak opioid[b] + paracetamol ± adjuvant therapy
3	Strong opioid[c] + paracetamol ± adjuvant therapy

[a] Adjuvant therapy may include non-steroidal anti inflammatory drugs (NSAIDS).

[b] For example, codeine.

[c] For example, morphine.

Table 11.6 Causes of neuropathic pain

Causes	Example
Infection	Postherpetic neuralgia; metabolic (e.g. diabetes mellitus) peripheral neuropathy
Trauma	Complex regional pain syndrome
Surgery	Phantom limb pain
Vascular	Central pain
Cancer	Cancer-induced neuralgia

Neuropathic pain—when does it occur?

Table 11.6 lists the causes of neuropathic pain and examples of some of the resulting conditions. Neuropathic pain is quite common, affecting 2.4% of younger people and 8% of elderly people.

Box 11.8 describes a case study of an elderly patient with postherpetic neuralgia.

> The population prevalence of neuropathic pain is about 2400 per 100 000 (2.4%), rising with age to 8000 per 100 000 (8%).

People with neuropathic pain complain of specific symptoms of pain such as burning, tingling, shooting, or stabbing. The signs of neuropathic pain are allodynia (pain caused by a stimulus that is not normally painful) and hyperalgesia (an increased response to a stimulus that is normally painful).

The diagnosis is confirmed by:

- diagnosis of an associated cause, such as diabetes
- classic symptoms
- positive clinical examination.

case study: Postherpetic neuralgia

BOX 11.8

An 86-year-old woman visited her GP with an active eruption of a vesicular rash 2 months ago. She told him that the rash started between her shoulder blades and continued round to the front just under her left breast. The rash was diagnosed as acute herpes zoster (shingles) and she was treated with antiviral agents (aciclovir) and analgesics.

Six weeks later she returned to her GP to say that the rash had cleared leaving a few scars but the area was agony. She described the constant pain as burning, with occasional electric shocks. She tells her GP that she cannot wear a bra because of the pressure (hyperalgesia) and if her husband tries to rub some ointment on her skin she screams with pain (allodynia).

The story of a herpes zoster infection and a verbal description of allodynia and hyper-algesia are common in this condition. The clinical examination confirmed the diagnosis of postherpetic neuralgia.

The GP prescribed additional medication of amitriptyline (an antidepressant) gabapentin (an anticonvulsant), and stronger analgesia.

She overcame the side effects of dizziness, dry mouth, and weight gain and found the medication ameliorated her pain to a tolerable level.

She was told by her GP that the future was uncertain as to whether she would ever come off the medication. She will probably be recommended to take the occasional 'drug holiday' (a period of time off medication to review efficacy) but no time frame can be put on the condition.

The diagnosis of neuropathic pain is important as the pharmacological treatment options are different. The pain is difficult to manage and requires a multidisciplinary approach. Treatment options include:

- **Non-pharmacological treatments**—physiotherapy (for example, for an immobilized limb), psychology (for coping strategies and rehabilitation) acupuncture and TENS.
- Pharmacological treatments, including
  - tricyclic antidepressants
  - anticonvulsants
  - analgesics.

SELF-CHECK 11.7

What are the types of chronic pain and how are they treated?

11.2.7 What influences the pain experience?

The experience of pain felt is not an isolated event. The life experiences the patient has had prior to the pain will influence their response.

Women are known to express pain more readily and generally seek help earlier than men. Elderly patients are less likely to report severe pain than younger equivalent patients, and are more prone to using maladaptive coping strategies.

The expression of pain also varies in different cultures; for example, a Nepalese person assumes that back pain is normal so the reported incidence of back pain in Nepal is virtually nil.

Previous painful experiences will also influence how much pain is expressed. Pain-related disability can be associated with ongoing litigation. Also, a study in the USA showed that litigants were more anxious and depressed than non-litigants.

11.2.8 Depression and chronic pain

What is the incidence of depression and pain?

Between 30 and 50% of people who have chronic pain are also depressed. The incidence is higher in chronic pain than in other chronic disorders, for example diabetes or chronic renal failure.

What factors do pain and depression have in common?

Not all people who have chronic pain develop depression; it usually affects the people who fail to adapt successfully to their pain. The factors that influence adaptation to pain are the same factors that influence the development of depression. These include the person's locus of control. An external locus of control—for example, a tendency to look to doctors to take the lead in your pain management—is linked to depression.

People who have a tendency to focus on the worse case (catastrophizing) are also more likely to develop depression. Other factors that influence the development of depression are a lack of confidence in your ability to carry out functional tasks (lack of self-efficacy), feeling that you are helpless, being fearful of evoking pain through activity (fear avoidance), and inappropriate reliance on passive coping strategies.

Why do people with chronic pain change their behaviour pattern?

We learn from an early age that movement exacerbates the pain evoked by an injury. As a result of this learning, we tend to rest an injury until healing takes place and the pain resolves. However, extended rest becomes unhelpful because joints become stiff and muscles lose tone and power.

A person in chronic pain may gain pain relief during the rest period, thus reinforcing the perceived benefit of the rest. When they begin normal activity again the pain intensity increases, again reinforcing the idea that pain is associated with activity and is relieved by rest. As the muscles weaken and the joints become stiff, the chronic pain sufferer's pain increases. An increase in pain is normally associated with tissue damage. Thus the pain sufferer has a further reinforcement that activity is harmful to them. Hence a cycle of rest and increased pain is set up.

> Depression does not cause pain but it does heighten the pain experience.

What is the association of pain and depression?

Rest leads to muscle weakness, joint stiffness, and increased pain. As this situation worsens, normal daily activities begin to evoke pain and are avoided. The chronic pain sufferer may avoid their normal employment for increasingly lengthy periods of time, often stopping work altogether. As work offered the person not only financial reward but social interaction, the chronic pain sufferer becomes increasingly isolated.

The person's role in society and in their family becomes eroded by the effects of pain upon them. The pain sufferer may no longer be able to fulfil their original role in the family and community. Those who care for the pain sufferer will find that they are unable to help except by offering emotional or physical support. Sometimes the support that is offered by carers contributes to the development of a new role for the pain sufferer, a sick role. This development is unhelpful in terms of potential for the pain sufferer to turn things around and recover.

Often pain makes people short-tempered, irritable, and frustrated. It also reduces concentration because it dominates attention. This means that the pain sufferer will find it difficult to occupy their time in an enjoyable or meaningful way. Some people cope and adapt, but many cannot and become angry and resentful. They look to the medical establishment for a cure, and cannot cope well with the inability of medicine to manage their pain effectively.

The patient who is more likely to become depressed is the one who looks outwards for answers, relies upon others for help, focuses on blame and failure, and is fearful about the future.

The patient less likely to become depressed tends to adapt to the limitations caused by pain, for example they do the same amount of activity as they used to but break it down into manageable chunks. People who do not become depressed by their pain tend to be able to utilize their inner resources to cope, they do not rely on others and do not catastrophize, tending to focus more on what they can do and achieve.

In summary, the burden of the impact of chronic pain can lead to depression if responses are maladaptive.

> **Not all people with chronic pain develop depression.**

What messages are there for patients with chronic pain?

Patients need to understand that immobility is not without consequence. The earlier a patient returns to normal activity, such as work, the better their outcome will be. The need to prescribe adequate and appropriate analgesia is important in the early stages, so that mobility is maintained.

The control of pain by self-management is important. Patients need to understand that pain does not mean ongoing tissue damage. Pain may not always be alleviated completely, nor will it necessarily get worse. The patient should expect the occasional flare-up but to try to continue as normal a routine as possible.

SUMMARY

- Episodic tension-type headache is extremely common, occurring in 24–74% of people over a 12-month period compared with 2% of people with chronic tension-type headache.

- Tension-type headache is described as a mild to moderate pressing or tightening feeling which is felt all over the head.

- People with tension-type headache may suffer from symptoms of anxiety and depression.

- Patients with tension-type headaches do not usually require any investigations.

- Most patients with tension-type headaches will respond to reassurance and lifestyle advice to reduce stress,

- Migraine affects 15–20% of women and 5–7% of men,

- The aura of a migraine attack is comprised of sensory, motor, and/or cortical dysfunction which evolves over 20–30 minutes and usually lasts less than 60 minutes.

- Migraine causes moderate to severe unilateral, throbbing headache, often with nausea and photophobia.

- Most patients with migraine do not need investigations.

- Cluster headache leads to short-lasting severe, unilateral, frontal or ocular pain associated with autonomic dysfunction such as watering of the eye.

- Medication overuse headache is a common cause of chronic daily headache.

- Idiopathic intracranial hypertension leads to headache and papilloedema.

- Temporal arteritis presents with headaches and, in some cases, scalp tenderness.

- Chronic pain is a complex phenomenon, the result of several interacting processes.

- A potentially damaging event stimulates nociceptors.

- The perception of pain is not directly related to the nociceptive stimulus because the nociceptive signal can be modified in many ways.

- There is an emotional response to the perception of pain, involving the patients' beliefs about pain, their previous experience, and their existing emotional state.

- The interaction of perceived pain, emotional response, and thoughts is manifested as a behavioural response.

- Pain behaviour elicits a response from medical staff, family, and other people. This gives a social context to the expression of pain.

- We observe behaviour, not nerve stimulation. We treat something that is affected by biology, psychology, and other people.

FURTHER READING

Headache

S. D. Silberstein, R. B. Lipton and D. J. Dalessio. *Wolff's headache and other head pain*, 7th edn. Oxford: Oxford University Press, 2001.
Detailed reviews of all types of headache disorders.

Neurology in practice: Issue 6—Headache. *Journal of Neurology, Neurosurgery and Psychiatry* 2002; **72** (Suppl. 11).
Advanced discussion of current issues.

Chronic pain

A practical guide to the provisions of chronic pain services for adults in primary care. London: British Pain Society and Royal College of General Practitioners, 2004.

Pain in Europe survey web site <*www.painineurope.com*>

CHAPTER TWELVE

Neurosurgery

Spyros Sgouros

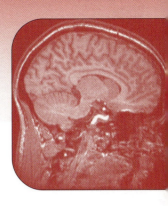

INTRODUCTION

In this chapter we examine how surgery can be used to:

- repair congenital abnormalities that present early in life, and other abnormalities that present later in life, and restore anatomy and function to as near-normal status as possible

- excise brain tumours that destroy nervous tissue and threaten function and life

- improve neural function in movement and mood disorders

- prevent further deterioration after a major vascular disorder or life-threatening trauma

- assist antibiotics in combating infection inside the central nervous system.

12.1 What are the goals of surgery of the central nervous system?

There are potentially severe risks and complications in any surgery of the central nervous system (CNS). Therefore, the surgeon must have very clear reasons for surgery, and be reasonably certain that the expected benefits from that operation significantly outweigh the risks. Neurosurgical operations allow a very small margin for error. As we have seen, the brain is a very compact structure, with a large number of highly organized, important, and indispensable structural units.

Whenever the brain or spinal cord is damaged, healing proceeds with the formation of scar tissue which is non-functional and simply binds adjacent structures together. This is called **gliosis**. In contrast to the cells of other organs, **neurons** and **axons** in the CNS are not reproduced after they have been damaged. As a general principle, the better the patient's functional state before surgery, the better the chance that they will be left unscathed by surgery.

We will now consider the goals of surgery of the CNS in more detail.

> Surgery of the central nervous system has potentially severe risks and complications.

12.1.1 Restoration of anatomical integrity

Once central nervous tissue has been damaged, it is impossible to repair it. However, there are many situations where nervous tissue has been compromised temporarily, and restoration of normal anatomy will lead to substantial gains of normal function. We can see examples of such restoration in the following sections.

Repair of congenital disorders

Congenital disorders of the brain and spine result from insults which affect the fetus in the first 20 weeks of intrauterine life. They are grouped broadly into **neurulation defects** and **post-neurulation defects** according to the timing of the insult with respect to the neurulation process (the development of the neural tube, which subsequently becomes the nervous system).

- **Neurulation defects** affect the normal anatomy of the brain more extensively because they happen before the nervous system has been shaped to its final form.

- **Post-neurulation defects** have more normal architecture preserved, as they happen later after the brain and spine have partially developed. Most congenital malformations of the nervous system affect structures in the midline. Some examples of these disorders are listed in Table 12.1.

Table 12.1 Congenital defects of the brain and spinal cord

Classification	Defect	Description
Neurulation defects	Anencephaly	Lack of development of the brain
	Cranio-rachischisis	Open midline defects in the head (encephalocele) and the spine (spina bifida or meningomyelocele)
Post-neurulation defects		
Cranial	Microcephaly	Various degrees of malformation or non-formation of brain tissue
	Hydranencephaly	
	Holoprosencephaly	
	Lissencephaly	
	Corpus callosum agenesis	
	Dandy Walker syndrome	
Spinal	Diastematomyelia	Abnormal formation of the spinal cord and the surrounding spinal column
	Neurenteric cyst	
	Dermal sinus	
	Dermoid cyst	

Surgical restoration of anatomical integrity is not always possible, and depends on whether there is tissue loss or just abnormal formation. In the case of tissue loss, there is no means of introducing new brain or spinal cord tissue, so no surgical treatment is possible. Examples of such conditions are hydranencephaly, holoprosencephaly, lissencephaly, and corpus callosum agenesis.

As we see in Figure 12.1, in the case of abnormal tissue formation, surgery can be used to partially reconstruct anatomical layers (such as in cases of myelomeningocele and diastematomyelia). Even then, any nervous tissue that was damaged during intrauterine development cannot be replaced.

Removal of compression of neural tissue

There are many circumstances where normal CNS tissues degenerate with time, resulting in compression of surrounding structures. We see a typical example of this in Box 12.1 in a patient with degeneration of the intervertebral discs in the spine. This leads to **disc prolapse** and compression of adjacent nerve roots and/or the spinal cord. Nerve root compression leads to severe pain in the arms, if it is in the neck region, or the legs, if it is in the lower back. If left untreated, the denervated muscles thin down (**atrophy**) and become weak. **Spinal cord compression** causes **myelopathy** (damage to the spinal cord substance) which results in weakness of the lower (**paraplegia**) or all four (**tetraplegia**) limbs.

Repair of damaged blood vessels

We considered the dangers of ruptured intracranial **aneurysms** in Chapter 5 and showed that surgical clipping of the neck of aneurysms can be curative. A more detailed description of the role of neurosurgery in other neurovascular conditions is given in section 12.2.3 below.

Removal of excess fluid from the brain

The brain contains cavities called **ventricles** which are filled with a water-like fluid, the **cerebrospinal fluid** (CSF).

Each day substantial amounts of CSF are produced, circulate in the brain and around the spine, and are then absorbed back into the bloodstream. If this circulation is blocked, CSF builds up within the brain, a condition which we call **hydrocephalus**. This increases the pressure within the head (the **intracranial pressure**, ICP) and, if left untreated, can lead to death. Surgery is employed to divert the fluid outside the brain. We shall learn more about hydrocephalus in section 12.3.4.

Head injuries can lead to a collection of blood and its breakdown products over the surface of the brain and underneath the dura in the subdural space.

This **subdural haematoma** or collection leads to increased ICP. Subdural haematoma can develop as a result of severe head injury (acute) and needs immediate surgical treatment, or can occur as a result of minor head injury (chronic), when it may not come to medical attention for a number of days or weeks after the injury. If a chronic subdural haematoma causes symptoms, the collection can be evacuated surgically by drilling small holes through the skull (**burr holes**). An example of such a case is described in Box 12.2.

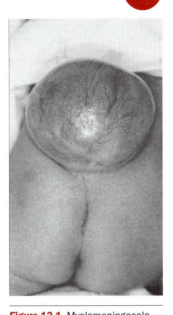

Figure 12.1 Myelomeningocele on the back of a newborn girl. The yellow-red area in the centre of the cystic malformation is the malformed spinal cord which is split in two parts and exposed to the environment. This was repaired on the first day of life to prevent meningitis and to protect the exposed spinal cord from further deterioration. A full-colour version of this image is shown in the plates section.

Subarachnoid haemorrhage and intracranial aneurysms are described in detail in section 5.2 on page 98.

The role of the ventricles and the production of CSF are described in section 1.2.3 on page 5.

The membranes that wrap and protect the brain (the meninges) are also described in section 1.2.3 on page 5.

case study: Cervical disc degeneration and cord compression

A 48-year-old man fell from a ladder while doing some repair work at home. Two days later he developed pain in his arms and walked with a clumsy gait.

On examination, upper limb power and reflexes were normal but there was numbness to pinprick in the lateral forearms, in keeping with root compression. Both legs were weak with brisk reflexes, suggesting a cord lesion.

We can see a midline MRI of his cervical spine in Figure 12.2. This shows that the C6/7 disc has degenerated and prolapsed, compressing the spinal cord. The discs at C2/3 and C3/4 levels are degenerate but are not compressing the spinal cord.

He had a cervical discectomy at the affected level. During that operation the abnormal disc was removed and the space that resulted was filled with normal bone harvested from the hip area.

His symptoms had cleared completely 3 months after the operation.

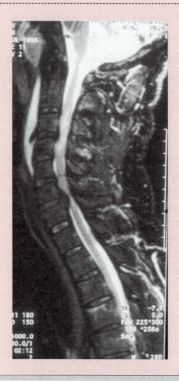

Figure 12.2 (*right*) Cervical spine MRI showing C6/7 disc degeneration and cord compression.

Reconstruction of the skull and spine

Damage to the skull or spine commonly occurs following severe trauma. Injury of the head by a sharp object (e.g. a golf club or ball) can result in a fracture of the skull in which the fractured piece of skull is pushed inwards forming a depressed **skull fracture**. Skull fractures with considerable depression require surgical elevation and repair.

In severe trauma, the facial bones can be fractured. Severe skull fracture can lead to damage of the underlying brain, and this is discussed in detail in section 12.3.1.

A fall from a height (e.g. from a horse or a first-floor window), or a car accident, can result in a fracture of the spine and possible injury to the spinal cord. As we see in the case described in Box 12.3, if the spinal fracture is extensive, and has made the spinal column unstable, it requires surgical fixation to prevent further destabilization and damage of the spinal cord.

Surgical reconstruction of the skull and the spine may also be required whenever these bony structures have been eroded and damaged by disease. We may see this in damage of the skull by a basal cell carcinoma of the skin in the head, or damage of the

case study: Chronic subdural haematoma

BOX 12.2

A 65-year-old man developed weakness of the left arm and leg gradually over 3 weeks. On closer questioning, he recalled injuring his head 6 weeks earlier on an open cupboard door in the kitchen.

The upper part of Figure 12.3 shows his CT scan, with a chronic subdural collection over the right hemisphere which is compressing the brain and causing shift of the midline structures.

He underwent burr hole evacuation (as shown in the lower part of Figure 12.3) of the subdural collection. The neurological deficit had recovered completely when he was seen 6 weeks later.

(a) (b)

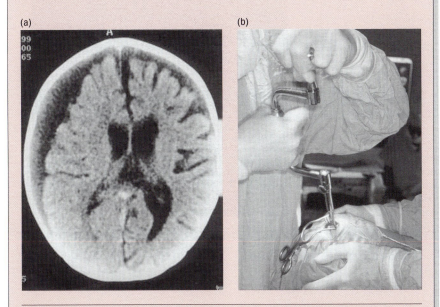

Figure 12.3 CT scan showing a chronic subdural collection over the right hemisphere causing midline shift (a). Intraoperative photograph of burr hole evacuation of the subdural collection (b).

spine by tuberculosis, **tumour**, or degenerative joint disease (for example, osteoarthritis or rheumatoid arthritis).

12.1.2 Excision of tumours that threaten normal neural tissue

Brain and spinal tumours are discussed in detail in section 12.3.2. However, it is important to stress here that, during surgical excision of such tumours, considerable effort is invested in to trying to preserve the surrounding non-affected structures, to avoid exacerbating the pre-existing neurological damage.

case study: Spinal trauma

BOX
12.3

A 4-year-old girl was hit by a car while trying to cross the road. She suffered severe head and spinal injuries.

We see her spinal radiographs in Figure 12.4, showing that the distance between the C2 and C3 vertebral bodies was greatly increased as a result of a distraction injury and severe disruption of the muscles and ligaments.

She required surgical stabilization of the cervical spine. After treatment of the head injury, she woke with paralysis in all four limbs.

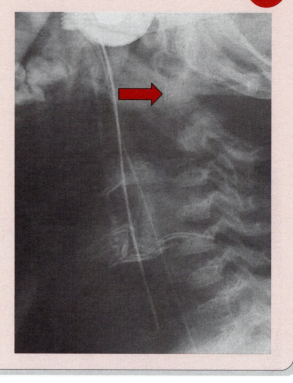

Figure 12.4 (*right*) Lateral radiograph of the cervical spine showing widening of the distance between vertebral bodies C2 and C3 with forward slip of C2 (arrow). These findings signify severe unstable spinal injury with complete disruption of all muscles and ligaments that keep the spine stable.

12.1.3 Improvement of neurological function (functional neurosurgery)

Certain disorders of the nervous system affect its function rather than its structure, so although the gross anatomical structure of the brain may be normal, there can be clinical expressions of significant dysfunction of the brain.

Details of such disorders and the different types of functional neurosurgery that may alleviate them can be seen in Table 12.2. It should be noted that for most of the conditions referred to in Table 12.2, the mechanism by which such surgery leads to clinical improvement is not well known, and many of these treatments were pioneered well before modern, accurate imaging was available.

Surgical ablation (elimination) or stimulation of an intracranial structure requires careful targeting of the structure involved. This is achieved using **stereotactic equipment** that allows precise placement of the ablating or stimulating electrode in deep parts of the brain based on radiological images.

Table 12.2 Types of functional neurosurgery

Type	Examples
Ablation of abnormally functioning nervous tissue	Cingulotomy for mood disorders (careful destruction of the cingulum in the brain)
	Rhizotomy for spasticity (selective division of nerves near the spinal cord to reduced tone in the legs)
	Cordotomy for pain (division of part of the spinal cord for pain in arm or leg)
Stimulation of dysfunctioning nervous tissue	Stimulation of the subthalamic nucleus or globus pallidus for severe Parkinson's disease
	Stimulation of the spinal cord in patients with chronic pain
Alteration of chemical environment of the nervous system by directly injecting medication	Continuous infusion of baclofen into the CSF for severe spasticity in multiple sclerosis
	Continuous CSF infusion of morphine for chronic pain due to malignancy.

12.1.4 Prevention of secondary neurological damage

Every time the brain suffers an insult, there is primary and secondary brain injury:

- **Primary brain injury** leads to direct physical damage to neurons and supporting cells.
- **Secondary brain injury** causes damage to, or destroys, neurons and supporting cells surrounding the area of the primary injury, due to lack of oxygen and other vital substances.

We see primary brain injury following an intracerebral haemorrhage from a ruptured aneurysm or an arteriovenous malformation, as we shall describe more fully in section 12.2.3. During the haemorrhage, blood is ejected from ruptured blood vessels under high pressure. This jet of blood directly injures or destroys tissue in its path.

Head injury also results in primary brain injury (**contusion** and haemorrhage) because of the shearing forces that are discharged on the brain.

In response to the primary injury, the surrounding brain swells leading to secondary brain injury. This swelling leads to:

- reduced oxygen (**hypoxia**)
- increased carbon dioxide (**hypercarbia**)
- the accumulation of neurotoxic substances (for example, dopamine) released from damaged neurons
- increased intracranial pressure
- disturbance of membrane potentials leading to epileptic activity.

All these processes interact with each other and make the swelling worse. They act as a positive feedback loop leading to further deterioration. If untreated, this leads to neuronal death and irreversible brain damage.

Similar processes take place in the spinal cord in response to trauma or haemorrhage. Irreversible damage of the spinal cord above the level of C3–4 leads to death because the ability to breathe is impaired. Irreversible damage of the spinal cord below the level of C3–4 leads to permanent paralysis below the level of the lesion.

Surgical strategies can be employed to prevent or minimize secondary brain swelling, and combat rising intracranial hypertension, and these include:

- Early removal of **intracerebral haematoma** or contusion. This aims to prevent deterioration due to pressure from the haematoma on the surrounding brain. In addition it reduces ICP by removing the volume of the haematoma from the head.

- Insertion of drains in the ventricles of the brain to remove CSF. This aims to prevent deterioration due to a build-up of CSF within the ventricles and reduce ICP by removing CSF from the brain.

- Removal of part of the skull (**craniectomy**) to allow the brain to expand. This aims to help reduce ICP by allowing the brain to expand once the rigid enclosure of the skull has been opened.

These strategies need to be deployed before irreversible damage occurs, and in conjunction with other medical treatments designed to reduce brain swelling.

12.1.5 Eradication of infection

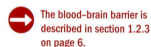

The blood–brain barrier is described in section 1.2.3 on page 6.

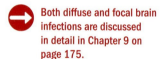

Both diffuse and focal brain infections are discussed in detail in Chapter 9 on page 175.

Penetration of antibiotics into the CNS is not easy, because of the **blood–brain barrier**. For the same reason, the natural defence of the body through the response of the immune system is not very effective in the brain. As a result, infection can be difficult to eradicate. Diffuse infections such as meningitis or encephalitis usually need only antibiotic therapy. However, infections that cause focal collections of pus require surgical evacuation as antibiotic treatment alone is not capable of clearing the infection.

Surgical treatment is necessary for **cerebral abscess** (collection of pus within the substance of the brain) and **subdural empyema** (collection of pus over the brain and underneath the dura). Brain abscess and subdural empyema are commonly caused by spread of infection from the air sinuses or the ears to the brain. Figure 12.5 shows an enhanced CT scan of a cerebral abscess.

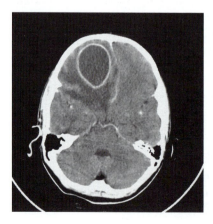

Figure 12.5 Contrast-enhanced CT scan of a cerebral abscess showing an enhancing round lesion in the right frontal lobe with considerable surrounding oedema.

SELF-CHECK 12.1

What is the difference between primary and secondary brain injury?

Bacterial infections are easier to treat than fungal infections, as, following evacuation of the pus, antibiotics clear the infection. It is not uncommon for more than one operation to be necessary, as collections can re-accumulate in the early stages.

12.2 Common neurosurgical conditions

Having considered the various goals of neurosurgery, we will now examine some of the more commonly occurring conditions that require such intervention.

12.2.1 Traumatic brain injury

How common is traumatic brain injury and who are most at risk?

Head injury can cause trauma to the skull or the brain. Traumatic brain injury (TBI) is the commonest cause of death in children and young adults, and the commonest cause of severe disability in young adults.

Up to 250 adults and 180 children per 100 000 of the population suffer a head injury every year. Thankfully, 80% of head injuries are minor and do not need hospitalization. Another 15% are moderate, needing hospitalization but no surgery. Only 5% are severe and require intensive care management and/or surgical treatment.

Often the terms **head injury** and TBI are used interchangeably, although strictly they should not. The term head injury is wider and includes trauma to the brain and skull, while the term TBI refers specifically to injury of the brain substance.

> TBI is the commonest cause of death in children and young adults, and the commonest cause of severe disability in young adults.

What are the likely causes of TBI?

Common causes of TBI are road traffic accidents and interpersonal violence. Children often fall from heights (trees, windows), and adolescents injure themselves during sports (fall from horses, injuries with hockey sticks or cricket bats). By far the most important cause is the motor car. The introduction of seat-belt legislation in the UK in the early 1980s reduced the incidence of severe head injuries dramatically.

What tissue changes are caused by TBI?

During head injury, we see primary injury as a result of the direct trauma and secondary injury as result of the subsequent biochemical event cascade (see section 12.1.4).

Primary injury can lead to **extradural haematoma**, subdural haematoma, **intracerebral haematoma**, brain contusion, and **diffuse axonal injury**.

Direct injury to the head can cause a skull fracture, which is a break in the continuity of the skull bones. It can be minor (a hairline fracture) or major (a depressed fracture, where the depressed fragment can be pushed into the brain).

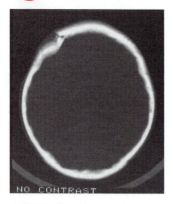

Figure 12.6 CT scan showing a depressed skull fracture in a 4-year-old boy who was hit on the head with a golf club. The skull is fractured and the fragments have been driven inwards.

 The nature and importance of the white matter tracts in the brain are discussed in section 1.2.1 on page 2.

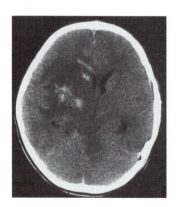

Figure 12.7 CT scan of brain contusion caused by a road traffic accident. There is damaged swollen brain with some blood collection in the right hemisphere and considerable surrounding brain swelling (the black low attenuation around the contusion).

We see an example of this in Figure 12.6. If the overlying skin is penetrated, the fracture is exposed to air (compound fracture) with considerably higher risk of infection. If the fracture is driven in to the brain significantly, the underlying brain substance is damaged causing a brain contusion. In the absence of brain damage, skull fracture does not cause long-term problems, provided that it is treated early, before infection sets in.

- An **extradural haematoma** is a collection of blood between the skull and the dura. It happens because the skull has fractured and torn a blood vessel in the extradural space.

- In contrast, a **subdural haematoma** is a collection of blood between the dura and the surface of the brain. It develops because veins that go from the brain surface to the dura are torn as a result of the injury to the head. An example of this was discussed in the case study in Box 12.2. As discussed already, it could be acute following severe injury, or chronic following minor injury to the head.

- An **intrecerebral haematoma** is a collection of blood within the substance of the brain itself. It occurs because the substance of the brain is disrupted by substantial injury, which ruptures the blood vessels within the brain white matter.

- Brain contusion is damage of the brain **parenchyma** (tissue) without a large collection of blood. This is the result of severe injury and we can see a CT scan from such a patient in Figure 12.7.

- Diffuse axonal injury is severe injury of the white matter tracts within the brain. This occurs as a result of intense acceleration–deceleration forces applied on the head during which the poles of the brain rotate within the head, and the white matter tracts are severed. It results in severe brain injury and often death. An example of a CT scan from such an injury can be seen in Figure 12.8.

Prevention of TBI relies on education of the general public about safety during everyday activities and sports. This includes the use of helmets by cyclists and motorcyclists, the use of seat belts in cars, and generally improving road safety.

> Primary brain injury can lead to extradural haematoma, subdural haematoma, intracerebral haematoma, brain contusion, and diffuse axonal injury.

What are the symptoms and signs of TBI?

TBI leads to impairment of consciousness and coma, focal neurological signs (such as **hemiparesis** and cranial nerve signs), **epilepsy**, and death.

Before the 1970s, it was difficult to describe the clinical state of a patient with a head injury. The **Glasgow Coma Score (GCS)** was then developed as a universal grading scale which facilitated communication between primary and secondary treatment centres. This standardized the description and classification of the clinical state of the patient.

As we can see from Table 12.3, the GCS is a numerical score ranging from a minimum score of 3 points to a maximum normal score of 15 points. It assesses three main areas of clinical response of the patient. These are motor function (M), verbal (V), and eye opening (E).

Table 12.3 Glasgow Coma Score

Area	Score	Meaning
Best motor response	1	No motor response
	2	Extension to pain
	3	Flexion to pain
	4	Withdrawal from pain
	5	Localizing pain
	6	Obeys commands
Best eye opening response	1	No eye opening
	2	Eye opening to pain
	3	Eye opening to verbal command
	4	Eyes open spontaneously
Best verbal response	1	No verbal response
	2	Incomprehensible sounds
	3	Inappropriate words
	4	Confused
	5	Orientated

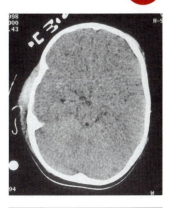

Figure 12.8 CT scan of diffuse axonal injury. The brain is swollen so the ventricles and the CSF spaces in the base of the brain are not seen.

The GCS should always be broken down into individual components. So 'E3V3M5' should be preferred to 'the GCS is 11', as using the number alone can be misleading.

Head injury is classified using the GCS into severe (GCS ≤ 8), moderate (GCS 9–12) and mild (GCS ≥ 13). In young children, a modification of the GCS is used to account for their developmental status: injury is severe when GCS ≤ 13, moderate when GCS = 14, and mild when GCS = 15.

What treatments are available for TBI?

Patients with mild head injury do not need any special treatment. After a short observation for an hour or so, they can be discharged home.

Patients with moderate head injury need a CT scan. If the scan is abnormal, they should be admitted to hospital for observation for 24 hours. This is because there is up to a 20% chance of further deterioration. If there has been no deterioration and the CT scan was normal, they can then be discharged home. If there is uncertainty, or there are CT scan abnormalities, longer observation may be required to ensure that they will not develop late brain swelling.

Patients with severe head injury require intensive treatment from the first minute they attend. First, the airway should be cleared and secured by passing an endotracheal tube down the patient's airway (**intubation**). Through the tube, the patient is ventilated artificially until transfer to a specialist centre. The head and neck should be secured in case there is associated spinal injury.

If the patient was involved in a high-energy impact (for example, a road traffic accident), it is common for them to have other injuries such as a torn liver or spleen, or broken

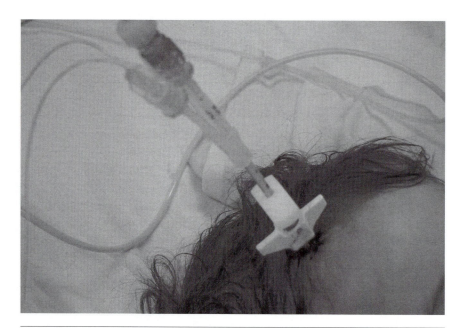

Figure 12.9 Intracranial pressure monitor (ICP bolt) secured on the skull of a patient following head injury.

long bones, from which they may have significant internal haemorrhage. An intravenous line is inserted and intravenous fluids administered to maintain adequate blood pressure.

Careful management of the patient in the first hour after severe trauma, with maintenance of adequate blood pressure and oxygenation, is crucial in improving the outcome. It is during this time that secondary injury begins, and hypoxia and hypotension may make this worse.

On arrival at the specialist centre, a CT scan is done to establish if there is intracranial damage. If there is any blood clot that needs evacuation, the patient is taken to the operating theatre as soon as possible and the clot is evacuated surgically. If there is only brain swelling, the patient is treated in intensive care.

A pressure monitor, to measure ICP, is inserted through a small incision in the scalp, as we can see in Figure 12.9. It is called a bolt because it screws on to the skull. A fine probe is then inserted through the hole in the skull which measures ICP. ICP is normally below 10–15 mmHg. An ICP of 15–20 mmHg is borderline but usually does not require treatment. However, an ICP above 20 mmHg for periods longer than a few minutes requires treatment with drugs, such as mannitol, to reduce swelling. If ICP rises above 40 mmHg for prolonged periods, **ischaemia** (reduction in blood flow) sets in and irreversible damage of brain tissue takes place.

SELF-CHECK 12.3

What is the importance of rising intracranial pressure and how can it be treated?

Other surgical treatments can be used to bring ICP down, such as insertion of a tube inside the ventricles of the brain to drain CSF, or removal of part of the skull to open up the rigid enclosure of the head. Treatment is continued until the ICP is down to normal. If ICP cannot be controlled, the patient will die.

What is the long-term outcome of TBI?

All patients who suffer head injury have a degree of **post-traumatic amnesia** (PTA). Commonly, the extent of PTA relates to the severity of head injury. This is often used to assess the severity of mild and moderate head injury, as it is a good indicator of the extent of cognitive and functional deficit after TBI.

Outcome following mild head injury is very good, often with no long-term problems. Many patients experience mild cognitive problems which settle within 3–6 months of the injury, although in a significant proportion long-term problems persist, affecting daily performance.

Outcome following moderate head injury is good from the survival point of view, but up to 40% experience long-term headaches, mood swings, anxiety, difficulties in concentration, and often social and professional problems due to emotional and behavioural disturbance. Social support is essential in order to maximize the chances of good recovery and social integration.

Good educational support is essential for children, who can suffer severe learning difficulties after moderate head injury. Up to 3% of patients who suffered moderate head injury can suffer from epilepsy in the long term. There is a 1% risk of **mortality** among adult patients with moderate head injury, usually from late deterioration after the injury.

Outcome from severe head injury varies. A GCS of 8 or less is associated with 48% mortality in adults and 28% in children.

Extradural haematoma has the best outcome of all causes of severe brain trauma, with an up to 25% risk of mortality and good functional outcome of those who survive. Subdural haematoma has up to 50% risk of mortality, and diffuse axonal injury has the worst prognosis of all, with up to 78% dying.

Survivors can have several problems ranging from headaches to cognitive deficits and severe neurological deficits, such as weakness or paralysis. A minority of survivors have few long-term problems and are functionally very good. Up to 20% of patients with severe head injury suffer from epilepsy in the long term.

Rehabilitation of patients who suffered TBI is a very important part of their overall management, and continues for several months, well after they have left the acute services. It contributes greatly to maximizing neurological recovery and to re-entry into the community.

12.2.2 Brain and spinal cord tumours

What tissue changes are caused by tumours of the nervous system?

Tumours of the nervous system can arise from overgrowth of:

- neurons (neuronal-neuroectodermal tumours)
- neuronal supportive cells—astrocytes (astrocytomas), oligodendrocytes (oligodendrogliomas), or ependymal cells (ependymomas), referred to collectively as gliomas
- supporting cells of the cranial nerves (schwannomas)
- meninges (meningiomas)
- other cell types (e.g. lymphoma, germinoma, craniopharyngioma).

Biological behaviour varies between tumours.

case study: Benign brain tumour: acoustic neuroma

BOX 12.4

A 32-year-old woman gradually noticed that she could not hear on the telephone. Her GP referred her to the local ear, nose, and throat (ENT) clinic who found that she had nerve deafness in the left ear.

As we can see in Figure 12.10, a CT scan showed a large mass in the left cerebellopontine angle, displacing the normal brain.

This was excised completely, leaving her deaf in the left ear but with no other deficit.

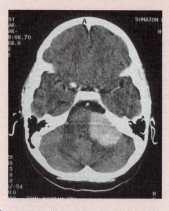

Figure 12.10 CT scan of a left acoustic neuroma.

Benign tumours usually compress and displace normal brain tissue, thereby disturbing the function of the structures that they compress. We give an example of a benign tumour in the case study described in Box 12.4.

In contrast to benign tumours, **malignant** tumours destroy and invade the surrounding brain or spinal cord. We describe an example of a malignant tumour, an astrocytoma, in the case study in Box 12.5. Because of the invasive properties of malignant tumours, surgery is not enough to combat tumour growth; at operation it is often impossible to differentiate normal from tumour tissue.

What are the symptoms and signs of tumours of the nervous system?

Tumours of the brain and spinal cord cause symptoms from compressing or infiltrating nearby normal structures. So, a tumour (e.g. a meningioma) compressing the motor cortex of the right hemisphere will present with a history of progressive weakness of the left arm or leg over a period of weeks.

Brain tumours can also cause symptoms not specific to their location, but from increasing ICP due to the growth of an expanding mass inside the closed box of the skull. Such symptoms include headaches and early morning vomiting.

SELF-CHECK 12.4

What is the difference between benign and malignant tumours?

Brain tumours give rise to symptoms and signs due to compression or infiltration of adjacent tissue and from increasing intracranial pressure.

---

case study: Malignant brain tumour: astrocytoma

BOX 12.5

A 4-year-old girl presented with attacks of jerking movements of her left hand which spread up the arm, then to the face, over 2 minutes (this is recognized as the typical Jacksonian march of focal motor epilepsy). She was a little confused afterwards.

Neurological examination showed that she had a mild left-sided weakness.

We can see her MRI scan in Figure 12.11, which shows a large mass in the right frontal lobe which invades the surrounding brain. An intraoperative biopsy showed that this was a malignant astrocytoma.

She was treated with surgery and radiotherapy but died 5 months later.

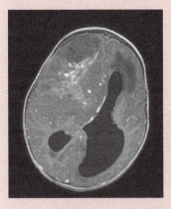

Figure 12.11 MRI of a malignant astrocytoma showing a large mass in the right frontal lobe which invades the surrounding brain.

What treatments are available for tumours of the nervous system?

Surgery for malignant tumours of neurons and glial cells is often restricted to removing as much of the abnormal tissue as appears safe at operation (this is known as **debulking**).

Adjuvant therapies are then used. **Radiotherapy** is often given to the entire brain and spine, irrespective of where the tumour is, as malignant tumours can spread through-out the nervous system. Most intrinsic brain tumours respond to radiotherapy, but unfortunately this treatment modality cannot be administered in children under the age of 3 years as it causes widespread destruction of the brain and spine.

Chemotherapy is given after surgery in certain types of malignant tumours, as they are responsive to various cytotoxic drugs. Often, a combination of radiotherapy and chemotherapy is given over many months following surgery.

In general, patients with malignant brain tumours spend considerable time in hospital for treatment, often without good outcome. As intrinsic tumours have a high risk of recurrence, patients may require many repeat scans for the first 5 years following surgery.

In contrast to tumours of neurons and glial cells, tumours that originate from cells external to the brain parenchyma (e.g. meningiomas and schwannomas) do not invade the normal brain or spinal cord and can be cured with surgery alone. An example of such a tumour can be seen in Figure 12.12.

(a)

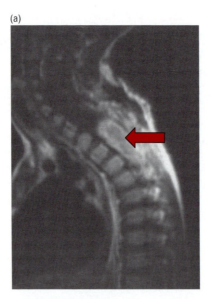

(b)

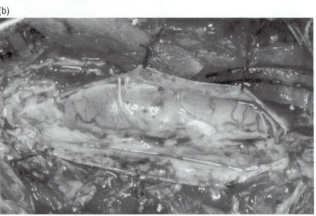

Figure 12.12 (a) Spinal MRI showing a ganglioglioma (arrow).
(b) An intraoperative photograph with the dura opened to reveal a
large tumour compressing the spinal cord.

However, in a small proportion of patients, even these tumours can recur after total
surgical excision, and for this reason patients require follow-up over a long period with
repeat scans.

Tumours of the spinal cord are not as common as brain tumours. Commonly, they cause
pain and weakness of arms or legs, and not uncommonly paralysis. They require surgical
excision and additional treatment depending on their malignancy.

SELF-CHECK 12.5

How can brain tumours be
treated?

If the stability of the spine is threatened, it may become necessary to stabilize the
bones with metal implants. Children treated for spinal cord tumour have a high risk of
developing spinal deformity years after surgery, and may require additional operations
to fix the spine with prosthetic metal implants to prevent further deterioration.

What is the long-term outcome of tumours of the nervous system?

Slower-growing benign tumours have a better outcome and can often be treated successfully with surgery alone. However, even benign tumours can recur years after the first surgery, requiring repeat surgical excision.

In contrast, malignant tumours have considerably worse outcome. Surgery alone is usually not enough to prevent the tumour from regrowing. Additional treatment in the form of radiotherapy or chemotherapy is necessary to control regrowth, and even then it is sometimes impossible to completely eradicate the tumour.

The severity of malignancy varies and different grading systems are used to classify malignant tumours. Survival varies from 5% to 50% in 5 years, depending on the type of tumour and severity of malignancy. Quality of life depends on the extent of neurological deficit before surgery and the severity of malignancy of the tumour.

12.2.3 **Neurovascular disorders**

The commonest neurovascular abnormalities that we see are:

- **arterial aneurysms** leading to subarachnoid haemorrhage
- **arteriovenous malformations** (AVM), which are abnormal blood vessels of medium calibre that form in a cluster within the substance of the brain; they directly connect the arterial to the venous circulation, thereby diverting blood from the brain substance
- **cavernous angiomas**, which are abnormal collections of small calibre vessels that form a small mass within the brain substance.

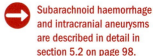 Subarachnoid haemorrhage and intracranial aneurysms are described in detail in section 5.2 on page 98.

Arteriovenous malformations

AVMs are formations of abnormal blood vessels that shunt blood from the arterial to the venous part of the circulation inside the brain. As a result, the part of the brain that would receive blood from these vessels cannot function properly. This is called a **steal phenomenon** as blood is being stolen from the brain, thus preventing it from functioning normally.

The high flow of blood within the malformation leads to growth of the vessels and eventually to rupture and haemorrhage which can be life threatening. Symptoms are similar to those of a ruptured aneurysm. AVMs can also present with epilepsy due to irritation of surrounding brain tissue, and headaches and weakness from malfunction of the adjacent brain due to the steal phenomenon.

Most AVMs are congenital but present clinically later on in life, at all ages but typically in the second and third decade of life.

As we can see by looking at Figure 12.13a, haemorrhage from an AVM is confirmed with a CT scan. An intracerebral clot may need to be evacuated surgically as an emergency, depending on the clinical condition of the patient. All patients with a suspected AVM will have an **angiogram** to establish the diagnosis, and an image demonstrating the abnormal collection of blood vessels is shown in Figure 12.13b.

Some malformations are too large to be excised directly so have to be shrunk by injecting a glue-like material that blocks up some of the abnormal vessels. There is also

(a)

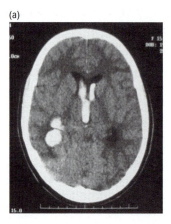

(b)

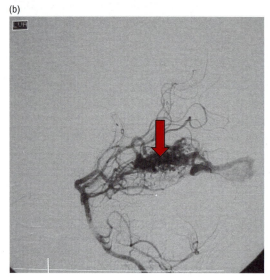

Figure 12.13 (a) CT scan of an arteriovenous malformation with blood in the ventricles and a haematoma in the right temporal lobe. (b) Digital subtraction angiography of same patient showing the AVM as an abnormal collection of blood vessels emerging from the right posterior cerebral artery (arrow).

the option to treat AVMs with stereotactic radiotherapy (radiosurgery). In this technique, a highly collimated beam of radiation is directed onto the AVM which over-heats and destroys the abnormal blood vessels. This can take up to 2 years to occlude the malformation.

The prognosis for AVMs is good, and the risk to life is much smaller than with aneurysms. Disability relates to the part of the brain that is affected.

Cavernous angiomas

Cavernous angiomas are small round lesions around 1–2 cm in diameter which are formed by abnormal blood vessels of small calibre. They present with intraparenchymal haemorrhage, epilepsy or dysfunction of surrounding brain.

A particular feature of cavernous angiomas is that they are frequently seen in highly crucial parts of the brain such as the thalamus or the brain stem. Sudden haemorrhage can cause devastating loss of neurological function or even death.

If we look at the CT scan of a cavernous angioma in Figure 12.14, we see the characteristic white round haemorrhage. MRI shows more details of these lesions. For reasons that are not understood, cavernous angiomas do not show up on angiography.

Treatment of cavernous angiomas depends on many factors, but many are best left untreated. The outcome of surgical excision varies according to the location of the lesion, how accessible it is, and how much damage was done by the haemorrhage. Sometimes multiple operations are necessary. Outcome is good provided that no permanent damage has taken place.

12.2.4 Hydrocephalus

We have already seen in Chapter 1 that the brain has four cavities within it called ventricles, which contain CSF. Throughout the day, 500 mL of CSF are produced which circulates in and around the brain and the spinal cord before being absorbed back into the bloodstream.

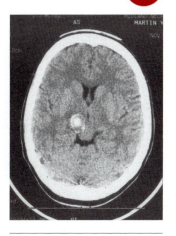

Figure 12.14 CT scan of a cavernous angioma with a round high-attenuation lesion (fresh haemorrhage) in the region of the right thalamus.

Hydrocephalus is due to obstruction of the CSF pathways within or outside the brain by a lesion (for example a tumour or a cyst) or congenital maldevelopment of the pathways (for example, **stenosis** of the aqueduct between the third and fourth ventricles).

In patients who have suffered brain injury or infection (such as meningitis), the site of CSF absorption in the head can be blocked by blood or infective material, causing hydrocephalus. On rare occasions, overproduction of CSF can be caused by tumours of the choroid plexus, the structure within the ventricles that produces the CSF.

 The ventricular system and the production and circulation of CSF are described in section 1.2.3 on page 5.

Hydrocephalus commonly presents in the first few years of life, in young adults, or in the fifth and sixth decades of life. The normal pressure of CSF inside the ventricles is below 12 mmHg, equal to the ICP. When hydrocephalus develops, ICP increases, and this is responsible for the symptoms.

Symptoms vary according to the age at presentation. Infants develop enlargement of the head circumference. Later the anterior fontanelle (the soft spot on the top of the baby's head) becomes full. If they are left untreated, they develop downward gaze, progressive lethargy, problems with breathing, and irregular circulation, and eventually stop breathing and die.

Older children develop headaches, blurred vision, poor school performance, vomiting, lethargy, and drowsiness; again, if left untreated, death may result. Young adults develop headaches, drowsiness, and progressive coma. Older adults develop difficulties with walking, intellectual decline, and urinary incontinence.

Neuroimaging with CT or MRI shows enlargement of the ventricles of the brain and any causative lesion. Examples of this can be see in the top two images of Figure 12.15.

There is no medical treatment for hydrocephalus; only surgery can control the accumulation of CSF. If the cause of hydrocephalus is a brain tumour, surgical excision usually resolves the build-up of CSF. In other circumstances, surgical treatment of hydrocephalus is achieved with redirection of CSF either internally in the brain or externally outside the brain.

(a)

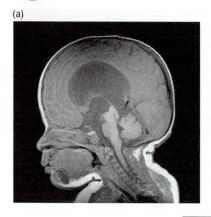

(b)

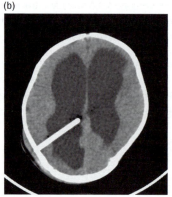

(c)

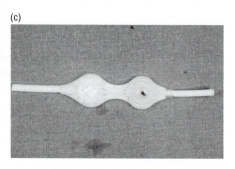

Figure 12.15 (a) MRI showing hydrocephalus which presented in a 6-month-old girl with increasing head circumference. Dilatation of the lateral and third ventricles is seen but not the fourth ventricle, suggesting obstruction of the aqueduct of Sylvius. (b) CT scan of a 14-month-old boy with postmeningitic hydrocephalus showing a shunt catheter in the right lateral ventricle. (c) A shunt valve with an inlet tube, the valve mechanism, and an outlet catheter.

Internal redirection of CSF can be achieved using a neuroendoscope. This small flexible or rigid telescope is inserted into the ventricles through the brain and can be used to create small holes in the walls of the ventricles to redirect the CSF. It is suitable for patients with aqueduct stenosis where a hole or stoma is made in the floor of the third ventricle. It can also be used to treat cysts in the brain by making holes in the walls of the cyst to collapse it.

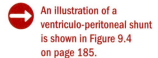

An illustration of a ventriculo-peritoneal shunt is shown in Figure 9.4 on page 185.

In many circumstances, a plastic tube system called a **shunt** is used to redirect the CSF out of the ventricles and into another place in the body, usually the abdominal cavity or the heart. As we can see in Figure 12.15c, the shunt system contains a tube which is inserted in to the ventricle, a one-way valve which controls the flow of fluid and which maintains normal pressure inside the ventricles by not allowing too much or too little fluid to flow, and a catheter which goes from the valve to the peritoneal cavity in the abdomen. The shunt is implanted under the skin and is not visible.

The most common complication of shunts is blockage. This occurs in 30% of patients in the first year after implantation, 50% in the first 5 years, and 80% by 10 years. When a shunt blocks, an operation is needed to replace the blocked part.

Another problem is infection, which can happen during surgery for implantation but may take months to declare itself. Infection requires removal of the shunt, temporary drainage of the CSF to an external bag, treatment with antibiotics to clear the infection, and implantation of a new shunt when the infection has cleared. Shunt infection in children is associated with intellectual impairment, so its prevention is paramount. A less common problem is shunt overdrainage, which may require surgical change of the type of the valve.

Shunts revolutionized the outcome of hydrocephalic patients. Before shunts were introduced in the 1950s, 80% of patients with hydrocephalus died and the survivors were mentally handicapped. Today, provided that the shunt is looked after correctly, patients are expected to survive indefinitely and death from hydrocephalus is rare.

Some children have other problems such as brain damage secondary to intraventricular haemorrhage, meningitis, or other congenital abnormalities, and these problems dictate their intellectual outcome. In the absence of other problems, outcome of hydrocephalus is very good.

SELF-CHECK 12.6

What is hydrocephalus and how can it be treated?

> If there is any obstruction to the circulation of CSF, build up of fluid occurs ahead of the obstruction. This accumulation of CSF inside the brain is called hydrocephalus.

12.3 **Neurosurgical tools**

Major technological developments over the last three decades have had a major impact on the development of neurosurgery. Some of these are listed below and we can see examples of them in Figure 12.16.

- Introduction of the operating microscope in the late 1970s provided illumination and magnification together with stereoscopic vision. This revolutionized intracranial surgery for brain tumours and vascular malformations.

- Development of the Cavitron ultrasonic surgical aspirator (CUSA) in the late 1980s dramatically improved the removal of brain tumours, allowing bigger excisions with less trauma to surrounding brain tissue.

(a)

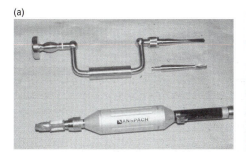

(b)

(c)

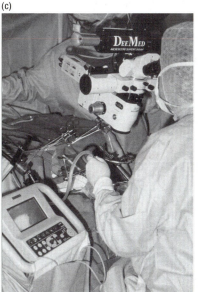

Figure 12.16 (a) Hudson brace and pneumatic drill, both designed to drill holes in the skull. (b) Cavitron ultrasonic surgical aspirator (CUSA) designed to liquefy brain tumours to facilitate their removal. The tip of the probe seen on the small table is used inside the head and the large equipment behind produces the ultrasonic pulses that break down the tumour. (c) Neurosurgeon removing a brain tumour, using the microscope to facilitate vision.

- Introduction of MRI in the 1990s enabled the brain and spinal cord to be visualized with a considerably higher level of detail.

In addition, neurosurgeons use many power tools to open the skull, or drill parts of the skull or spine. They use many prosthetic materials such as metal rods and screws to stabilize the bones of the spine or metal plates to repair damage to the craniofacial bones. The coupling of improved neuroimaging with these surgical tools in image-guided surgical equipment will provide an even higher level of refinement in the future. Progress in neurosurgery is intimately linked with such technological developments.

SUMMARY

- Surgery of the CNS has potentially severe risks and complications.
- Head injury or traumatic brain injury (TBI) is the commonest cause of death in children and young adults and the commonest cause of severe disability in young adults.
- Primary brain injury can lead to extradural haematoma, subdural haematoma, intracerebral haematoma, brain contusion, and diffuse axonal injury.
- The Glasgow Coma Score (GCS) was developed as a universal grading scale for head-injured patients which facilitates communication between primary and secondary treatment centres.
- Intracranial pressure (ICP) is monitored in severe head injury with an ICP monitoring device.

- Rising ICP is treated with mannitol, insertion of a ventricular drain, and/or removal of any intra-parenchymal haematoma.
- Brain tumours give rise to symptoms and signs due to compression or infiltration of adjacent tissue, and increasing ICP.
- Benign tumours usually compress and displace normal brain tissue, thereby disturbing the function of the structures that they compress.
- Malignant tumours destroy and invade the surrounding brain or spinal cord.
- Brain tumours can be treated with surgery, radiotherapy, and chemotherapy.
- If there is any obstruction to the circulation of CSF, fluid builds up ahead of the obstruction. This accumulation of CSF inside the brain is called hydrocephalus.

FURTHER READING

F. Ali-Osman. *Brain tumours*. Totowa, NJ: Humana Press, 2005.
A comprehensive review of brain tumours.

G. Cinalli, W. J. Maixner, and C. Sainte-Rose. *Pediatric hydrocephalus*. Milano: Springer, 2004.
A clear and comprehensive account of the various forms of hydrocephalus in children.

S. S. Rengachary and R. G. Ellenbogen. *Principles of neurosurgery*, 2nd edn. Philadelphia: Elsevier, 2004.
An entry-level book on neurosurgery, offering clear explanations of the principles of neurosurgical diseases.

G. Teasdale and B. Jennet. Assessment of coma and impaired consciousness. A practical scale. *Lancet* 1974; 2(7872); 81–84.
The seminal publication of the Glasgow Coma Scale, which transformed the management of head injuries.

A. C. Williams. Patient care in neurology. Oxford: Oxford University Press, 1999.
Offers a good account of neurological and neurosurgical disorders, at an intermediate/advanced level.

CHAPTER THIRTEEN

Anxiety and related disorders

Tom Clark

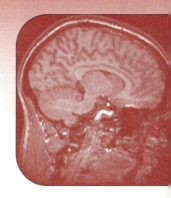

INTRODUCTION

In this chapter we look at psychiatric disorders that are characterized by anxiety. First of all we look at the normal human emotion of anxiety and consider how we recognize when anxiety becomes pathological. Then we look at the symptoms and signs of the five main anxiety disorders, before considering their causes, epidemiology, and treatment. The disorders considered in this chapter are:

- generalized anxiety disorder
- panic disorder
- phobic anxiety disorders
- post-traumatic stress disorder
- obsessive-compulsive disorder.

13.1 Normal anxiety

Anxiety is a normal human emotion—everyone experiences it on occasions. Indeed, it is an important part of our response to stress and in some situations it is useful and adaptive. For example, musicians and sportspeople tend to regard a degree of anxiety as important in determining top performance. Similarly, it is helpful for students to experience some anxiety before exams, as this may improve performance. But if the anxiety is too severe, or occurs in situations in which it is not adaptive, then it may be regarded as pathological.

> Anxiety is a normal and important human emotion, which is usually not pathological.

Some people are **dispositionally** anxious. This means that their personality is such that they tend to experience anxiety and tension more than most people. Such individuals

Table 13.1 Components of anxiety

Abnormal mood state	Fearfulness
	Apprehension
Abnormal thinking style	More likely to think that something bad will happen
	Less likely to feel able to cope with it
Increased arousal	Restlessness
	Irritability
	Difficulty sleeping
	Sensitivity to noise
Somatic symptoms	Increased heart rate
	Palpitations
	Sweating
	Dry mouth
	Tremor
	Shortness of breath
	Chest tightness
	Urinary frequency
	Diarrhoea
	Headaches
	Muscular pains and tension
Changes in behaviour	Reduced purposeful behaviour
	Restless purposeless behaviour
	Avoidance of anxiety-provoking situations

SELF-CHECK 13.1

What is the difference between dispositional anxiety and an acute anxiety disorder?

have been like this since their adolescence, and will probably always be like this. They tend to meet all of life's challenges with an excessive degree of anxiety and may feel that they cannot cope with such challenges. This dispositional anxiety is rather different from the more acute anxiety states or mental illnesses that we will discuss in this chapter. But anxiety-related disorders are more likely to occur in people with a **pre-morbidly** anxious personality.

Table 13.1 shows us the symptoms and signs associated with anxiety. The essential feature seems to be a subjective sense of fear and apprehension, so the fear is directed towards the future and related to some perceived threat. It has been demonstrated that individuals who are prone to anxiety tend to think in two characteristic ways. They are more likely to think that something bad will happen to them, and they are less likely to think that they will be able to cope with this. It is easy to see how these two types of thought may combine to make someone anxious.

The changes in behaviour are also important. The student described in Box 13.1 is demonstrating reduced purposeful activity by not revising as much as he should, and restless, purposeless activity by doing the washing up. His tendency to do the house-work rather than revise may also be seen as an avoidance strategy: revising is liable to

---

case study: Normal anxiety

BOX 13.1

A 21-year-old male undergraduate had his final examinations approaching. He began to find that he was revising less than he knew he should (constriction of purposeful activity), and he found himself doing the washing up and even getting out the vacuum cleaner occasionally (restless purposeless activity).

Although he had always passed previous exams, he couldn't help worrying that this time he would fail. As the exams approached, his sleep began to deteriorate. He coped with this by drinking a moderate amount of alcohol at night.

On the day of the exam, he felt increasingly anxious, his palms were sweaty, his mouth was dry, and he had to go to the toilet three times before entering the examination hall.

---

remind him of the forthcoming examination, and therefore may exacerbate his anxiety. Avoidance strategies are of great importance in maintaining anxiety disorders, and therapeutic approaches are often based on enabling a patient to repeatedly experience their anxiety.

This student also begins to experience some of the physical or somatic symptoms of anxiety as his exams approach. These are predominantly mediated by the sympathetic division of the autonomic nervous system. This is responsible for the 'flight or fight' response—the way in which an individual responds physiologically to threat or danger. The autonomic nervous system is not under conscious control. Target organ synapses are activated physiologically by adrenaline or noradrenaline. The symptoms are important in perpetuating anxiety, and peripheral adrenergic receptors may be manipulated pharmacologically in treating anxiety disorders.

> Avoidance strategies are very important in maintaining anxiety disorders and as a target for therapeutic intervention.

Of course, usually when we feel anxious about something we do not experience all of these components, but the more severe the anxiety, the more of these we may feel. It may be difficult to decide when the anxiety experienced by an individual should be considered pathological, or in need of medical attention.

There are two aspects to consider: situation and degree.

In some cases, the **situation** in which the anxiety occurs may suggest a pathological process. For example, in phobic anxiety disorders, the anxiety is out of proportion to the demands of the stimulus. A patient who experiences significant anxiety when confronted by a spider may be considered to have a phobia, but the same degree of anxiety before making one's first parachute jump may be considered entirely normal.

However, in other cases the **degree** of anxiety described by the patient is of itself so severe that it is clearly beyond normal experience.

SELF-CHECK 13.2

What factors are important to consider in deciding whether anxiety is pathological or not?

13.2 What are the symptoms and signs of anxiety-related disorders?

For all of these disorders the central symptom of anxiety is the same. They are distinguished by other associated symptoms, or by the different ways in which the anxiety presents.

13.2.1 Generalized anxiety disorder

People who suffer from generalized anxiety disorder (GAD) are always anxious. Their anxiety is not related to any particular circumstance or situation. Such patients complain of a persistent feeling of tension and apprehension, and may appear on the verge of tears. They are likely to experience a variety of the physical symptoms of anxiety. The degree of anxiety is not usually as severe as that experienced by patients with some of the other disorders in this chapter (such as panic disorder and phobic anxiety disorders), but GAD may be extremely disabling because of the persistent and relentless nature of the anxiety.

SELF-CHECK 13.3

What aspect of the anxiety in generalized anxiety disorder leads to it being particularly disabling?

This sense of subjective tension and apprehension dominates a patient's life from waking in the morning until they go to sleep at night. Typically they will struggle to get to sleep at night and then will wake frequently throughout the night. This poor sleep is likely to exacerbate the irritability and short temper that is also a feature of the disorder. The anxiety pervades their whole life and may have a very significant effect on their ability to work effectively, on their relationship with their spouse or children, or on other aspects of their life.

13.2.2 Panic disorder

Panic disorder is characterized by episodic anxiety. So, in contrast to GAD, patients with panic disorder do not feel anxious most of the time. However, they experience repeated episodes of acute anxiety (panic attacks) of great severity. These attacks of anxiety begin suddenly and develop quickly, usually reaching a peak within 10 minutes. The attack may last for up to 30 minutes before gradually beginning to subside. It is common for patients to be left feeling tense, tremulous, or physically exhausted for some hours afterwards.

In Table 13.2, we can see common symptoms that occur during panic attacks. Many of these have already been mentioned before as common symptoms of anxiety. It is particularly common for patients with panic disorder to describe a severe sense of impending doom, imminent death, or going mad. Even if the patient has experienced panic attacks many times before, they may continue to experience these thoughts in the throes of their panic. Depersonalization is an unpleasant feeling of unreality, or detachment from surroundings.

In panic disorder, in contrast to the phobic anxiety disorders described below, the panic attacks are unpredictable, and not associated with any specific stimulus. However, it is

Table 13.2 Symptoms of panic attacks

Rapidly escalating anxiety and panic
Racing or pounding heartbeat
Flushing and sweating
Shortness of breath and chest pain
Dizziness or lightheadedness
Nausea
Tingling or numbness
Tremulousness
Depersonalization
A fear of losing control, going mad, or impending death

quite common for situational anxiety to develop in patients with panic disorder. For example, an individual may begin to feel particularly anxious about the prospect of experiencing a panic attack in public, or away from home. The patient may become house-bound, and their panic disorder may merge into a presentation typical of agoraphobia (see below).

SELF-CHECK 13.4

How long do panic attacks usually last?

13.2.3 Phobic anxiety disorders

In some ways phobic anxiety disorders are similar to panic disorders. Patients experience panic attacks in just the same way as patients with panic disorder. Between attacks they are characteristically free of anxiety, but phobic anxiety disorders differ in that panic attacks only occur in response to a particular, well-defined situation. To this extent they are predictable in a way that the anxiety of panic disorder is not. Furthermore, the anxiety is out of proportion to the demands of the stimulus. It is frequently recognized as silly or irrational, but despite this the patient cannot reason it away or prevent themselves from feeling anxious. As a result of their anxiety, patients avoid the anxiety-provoking situation. This avoidance is very important because by avoiding the stimulus, and thereby avoiding the experience of anxiety, patients perpetuate their own disorder.

The term phobia is used commonly in English with a variety of different prefixes. So a fear of spiders is known as arachnophobia and a fear of small enclosed spaces as claustrophobia. However, in psychiatric classifications only three forms of phobia are recognized: agoraphobia, social phobia, and specific phobias.

> Phobic anxiety disorders are characterized by anxiety which is out of proportion to the demands of the stimulus, and consequent avoidance of the stimulus.

Agoraphobia

Agoraphobia occurs much more commonly in women than in men. It is a term that is literally translated as a fear of the market place, and has come to mean a fear of crowds, or a fear of open spaces. None of these accurately reflects the clinical picture of agoraphobia.

The usual presentation is of a patient who becomes anxious when they are away from home or in situations that they cannot leave easily. Typically the disorder starts when the patient unexpectedly experiences a panic attack while away from home. As a result of this they rush home and eventually the panic dissipates. Subsequently the patient associates their experience of panic attacks with being away from home. This leads to the patient becoming increasingly housebound, and often increasingly dependent on others, such as friends or their partner, to run errands for them.

It can be seen that agoraphobia has much in common with panic disorder. The initial panic attack is often unpredictable and characteristic of panic disorder. Even when patients become housebound they often experience unpredictable panic attacks in addition to their anxiety related to leaving home. It is also notable that these patients often experience a great deal of anticipatory anxiety even when they are at home, so it may resemble GAD as well.

Social phobia

Social phobia is a fear of being in situations in which one is expected to perform socially or in which one may be subject to critical observation by others. So it is often manifest as a fear of social gatherings, working on committees or in small groups, or eating or drinking in public.

In contrast to agoraphobia it is equally common among both men and women, and it has its onset at an earlier age, usually in adolescence. To this extent it may be seen as initially developmentally appropriate, in that it is normal for adolescents to be some-what socially awkward. In most people this improves as they grow older and mature. When encountered in adults, social phobia may be seen as an abnormal persistence of this normal developmental stage.

Often patients complain of symptoms that would be observable to others and perhaps humiliating, such as blushing, trembling, or vomiting in public. Alcohol and substance misuse are very common in social phobia, because these substances may reduce a patient's anxiety while intoxicated. This may be seen as a reflection of the adaptive and socially acceptable use of alcohol (and illegal drugs within certain subcultures) as social lubricants.

---

case study: Specific phobia

BOX 13.2

A 35-year-old man has a fear of moths. He has always disliked moths, for as long as he can remember. He remembers as a child that if there were a moth in his bedroom when he went to bed he would have to kill it or otherwise remove it from his room before he could go to sleep.

Even as an adult he becomes anxious if he is in enclosed spaces with a moth, and he takes steps to avoid them. For example, if he opens the front door of the house at night, he ensures that the hall light is turned off so that the moths outside are not attracted in. He knows that moths cannot hurt him but he cannot stop himself from feeling anxious in their presence.

It puzzles him that he feels so anxious around moths but does not have a similar anxiety relating to butterflies, which seem superficially similar.

Often social phobia is difficult to distinguish from people who have an abnormal personality characterized by anxiety, shyness, or low self-esteem. So psychological treatment approaches targeting these underlying dispositional characteristics may be beneficial, as well as approaches aimed more specifically at social anxiety.

Specific phobias

All other phobias are termed specific phobias. A fear of animals is particularly common, as is a fear of dental treatment, of flying, or of blood and injections. These phobias typically begin in childhood and in many cases the patient will be able to recall a specific incident that led to their fear. As with social phobias, they may be seen as developmentally appropriate when they begin in childhood. Specific phobias are extremely common, but relatively few come to medical attention.

> **SELF-CHECK 13.5**
>
> How many different types of phobic anxiety disorder are recognized in contemporary psychiatric classifications?

13.2.4 Post-traumatic stress disorder

Post-traumatic stress disorder (PTSD) is almost unique among psychiatric disorders in that the disorder is in part defined by the assumed cause. The ability of significantly stressful events to produce long-standing psychological **morbidity** has been recognized for well over 100 years, particularly in relation to armed conflict. Shell shock and battle fatigue were commonly used terms in the First World War, and in the late 1960s the experiences of US soldiers in Vietnam led to the disorder gaining increasing prominence within psychiatry and expanding beyond the medical arena, into day-to-day usage.

PTSD is characterized by the presence of four groups of symptoms, which are illustrated in Box 13.3 and described below. These symptoms may develop immediately after the stressful event, but in many patients there is an initial period of normal functioning, the onset of symptoms being delayed for up to 6 months in some cases.

---

case study: Post-traumatic stress disorder **BOX 13.3**

A policeman presented to see a psychiatrist. He had been on the beat for 20 years. Six months previously, while off duty, he had come across a group of youths on the street vandalizing a car. He had approached them and told them to stop it, but rather than running off as he had anticipated, they assaulted him.

They did not cause serious physical injuries, but the assault so shook his confidence that he struggled to get over it and return to his job. Amongst other symptoms he complained that on repeated occasions every day, memories of the assault would enter his mind. These memories would be so vivid that he would feel the sense of anxiety he had felt originally when he was assaulted. It felt, to him, almost as though he was being assaulted again. He complained of avoiding going out of the house after dark, for fear he would be assaulted again.

His alcohol intake had begun to increase and his wife complained that he was increasingly irritable and tended to lose his temper at the slightest provocation. This was in contrast to his previously placid personality. His sleep was usually interrupted at night, he had stopped socializing with long-standing friends, and he had not played golf, previously his main hobby, for months.

Re-experiencing phenomena

The cardinal re-experiencing phenomenon is the **flashback**. A flashback occurs when the individual subjectively feels as though they are re-living their traumatic event. They may re-experience the sensations, thoughts and emotion they felt at the time, and in severe cases may even behave as they did at the time. Other re-experiencing phenomena are repetitive, intrusive thoughts or memories of the traumatic event, and recurrent nightmares.

Avoidance behaviour

Individuals with PTSD usually avoid things that remind them of the traumatic event. An individual who has symptoms of PTSD after a car accident may avoid travelling in cars, or may avoid the road or area in which the accident occurred. Patients also commonly complain of symptoms of **anhedonia** (an inability to enjoy life), reduced emotional responsiveness, social withdrawal, and reduced experience of pain or pleasure. They may tend to withdraw into fantasy and engage less well with their real life, with friends or family. They may also find that they engage in excessive pointless activity, always having to keep busy and active. All of these symptoms may be seen as strategies for avoiding the anxiety that is associated with the stressful event.

Hypervigilance

Individuals with PTSD feel subjectively on edge, tense, and unable to relax. Sleep is typically impaired, individuals feeling that they sleep more lightly than before, and that they do not feel rested in the mornings. Often they wake up repeatedly during the night. They are more irritable than usual, more likely to lose their temper and be distractable, with impaired concentration and memory. They may also complain of being oversensitive to noise. This may lead to an observable increased startle reaction, shown for example when they jump in response to a door being slammed.

Associated symptoms

> **SELF-CHECK 13.6**
>
> What are the four groups of symptoms that are characteristic of PTSD?

Finally, it is very important to be aware of the associated problems of depressive mental illness and substance misuse which may complicate PTSD. Alcohol and drug misuse are common problems because they may help to mask the symptoms of anxiety and re-experiencing phenomena. This may be seen as a way of self-medicating to reduce anxiety, or as an avoidance strategy which impedes treatment. It is also very important to exclude co-morbid depression because this may be relatively easy to treat, in comparison to the underlying PTSD.

13.2.5 Obsessive-compulsive disorder

Obsessive-compulsive disorder (OCD) is characterized by the symptoms of obsessions and compulsions. Anxiety is an important associated symptom.

Obsessions are repetitive, intrusive stereotyped thoughts, images, or impulses that are resisted by the patient but recognized as their own. This means that the obsessional thought repeatedly enters a patient's mind. The patient may well recognize that the thought is untrue, irrational, or even foolish, but despite trying, they cannot stop themselves from thinking it. It is intrusive in the sense that it seems to push its way to the front of their mind even when they are engaged in some other unrelated task. 'Stereotyped' means that it occurs in just the same way each time. Despite all this, the patient recognizes the obsession as being a product of their own mind, thus differentiating obsessions from the symptom of thought insertion, which is characteristic of schizophrenia.

Compulsions are voluntary motor actions which are performed reluctantly despite being recognized as silly or absurd. They are almost always associated with an accompanying obsession, and a compulsion is designed to reduce the anxiety which the obsession causes.

Any thought or impulse may be obsessional in nature, but it is particularly common for obsessions to centre around themes of dirt or contamination, obscenities or blasphemies, abhorrent sexual practices, orderliness, tidiness, or the possible presence of serious illness in the patient. Often obsessions are particularly distressing because their content is so abhorrent to the patient, and it is difficult for them to understand why they would think such a thing. A good and common example of this is seen in new mothers who report experiencing distressing images of their baby coming to harm. They might repeatedly experience an intrusive image of dropping their baby as they carry it down the stairs.

 See section 15.1.1 on page 307 for a description of the psychotic symptom of thought insertion.

SELF-CHECK 13.7

What are the commonest types of obsessional thought?

---

case study: Obsessive-compulsive disorder   **BOX 13.4**

A 24-year-old woman was referred to see a psychiatrist by her GP. She had always been a somewhat anxious, fastidious, and tidy person but over the last 6 months her family were complaining that this was becoming intolerable. She was constantly cleaning the house, had given up all of her previous hobbies and interests, and was struggling to cope with her part-time job. On occasion she would stay up until the early hours of the morning cleaning and then would get up and clean before going to work the next morning.

She was becoming increasingly irritable with her husband and two young children because she felt that they were not helping her to keep the house clean. She had begun to insist that the children bathed at least three times every day. She was changing all the sheets on the beds in the house every day. She insisted that her family changed their clothes as soon as they came into the house from outside and she repeatedly washed her hands up to 20 times a day, to the extent that the skin on her hands was becoming red and inflamed because of the repeated scrubbing with a nail brush.

She acknowledged to the psychiatrist that she was becoming stressed by these issues and finding it difficult to cope. But she said she was troubled repeatedly with the thought that her children or the house were dirty, and that as a result her children might develop some infection or serious illness.

With regard to the hand washing, she said that washing her hands makes her feel more relaxed for a period of time but then the thoughts that her hands are dirty, and that she might spread some infection or disease, recur. Although she knows that she does not have any infection, the thought will not go away. She becomes increasingly stressed and tense and the only strategy that resolves these feelings is washing her hands. Unfortunately it only works for a short period. Then the thoughts and associated tension return.

13.3 What causes anxiety disorders?

Anxiety disorders have multiple causes. These may be factors that make an individual more likely to develop an anxiety disorder at some stage, or factors that actually precipitate an episode of illness in a predisposed individual. Such factors may be thought of as being biological, psychological, or environmental, but in practice these three broad categories interact with each other and may not be wholly distinct from one other.

13.3.1 Genetics

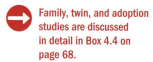
Family, twin, and adoption studies are discussed in detail in Box 4.4 on page 68.

Family studies demonstrate that in general, anxiety disorders run in families. So, the relatives of a patient with an anxiety disorder show an increased rate not just of that disorder, but of all anxiety disorders. Similarly, twin studies suggest that rather than inheriting specific anxiety disorders, a more general tendency to **neuroticism** is inherited, which may become manifest clinically as any of the disorders in this chapter. There are no adequate and relevant adoption studies. The anxiety disorders for which there is best evidence of a specific genetic contribution are panic disorder and OCD.

It seems likely that all individuals have a varying predisposition to develop anxiety or neurotic disorders, and that this is in part determined genetically. The actual mental illness that they develop depends on the degree of that predisposition and various other environmental or other precipitating factors.

> The evidence for a strong genetic contribution to specific anxiety disorders is limited, but there is a genetic contribution to a more general tendency to anxiety.

13.3.2 Environmental stressors

It is usual for anxiety disorders to be precipitated by some life event or stressor. This might be losing a job, the break-up of a marriage, the death of a spouse, some physical illness, or any other stressful situation. Often it seems that such an event has tipped an individual who had some previous dispositional tendency to anxiety 'over the edge', into a more severe anxiety state. An individual may experience repeated episodes of their disorder at times of stress, with relatively good mental health in between.

In addition to these precipitating factors, environmental factors may also be important in predisposing an individual to develop anxiety disorders in later life. Major factors during childhood that may be associated with an increased likelihood of neurotic mental illness include a history of childhood physical, sexual or emotional abuse, inconsistent parenting, and difficulties in peer relationships.

PTSD warrants special mention here. It is the only psychiatric disorder that by definition is caused by a stressful environmental event. Current classifications suggest that the event which led to the disorder should be severe enough to cause such distress in anyone. This implies that predisposing vulnerabilities, such as predispositional anxiety, are not relevant. In clinical practice, psychiatrists see symptoms of PTSD after varying degrees of psychological trauma. The greater the predispositional tendency to neurosis, the less the degree of environmental stressor required to precipitate neurosis.

13.3.3 Psychological theories

Psychodynamic theories

Psychodynamic theories began with the work of Sigmund Freud, who was mostly concerned with anxiety neuroses. These theories all have in common the idea that neurotic symptoms and anxiety in the present are a function of some disturbance or problem in early life. This may relate to problems in forming attachments to parental figures, to encountering difficulties during particular hypothetical stages of childhood development, or even to issues in the prenatal environment.

Psychoanalytic theory is introduced in section 4.3.4 on page 72.

Cognitive behavioural theories

People who are prone to suffer anxiety disorders tend to overestimate the likelihood of bad things happening to them, and tend to lack confidence that they will be able to cope with those things. These thoughts are liable to lead to a vulnerability to anxiety.

Also, patients with anxiety disorders tend to have greater fears than others about the physical symptoms of anxiety. This leads to a vicious circle of anxiety in which thoughts, emotions, and somatic symptoms combine to lead to ever-increasing levels of anxiety, and this is illustrated in Figure 13.1. This theory is commonly used therapeutically to help patients understand how their panic attacks escalate.

Avoidance behaviour is characteristic of all anxiety disorders. Patients with phobic anxiety disorders avoid experiencing anxiety by avoiding the anxiety-provoking stimulus. Patients with OCD avoid anxiety by performing their compulsions promptly. Patients with PTSD avoid things that remind them of the traumatic event, and all of these patients may also avoid anxiety by taking alcohol or other drugs, or by withdrawing socially. It is postulated that this avoidance leads to potentiation of the association of the stimulus with the anxiety, so this avoidance is itself perpetuating and exacerbating the disorder. This concept is used in psychological treatment of all anxiety disorders.

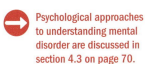
Psychological approaches to understanding mental disorder are discussed in section 4.3 on page 70.

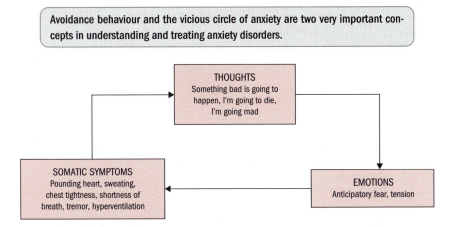

> Avoidance behaviour and the vicious circle of anxiety are two very important concepts in understanding and treating anxiety disorders.

Figure 13.1 A vicious circle of anxiety. Patients with panic disorder are more likely than others to interpret physical symptoms negatively.

13.3.4 Neurophysiology

Neuroanatomy

There is considerable circumstantial evidence for involvement of the structures of the **limbic system** in generating both normal anxiety and anxiety disorders. In animal studies stimulation of the limbic system produces fear. A human corollary of this occurs in temporal lobe epilepsy, of which fear and anxiety are common symptoms. In severe and treatment-resistant cases of OCD, **limbic leucotomy** has been demonstrated to be effective. Finally, PET scanning studies also suggest the involvement of the temporal poles in both normal and pathological human anxiety.

One theory is that the septohippocampal circuit, in combination with the associated circuit of Papez, acts as a comparator, comparing expected with actual stimuli. An apparent mismatch leads to interruption of behaviour through increased arousal and attention, and a consequent search for alternatives. Importantly, the hippocampus is associated with the **locus ceruleus**, on the floor of the fourth ventricle. The locus ceruleus, stimulation of which leads to anxiety in animals, has descending pathways to the sympathetic division of the autonomic nervous system, thus providing a potential pathway to generate the physical symptoms of anxiety. We can see a schematic representation of this circuitry in Figure 13.2.

Another limbic nucleus that may be important is the **amygdala**. Lesions of the amygdala lead to dramatic effects on the anxiety response as well as on levels of aggression, and

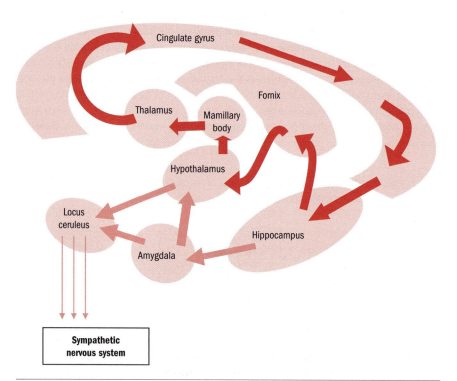

Figure 13.2 A schematic and simplified representation of the circuit of Papez and some related pathways.

there are very many **benzodiazepine** receptors within the amygdala. The apparent importance of the amygdala may be reconciled with the septohippocampal theory by the suggestion that there are differences in the systems subserving fear and anxiety, the amygdala being most important for the former and the septohippocampal system for the latter.

> There is good evidence for the importance of the limbic system and temporal poles of the brain in human emotion and anxiety.

Neurotransmitters

Serotonergic systems are most commonly implicated in anxiety disorders. Circumstantial evidence for this comes from clinical observations of the therapeutic effect of drugs which act on serotonergic systems. It has been shown robustly that urinary and plasma **catecholamines** are increased in anxiety disorders, suggesting that other neurotransmitters, particularly **noradrenaline** and **dopamine**, are important, perhaps in determining different aspects of anxiety.

There is also considerable evidence that panic attacks can be induced in susceptible subjects experimentally, supporting biological theories and offering further methods of investigating physiological correlates of anxiety (see Box 13.6 for examples of this).

Hormonal changes

There is relatively limited evidence for consistent hormonal changes in the anxiety disorders. **Hyperthyroidism** is often associated with anxiety, and many of the physical symptoms are similar. There have been occasional reports of diminished **thyroid stimulating hormone** (TSH) response to **thyrotropin** in panic disorder, but basal levels of TSH and routine thyroid function tests are normal. Similarly there is no consistent evidence of changes on the **dexamethasone suppression test** or other common endocrine challenges.

SELF-CHECK 13.8

Which three neurotransmitter systems are particularly implicated in anxiety disorders?

---

extension: Inducing panic

BOX 13.6

The observations that intravenous infusions of adrenaline induce physical symptoms of anxiety, and that noradrenaline stimulates lactic acid production, have led to the investigation of lactic acid in inducing anxiety. Intravenous infusions of lactate have been shown to induce panic in almost all anxious patients, but not in normal controls.

There is some evidence that this is a central effect, though the mechanism is not clear. The effect may be blocked by imipramine, an antidepressant which is predominantly serotonergic in action, and which is therapeutically effective in panic disorder.

Yohimbine is another substance which induces panic in susceptible patients. It stimulates the locus ceruleus and increases noradrenaline release. Yohimbine-induced anxiety is accompanied by an increase in urinary and plasma MHPG, a metabolite of noradrenaline. Its effect may also be blocked by imipramine.

Other factors that may induce panic in this way include caffeine and hyperventilation. Sometimes, patients (if young and healthy) are encouraged to hyperventilate in clinic, to demonstrate the effect that overbreathing can have on anxiety. They are then taught breathing exercises as a therapeutic manoeuvre.

Table 13.3 Approximate prevalence rates of anxiety disorders in the general population

Generalized anxiety disorder	5%
Panic disorder	1%
Phobic anxiety disorders	10%
Obsessive compulsive disorder	1%
PTSD	1%

13.4 How common are anxiety-related disorders?

Anxiety disorders are very common in the general population, and actually present more often to GPs than to psychiatrists. Epidemiological studies have often used different methods of identifying individuals and cases, so accurate prevalence rates are not available, but the figures in Table 13.3 give a rough guide to the relative frequency of these disorders in the general population.

Specific phobias are the most common form of phobic anxiety disorder, but these usually don't present to psychiatric clinics, in which agoraphobia is the most common type of phobia encountered.

Anxiety disorders also present to doctors in other specialties, because patients may assume that the physical symptoms of anxiety are caused by some physical disorder. In particular, patients may present to the hospital emergency department with a suspected heart attack, when in fact their symptoms are due to panic disorder.

13.5 What treatments are available for anxiety-related disorders?

13.5.1 Pharmacological treatments

Benzodiazepines

These drugs have only a limited role in the treatment of anxiety disorders. They are extremely effective and work more quickly than other treatments, so they may be of benefit in very acute situations. However, after more than a few weeks of use they induce tolerance and dependence, meaning that larger doses are required to achieve the same effect. This limits their more widespread use in contemporary medicine, though in previous decades they were very widely prescribed, before their dependence-inducing potential was recognized.

Commonly used examples include diazepam, lorazepam, and temazepam. They bind to benzodiazepine receptors, which are themselves linked to GABA$_A$ receptors. In this way they potentiate the effect of endogenous GABA, which is the most widespread inhibitory

Table 13.4 Side effects of anti-anxiety treatments

Benzodiazepines	Sedation
	Blurred vision
	Gastrointestinal upset
	Ataxia
	Headache
	Low blood pressure
	Restlessness
	Rashes
Tricyclic antidepressants	Raised heart rate
	Cardiac arrhythmias
	Postural hypotension
	Weight gain
	Dry mouth
	Blurred vision
	Constipation
	Nausea
	Drowsiness
	Sexual dysfunction
	Confusion (particularly in the elderly)
Selective serotonin reuptake inhibitors (SSRIs)	Nausea
	Diarrhoea
	Insomnia
	Headache
	Restlessness
	Sexual dysfunction

neurotransmitter in the brain. The common side effects of benzodiazepines are listed in Table 13.4.

Benzodiazepines should only be prescribed for short periods of time, so they are rarely appropriate for use as the main pharmacological treatment of an anxiety disorder. However, they may be useful in combination with other less rapidly acting medications and occasionally they may be used to augment or enable effective psychological treatment.

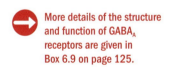

More details of the structure and function of GABA$_A$ receptors are given in Box 6.9 on page 125.

> Although benzodiazepines are very effective anxiolytics, their tendency to induce dependence severely limits their clinical use.

Antidepressants

Most antidepressant medications are also effective **anxiolytics**, particularly those which preferentially affect serotonergic systems (see Box 13.7). They are the first-line treatment for both GAD and panic disorder. There is also some evidence to support their use in PTSD, although it is worth noting that response to treatment is predicted by the

> ### extension: Antidepressant medication
>
> **BOX 13.7**
>
> -------
>
> All of the antidepressants that are commonly used today inhibit neurotransmitter re-uptake into presynaptic terminals. In this way they potentiate the effect of the neurotransmitter and increase synaptic transmission.
>
> It is not entirely clear that this is how their therapeutic effect is mediated. They also have important effects on receptor density and sensitivity, effects that develop much more slowly than the almost immediate effect on reuptake. It so happens that their anti-anxiety effect takes 2–3 weeks to develop, which might suggest that it is changes in receptor density which are of prime importance rather than reuptake inhibition.
>
> However, the drugs tend to be categorized depending on whether they act primarily on serotonin or noradrenergic systems. Those that act primarily on serotonergic systems tend to be the most effective in anxiety disorders.

The reuptake of neurotransmitters from the synaptic cleft, and the blockade of these transporters by drugs, is described in Box 2.3 on page 30.

presence of depressive symptoms. So it may be that the treatment is really just treating a depressive syndrome, which, as we have seen, is commonly **co-morbid**.

Examples of antidepressants include amitryptiline, imipramine, fluoxetine, and paroxetine. Their common side effects are listed in Table 13.4. Note that apart from sedation, the other side effects of benzodiazepines are relatively uncommon. These drugs are usually very well tolerated. The newer **selective serotonin reuptake inhibitor** (SSRI) antidepressants are usually tolerated better than the tricyclics. Importantly, they are much less cardiotoxic and tend to be safer in overdose.

For most anxiety disorders, relatively low doses of antidepressant medication are required. However, OCD differs in that often high doses are needed, perhaps 60 mg of fluoxetine, as opposed to the normal antidepressant dosage of 20 mg.

Beta-blockers

These drugs act on peripheral adrenergic receptors and do not have any anxiolytic effects within the central nervous system. They may be useful in patients who have prominent somatic symptoms of anxiety, and may help particularly with tremor and palpitations. However, they are not an adequate treatment for most anxiety disorders. They are sometimes used for situational anxiety; for example musicians might use them before a performance to stop their hands shaking. Snooker players have been known to use them for the same reason, though this of course is against competition rules.

13.5.2 Psychological treatments

As discussed previously, the concept of avoidance is central to all psychological approaches to treating anxiety. Psychological approaches to treatment are based on enabling and encouraging patients to repeatedly expose themselves to, and habituate to, their anxiety. Then the anxiety and associated symptoms will begin to dissipate.

Anxiety management

This is a **cognitive behavioural treatment** which may be useful for any patient who experiences anxiety. It is particularly used in GAD and panic disorder. It may be delivered either to a group of patients or on an individual basis. Patients are educated about anxiety disorders, particularly about the vicious circle of anxiety and the way in which the physical symptoms of anxiety are caused. The importance of avoidance in perpetuating the disorder and the principle of exposure to anxiety in treating the disorder is explained. Relaxation techniques such as breathing exercises or **progressive muscular relaxation** are taught. Patients are expected to keep a diary of their anxiety symptoms, noting precipitants, accompanying thoughts, and instances of avoidance behaviour. Maladaptive thinking is challenged, partly through education but also by correcting logical errors and offering alternatives.

Exposure therapy

The importance of exposure to anxiety is particularly applied to the psychological treatment of phobic anxiety disorders. Essentially, this involves supporting patients in repeatedly exposing themselves to their feared situation. This is termed **flooding** when the patient is suddenly and rapidly exposed to very severe anxiety. If they are able to remain in the situation then their anxiety will gradually dissipate. However, it is usually very difficult to persuade a patient to tolerate that level of anxiety, so **graded exposure** is used more frequently. This is the exposure of a patient to a series of stages of gradually increasing levels of anxiety. The therapist helps the patient draw up a **hierarchy of anxiety-provoking situations**. This begins with a situation which will cause a relatively low level of anxiety, and progresses until the final step is some very anxiety-provoking situation and also some important goal that will be sufficiently motivating for the patient. The patient starts at the bottom of the hierarchy and works their way to the top, practising each stage until they no longer feel anxious. We can see an example of this in Box 13.8.

This form of treatment requires considerable effort from the patient; it is time consuming and may be difficult, but may lead to major improvement in functioning. In general terms, simple phobias tend to be easier to treat in this way than social phobia or agoraphobia, and the prognosis is better in the absence of any other psychiatric or neurotic symptoms and in the absence of a history of psychiatric disorder.

Response prevention

In order to help a patient with OCD experience their anxiety, it is necessary to encourage him or her to avoid performing compulsions. This behavioural treatment is known as **response prevention**. The quickest way of achieving this is to support the patient in not performing the compulsion until the consequent anxiety dissipates. However, this may be more than a patient can manage, so an approach analogous to graded exposure may be used, whereby a patient is encouraged to avoid performing compulsions for gradually increasing periods.

It is interesting that cognitive therapy, which focuses on a patient's thoughts and thinking patterns, has not proved particularly effective in treating OCD. Effective treatment is behavioural and focuses on the compulsion. The evidence suggests that if the compulsion can be eradicated then the obsessions will wane too.

case study: Graded exposure for agoraphobia

BOX 13.8

A 45-year-old woman had been housebound for nearly 1 year because of her fear of experiencing a panic attack when away from home. She drew up the following hierarchy of anxiety-provoking situations with her therapist:

1. Opening the front door
2. Stepping on to the porch
3. Walking down the garden path
4. Opening the garden gate
5. Walking to the bus stop
6. Travelling one stop on the bus
7. Travelling to the supermarket
8. Travelling to the supermarket and completing her shopping.

Opening the front door was chosen as the first stage because although she reported that this would make her feel anxious, she felt that it was realistic for her to be able to tolerate the degree of anxiety that she anticipated this would cause.

The therapist then supported her in practising this first stage. She was taught some relaxation exercises, and educated about anxiety and the nature of the symptoms. After some practice she found that she no longer felt anxious when she opened the door and looked out, though the thought of going shopping was still extremely anxiety provoking.

However over a period of several months she managed to work her way up the hierarchy and complete some shopping. On a few occasions she had to go back a step, but with perseverance she made progress again. Eventually she was able to go shopping, though she remained anxious to some degree. It took continued effort to ensure that she did not go back to avoiding leaving the house.

> All psychological treatments for anxiety disorders depend on the idea that the disorder is maintained by avoidance behaviour, and successful treatment is dependent upon repeated exposure to anxiety.

13.5.3 How do doctors choose a treatment for individual patients?

In clinical practice, doctors need to consider a variety of issues in agreeing on a treatment plan with a patient. Different patients differ greatly in their expectations of doctors. Some want their doctor to reassure them and tell them what the best treatment is. Others want to engage in a detailed discussion of the options, and may bring their own strong opinions and preferences to this. The efficacy of any treatment will be improved if it is acceptable to the patient, and the patient feels that they are receiving the most appropriate treatment.

For all of these disorders it is essential to rule out co-morbid mental illness, particularly depression, before embarking on treatment. Anxiety is a very common, perhaps universal, concomitant of depression, which may present with a picture suggestive of any of the disorders in this chapter. Similarly, it is essential to identify maladaptive avoidance strategies, such as drug or alcohol misuse. It will be much more difficult to treat the disorder while these are still being used.

For panic disorder, GAD, and OCD in particular, antidepressant treatment will usually be recommended, but this may well be carried out in combination with anxiety management or some other psychological treatment. Phobic anxiety disorders and PTSD are more likely to be treated using a psychological approach in the first instance.

13.6 What is the outcome of anxiety-related disorders?

For all the anxiety disorders, a good prognosis is more likely if the disorder is of acute and recent onset, in a patient with no history of anxiety disorders and no apparent dispositional anxiety.

However, it is more usual for the disorder to have been present for a considerable time (sometimes several years) before it comes to the attention of a doctor. It is often difficult to distinguish between a long-standing dispositional anxiety and the acute anxiety disorder superimposed on this. In these cases the prognosis is poorer. Although treatment is likely to alleviate the symptoms to some degree, the patient may well continue to experience anxiety symptoms persistently, and may fail to regain their previous level of functioning. Typically the disorder will fluctuate in severity, becoming worse at time of stress.

Panic disorder tends to present more acutely than other anxiety disorders, because of its acute and severe nature. Perhaps this is one of the reasons why it tends to show a better response to treatment.

SUMMARY

- Anxiety is a normal human emotion which is usually not pathological.

- It is important to distinguish dispositional anxiety from acute anxiety states.

- The experience of anxiety may be separated into associated mood state, types of thought, physical symptoms, and behaviours.

- Avoidance of the experience of anxiety tends to perpetuate anxiety disorders. This concept is crucial to our understanding of anxiety and to psychological therapeutic techniques.

- Deciding when anxiety is pathological often depends on considering the situations in which the anxiety occurs, and the degree of the anxiety.

- Generalized anxiety disorder (GAD) is characterized by constant free-floating anxiety.

- Panic disorder is characterized by discrete episodes of severe and acute anxiety, interspersed by relatively anxiety-free periods.

- Phobic anxiety disorders are characterized by episodes of acute anxiety which is out of proportion to the demands of the stimulus, and by avoidance of the anxiety-provoking stimulus. Three types are recognized in psychiatric classifications: agoraphobia, social phobia, and specific phobia.

- Post-traumatic stress disorder (PTSD) is characterized by re-experiencing phenomena, avoidance, and hypervigilance.

- Obsessions are repetitive, intrusive stereotyped thoughts, images, or impulses that are resisted by the patient but recognized as their own.

- Compulsions are voluntary motor actions which are performed reluctantly despite being recognized as silly or absurd. They are designed to reduce the anxiety associated with an accompanying obsession.

- The causes of anxiety disorders are multifactorial. In most cases the genetic vulnerability is probably a general predisposition to anxiety, rather than to a specific disorder.

- Both psychological and pharmacological treatments are important in treating anxiety disorders. They can often be combined to good effect.

- Possible pharmacological treatments include benzodiazepines, antidepressants, and beta-blockers.

- Psychological approaches to treatment include anxiety management for any anxiety disorder, exposure therapy for phobic anxiety disorders, and response prevention for OCD.

FURTHER READING

General

World Health Organization. *The ICD-10 Classification of Mental and Behavioural Disorders*. Geneva: World Health Organization, 1992.
The WHO's classification of all psychiatric disorders including the anxiety disorders. It contains some excellent clinical descriptions of the syndromes.

Panic and anxiety

D. F. Klein. Delineation of two drug responsive anxiety syndromes. *Psychopharmacologia* 1964; **5**: 397–408.
The seminal study which led to the distinction of panic disorder from generalized anxiety disorder on the basis of response to antidepressant treatment.

D. J. Nutt and C. Lawson. Panic attacks: a neurochemical overview of models and mechanisms. *British Journal of Psychiatry* 1992; **160**: 165–178.
Review of the neurobiology of panic disorder.

Obsessive-compulsive disorder

A. J. Lewis. Problems of obsessional illness. *Proceedings of the Royal Society of Medicine* 1935; **29**: 325–336.
The classic description of obsessive-compulsive disorder.

PTSD

M. J. Friedman. Biological and pharmacological aspects of the treatment of PTSD. In *Handbook of post-traumatic stress disorder therapy*, ed. M. Williams, M. Sommer, and M. Westport. Westport, CT: Greenwood Press, 1994.
Contains a review of animal models and the neurobiology of PTSD.

R. Ramsay. Post-traumatic stress disorder: a new clinical entity. *Journal of Psychosomatic Research* 1990; **34**: 355–365.
A review of the multifactorial aetiology of PTSD.

M. R. Trimble. *Post-traumatic neurosis*. Chichester: Wiley, 1981.
Contains an account of the historical development of PTSD and related post-traumatic neurotic syndromes.

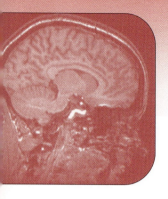

CHAPTER FOURTEEN

Mood disorders

Lisa Jones and Femi Oyebode

INTRODUCTION

Mood disorders, a term used interchangeably with affective disorders, are a group of syndromes where the main feature is a pathological mood state. This can be either depression (extreme low mood) or, its polar opposite, mania (extreme high mood).

The changes in mood are much more severe and persistent than the normal ups and downs of everyday life. People with mood disorders suffer severe distress and often struggle to function at their normal level during episodes of illness. For example, they may have to take time off work and may stop engaging in social activities. However, it is usual for sufferers to recover between episodes and return to normal levels of social and occupational functioning.

In this chapter we consider the two types of major mood disorders: unipolar depression and bipolar affective disorder (manic depression). We describe the symptoms and signs of these disorders and how they are assessed; and discuss the epidemiology and what is currently known about the aetiology. We end with a brief introduction to the most commonly used treatments for mood disorders including pharmacological and psychological interventions.

14.1 Unipolar depression

Unipolar depression describes an illness characterized by episodes of depression, and the absence of episodes of mania. Each episode of depression usually lasts for at least 2 weeks, and often for considerably longer than this. The average length of a treated episode of depression is 2–3 months.

Some sufferers may only experience a single episode of depression during their life (described as a **single major depressive episode**), whereas others may suffer two episodes or many more. In the latter case, the illness is described as **recurrent unipolar depression** (or recurrent major depressive disorder). At least half of people who experience one episode of depression will go on to have another episode. Unipolar depression is not a current diagnostic term in the major psychiatric classification systems, but is often used, as it is here, to describe diagnoses of either single major depressive episode or recurrent major depressive disorder.

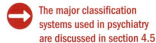

The major classification systems used in psychiatry are discussed in section 4.5 on page 81.

> Unipolar depression is characterized by episodes of depression, and the absence of episodes of mania.

14.1.1 What are the signs and symptoms of unipolar depression?

The core symptom of depression is severe low mood. This is different from normal sadness or feeling blue, which is experienced by all of us in relation to unfortunate events in our life. Normal sadness is usually understandable and is a meaningful response to adverse events in our life, such as bereavement or a relationship breakdown, and is usually transient.

The deep unhappiness associated with severe depression feels qualitatively different from normal sadness, is much more distressing, persistent, and uncontrollable, and is often unrelated to adverse life events. Typically, mood is lower in the morning than at other times of the day (**diurnal mood variation**). Other core symptoms are loss of interest and pleasure in activities that the sufferer usually finds interesting and pleasurable (this is known as **anhedonia**), and unaccountably low levels of energy and increased tiredness (known as **anergia**).

Aside from these core symptoms, there are a number of other symptoms that may be experienced as part of the depression syndrome. Sufferers may experience negative cognitions about themselves, such as feelings of worthlessness, hopelessness, and inappropriate guilt (for example, 'I am a useless person, and I do not deserve help because of all the bad things I have done in my life'). Self-confidence is often very low and there can be social withdrawal such that depressed patients avoid contact with other people (for example, by not answering the telephone or the doorbell). Sufferers often describe an inability to concentrate, even on simple things like reading the daily newspaper or following their favourite television programme, and an inability to remember things or to make basic decisions. There may be a wish to be dead. This can be a passive desire to not wake up in the morning (**tedium vitae**), or an active desire to take one's own life (**suicidal ideation**). In severe cases, there may be suicide attempts, or, tragically, successful suicides.

Biological symptoms (sometimes known as **endogenous features**) are typical in severe depressive episodes. Sufferers may experience appetite change (typically decreased appetite, although appetite can be increased in some patients who describe comfort eating) and associated weight change. They may also have sleep disturbance. This may take the form of waking up very early in the morning (**late insomnia**), waking during the night (**middle insomnia**), or finding great difficulty in falling asleep at night (**initial insomnia**). Early morning wakening twinned with diurnal variation of mood is particularly upsetting. In other cases, there may be excessive sleep (**hypersomnia**) whereby sufferers sleep solidly during the night, have trouble waking in the morning, and fall asleep during the day. Another common biological symptom of depression is markedly reduced sexual drive (**diminished libido**).

> Biological symptoms, such as appetite and sleep disturbance and diminished libido, are common in severe depression.

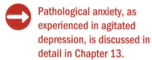 Pathological anxiety, as experienced in agitated depression, is discussed in detail in Chapter 13.

In addition to these symptoms (subjective experiences), there are a number of signs (objective, observable behaviour) associated with depression. Sufferers have a sad and downcast appearance, and may well have long bouts of crying. They may appear to be very slow in their actions and thoughts (**psychomotor retardation**), or anxious, irritable, and restless. The latter is described as **agitated depression**, and in severe cases may manifest itself in an inability to sit down for any length of time, or wringing the hands or even banging the head repeatedly against a wall. Severe psychomotor retardation can progress to mutism and depressive stupor. Depressed patients may appear unkempt in appearance, as a result of poor self-care associated with anhedonia and anergia. Some depressed patients will try to mask their depression; this is sometimes known as **smiling depression**. Table 14.1 summarizes the signs and symptoms of depression. A typical case of unipolar depression is outlined in Box 14.1.

Of course, some people are miserable and pessimistic by nature. They may be described as having a dysphoric personality. The key feature in deciding whether or not someone is experiencing an episode of unipolar depression is that the pattern of signs and symptoms is considered, by the sufferer and by others, to be a distinct change

Table 14.1 Signs and symptoms of depression and mania

	Depression	Mania
Core	Low mood	Elated/irritable mood
	Anhedonia	Overactivity
	Anergia	
Biological	Diurnal variation of mood	Reduced need for sleep
	Appetite/weight change	Increased appetite
	Sleep disturbance	Increased libido
	Diminished libido	
Other	Low self-confidence/self-esteem	Increased self-esteem
	Inappropriate guilt	Disinhibited behaviour
	Impaired concentration, memory and decision-making	Recklessness
	Tedium vitae/suicidal ideation	Distractibility
	Psychomotor retardation	Pressure of speech
	Agitation	Flight of ideas
	Psychosis	Psychosis

> ## case study: Unipolar depression
> ---
> **BOX 14.1**
>
> A 45-year-old married woman first came to attention after a failed suicide attempt. She had taken 32 tablets of paracetamol and a bottle of wine with the intention of killing herself. She was found unconscious by her husband and taken to the emergency department of the local hospital.
>
> On assessment she gave a 6-month history of gradual onset of low spirits which she described as awful and horrible. Her mood was said to be persistently low, and usually worse first thing in the morning. She had difficulty getting out of bed and did not look forward to the day ahead. She lost interest in her appearance and for someone who was usually house-proud, found that she no longer cared about her home. Gradually she became more pessimistic in her outlook and felt hopeless about the future. Life did not seem worth living to her.
>
> Her sleep became disturbed, such that she woke at 3 a.m. She could not get back to sleep and spent the time ruminating on her life and became preoccupied with the idea that she was worthless, a bad mother and wife, and that her family were better off without her. She had noticed that her appetite was poor and she had lost about a 6 kg in weight over a period of 6 months. She managed to continue to cope with her domestic responsibilities, including the care of two children. Her husband and friends were not aware of her condition. The clinical diagnosis was moderate depressive episode.

from what is normal for the individual concerned. Moreover, there will be some degree of impaired functioning, such as taking sick leave from work, relationship difficulties, or neglecting the housework.

> Episodes of depression involve a distinct change from the sufferer's normal state, and impaired occupational and social functioning.

There are other psychiatric conditions that commonly co-occur with unipolar depression, such as anxiety, phobias, hypochondriasis, and obsessive-compulsive symptoms. In very severe cases of depression there may be psychotic symptoms (hallucinations and delusions). Typically these are **mood-congruent**, in that the subject matter has a depressive theme. For example, a sufferer may harbour abnormal beliefs such as persecutory delusions that people want to harm them in some way and that this is deserved, or nihilistic delusions that part of them, often the brain or intestines, has disappeared or rotted away. Mood-congruent auditory hallucinations involve a hallucinatory voice telling the sufferer that, for example, they are worthless and deserve to die.

Mood-incongruent psychotic symptoms, where the subject matter has no relation to the depressed mood, may also occur.

> Psychotic symptoms may be present in severe cases of depression.

Psychosis is introduced in section 4.4 on page 73 and discussed in more detail in Chapter 15.

Anxiety, phobias, and obsessive-compulsive disorder are discussed in Chapter 13.

SELF-CHECK 14.1

How does an episode of depression differ from normal periods of sadness experienced by all of us?

14.2 Bipolar affective disorder

Bipolar affective disorder, otherwise known as manic-depression, describes an illness characterized by at least one manic episode which is often, although not always, accompanied by one or more episodes of depression. Each episode of mania will usually last for at least 1 week. The average duration of episodes of mania is around 2–3 months.

Hypomania is a milder and less disruptive form of mania, which may only last for 4 days. Hypomania in the absence of mania, with or without episodes of depression, is classified as **bipolar II disorder**, and we describe a typical case of bipolar II disorder in Box 14.2. **Bipolar I disorder** describes mania, with or without episodes of depression.

Table 14.2 summarizes the principal categories of mood disorder.

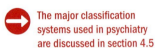 The major classification systems used in psychiatry are discussed in section 4.5 on page 81.

> Bipolar affective disorder is characterized by at least one episode of mania, which is often, although not always, accompanied by one or more episodes of depression.

---

case study: Bipolar II disorder   BOX 14.2

A 24-year-old woman who works as a teacher has been referred to a psychiatrist in the past because of recurring episodes of depression with thoughts of self-harm. She has had short periods of high mood, but has never discussed these with the psychiatrist as she feels they are not really a problem. In fact she finds these periods rather pleasurable.

During the high periods, which last for around 5 days at most, she feels very happy and does not need as much sleep as usual. She finds that she can achieve a lot more than usual because she has a lot of mental and physical energy. She feels more intelligent than usual during these periods, and is more sociable and entertaining. Her boyfriend has suggested that she 'calms down' when she feels like this, as he finds it difficult to keep up with her activities and ideas, and sometimes finds her jokes a little difficult to take. She noticed that the most recent of these episodes occurred after she started a course of antidepressant medication.

Table 14.2 Principle categories of mood disorder

Category	Episodes of illness
Single major depressive episode	One episode of depression
Recurrent major depressive episode	Two or more episodes of depression
Bipolar I disorder	One or more episodes of mania with or without episodes of depression
Bipolar II disorder	One or more episodes of hypomania with or without episodes of depression

14.2.1 What are the signs and symptoms of mania?

The core symptom of mania is elated, euphoric mood. This extreme happiness and optimism is out of character for the sufferer and seems unnatural, though often infectious, to observers. Sometimes the prevailing mood state in an episode of mania is irritability and hostility, sometimes leading to violence, rather than elevated mood. In some cases, irritable and elevated moods may co-occur and the predominant mood state may be described as **labile**.

Like depression, mania is a syndrome characterized by a number of other symptoms and signs in addition to the core alteration in mood. Sufferers are usually overactive and physically restless. Their behaviour may be reckless or socially inappropriate and disinhibited, often leading to painful consequences. For example, they may spend or give away all of their money, drive recklessly, or have unprotected sexual relations with a number of different partners. Sufferers are often distractable, in that they are unable to complete tasks because they are constantly changing activities and plans.

Speech is usually increased in quantity, uninterruptible, and very fast, often so fast that it is difficult to understand what is being said (**pressure of speech**). This reflects the experience of **flight of ideas**, whereby thoughts are crowded in the mind and there are rapidly changing thought patterns that are not clearly linked (racing thoughts). Sometimes thoughts are linked by rhymes (**clang associations**).

The content of thought is often expansive, and associated with increased self-esteem. For example, sufferers may believe that their opinions are of paramount importance, and that their work is of exceptionally high quality. Biological symptoms are also typically present. Sleep is reduced, but the sufferer does not feel tired. Appetite is often increased, although patients may not find the time to eat. There is usually a marked increase in sexual energy.

> Behaviour in episodes of mania may be reckless, leading to painful consequences.

As in depression, psychosis may be present in severe cases. Mood-congruent psychotic symptoms typically take the form of **grandiose delusions**. These delusions may be related to identity; for instance, sufferers may be convinced that they are a member of a royal family, a great statesman, or a famous religious figure (for example, 'I am God'). Grandiose delusions may also be centred on abilities; for example, the sufferer may believe that they possess extraordinary powers to heal the sick or control the weather. Mood-congruent delusions may also be persecutory in nature. In such cases, the belief is that people are out to harm the sufferer because of their special identity or abilities. Hallucinations usually involve voices telling the sufferer that they are a wonderful and special person.

The signs and symptoms of mania are summarized in Table 14.1. A typical case of bipolar I affective disorder is described in Box 14.3.

> Delusions in episodes of mania are often convictions of grandiose identity or grandiose abilities.

SELF-CHECK 14.2

Why are manic patients often at high risk of causing harm to themselves, or to other people?

> **case study:** Bipolar I disorder
>
> ---
>
> A 27-year-old electronic engineer was arrested by the police because he was found in a public place taking his clothes off and proclaiming himself as the new Messiah.
>
> When he was assessed by a psychiatrist in the police cells he was found to be both elated and irritable in mood. He was talking rapidly and shouting so loudly that his voice was hoarse. It was difficult to understand exactly what he was saying because it appeared as if his thoughts were jumbled. He seemed to be saying that he was a reincarnation of Jesus Christ and that he had special powers including the powers to raise the dead, heal the sick, and feed the poor. He was angry that the police were holding him, and was surprised that they could not see that he was not an ordinary person.
>
> He was also restless, could hardly sit still, and his gestures were expansive and exaggerated. He denied that anything was wrong with him. He refused to be transferred to hospital and had to be detained under the Mental Health Act.

14.3 Subcategories of mood disorders

14.3.1 Mixed mood states

In some cases, symptoms of mania and symptoms of depression occur simultaneously (this is known as a **mixed mood state**). A typical example of mixed mood state involves low mood with suicidal ideation, along with overactivity, pressured speech, and flight of ideas.

14.3.2 Rapid cycling

Rapid cycling may occur in mood disorders, whereby sufferers experience four or more episodes of depression, mania, or mixed mood state in a single year. Some patients experience even more rapidly alternating mood states, which is known as ultra-rapid cycling.

14.3.3 Mood disorder following childbirth

Mild depression occurring in the first few days after giving birth (**baby blues**) is common and usually transient, but approximately 10% of new mothers develop a major episode of depression within 3 months of childbirth (**postnatal depression**).

A more severe postnatal disorder, **puerperal psychosis**, occurs in fewer cases (about 1 in 500 births), and usually begins within the first few weeks after the birth. Women with a previous history of psychiatric illness are at greatest risk of puerperal psychosis, which is a severe disorder presenting with symptoms of mood change, psychosis, perplexity, and confusion. A typical case of puerperal psychosis is presented in Box 14.4.

case study: Puerperal psychosis
BOX 14.4

A 28-year-old single woman, delivered her first child, a girl, at term by a normal vaginal delivery 4 days before her presentation to the GP.

Her partner first became concerned when he noticed that she was not sleeping at all and that she was neglecting the newly born child. Her mood appeared to be shifting from being cheerful to unprovoked inconsolable tearfulness. She had also stopped eating.

Her partner became very worried when she started to say that their daughter was the Devil's child, and had brought an evil presence to their home. The partner became concerned that she might harm the child.

When she was seen by the GP she appeared perplexed, agitated, and hostile. She refused to speak to the GP. She seemed to be listening to 'voices' and the GP suspected she was experiencing auditory hallucinations. Although she did not have a past psychiatric history, there was a history of puerperal psychosis in both her own mother and another sister.

14.3.4 Seasonal affective disorder

Seasonal affective disorder (SAD) is characterized by episodes of depression that occur annually in autumn and winter, and may well be related to reduced hours of daylight. Typical symptoms of SAD are low mood, hypersomnia, social withdrawal, increased appetite, and tiredness. Symptoms of SAD resolve in the spring and summer.

14.4 How common are mood disorders?

Mood disorders are common. The World Health Organization (WHO), on behalf of the World Bank, has identified that mood disorders will be the second major cause of global health burden in 2020 (ischaemic heart disease is identified as the leading cause). **Mortality** rates among sufferers of mood disorders are high. Approximately 15% of sufferers, particularly those with a young age of illness onset, will commit suicide.

14.4.1 Unipolar depression

Major depressive disorders are very common. Estimates of the lifetime risk of suffering from major depression differ markedly according to the diagnostic criteria, methodology, and sample employed, but risk is probably around 7% in men, and 14% in women. At any one time in the UK, there are approximately 20–30 men in every 1000 experiencing a depressive episode, and approximately 40–90 affected women in every 1000. It is not clearly understood why there is a significantly greater risk in women.

Depression is particularly common among those who live in urban environments, and those in lower socio-economic groups. Men, and to a lesser extent women, who are

SELF-CHECK 14.3

What reasons can you think of to explain why women are twice as likely as men to suffer from unipolar depression?

divorced or separated have a greater risk of depression. The average age of onset of unipolar depression is in the late twenties.

> Women are twice as likely as men to suffer from unipolar depression.

14.4.2 Bipolar affective disorder

Bipolar affective disorder is less common than unipolar depression, with a lifetime risk of approximately 1%. Unlike unipolar depression, there is an equal risk in men and women. The **point prevalence** is approximately 1–6 per 1000 of the population. Bipolar disorder usually manifests for the first time in the early twenties. Over half of bipolar patients present first with an episode of mania, rather than depression. Some research has shown that bipolar disorder is associated with higher socio-economic status, which is opposite to the relationship between depression and socio-economic status.

> Bipolar disorder is less common than unipolar disorder, although it is still fairly common as it will affect approximately 1% of the general population at some time during their life.

14.5 What are the likely causes of mood disorders?

We know that the causes of mood disorders are complex and multifactorial. There are important biological (including genetic) factors and environmental (including physical and psychosocial) factors that act together to cause mood disorders.

> Mood disorders are caused by complex interactions between nature and nurture.

14.5.1 Genetics

Mood disorders run in families. Individuals with a close relative who suffers from depression have an increased risk of developing depression compared to the general population. Close relatives of bipolar disorder sufferers have an increased risk of bipolar disorder and of unipolar depression.

Twin studies (so-called 'experiments of nature') show that the shared risk of mood disorders in families is mainly due to the fact that family members share genes, rather than simply because they share life experiences. **Monozygotic** (identical) twins share 100% of their genes. If one member of a monozygotic twin pair suffers from a mood disorder, then the co-twin has a greatly increased risk of developing a mood disorder (the **concordance** is approximately 65%). **Dizygotic** (fraternal) twins have only half of their genes in common. Concordance for mood disorder in dizygotic twin pairs is approximately 20%.

The significantly higher concordance rate in monozygotic twin pairs, compared to the concordance rate in dizygotic twin pairs, is strong evidence for the importance of genetic factors if we assume that monozygotic and dizygotic twin pairs share their environment to the same degree. Importantly, the increased risk to the co-twin of an affected mono-zygotic twin is the same even if the twins have been separated at birth and brought up with different families; in other words, even if they have not shared any life experiences. The fact that concordance between monozygotic twins is not 100% also tells us that genes are not the whole story in understanding the causes of mood disorders; non-familial environmental factors must also be important. We discuss this in more detail in section 14.5.3.

Studies of individuals who have been adopted also confirm that genes are an important cause of mood disorders. Individuals who have a biological parent with a major mood disorder, but who have been raised by healthy adoptive parents, have an increased risk of developing a mood disorder similar to those individuals who have been born and raised by a parent with a mood disorder. This risk is significantly greater than that in individuals who were born to healthy parents and raised by an adoptive parent suffer-ing from a mood disorder. This evidence, together with the evidence from twin studies, strongly suggests that shared genes, and not shared life experiences, account for the observation that mood disorders run in families.

Despite this compelling evidence, no genes have yet been identified that are consistently associated with increasing the risk of developing a major mood disorder. However, large studies are currently under way in many centres around the world and researchers feel optimistic that susceptibility genes will be identified in the coming years.

We know that mood disorders are not caused by a single major gene because of the complex patterns of inheritance in families. More likely, a number of genes act together to increase susceptibility to mood disorders. The identification of such genes will give important clues to the underlying pathophysiology of mood disorders, which will lead to a better understanding of the gene–environment interplay and more effective, better-targeted treatments.

> **SELF-CHECK 14.4**
>
> How does studying twins and adoptees tell us that shared genes more than shared family environment accounts for the fact that mood disorders run in families?

> Family studies show that mood disorders run in families. Studies of twins and adoptees show that this observed familial aggregation is mainly due to shared genes rather than shared family environment.

Family, twin, and adoption studies are discussed in detail in Box 4.4 on page 68.

14.5.2 Personality and cognitive style

The genes that predispose an individual to a mood disorder may also be expressed in their personality. Alternatively, an individual's personality may put them at risk of, or protect them from, developing a mood disorder. There is evidence that some aspects of personality are related to mental illness generally, and that some traits are related to depression and mania specifically.

Neuroticism (N), a personality trait involving emotional instability, may be related to depression. Some researchers have shown that having a highly N personality increases the risk of a major depressive episode within the next year by more than 100%. Some evidence suggests that having an **extravert** personality (outgoing, fun, optimistic) might protect against the onset of depression. Mania has been associated, although not robustly, with **sensation seeking** (seeking out new and varied experiences which are often risky), and with traits such as obsessionality and perfectionism.

Cognitive style, a related concept, describes one's characteristic way of thinking. Low self-esteem (negative thoughts about oneself), pessimistic views about the future, and dysfunctional attitudes (such as unhealthy levels of dependency on others, for example, 'If others dislike you, you cannot be happy' and a high need for achievement, for example 'Unless I do everything right I am a failure') may well predispose to depression, and perhaps even to bipolar disorder.

Psychologists also talk about a **depressogenic attributional style** in individuals vulnerable to depression. This means that events are attributed to external factors outside of their control and consequently they view themselves as helpless (this is known as **learned helplessness**), and ultimately hopeless.

Research also suggests that depressed patients have a **negative recall bias**, that is, they preferentially recall unpleasant memories rather than pleasant memories. Negative recall bias is particularly marked when the memories relate to themselves.

A major problem with research in this area is that most studies are cross-sectional and involve measuring personality and cognitive style after the onset of mood disorder. Therefore, researchers cannot be sure whether characteristic personality profiles and cognitive styles of individuals with mood disorders are a cause or a consequence of mood disorder.

> **SELF-CHECK 14.5**
>
> Why can we not be certain that aspects of personality and cognitive style associated with mood disorders are a root cause?

The suggestion that changes in personality are a consequence of illness is known as the **scarring hypothesis**. Even so, negative and pessimistic thought patterns associated with episodes of depression certainly prolong the episode as they contribute to the low mood, which, in turn, contributes to the negative thinking. Tackling the negative thought patterns associated with depression is a major goal of psychological therapies used in depression, as we shall see below.

> Mood disorders may be associated with characteristic personality profiles or styles of thinking.

14.5.3 Environmental stressors

If genes were solely responsible for mood disorders, then the concordance between pairs of monozygotic twins would be 100%, given that they share 100% of their genetic material. This is not the case. As we saw above, concordance is around 65%. This tells us that non-genetic factors must also be important in determining who develops, or does not develop, a mood disorder. It is therefore important that explanations of the aetiology of mood disorders take account of both genetic and **non-shared environmental factors**.

> Twin studies show that non-familial environmental factors are important causal factors in mood disorders.

Environmental stressors may be predisposing or precipitating; that is, there may be chronic life difficulties or an acute stressor that occurred many years before the onset of illness (**predisposing factors**), or there may be an acutely stressful life event which immediately precedes the onset of illness or the onset of an episode of illness (**precipitating factor**). There is evidence that both may play a part in mood disorders.

Individuals who have suffered a trauma in childhood, such as physical, sexual, or psychological abuse or family break-up, are at higher risk of developing a mood disorder in adulthood. Those with prolonged periods of stress in their lives are also at higher risk. Prolonged stress may involve difficulties at work, marital difficulties, poor socio-economic circumstances, being a mother with two or more young children at home, chronic physical illness, being socially isolated, or combinations of all of the above.

Acute adverse life events include bereavement, loss of a job, relationship break-up, major financial crisis, and physical assault. Research shows that risk of a mood disorder is substantially increased during the 6 months following an adverse life event. However, for some life events it is difficult to be sure whether they are independent of the early stages of a yet-to-be-diagnosed mood disorder. For example, losing one's job and a marriage break-up may be due to poor performance at work and impaired interpersonal relations occurring as a result of depression.

Some adverse life events, however, are clearly independent of illness and not within the person's control, such as bereavement, and there is clear evidence that they may lead to a depressive disorder. Adverse life events may also predispose to, or precipitate, mania. The onset of mania has also been related to loss of sleep caused by, for example, shift work and long-haul aeroplane flights.

> Adverse life events, such as bereavement or divorce, increase the risk of mood disorders.

SELF-CHECK 14.6

In what ways can life stresses contribute to the onset of mood disorders?

Other factors linked to mood disorders, but not by clear biological mechanisms, are viral infections, use of psychoactive substances, treatment with corticosteroid medications, and brain injury. Some of these are further discussed below.

14.5.4 Biochemical abnormalities

Our understanding of the neurobiology of mood disorders is limited. However, the **monoamine hypothesis** has received much attention. The foundation of the monoamine hypothesis lies in the following observations:

- Drugs that modulate levels of monoamines (noradrenaline, dopamine, serotonin, acetylcholine) in the brain can induce depressed and euphoric mood in humans.
- Animal studies have shown that monoamine activity is important in regulating behaviours which are affected in mood disorders, such as sleep cycles, sexual behaviour, appetite, and motivation.
- Medications effective in treating mood disorders act on monoamine systems.

Monoamine oxidase inhibitors (MAOIs) are a class of antidepressants which reduce the enzymatic breakdown of noradrenaline, dopamine, and serotonin (also known as 5-hydroxytryptamine or 5-HT), leading to increased presynaptic levels of neurotransmitters available for release.

Tricyclic antidepressants (TCAs) inhibit the reuptake of serotonin and noradrenaline, thus increasing and prolonging their activity at synapses during transmission. More recently, medications that selectively increase either serotonergic transmission (**selective serotonin reuptake inhibitors**; SSRIs) or noradrenergic transmission (**noradrenaline reuptake inhibitors**; NARIs) have also been shown to have antidepressant effects.

Neurotransmission and the pharmacological blockade of neurotransmitter uptake are discussed in section 2.2.4 on page 29 and in Box 2.3 on page 30.

The **indoleamine hypothesis** of depression states quite simply that low synaptic concentrations of serotonin bring about depression. However, as we know the brain is very complex and made up of many interconnected and interdependent systems, so increasing serotonin levels to relieve depression does not necessarily imply that reduced serotonergic function is the root cause of depression.

> Mood disorders may be caused by altered activity of the neurotransmitters serotonin and noradrenaline.

Other evidence points to a central role for serotoninergic neurotransmitter systems in mood disorders, although this evidence is far from conclusive. Some studies show that there are reduced concentrations of 5-HIAA (the main serotonin metabolite) in the cerebrospinal fluid (CSF) of patients with depression compared to controls, and that concentrations of serotonin are reduced in the brains of depressed patients who have committed suicide. Increased CSF concentrations of 5-HIAA have also been found, though not consistently, in manic patients. Depletion of **tryptophan** (the amino acid precursor of serotonin) provides the most compelling evidence that serotonin is involved in the aetiology of mood disorders. Tryptophan depletion leads to reduced synthesis and release of serotonin, which, in turn, leads to depressive symptoms. Normalizing tryptophan levels, by resuming a normal diet, leads to alleviation of the depression.

Neuroimaging in psychiatry is introduced in section 4.2.3 on page 69.

Positron emission tomography (PET) studies have shown altered brain metabolism in the prefrontal cortex of depressed patients following tryptophan depletion. This finding is consistent with other neuroimaging studies that have implicated the prefrontal cortex in mood disorders. Other studies have implicated a critical role for the amygdala.

> Neuroimaging studies implicate areas of the prefrontal cortex and the amygdala in mood disorders.

SELF-CHECK 14.7

What is the monoamine hypothesis of mood disorders?

Dopamine is implicated in the development of mania, but this hypothesis has received very little scientific investigation. Drugs that displace dopamine from presynaptic terminals, thus increasing synaptic dopamine availability (such as amphetamine) do produce manic-like states, and dopamine antagonists (antipsychotic drugs) are effective in reducing the symptoms of acute mania. It is not difficult to purport that dopamine underactivity may play a role in depression, given that dopamine release is a well-established reward/ pleasure mechanism.

14.5.5 Hormonal abnormalities

The increased risk of mood disorder after childbirth, and at the menopause, suggests that endocrine changes may be an important causal factor. Furthermore, mood disorders have been associated with endocrine disorders, such as **Addison's disease**, **Cushing's syndrome**, and **hypothyroidism**, and are common in patients taking high doses of corticosteroid medications.

Most work in this area has concentrated on the **hypothalamic–pituitary–adrenocortic (HPA) system** which we can see illustrated in Figure 14.1. HPA overactivity undoubtedly occurs in depression. Plasma concentrations of the 'stress hormone', cortisol, are increased (**hypercortisolaemia**) in approximately 50% of patients with depression, and in some patients with mania. Elevated levels of corticotrophin releasing hormone (CRH) have been shown in the CSF of depressed patients. CRH is released by the hypothalamus, which stimulates the release of adrenocorticotrophic hormone (ACTH) in the pituitary, which in turn acts on the adrenal cortex to stimulate the release of cortisol. Furthermore, CRH receptors have been shown to be downregulated in the brains of people who have died by suicide. Some researchers think that elevated cortisol occurs in those patients who have experienced chronic life stressors, and may cause depression by reducing serotonin function in the brain. However, the cortisol story is far from clear. Other researchers think that cortisol is a mood elevator (euphoriant) and that the overactive HPA activity seen in depressed patients represents the body's effort to fight depression naturally.

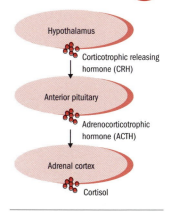

Figure 14.1 A schematic and simplified representation of the hypothalamic–pituitary–adrenal (HPA) axis.

> Mood disorders are associated with increased levels of the stress hormone cortisol, but it is not known whether this is a cause or consequence of mood disorder.

SELF-CHECK 14.8

How might overactivity of the HPA axis lead to depression?

14.6 How are mood disorders assessed?

Doctors use interviews, and their observations of the patient's behaviour, to assess whether or not a patient is suffering from a mood disorder, along with a physical examination to ensure that the mood symptoms are not secondary to a physical illness. The interview will involve a thorough assessment of the patient's history and current mental state. Whenever possible, doctors will also interview an informant. This is especially important when assessing a manic patient, as **insight** may be limited or absent. The doctors will not only be interested in the current presence or absence and severity of symptoms and signs, but also in possible aetiological factors and social consequences of the illness.

Of particular importance in mood disorders is assessing the risk that patients pose to themselves, and to others. For example, some patients will be at a high risk of suicide, or of endangering themselves and others by impaired judgement and reckless behaviour, such as continuing to drive or operate machinery, or of neglecting their children. In severe cases, patients may require hospitalization. Hospitalization, often compulsory admission under a section of the Mental Health Act, is common in cases of mania.

SELF-CHECK 14.9

How do doctors assess the signs and symptoms of mood disorders?

> Assessments of risk, to self or others, are important when assessing mood disorders.

14.7 What treatments are available for mood disorders?

There are a number of treatments available for mood disorders. The treatment package is tailored to the severity of the disorder, the likely aetiology, the patient's preferred treatment option, and the availability of different types of treatment.

There is a need to carefully monitor the treatments of patients with mood disorders, as antidepressant treatment can lead to an episode of mania or hypomania (as we saw in the case study in Box 14.2) and treatment of mania can lead to depression. Patients and their families are likely to be very distressed by the diagnosis of depression or manic depression, thus providing basic levels of psychological support and encouragement is very important. Furthermore, advice to patients about what they can do to help themselves, such as seeking social support, eating healthily, taking some exercise, and taking steps to improve their chances of sleeping at night, are all important.

> Doctors tailor treatment packages for each individual mood disorder patient.

14.7.1 Treatment of depression

Antidepressant medication

Antidepressant drugs are used widely in the treatment of depression, and are effective in most cases of moderate or severe depression. They are particularly effective in patients with biological symptoms of depression (sleep disturbance, appetite/weight changes, diminished libido). The best predictor of good response to a particular antidepressant medication is a previous good response.

As discussed above, the major classes of antidepressants are reuptake inhibitors (TCAs, SSRIs, and NARIs) and inhibitors of monoamine oxidase (MAOIs). The first-line drug treatment in contemporary practice is usually a SSRI such as fluoxetine (Prozac). The most common unwanted side effects of SSRIs are nausea, tension, and restlessness. SSRIs are preferred to the older TCAs because of the potential side effects of TCAs which include tremor, dry mouth, urinary retention, constipation, sexual difficulties, drowsiness, and potential disruption to cardiac rhythm.

Non-adherence to antidepressant medication can be a problem; it often results from the adverse effects of the medication. Also, some patients with depression may feel so hopeless that they believe that medication cannot help them and therefore stop taking it. Some patients will be advised to stay on antidepressant medication even after they have recovered from the depressive episode, usually for 6 months but sometimes for 2 years or longer. This is known as **maintenance medication** and can be important in reducing the risk of relapse.

> Antidepressant medication is effective in moderate and severe depression, although non-adherence can be a problem.

Electroconvulsive therapy

There is undeniable evidence, including a number of randomized controlled trials, that electroconvulsive therapy (ECT) is effective in alleviating severe depression. Because it causes adverse effects such as short-term impairment of memory, it is mainly used to treat severe cases of depression that have failed to respond to antidepressant medication. Its antidepressant action is quicker than that of antidepressant drugs. Hence, it is used in cases where a rapid response is highly desirable, such as in cases where there is a risk of death from lack of eating or drinking.

ECT involves applying an electrical current, usually bilaterally, to the skull of an anaesthetized patient to produce a seizure. The treatment is given two or three times per week, and the average number of administrations required is between four and eight. Its beneficial effects probably result from changes in the serotonergic and noradrenergic neurotransmitter systems.

Psychological treatments

Psychological and social support is important for patients with depression and their families. Acceptance, reassurance, and moral support are undoubtedly necessary and beneficial. Such support can help to minimize the stressors that play an important role in maintaining depression. Informal psychological and social support can be an effective treatment in many cases of mild depression.

Formal **cognitive behavioural therapy** (CBT) is an effective treatment in mild to moderate depression. There is some evidence that CBT can reduce the risk of relapse after moderately severe episodes of depression. CBT is a therapy used to treat maladaptive thoughts and behaviours. It has its roots in cognitive psychology, which emphasizes the importance of thoughts in influencing mood (as discussed in section 14.5.2 above). Therapists work with patients to draw attention to their negative thoughts and behaviours, and then to modify them. The aim is to encourage positive thinking and handling of situations, and a positive outlook for the future. CBT requires high levels of motivation and commitment from patients because they have to work hard between therapy sessions at identifying maladaptive thoughts and behaviours (through use of a diary), and then at practising the new ways of thinking and acting. CBT is complicated, and patients require a great deal of training to use it effectively.

Interpersonal psychotherapy (IPT) focuses on improving the patient's relationships with other people, and has been shown to be effective in outpatients with non-psychotic depression. However, IPT is much less widely used than CBT.

'Talk therapies', such as CBT and IPT, are effective in treating mild to moderate cases of depression.

SELF-CHECK 14.10

What is cognitive behavioural therapy (CBT)?

14.7.2 Treatment of mania

Antipsychotic medication

Antipsychotic drugs (dopamine receptor antagonists, sometimes known as major tranquillizers) are usually the first treatment given to acutely manic patients. These are

Antipsychotic drugs are discussed in section 15.5.1 on page 318.

usually administered very quickly because of the high likelihood of reckless behaviour with painful consequences.

Lithium

Lithium is commonly used as a prophylactic agent in bipolar disorder because of its mood-stabilizing effect, although it is more effective at preventing manic episodes than depressive episodes. Patients being treated with lithium have to have their plasma concentrations of lithium checked regularly because lithium concentrations can rise to dangerous levels, and the therapeutic and toxic doses are close together.

Non-adherence can be a problem in patients on lithium maintenance therapy. Patients may miss the exhilaration of episodes of mania, or may be unwilling to tolerate the side effects, which include tremor, hair loss, weight gain, sedation, impaired memory, and acne. When lithium prophylaxis is discontinued there is greatly increased risk of manic relapse, so indefinite continuation is often recommended.

The biochemical action of lithium is poorly understood, although it may work on the inositol-phosphate-dependent second-messenger pathways. Its suggested biochemical effects in the brain have not been clearly linked to its therapeutic action in bipolar disorder. Some researchers think that lithium stabilizes the population of serotonin receptors, thus preventing wide shifts in neural sensitivity. Others believe that lithium may increase the production of neuroprotective proteins, thus preventing cell death and facilitating neural or glial growth.

> **SELF-CHECK 14.11**
>
> Why does non-adherence with medication occur in patients with mood disorders?

> Lithium is a widely used effective treatment in bipolar disorder, although its mechanism of action is not understood.

Antiepileptic drugs

 More detail of the mechanism of action of these anticonvulsants is provided in section 6.7.2 on page 123.

Sodium valproate, carbamazepine, and lamotrigine are anticonvulsants usually used in the treatment of epilepsy, all of which now have a role in the treatment of bipolar disorder. These drugs are alternatives to lithium and have mood-stabilizing effects. Lamotrigine, in contrast to lithium, is thought to be superior in preventing recurrence of depressive episodes in bipolar disorder.

Psychological treatments

CBT and **family therapy** can help to reduce relapse in bipolar disorder, although the evidence for effectiveness is not as strong as that for reducing relapse in unipolar depression.

SUMMARY

- The two types of major mood disorders are unipolar depression and bipolar affective disorder.

- Unipolar depression is characterized by episodes of depression and the absence of episodes of mania.

- Bipolar I affective disorder is characterized by at least one episode of mania, which is often, though not always, accompanied by one or more episodes of depression.

- Bipolar II affective disorder is characterized by at least one episode of hypomania, accompanied by one or more episodes of depression.

- Mood disorders are common. Lifetime risks of unipolar depression and bipolar disorder are approximately 10% and 1% respectively.

- Women are twice as likely as men to suffer from unipolar depression.

- The causes of mood disorders are complex and multifactorial.

- Genetic and non-genetic factors both play an important role in the aetiology of mood disorders.

- Patients with mood disorders show characteristic patterns of personality traits and cognitive style.

- Adverse life events can predispose to, and precipitate, mood disorders.

- There is evidence of decreased monoamine transmission and altered brain metabolism in mood disorder patients.

- Depression is associated with overactivity of the HPA axis.

- Antidepressant drugs are widely used in the treatment of depression.

- ECT is effective in alleviating severe depression.

- Psychological therapies are effective in treating mild to moderate cases of depression.

- Lithium is commonly used as a prophylactic agent is bipolar affective disorder.

- Non-adherence to medication can be a problem when treating mood disorder patients.

FURTHER READING

Books

N. Andreasen. *Brave new brain: conquering mental illness in the era of the genome.* Oxford: Oxford University Press, 2004.
Engaging, readable and comprehensive overview of modern approaches to understanding mental illness.

F. K. Goodwin and K. R. Jamison. *Manic-depressive illness.* Oxford: Oxford University Press, 1990.
An encyclopedic guide to all aspects of bipolar affective disorder.

K. R. Jamison. *An unquiet mind: a memoir of moods and madness.* London: Picador, 1997.
Extremely well written and readable account of coming to terms with mood disorder and psychiatric treatment.

L. Wolpert. *Malignant sadness: the anatomy of depression.* London: Faber & Faber, 2001.
Readable and intelligent account of the experience of depression, and the epidemiology, underlying causes and treatments.

Review papers

L. B. Alloy, L. Y. Abramson, S. Urosevic *et al.* The psychosocial context of bipolar disorder: environmental, cognitive, and developmental risk factors. *Clinical Psychology Review* 2005; **25**(8): 1043–1075.

N. Craddock, M. C. O'Donovan, and M. J. Owen. Genes for schizophrenia and bipolar disorder? Implications for psychiatric nosology. *Schizophrenia Bulletin* 2006; **32**(1): 9–16.

T. Deckersbach, D. D. Dougherty, and S. L. Rauch. Functional imaging of mood and anxiety disorders. *Journal of Neuroimaging* 2006; **16**(1): 1–10.

K. P. Ebmeier, C. Donaghey, and J. D. Steele. Recent developments and current controversies in depression. *Lancet* 2006; **367**: 153–167.

A. R. Hariri, E. M. Drabant, and D. R. Weinberger. Imaging genetics: perspectives from studies of genetically driven variation in serotonin function and corticolimbic affective processing. *Biological Psychiatry* 2006; **59**(10): 888–897.

J. P. Herman, M. M. Ostrander, N. K. Mueller, and H. Figueiredo. Limbic system mechanisms of stress regulation: hypothalamo-pituitary-adrenocortical axis. *Progress in Neuro-Psychopharmacology and Biological Psychiatry* 2005; **29**(8): 1201–1213.

D. F. Levinson. The genetics of depression: a review. *Biological Psychiatry* 2006; **60(2)**: 84–92.

J. Scott. Psychotherapy for bipolar disorders—efficacy and effectiveness. *Journal of Psychopharmacology* 2006; **20**: 46–50.

CHAPTER FIFTEEN

Schizophrenia and related psychoses

Lisa Jones and Femi Oyebode

INTRODUCTION

Schizophrenia (meaning 'splitting or fragmenting of the mind') and related psychoses are a group of serious mental disorders characterized by psychotic symptoms such as **hallucinations** (false perceptions) and **delusions** (firmly held false beliefs), which involve a loss of contact with reality. Schizophrenia does not imply a split personality or multiple personalities, as is often believed by lay people.

As we shall see, schizophrenia is a puzzling and relatively common debilitating condition that causes a great deal of suffering and distress. It is most unfortunate that 'schizo' has come to be used as a slang derogatory term that adds to the severe stigmatization experienced by sufferers. The course of schizophrenia is often chronic with a poor long-term prognosis, which means that sufferers are usually unable to work or enjoy normal social functioning. Some patients experience recurrent episodes of acute illness, but often do not return to their usual level of functioning between episodes and gradually deteriorate. A minority of sufferers recover completely after a single acute episode of schizophrenia.

In this chapter we describe the symptoms and signs of schizophrenia, discuss the epidemiology and who is most at risk of developing schizophrenia. We discuss what is known about the biological and non-biological causes of schizophrenia, and outline common pharmacological and psychological treatments. We end with a brief discussion of psychotic disorders related to schizophrenia.

Schizophrenia does not imply that sufferers have split or multiple personalities.

15.1 What are the clinical features of schizophrenia?

Schizophrenia is a **syndrome**, which means that different patients present with very different clinical pictures. No symptom is defining of schizophrenia because each is present in some patients, and none is present in all patients. Schizophrenia affects all aspects of the mind (perceptions, thoughts, emotions, motivations) and behaviours. Psychiatrists classify the signs and symptoms of schizophrenia into those that are present in schizophrenia and not in healthy individuals (**positive symptoms**) and those that are a loss of normal abilities (**negative symptoms**).

> Positive symptoms are characterized by their presence in schizophrenia and negative symptoms are characterized by loss of particular functions in schizophrenia.

15.1.1 Positive symptoms

The core positive symptoms are hallucinations and delusions. One of the most common symptoms of schizophrenia is the experience of **auditory hallucinations**. These occur in approximately 75% of schizophrenia sufferers. Typically they take the form of voices, although may be simple sounds such as birdsong, tapping, or music. The voices may utter single words or short phrases to the patient, but typically are longer sentences that either provide a running commentary on the individual's behaviour or refer to them in the third person, for example, 'now he's going to bed', or 'she's going out of the front door'. Some patients experience two or more voices discussing them in the third person. Often the voices are derogatory or threatening. Sometimes they can give commands. Other patients may hear voices repeating their own thoughts aloud (**thought echo**).

Visual hallucinations also occur, but are less common than auditory hallucinations. They can be perceptions of simple flashes of light or shadows, more complex images of objects or people, or sometimes visions of whole scenes. There may also be **tactile** (such as a crawling sensation on the skin), **gustatory** (such as tasting poison in food), or **olfactory** (such as smelling gas) hallucinations.

> Auditory hallucinations are very common in schizophrenia.

Several types of delusion occur in schizophrenia. Some patients experience **delusional mood** before the onset of actual delusions. In this state, patients strongly suspects that something strange and often sinister is happening, and that it refers to them in some way, but they are not sure exactly what is going on. **Persecutory delusions** are common, where sufferers believe that someone wants to harm them in some way. They may believe that whole groups of people are conspiring against them. **Delusions of reference** are also common in schizophrenia. These are false beliefs that events, objects, or people have a special personal significance. For example, sufferers may believe that a story in the news is directed at them or that the arrangements of objects in a room is sending a secret message to them. Some patients experience **delusional perception** where a delusion arises suddenly as a result of a normal everyday occurrence, for example, a falling leaf touched a patient on the head and therefore he knew that he was going to be murdered. Less specific, but still bizarre, delusions with religious and sexual themes may also be present.

Other types of delusions that occur in schizophrenia can be particularly difficult for non-sufferers to understand. **Delusions of passivity** involve beliefs that a mysterious external alien force has taken control of one's will or actions. Sometimes these can involve loss of control of one's own thoughts. Sufferers can believe that alien thoughts are being inserted into their mind (**thought insertion**), that their own thoughts are being withdrawn from their mind (**thought withdrawal**), or that their thoughts are leaking out of their mind and somehow are being broadcast to others (**thought broadcasting**). Streams of thought may stop suddenly so that the mind is distressingly empty of thoughts, known as **thought block**. Some patients believe that a member of their family or close friend has been replaced by an impostor who is very skilled at impersonating the family member or friend (**delusions of misidentification**, or Capgras syndrome). In some patients, the psychosis can be described as systematized, in that their hallucinations and delusions are centred on a common theme.

> Several types of delusions occur in schizophrenia.

The unusual experiences associated with schizophrenia can make sufferers appear odd, eccentric, or bizarre in their behaviour. Patients with schizophrenia may appear frightened, perplexed, suspicious, angry, or withdrawn. Some patients will smile or laugh for no apparent reason, or show emotion that is incongruous to the circumstances, such as giggling while a serious or distressing event is taking place (**inappropriate affect**). Others will spend a lot of time apparently talking to themselves, which is often because they are responding to auditory hallucinations.

Some sufferers demonstrate **positive formal thought disorder**, which means that there are abnormalities in the form of their thoughts that are reflected in their speech (contrast this to delusions, where there are abnormalities of the content of thoughts). These abnormalities take many forms. There may be a general vagueness (**poverty of content of thought**), a lack of connection between ideas (**loosening of associations**, also known as knight's-move thinking, from a chess analogy), responses to questions may be illogical (**tangentiality**), new words (neologisms) may be created, or thought and speech may be completely incoherent and make no grammatical sense (**word salad**).

> Positive formal thought disorder describes abnormalities in the **form** of thoughts, whereas delusions are abnormalities in the **content** of thoughts.

 Delusions, hallucinations and other psychotic symptoms are introduced in section 4.4 on page 73.

Table 15.1 First-rank symptoms of schizophrenia

Auditory hallucinations of the following types:	Two or more voices discussing the patient in the third person
	Thought echo
	Voices commenting on the patient's behaviour
Thought interference of the following types:	Thought insertion
	Thought withdrawal
	Thought broadcasting
Delusions of passivity	
Delusional perception	

---

case study: Acute schizophrenia

BOX 15.1

A 19-year-old single man began to behave strangely shortly after he left home to go to university. Within the first 4 weeks at university his flatmates noticed that he became socially withdrawn to the degree that he hardly left his room. He was neglecting his personal hygiene, appeared distracted and uncommunicative, and occasionally was seen to be laughing for no apparent reason and talking to himself. At night, he paced his bedroom, banged on the walls, and shouted out obscenities.

When he was assessed by psychiatrists he claimed that everyone could read his mind and that his thoughts were no longer private. He believed that there was a conspiracy to kill him, even though he was not sure who was responsible for this conspiracy and why he was a target. He also believed that he was being watched and followed everywhere. He claimed that light bulbs held microphones that were used to eavesdrop on his conversations.

Furthermore, he described hearing voices of two people, a man and woman, who talked endlessly about him, commenting on his actions and what he was wearing. These voices also shouted obscenities at him and forced him to shout out obscenities in turn. He agreed to be admitted into hospital on condition that the hospital authorities protect him from his enemies.

SELF-CHECK 15.1

What are the main types of positive symptoms that occur in schizophrenia?

Not all of the symptoms we have described are specific to schizophrenia. However, some are highly predictive of schizophrenia and, as such, are called **first-rank symptoms**. Table 15.1 summarizes the first-rank symptoms of schizophrenia.

Box 15.1 describes a typical patient with acute schizophrenia, displaying florid psychotic symptoms.

15.1.2 Negative symptoms

Chronic negative symptoms often follow on from the acute phase of schizophrenia, and are sometimes referred to as a 'defect state'. However, it is not thought that they are secondary to the positive symptoms, or to medication, as some patients experience negative symptoms before the onset of florid psychosis and unmedicated patients also experience negative symptoms.

Avolition and **apathy** are core negative symptoms. Patients lack motivation, drive, and initiative, and often spend many hours doing nothing at all. They often become very socially withdrawn (**asociality**), and loss of contact with family and friends is common. Self-care usually deteriorates, as does upkeep of the home, resulting in a dirty, often squalid, living environment.

People with schizophrenia commonly lack the normal variations in mood experienced by healthy individuals. This is known as **affective blunting** or affective flattening, and is often shown in a lack of facial expression, a lack of expressive gesture, and a monotonous voice. Affective blunting is present in around two-thirds of schizophrenia patients. There may be reductions or slowness in the stream of thoughts, known as **poverty of thought**.

Researchers have also shown that patients with chronic schizophrenia have cognitive decline, that is, their intellectual abilities seem to be reduced from **pre-morbid** levels. These chronic negative symptoms are severely disabling for many patients, and make it impossible for them to hold down a job, enjoy life's pleasures, or have a meaningful relationship.

> Negative symptoms in schizophrenia tend to be chronic and are severely disabling.

A typical patient with chronic schizophrenia displaying negative symptoms is described in Box 15.2.

---

case study: Chronic schizophrenia

BOX 15.2

A 37-year-old man was brought to the outpatient clinic by a community psychiatric nurse (CPN) for review of his treatment. He lived alone in a block of flats in an inner city area. He had been known to the psychiatric service since the age of 17 years when he was first admitted and treated for schizophrenia.

Since that first episode he had been admitted on eight further occasions, some under the Mental Health Act. In the 20 years that he had been known to the services, he had never been fully recovered. He continued to express delusions of persecution and delusions of passivity, and experience auditory hallucinations. Although he was receiving a combination of antipsychotic medication administered as a depot injection every 4 weeks and oral anticholinergic medication for the treatment of the extrapyramidal side effects of his medication, he continued to exhibit the psychotic symptoms described above.

In addition to the positive symptoms, the CPN confirmed that he was lacking in energy, drive, and motivation. This was apparent from the fact that he rarely got out of bed before midday, and he did very little when he was out of bed. He did not go out socially, nor did he visit family or friends. His personal hygiene was quite poor. He did not change his clothing from day to day. He hardly washed. His flat was dirty and untidy.

On examination in the clinic, his affect was flat, and his speech was monosyllabic and impoverished in content. There was an absence of spontaneous speech. His gestures were markedly reduced in rate and intensity. He seemed to be preoccupied with his internal experiences.

SELF-CHECK 15.2

What are the main types of negative symptoms that occur in schizophrenia?

15.1.3 Mood symptoms

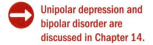

Unipolar depression and bipolar disorder are discussed in Chapter 14.

Patients with schizophrenia often have changes in mood such as depression, elation, or irritability. It is unclear whether the mood changes are an integral part of the disorder, or secondary responses to either the experience of having schizophrenia or the treatment of schizophrenia. In some cases it is difficult to know whether the symptoms of schizophrenia or the mood disorder are most prominent. Such cases are described as **schizoaffective disorder**. Cases can be either schizoaffective disorder–depressed type or schizoaffective disorder–bipolar type, according to whether the co-morbid mood disorder is unipolar depression or bipolar disorder.

> A psychotic illness with equally prominent mood symptoms is described as schizoaffective disorder.

15.1.4 Other symptoms

Sometimes patients with schizophrenia exhibit **stereotypies**, which are odd movements repeated over and over again (such as rocking to and fro on a chair or rubbing the head round and round with one hand). When these strange repetitive movements are goal-directed they are called **mannerisms** (for example, saluting three times before entering a room).

In severe rare cases, patients may become **catatonic**. A catatonic stupor is characterized by mutism and unresponsivity, although the patient is fully conscious. Patients may adopt statuesque posturing, whereby the muscles are held in a pliant state called **waxy flexibility**, and sufferers obediently permit themselves to be rearranged into awkward, uncomfortable positions that they may subsequently hold for hours. Catatonic excitement is characterized by hyperactive, sometimes violent, behaviour and continuous shouting with no clear antecedents and no clear purpose.

15.2 How common is schizophrenia?

The lifetime risk in the general population of developing schizophrenia is 1%, and this is equal in men and women. The **point prevalence** is around 4 per 1000 of the population, and the **annual incidence** is 10–20 new cases per 100 000 of the population.

The incidence of schizophrenia appears to be fairly stable across different cultures and ethnic groupings. There is some evidence that immigrants and Afro-Caribbeans born in the UK have higher rates of schizophrenia, although reasons for this are unclear. Given the long-term care needed by most sufferers, schizophrenia represents a major burden for health services. In the USA, the monetary cost of schizophrenia exceeds that of all cancers.

The illness usually begins in the late teenage years or early twenties, although men generally have an unexplained earlier age of onset than women. Evidence also suggests that the course of the illness is generally more severe in men, with a worse prognosis.

Unmarried people and people living in social deprivation have a significantly increased risk of schizophrenia; for example, the point prevalence among homeless people is 100 per 1000 of the population. This is further discussed later in section 15.3.5. Approximately 10% of schizophrenia sufferers, particularly young people in the early stages of the illness, will commit suicide.

> The lifetime risk in the general population of developing schizophrenia is 1%.

> The risk of developing schizophrenia is equal in men and women, although men tend to develop the illness earlier in their life, and may have a more severe and chronic illness.

SELF-CHECK 15.3

Why do you think the annual incidence of schizophrenia is much lower than the point prevalence?

15.3 What are the likely causes of schizophrenia?

We do not know what causes schizophrenia. However, we know for certain that the causes are complex and multifactorial. There is strong evidence for a biological (including genetic) basis, and evidence that other environmental risk factors (such as obstetric complications and excessive cannabis use) predispose to, or precipitate, the illness. We know that schizophrenia is caused by complex interactions between nature and nurture.

15.3.1 Genetics

Schizophrenia is more common in the family members of patients with schizophrenia than in the general population. First-degree relatives (parents, siblings, offspring) of a schizophrenia sufferer have a 10-fold increased risk of schizophrenia compared to the general population (10% versus 1% lifetime risk respectively). However, this familiality could be due to the fact that families share environments as well as sharing genes.

> Close family members of schizophrenia patients have a 10-fold increased risk of schizophrenia compared to the general population.

Twin studies demonstrate that it is mainly the shared genes, rather than the shared environment, that increases the risk of schizophrenia in family members of sufferers. Studies consistently show that the **concordance** is much higher between **monozygotic** (identical) twins (around 48%) than between **dizygotic** (fraternal) twins (around 10%). The increased concordance between monozygotic twins is presumably because they have 100% of their genes in common, compared to dizygotic twins who share only half of their genetic material.

The findings of twin studies are strengthened by adoption studies. Adoptions create pairs of relatives who share (1) genes but not environment (biological relatives) and (2) environment but not genes (adoptive relatives). Again, the findings from adoption studies are consistent. Adoptees with schizophrenic biological relatives and healthy adoptive relatives have the same increased risk of schizophrenia as individuals who have been born to, and raised by, relatives with schizophrenia. Adoptees who were born to healthy biological parents, but raised by a schizophrenic adoptive parent, do not have an increased risk of schizophrenia. The concordance rate for schizophrenia among monozygotic twins who have been adopted apart, and raised by two healthy families, is the same as that among monozygotic twins who have been reared together. This evidence all suggests that shared genes, and not shared environment, explain the familial aggregation of schizophrenia.

> Studies of twins and adoptees show that familial aggregation of schizophrenia is mainly due to shared genes rather than family culture.

 The diathesis–stress model is introduced in section 4.2.1 on page 69.

The evidence for genetic factors in the aetiology of schizophrenia is highly convincing. We are fairly certain that heredity accounts for at least two-thirds of the variance in liability to schizophrenia. Complex patterns of familial resemblance make it clear that schizophrenia is not caused by a single major gene (a gene that always results in the disease in those who carry it). Rather, a number of different genes (perhaps many) are involved in a complex interplay with non-genetic factors (the **diathesis–stress model**).

Some of the genes that may be associated with schizophrenia risk are described in section 3.5.2 on page 55.

However, the search for specific susceptibility genes using modern molecular genetic techniques has yet to yield incontrovertible findings. There are a number of genes that have strong evidence to implicate their involvement in schizophrenia (such as *neuregulin 1*, *DISC1*, and *dysbindin-1*, which are currently causing much excitement among schizophrenia researchers), although the size of the increased risk that they confer is likely to be small.

An important reason for the lack of success in molecular genetic studies might be **phenotypic heterogeneity**. As we discussed above, different patients can present with very different clinical pictures. Therefore, the phenotypic heterogeneity might well reflect genetic heterogeneity in that schizophrenia could be several disorders, each with a different underlying genetic cause.

SELF-CHECK 15.4

What benefits can you think of in identifying susceptibility genes for schizophrenia?

Much work is currently being undertaken in this area, and experts feel confident that definite susceptibility genes for schizophrenia, or for certain aspects or types of schizophrenia, will be located in the near future. This will undoubtedly lead to breakthroughs in risk prediction and understanding the pathogenesis of schizophrenia and will be key to developing new and improved treatments.

Family, twin, and adoption studies are discussed in detail in Box 4.4 on page 68.

> Strong evidence is emerging for the involvement of specific genes in schizophrenia, such as *neuregulin 1*, *dysbindin-1*, and disrupted-in-schizophrenia (*DISC1*).

15.3.2 Neurodevelopmental abnormalities

The **neurodevelopmental hypothesis of schizophrenia** has attracted much attention. This states that schizophrenia is a result of a pathological process that begins very early in life and results in abnormal development of the central nervous system.

As we discuss below, obstetric complications are more likely in schizophrenia sufferers than in the general population, which is suggestive of an early insult. Sufferers are also more likely to have developmental delays during childhood. Studies of 'high risk' children of people with schizophrenia show cognitive deficits (particularly in attention) and poor motor coordination. Mothers of patients with schizophrenia recall that their children had developmental delays, particularly with reading. Studies of the childhood medical records of adult patients with schizophrenia show evidence of low IQ, poor performance at school, behavioural and motor abnormalities (such as clumsiness, and **ambidextrousness**), and language difficulties.

As adults, patients with schizophrenia have been shown to have more neurological 'soft' signs and minor physical abnormalities than controls and dermatoglyphic (finger and palm prints) abnormalities, which are all suggestive of a developmental disorder.

> The neurodevelopmental hypothesis of schizophrenia states that schizophrenia results from a pathological process that begins early in life and leads to abnormal development of the central nervous system.

Post-mortem studies and neuroimaging studies have consistently shown brain abnormalities in schizophrenia patients. There are increased ventricular spaces and reduced cortical volumes in schizophrenia, and many studies have specifically implicated the involvement of the temporal lobes. Subtle abnormalities in the architecture of the hippocampus (such as disarrayed pyramidal cells), and its connections to the frontal lobes, have been widely reported.

Some researchers have used functional brain imaging to show that the positive symptoms of schizophrenia are associated with increased brain activity in the left hippocampal region, and the negative symptoms are associated with decreased activity in left frontal areas (the **hypofrontality hypothesis**). These brain abnormalities do not seem to progress with the course of the disorder, which suggests that they may have been present before the onset of illness, and are not simply artefacts of chronicity or treatment. Many neuroscientists believe schizophrenia, rather than being due to dysfunction in particular regions of the brain, is due to faulty connections between the different regions of the brain (that is, abnormal wiring or synaptic connections).

Neuroimaging techniques are discussed in relation to psychiatry in section 4.2.3 on page 69.

> Neuroimaging studies and post-mortem studies consistently demonstrate structural and functional brain abnormalities in patients with schizophrenia.

All the above evidence strongly suggests that schizophrenia is a disorder of neurodevelopment, in at least a substantial proportion of sufferers, which may be observable during childhood. This theory is consistent with there being a genetic basis to schizophrenia, as brain growth and development is largely under genetic control. However, it does not explain why the onset of schizophrenia does not occur until later in life, and does not account for the fact that schizophrenia can be an episodic illness.

SELF-CHECK 15.5

Outline the major lines of evidence that suggest schizophrenia is a disorder of neurodevelopment.

15.3.3 **Biochemical abnormalities**

The observation that amphetamine (which displaces dopamine from presynaptic terminals, thus increasing synaptic dopamine availability) can produce auditory hallucinations and delusions partly led to the theory that schizophrenia is caused by increased dopaminergic transmission. Dopaminergic dysfunction in schizophrenia is also implied by the efficacy of antipsychotic medications, which are dopamine antagonists as we shall see below. The potency of most typical antipsychotic medications is related to their ability to block dopamine D_2 receptors.

However, the **dopamine hypothesis of schizophrenia** has become less dominant since the advent of atypical antipsychotic medications, such as clozapine, which have a much wider ranging pharmacological profile. Additionally, very little support for excessive dopamine activity in schizophrenia has emerged from post-mortem studies and functional neuroimaging studies.

> The dopamine hypothesis of schizophrenia states that schizophrenia is caused by increased transmission of the neurotransmitter dopamine.

 GABAergic transmission is described in section 2.2.4 on page 29.

More recently, increasing interest has been shown in the possible roles that increased glutamatergic and serotonergic transmission, and reduced GABAergic (gamma-aminobutyric acid (GABA) is an inhibitory neurotransmitter) transmission, may play in the pathogenesis of schizophrenia.

For example, reductions in GABAergic neuronal density and abnormalities in receptors and reuptake sites have been identified in several cortical and subcortical GABA systems, and the use of GABA agonists has been associated with improvement in schizophrenia symptoms in several clinical studies.

The mechanisms of neurotransmission are described in sections 2.2.3 and 2.2.4 from page 28.

However, the biochemical basis of schizophrenia is still far from clear. Together with modern molecular genetic and neuroimaging approaches, further biochemical investigations in both animals and humans are crucial to our understanding of the complex biological basis of schizophrenia. Improved knowledge of the underlying pathophysiology will surely lead to important advances in treatment for this devastating illness.

> Altered transmission of the neurotransmitters glutamate, serotonin, and GABA have been implicated in schizophrenia.

15.3.4 **Pre-morbid personality**

There is evidence that some patients with schizophrenia displayed unusual pre-morbid personality traits. These are known as **schizoid** or **schizotypal** personality traits, and involve solitariness, suspiciousness, and odd thought and speech patterns. Such personality characteristics may be early manifestations of the underlying schizophrenia genotype or neurodevelopmental pathology, or may be independent risk factors for the disorder.

Importantly, studies show that by no means all patients with schizophrenia demonstrated evidence of abnormal pre-morbid personality, and some showed evidence of very high levels of pre-morbid social functioning. Evidence of pre-morbid personality abnormalities may well be predictive of poor prognosis in schizophrenia.

> Some patients with schizophrenia had unusual pre-morbid personality traits.

SELF-CHECK 15.6

Can you think of any difficulties in assessing the pre-morbid personality of an individual with schizophrenia?

15.3.5 Environmental factors

We know that non-genetic factors must play an important role in the aetiology of schizophrenia by looking at the concordance rate between pairs of monozygotic twins. As discussed in section 15.3.1, approximately half of members of monozygotic twin pairs do not suffer from schizophrenia when their co-twin is a sufferer. This would be an unlikely observation if genes were the sole cause of the disorder, given that monozygotic twin pairs share 100% of their genetic material. Therefore, we know that **non-shared environmental factors** are important, whether it be in precipitating, or predisposing to, schizophrenia.

> Twin studies show that non-shared environmental (non-genetic) factors are important in the aetiology of schizophrenia.

SELF-CHECK 15.7

What do we mean by a predisposing factor and a precipitating factor?

As mentioned in section 15.3.2, obstetric complications have been associated with an increased risk of developing schizophrenia later in life. The complications can be during pregnancy (bleeding, maternal diabetes, rhesus incompatibility, pre-eclampsia, maternal influenza during the second trimester, fetal malnutrition), labour (asphyxia, emergency Caesarean section, winter birth), or fetal development (low birth weight, congenital abnormalities, reduced head circumference). However, the size of the increased risk is very small, and the studies are not always easy to interpret as many of them are based on retrospective data.

It is also not clear how these factors work to increase the risk of schizophrenia. There is also a question mark over the direction of causality between schizophrenia and birth complications; that is, it is perfectly plausible that a pre-existing, presumably genetic, neural defect could cause perinatal complications rather than the other way around.

> Obstetric complications have been associated with an increased risk of schizophrenia.

Low socio-economic status is associated with schizophrenia. However, it is not clear whether this is a cause or a consequence of the disorder. Both arguments are plausible. Living in social deprivation, especially homelessness, increases exposure to a number of proposed risk factors (poverty, poor nutrition, inadequate education, poor health care), and people who develop schizophrenia are likely to become more socially deprived because they are unable to function in daily life. The latter argument is known as the **downward social drift** hypothesis.

Heavy consumption of cannabis, particularly starting in the early teenage years, has also been proposed as a precipitating factor for schizophrenia, but this may well be related to pre-morbid personality difficulties, or a consequence of the early stages of undiagnosed schizophrenia.

Other possible precipitating factors are stressful adverse life events occurring shortly before the onset of schizophrenia, such as a relationship break-up, joining the army, or

Table 15.2 Features of high expressed emotion (high EE) among relatives of schizophrenia patients

	Examples
Critical and hostile attitudes	
Dislike, disapproval, or resentment	'He never gets out of bed. He's still watching TV at 1 a.m. and then he falls asleep with the TV still on and it buzzes all night. He then can't get up the next morning. It really annoys me.'
Aggression	'He never washes, it's embarrassing. We go out shopping and he hasn't washed or shaved. He hasn't even combed his hair. I feel so angry I could hit him.'
Blame	'It's her fault her father left us. He just couldn't cope with her behaviour any more. I have to look after her, so I can't work to save up for a better life.'
Perception that the patient has control of the illness	'She should pull herself together. She should tidy herself up a bit and find a nice boyfriend.'
Emotional overinvolvement	
Statements of attitude	'I love her so much, I would do anything for her.'
Dramatization	'All his friends from school are doctors now. They are so very clever. He was clever too. He was top of the class in everything.'
Exaggerated emotional responses	'Her Dad has had to have a heart bypass operation. It's such a shame. He's very seriously ill you know, and getting worse every single day.'
Reports of self-sacrifice/devotion	'I don't work so that I can be here whenever she needs me. If I have to go out I use the bus so that the car is here in case she needs it.'
Lack of objectivity	'They're not leaving him alone. They're watching him all the time and talking about him. I wish they would leave him alone and stop troubling him for a few hours at least.'
Overprotective behaviour	'He can't be trusted to take his tablets. I get him out of bed at 8 a.m. every morning to make sure he has his tablets. We have our breakfast together and then I like him to come shopping with me. I always attend his appointments with him. I like to make sure he's telling the doctors the right information. I also like to be sure the nurses are giving him the right medication.'
Emotional displays	Crying

failing an examination. Stressful life events after onset are also thought to contribute to relapse and a poor outcome in schizophrenia.

High levels of **expressed emotion** (high EE) among the family members of patients with schizophrenia, especially high levels of critical and hostile comments and emotional over-involvement, have been shown to lead to increased relapse rates among sufferers. See Table 15.2 for more specific details about the features of high EE. One important study of schizophrenia patients living with their families showed that the relapse rate for high-EE cases was 50% compared with 21% in low-EE cases. However, there is very little evidence that early family relationships contribute to the development of schizophrenia. The prevailing and blame-levelling idea developed in the 1940s of a so-called **schizophrenogenic mother**, who causes schizophrenia in her child by being dominant, hostile, and overprotective, is thankfully no longer widely accepted.

> Family relationships can be important in determining the likelihood of relapse in schizophrenia, but there is little evidence that they are causal factors.

15.4 How is schizophrenia assessed?

Because the aetiology of schizophrenia is still obscure, it is defined purely in terms of its symptoms and signs. A thorough examination of the patient's psychological, physical, and social status is usually conducted. A clinical interview with an individual presenting with the symptoms and signs described above can pose particular challenges.

Invariably **insight** into their own mental state is absent in psychotic patients. Sometimes patients can find it difficult to describe their psychotic symptoms. This might be because of embarrassment or because of fear of being classed as 'insane'. Some patients may be too frightened to divulge the content of their voices or beliefs of being persecuted. Indeed, some patients may believe that the doctor assessing them is part of the conspiracy against them.

Collateral information from a reliable informant such as a parent or carer is invaluable. Although media portrayals of schizophrenia emphasize violence, the reality is that violence to other people is uncommon and homicide is rare. Nevertheless, the risk of violence is increased in the presence of command hallucinations, and delusions of passivity and persecution. It is, therefore, important for the risk of violence to be carefully assessed in all schizophrenia patients. Patients at high risk of violent behaviour usually require hospitalization, often compulsorily, and may need to be placed in a special area (an intensive care unit) of a psychiatric hospital with highly trained staff until the risk is reduced. The risk of violence usually abates as acute psychotic symptoms are brought under control with medication.

> It is important that doctors assess the risk of violence to self or others in schizophrenia although, contrary to popular belief, the risk of violence to others is usually low.

15.5 What treatments are available for schizophrenia?

There are a number of pharmacological, psychological, and social approaches to the treatment of schizophrenia. The wide-ranging needs of patients are often met by a multidisciplinary care team, which includes psychiatrists, mental health nurses, psychologists, social workers, and occupational therapists. Treatment packages will be individually tailored for each patient.

> Multidisciplinary treatment packages are tailored for each individual patient with schizophrenia.

15.5.1 Antipsychotic medication

The most effective treatment for acute psychosis is antipsychotic medication (sometimes known as neuroleptics or major tranquillizers). However, their effectiveness in treating the negative symptoms of schizophrenia is less clear.

There are many antipsychotic drugs available. They can be divided into two categories: conventional antipsychotics (also known as first generation) and atypical antipsychotics (also known as second generation).

The conventional antipsychotics block dopamine D_2 receptors. They are effective in about two-thirds of schizophrenia patients, but can cause severe and distressing adverse effects, such as, extrapyramidal effects (parkinsonism, acute dystonia, akathisia, and tardive dyskinesia). See Table 15.3 for a summary of the clinical features of these extrapyramidal side effects. Anticholinergic medication can be prescribed alongside antipsychotics to prevent the development of extrapyramidal symptoms, although anticholinergics have side effects of their own and may reduce the efficacy of antipsychotics.

Atypical antipsychotics vary in the extent to which they block D_2, D_4, and $5HT_{2A}$ receptors. They also bind to adrenergic and muscarinic receptors. They cause fewer extrapyramidal side effects, but can still cause unpleasant effects such as weight gain and sexual dysfunction.

> Antipsychotic drugs are the most effective treatment for acute psychosis.

Antipsychotics are commonly used as **maintenance medication** in schizophrenia to reduce the risk of relapse, and their efficacy in this regard has been clearly demonstrated by a number of controlled studies. Adherence with medication is often very poor among schizophrenia sufferers, so intramuscular depot injections, which are slow-release and administered every 2–4 weeks, are often used rather than oral medication.

Table 15.3 Clinical features of extrapyramidal side effects of antipsychotic medication

Extrapyramidal effect	Clinical features
Parkinsonism	Expressionless face
	Shuffling gait and lack of associated movements when walking
	Stooped posture
	Muscle rigidity
	Coarse tremor
	Slowed, awkward movements
Acute dystonia	Tongue protrusion
	Grimacing
	Spasm of ocular muscles (oculogyric crisis)
	Twisted or bent neck (torticollis)
	Spasm of the spine (opisthotonus)
Akathisia	Physical restlessness of the arms and legs
	Inability to keep still while standing, sitting, or lying
Tardive dyskinesia	Chewing and sucking movements
	Grimacing
	Akathisia
	Uncontrollable writhing movements of the limbs and body (choreoathetoid movements)

15.5.2 Psychological treatments

Psychological support and education about the illness and treatment are crucial in schizophrenia. Similar counselling also benefits the sufferer's family. **Family therapy** can help to reduce the levels of emotional involvement and criticism among relatives, which as we discussed above may be important in reducing the risk of relapse. Such therapy includes providing education about schizophrenia to relatives, and group meetings with other relatives to share experiences and coping techniques.

Some evidence suggests that formal **cognitive behavioural therapy** may help patients to cope with chronic hallucinations and delusions. An example is giving alternative explanations of delusional beliefs in a non-confrontational and non-threatening environment.

SELF-CHECK 15.10

How might family therapy help in the treatment of schizophrenia?

15.5.3 Social care

Patients with chronic schizophrenia often have many social needs, such as housing, social networks, and occupation. There is evidence that both overstimulation and understimulation can be harmful in schizophrenia, so attempts are usually made to place patients in environments where they have ordered daily routines with some limited responsibilities.

Discharging patients from psychiatric hospitals and providing their care 'in the community' has been a major aim for the last 40 years or so. Hostels, 'halfway houses', day centres, and sheltered workshops offering rehabilitative programmes have become common, although demand for such facilities far outweighs provision. The lack of adequate support in the community can have disturbing, and very occasionally violent, consequences.

> It is important to recognize the wide-ranging social needs of patients with schizophrenia.

15.5.4 Antidepressants and lithium

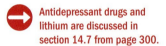

Antidepressant drugs and lithium are discussed in section 14.7 from page 300.

Medications used to treat mood disorders may be beneficial in schizophrenia, particularly in schizoaffective disorder. Antidepressants are helpful in schizoaffective disorder–depressed type, and lithium may be useful in schizoaffective disorder–bipolar type.

15.6 Other psychotic disorders related to schizophrenia

There are a number of psychotic disorders that resemble schizophrenia but do not share all of the features. The key difference is usually that they lack the chronicity of schizophrenia but share some of the acute positive symptoms. The psychosis is treated in the same way as the acute positive symptoms of schizophrenia, as we have discussed above.

15.6.1 Schizophreniform psychosis

Schizophreniform disorder is characterized by the same symptoms and signs of schizophrenia, but is a much shorter, transient disorder. A schizophreniform disorder lasts no longer than 1 month.

15.6.2 Delusional disorder

Delusional disorder is characterized by persistent delusions in the absence of any other features of schizophrenia. Delusional disorders often begin in middle age or later in life, and can be an early stage of schizophrenia.

An example of a delusional disorder is **morbid jealousy** (or Othello syndrome), where the sufferer has a false, unshakeable conviction that their sexual partner is being unfaithful. The delusion is usually accompanied by obsessive behaviour, such as checking the partner's diary and underwear, constantly questioning the partner about their whereabouts, or following them. The risk of violence in morbid jealousy sufferers is quite high, and needs careful assessment by a mental health specialist. Morbid jealousy is more common in men than women.

Erotomania (also known as de Clerambault syndrome) is another example of a delusional disorder. The sufferer is usually, though not always, female and is convinced that another person who is usually, but not necessarily, of a higher status, secretly loves her. She will pester her supposed lover with letters and gifts, and may follow him and try to visit his home or place of work. As with morbid jealousy, erotomania can have disastrous consequences for both the sufferer and the supposed lover.

SELF-CHECK 15.11

How does delusional disorder differ from schizophrenia?

SUMMARY

- Schizophrenia and related psychoses are serious mental disorders characterized by psychotic symptoms, which involve a loss of contact with reality.

- The clinical features of schizophrenia can be classified into positive symptoms and negative symptoms.

- Positive symptoms include hallucinations (false perceptions), delusions (false beliefs), and positive formal thought disorder.

- Negative symptoms are usually chronic, and include avolition, apathy, asociality, poverty of thought, and affective blunting.

- Schizoaffective disorder involves symptoms of schizophrenia and symptoms of mood disorder in equal prominence.

- The lifetime risk of developing schizophrenia is 1%.

- Schizophrenia is equally common in men and women.

- The causes of schizophrenia are complex and multifactorial.

- Genetic and non-genetic factors both play an important role in the aetiology of schizophrenia.

- Strong evidence is emerging for the involvement of specific genes in schizophrenia such as *neuregulin 1*, *dysbindin-1*, and *DISC1*.

- There is compelling evidence that at least some cases of schizophrenia are disorders of neuro-development.

- Post-mortem studies and neuroimaging studies have consistently shown brain abnormalities in patients with schizophrenia.

- Altered serotonin, glutamate, GABA, and possibly dopamine, neurotransmission have been implicated in schizophrenia.

- Some patients with schizophrenia showed evidence of unusual pre-morbid personality traits.

- Obstetric complications, low socio-economic status, heavy consumption of cannabis, and stressful life events have all been associated with schizophrenia.

- High levels of expressed emotion from family members increase relapse rates in schizophrenia.

- Patients with schizophrenia are usually treated by a multidisciplinary team.

- Antipsychotic medication is the most effective treatment for acute psychosis, but can cause severe and distressing side effects.

- Psychological and social support is important in meeting the needs of patients with schizophrenia.

- Schizophreniform psychosis and delusional disorder are examples of psychotic disorders related to schizophrenia.

FURTHER READING

N. Andreasen. *Brave new brain: conquering mental illness in the era of the genome.* Oxford: Oxford University Press, 2004.
Engaging, readable. and comprehensive overview of modern approaches to understanding mental illness.

D. Cichetti and E. F. Walker (eds). *Neurodevelopmental mechanisms in psychopathology.* Cambridge: Cambridge University Press, 2003.
Well-written, authoritative account of contemporary neurodevelopmental perspectives on mental illness.

Gottesman, I. I. *Schizophrenia genesis: the origins of madness.* New York: Freeman, 1990.
Comprehensive, readable, and compassionate account of the complex interactions of genes and environmental factors in causing schizophrenia.

McGrath, P. *Spider.* London: Penguin, 1992.
Harrowing novel that provides a frighteningly realistic portrayal of the experience of schizophrenia.

Review papers

M. R. Broome, J. B. Woolley, P. Tabraham *et al*. What causes the onset of psychosis? *Schizophrenia Research* 2005; **79**: 23–34.

M. C. Clarke, M. Harley, and M. Cannon. The role of obstetric events in schizophrenia. *Schizophrenia Bulletin* 2006; **32**: 3–8.

N. Craddock, M. C. O'Donovan, and M. J. Owen. Genes for schizophrenia and bipolar disorder? Implications for psychiatric nosology. *Schizophrenia Bulletin* 2006; **32**(1): 9–16.

F. B. Dickerson and A. F. Lehman. Evidence-based psychotherapy for schizophrenia. *Journal of Nervous and Mental Disease* 2006; **194**: 3–9.

M. J. Owen, N. Craddock, and M. C. O'Donovan. Schizophrenia: genes at last? *Trends in Genetics* 2005; **21**(9): 518–525.

J. L. Rapoport, A. M. Addington, and S. Frangou. The neurodevelopmental model of schizophrenia: update 2005. *Molecular Psychiatry* 2005; **10**: 434–449.

K. Seeber and K.S. Cadenhead. How does studying schizotypal personality disorder inform us about the prodrome of schizophrenia? *Current Psychiatry Reports* 2005; **7**: 41–50.

R. Tandon and W. W. Fleischhacker. Comparative efficacy of antipsychotics in the treatment of schizophrenia: a critical assessment. *Schizophrenia Research* 2005; **79**: 145–155.

A. J. Wearden, N. Tarrier, C. Barrowclough, T. R. Zastowny, and A. A. Rahill. A review of expressed emotion in health care. *Clinical Psychology Review* 2000; **20**(5): 633–666.

Psychoactive substance use and addiction

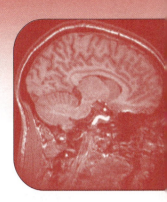

Ed Day and Alison Cooper

INTRODUCTION

The human race has long had a close relationship with substances that produce psychoactive effects, and our capacity for finding, eating, drinking, chewing, or smoking vegetable products with stimulant, sedative, euphoriant, or intoxicating properties is unique amongst living organisms.

Alcohol is known to have been produced by the earliest civilizations, and prescriptions for beer were written by physicians on clay tablets more than 4000 years ago. For centuries, opium has been extracted from the immature fruits of the opium poppy, cannabis from the Indian hemp plant, and cocaine from the leaves of the South American coca plant.

Table 16.1 lists a selection of the more commonly used psychoactive substances, and their effects. The effect that each has depends on the amount used, the frequency of use, the route with which it is taken (whether it is swallowed, smoked, sniffed, or injected), the user's past experience with this or other substances, and a variety of other factors. There also appears to be a trend towards taking combinations of drugs, and this can alter the benefits and risks of each of them.

Most substances produce some form of initial pleasure or gain for the individual, such that some people develop such a strong attachment to them that they find it hard to moderate their use. This may develop into a degree of 'necessity' or 'addiction', and with this comes a loss of personal control over use of the substance. This can lead to a range of physical, psychological, and social harms.

Table 16.1 The effects of some psychoactive substances

Name	Examples	Main effects	Withdrawal effects
Alcohol		At low doses it is both stimulating and relaxing, leading to pleasant social disinhibition. At higher doses it causes incoordination, slurred speech, unconsciousness, and even coma	Sweating, nausea and vomiting, headache, weakness, faintness, tremor, insomnia, seizures, high blood pressure, heart rhythm abnormalities
Cannabis		Euphoria, muscular relaxation, sleepiness, intensified sights and sounds, a feeling of increased creativity and an altered sense of time and space. The user may have problems with attention and short-term memory, as well as decreased coordination and increased reaction time	Fatigue, anxiety, problems concentrating, yawning, change in appetite, feelings of depression and difficulty sleeping may be experienced after stopping frequent use
Stimulants	Amphetamine, cocaine	Increased energy and stamina, euphoria, improved confidence, less need for food or sleep	Depressed mood, fatigue, irritability, hunger
Anxiolytics and Hypnotics	Benzodiazepines such as diazepam (Valium), nitrazepam (Mogadon)	Reduce anxiety and promote sleep. Alleviate alcohol withdrawal symptoms and can produce euphoria at high doses	Anxiety, panic, insomnia, low mood and epileptic seizures if high doses are used
Opioids	Heroin, morphine, opium, codeine	A sense of warm, drowsy, dreamy euphoria, relief of pain and distress, sedation and sleep	Sweating, running eyes and nose, sneezing, yawning, shivering, agitation and restlessness, insomnia, pains in muscles and joints, nausea and vomiting, abdominal cramps, diarrhoea
Hallucinogens	LSD, magic mushrooms	Depends on the emotional state of the user. Experience of sights and sounds is altered, heightened, or misinterpreted. Unusual or original thinking patterns emerge	Unpleasant 'flashbacks' may occur
Others	Ecstasy	Has effects similar to both LSD and amphetamines. Leads to prominent mood changes, with euphoria and a feeling of closeness, but also to cognitive changes, anxiety, dry mouth, and a labile mood	Users may experience problems with mental arithmetic, memory, low mood, and sleep a day or so after taking the drug
	Phencyclidine, ketamine	Dose-related effects include euphoria, incoordination, heightened emotions, disorganized thinking, feelings of unreality, and misperceptions	Sleepiness, tremor, diarrhoea, and teeth grinding have been reported in animals

16.1 How is addiction defined and what are the signs and symptoms of substance misuse and addiction?

The term **psychoactive substance** (or just substance) means any medication or drug that alters the mind. Addiction is not an all-or-none phenomenon, and can be thought of as existing along a spectrum of severity:

use—misuse—harmful use/abuse—dependence

The point at which an individual moves from one category to another is often not clear, and it is not necessary to pass through all of the stages before reaching dependence (for example, dependence can occur on low prescribed doses of benzodiazepines, or with opioids prescribed for pain relief).

Medical systems of classification such as ICD-10 or DSM-IV provide some definitions for these terms:

Classification systems for psychiatric disorders, such as ICD-10 and DSM-IV are considered in section 4.5 on page 81.

- **Misuse** indicates that the substance is either not legal, or else is used in a way that does not comply with medical recommendations, for example drinking more alcohol than the recommended daily limits as described below.

- **Harmful use** or **abuse** is defined as a pattern of substance use that is causing damage to health but does not meet the criteria for dependence.

The term **dependence** has now largely replaced the broader term **addiction**, and can be thought of as a chronic, recurring condition with physical, psychological, and social dimensions. It is typically characterized by a loss of control over one's substance use, and is usually associated with unsuccessful attempts to cut down or control use. Substances are taken in larger amounts or over a longer period than was intended, and considerable time is spent in obtaining, using, or recovering from the effects of the drugs.

This leads to a reduction in other social, occupational, or recreational activities, but use continues despite the drug-related problems. Physical **tolerance** to the substance, and a **withdrawal** syndrome on reduction or cessation of use, are usually present. Most psychoactive substances, if used regularly, can produce some degree of dependence. The diagnostic criteria for dependence are listed in Table 16.2, and the case studies in Boxes 16.1, 16.2, and 16.3 illustrate the spectrum of severity of addiction.

Binge drinking of alcohol may be considered a form of misuse or harmful use, and is defined as drinking over twice the daily recommended limits in one day (more than 8 units for men and more than 6 for women). In the UK, a unit is defined as 8 g of alcohol. This is equivalent to half a pint of beer (3–4% alcohol), a small (125 mL) glass of wine (9% alcohol), or one pub measure of spirits. The UK Government recommends that men

Table 16.2 The ICD-10 definition of dependence states that three or more of the following must be experienced at some time during the previous year for a diagnosis of dependence:

A strong desire to take the substance

Difficulties in controlling the use of the substance

A withdrawal syndrome when substance use has ceased or been reduced. The physical symptoms of withdrawal vary across drugs, but psychological symptoms include anxiety, depression and sleep disturbance. The individual may also report the use of substances to relieve the withdrawal symptoms

Evidence of tolerance, i.e. higher doses are required to achieve the same effect

Neglect of interests and an increased amount of time taken to obtain the substance or recover from its effects

Persistent substance use despite evidence of its harmful consequences.

case study: Drug misuse

BOX 16.1

A 29-year-old single man lives alone and works as a financial adviser. He was brought up in a prosperous middle-class area, and was happy and supported as a child.

He first tried cannabis whilst at school, and continued at university. He has also tried LSD, ecstasy, and amphetamines at clubs. He drinks five or six pints of lager most Friday and Saturday nights with friends. He wouldn't dream of injecting drugs. He grows cannabis plants in his flat for himself and his friends to smoke.

case study: Drug abuse

BOX 16.2

A 31-year-old man lives with his girlfriend. He was adopted as a baby, and knows nothing of his biological parents. His adoptive parents separated when he was 6, and he now has little contact with them. He was bullied at school, and his reports described him as overactive with poor concentration.

He tried a variety of substances in his early teens, including cannabis, LSD, and ecstasy. He has been injecting amphetamines since the age of 20, having been introduced to them by a friend. He was initially worried about injecting, but soon fell into a regular pattern of use at the weekends. He never uses during the week, and never spends more on drugs than he can afford. His mood has always been 'up and down', but he feels that this is improved when he takes drugs. He works in a fast food restaurant 4 days per week, but has recently had to have several days off sick when he developed an infection at one of his injecting sites.

case study: Alcohol dependence

BOX 16.3

A 56-year-old woman had her first alcoholic drink at the age of 10. She describes 'taking to alcohol like a duck to water', and found that it helped her cope with her anxiety in social situations. She had a happy upbringing, but her father was a heavy drinker throughout his life and died of a stroke in his late fifties.

She was successful in her work as a publisher and was promoted to a senior position that she found very stressful. She suffered a 'nervous breakdown' aged 31 and was admitted to a psychiatric hospital. She had a further three admissions to hospital in the next 10 years, each time requiring medication to cope with the symptoms of alcohol withdrawal. She managed a period of 12 years of abstinence from alcohol after the last admission with no professional help.

Three years ago she met a group of friends while working away from home and was persuaded to have her first drink. Her consumption increased slowly from this point, and she now drinks over 50 units per week. She feels that her life has been a failure and is guilty about her drinking and the effect that it has had on others.

should consume no more than 21 units per week, with no more than 3–4 units per day. The equivalent figures for women are 14 units/week and 2–3 units/day.

> Dependence on a psychoactive substance has both physical and psychological components.

SELF-CHECK 16.1

What are the six key features of the dependence syndrome? What is the significance of making this diagnosis for treatment?

16.2 What is the extent of the problem?

Since the 1960s, increased availability of drugs and alcohol has led to an escalation in the use of a variety of both legal and illegal substances. Evidence gathered from many different sources (information on drug seizures, quantities of alcohol sold, surveys, and numbers attending treatment services) indicates that substance use has increased in the last 30 years.

Over 90% of adults in Britain drink alcohol, and more than 20% drink more than recommended limits. Around 5% of the population have alcohol dependence as defined above, and alcohol use accounts for up to 150 000 hospital admissions each year and 20 000 deaths. Those aged 16–24 drink the most, but those over 45 are more likely to drink every day.

The UK also has one of the highest rates of illicit substance use in Europe, with over 30% of adults (aged 15–64) having tried cannabis at least once, 12% amphetamines, 7% cocaine, and 1% heroin. Furthermore, the number of people under 18 trying illicit drugs has increased dramatically since the 1970s, with over 40% of 15–16-year olds reporting use of an illicit drug at some point. The **prevalence** of most types of drug use is greatest between 16 and 24 years, with 15% reporting use of cannabis in the last month.

Men are more likely than women to report use of all substances, although these differences lessen with age. Approximately three times as many men as women are currently attending drug treatment services in the UK.

Although survey data shows the use of illicit drugs to be higher in whites than non-whites, drug use is not limited to any one specific ethnic group. Ethnic minority groups are under-represented in treatment populations.

Being unemployed is associated with higher levels of illicit drug use, but higher income is often associated with higher consumption of alcohol and some other drugs.

> Rates of alcohol and illicit substance use are increasing in the UK.

16.3 What are the causes of addiction?

Multiple factors are usually involved in the development of a substance misuse problem in an individual. These may include genetic predisposition, family factors, adverse life events, psychological symptoms, availability and social acceptability of the substance, peer pressure, and limited educational or work opportunities. Causation is seldom straightforward, and it is usually possible to identify a combination of significant factors in any one person.

When asked why they use psychoactive substances, people give a variety of reasons: curiosity, the pleasure of trying a new experience, pressure from friends, boredom, fashion, the thrill of doing something potentially dangerous, escape from problems at home, school or work, or the need for a confidence boost.

The 'moral model' of alcoholism predominated until the nineteenth century. This attributed the cause of addiction to personal responsibility or sin, and treatment tended to concentrate on punishment, or on 'saving' the person by religious conversion. The mid to late nineenth century saw the rise of the Temperance Movement, where people began to believe that alcohol itself was the cause of alcoholism and that society was responsible for allowing alcohol to be available. This led to a period of complete prohibition of alcohol in the USA in the early twentieth century. More recently a 'medical model' has evolved, whereby the drinker is seen as a victim suffering from a disease and in need of treatment.

16.3.1 Biological factors

One of the curious observations associated with humans misusing psychoactive drugs is why one person can use a drug recreationally, while another can become dependent on it. Clearly this suggests that there are factors which vary between people but which can influence how they react to taking the drug.

One of these factors is the biology of the individual. To explore the possibility that a person's biology can influence how they respond to a drug and whether or not they will become dependent upon it, we need to know something about the effect the abused substance can have on biological processes.

What biological processes are linked to drug-taking?

If we consider the list of abused drugs in Table 16.1, we can see that all of them exert their effects on the brain. However, they appear to act on different regions of the brain, as well as on different neurotransmitter systems. As we saw in Chapters 1 and 2, we might expect that the brain region and neurotransmitter system that a substance acts upon would influence the behaviour seen in the individual. This might seem to contradict the idea that there is a single region of the brain responsible for promoting drug-taking.

However, research has demonstrated that, despite these differences, all drugs that humans are known to abuse ultimately affect a common pathway. This pathway uses the neurotransmitter **dopamine** and, as can be seen in Figure 16.1, this pathway has widespread projections to many regions of the brain.

 The dopaminergic neurons of the substantia nigra, and movement disorders related to their dysfunction, are discussed further in section 8.1.3 on page 153.

The dopaminergic neurons of the reward pathway have their somata (the plural of **soma**) located in the **ventral tegmental area**, which is found close to, but is distinct from, the dopaminergic neurons of the **substantia nigra**, a brain region that is crucially important in movement control.

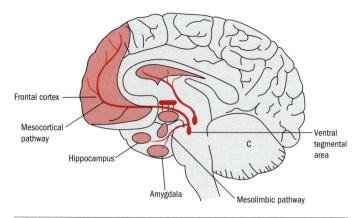

Figure 16.1 Line drawing of sagittal view of brain showing mesolimbocortical projections. Reproduced with permission from H. P. Rang *et al.*, *Pharmacology*, 5th edn. Elsevier, 2003.

Furthermore, experimental work has shown that activity of this pathway is related to the feelings of pleasure or reward, probably via its projections to the limbic structures of the temporal lobe and the prefrontal cortex. It is important to note that the precise role of dopamine and the reward circuitry in mediating the pleasurable effects and abuse of drugs is still poorly understood.

> All known drugs of abuse affect one pathway in the brain.

The role of the reward pathway in normal brain function

It may seem strange that the brain has evolved to have neural circuitry that is activated by psychoactive drugs! In fact, the normal function of this pathway appears to be to make activities such as feeding and reproduction, which are necessary for the long-term survival of the individual and the species, more pleasurable and therefore more likely to be undertaken. Psychoactive drugs merely hijack this process.

Finding evidence for genetic influences on drug-taking behaviour

It is important to remember that dopamine is released upon activation of the reward pathway in all people in response to abused drugs. So, it is possible that some parameter about this pathway is different between those people who become dependent upon a drug, and those who don't. These differences could be due, in part, to the genetic make-up of the individual.

To study the genetic influence on biological processes in humans we usually use identical and non-identical twins, since identical twins share 100% of their genes but non-identical ones only share 50%. We can assume that all other factors such as the social situation of each twin are then equivalent. To have any statistical meaning these studies must use many sets of twins. It is often difficult to find twins who either use or do not use particular drugs. For this reason, most of the studies on the influence of a person's genetics on the likelihood of their having become dependent upon a drug have been conducted in alcoholics, since alcohol is the most commonly abused substance.

Strategies for investigating the contribution of genetics to illnesses or disorders are introduced in Box 4.4 on page 68.

The study of alcoholics has demonstrated that identical twins are more likely to both develop alcoholism than are non-identical twins. When the influence of all other contributing factors is taken into account, this strongly supports the idea that there is a genetic component to the likelihood of developing alcoholism.

> Most studies on the role of genetics in drug abuse have focused on alcohol.

How might genes influence the likelihood of developing alcoholism?

Studies on human alcoholics have demonstrated that they have less dopamine in their reward pathway but normal levels in other dopaminergic pathways. However, what causes this decrease is unknown; it may be that the genetic make-up of these individuals means that they have fewer dopaminergic neurons, or that they have the correct number of neurons but that those neurons release a lower level of dopamine. Furthermore, other studies have concentrated on the receptors for the dopamine and their genes. The results for these studies are inconclusive since some found changes in the number of receptors but others did not.

Another neurotransmitter that has been implicated in alcoholism is **serotonin** or **5-hydroxytryptamine** (5-HT). Like dopaminergic pathways, serotonin pathways extend throughout the brain including a large projection to the prefrontal cortex. Hence, it is possible that these two neurotransmitter systems interact to determine an individual's response to abused drugs.

SELF-CHECK 16.2

Which neurotransmitters have been implicated in drug abuse?

So, there is evidence for an inheritable influence on alcoholism and there is some evidence to suggest that this may extend to other drugs of abuse too. However, it is clear that any genetic component is likely to be complex, possibly involving many genes. However the genetic influence is likely only to be a small contributing factor and there are very many non-genetic factors too.

16.3.2 Psychological models of addiction

A variety of psychological theories have been put forward to explain addiction to psychoactive substances, but none provides a definitive answer. As mentioned above there are multiple reasons why people first start using psychoactive substances, but most centre around pleasure or the expectation of increased efficiency or creativity. Initially most substances produce a desirable effect such as euphoria, or relief from anxiety, tension, sadness, or boredom. This may be enhanced by the social circumstances that the individual finds themselves in, and many substances allow the user to forget about a range of adverse life circumstances. Alcohol or drugs may also give a boost to self-confidence, and provide access to new groups of friends.

In the longer term, however, many substances create a new set of problems. Difficulties are ignored, minimized or denied, or wrongly attributed to other causes, and users tend to have difficulty in evaluating the advantages and disadvantages of continuing substance use. Further substance use may then be the preferred way of coping with such problems, leading to the development of a vicious circle.

Once physical dependence on a substance develops, it is likely that withdrawal symptoms will occur when the user stops taking it. These are often a strong disincentive to stopping, and can lead to a perpetuation of the addiction. However, withdrawal effects vary enormously from person to person, and the impact on the individual is partly determined by the psychological meaning attached to the symptoms.

Substance users often ascribe their drug or alcohol use to 'uncontrollable urges or cravings'. A craving is a desire for the substance, and an urge is the internal drive or stimulus to act on the craving. If a craving for one experience (for example, affection) cannot be satisfied, an individual may turn to another (such as substance use). Cravings and urges tend to be automatic and may become **autonomous** or self-perpetuating.

Behavioural factors

Behavioural theory suggests that the frequency of a behaviour is influenced by its consequences or **reinforcers**, and the likelihood of behaviour being reinforced depends on the balance of rewards and punishments involved. Psychoactive substances may be reinforcing in two different ways: through the direct effects of drugs on the brain (as seen in section 16.3.1 above), or through its effects on other reinforcers, such as social status or sexual functioning.

Just as Ivan Pavlov's dogs in the nineteenth century learnt to associate feeding with the ringing of a bell, cravings and urges can become attached (**conditioned**) to a stimulus (such as being with particular friends). Over time a process of stimulus generalization takes place, whereby the cravings and urges become associated with a wider range of people, places, or emotions (for example, originally a person may crave for a drink when with certain friends, but later it occurs at any point when they are upset, bored, or lonely). This in turn leads to an expansion of the dysfunctional beliefs, such that 'I should have a drink to be part of the group' becomes 'I need a drink to be accepted', and later 'I have to drink to relieve my loneliness and distress'.

 Learning and conditioning theory are introduced in section 4.3.1 on page 70 and the neuronal basis of Pavlov's experiments is discussed in section 2.3.1 on page 34.

Although cravings for drugs are involuntary, the subsequent urge to take them is under voluntary control (often called 'willpower'). Furthermore, there is a delay between the experience of craving and acting on the urge that provides an interval for a therapeutic intervention. Fostering a delay between craving and drug use allows the acute craving to dissipate naturally, thus lowering the chances that the person will act on it. Individuals can also be taught techniques to enhance their ability to resist the urge to use substances.

Cognitive factors

A major obstacle to eliminating substance use is the range of dysfunctional beliefs that form around drugs or alcohol. One example might be the belief that 'I can't be happy unless I take cocaine'. Stopping drug use may mean the loss of a valued safety mechanism and way of coping with problems. When a user stops taking the drug they are likely to then experience cravings, often in the context of low mood or exposure to drugs or related stimuli. The intolerable sense of loss and disappointment that then appears means that they feel driven to give in to the craving in order to feel better.

The range of dysfunctional ideas exhibited by substance users includes the belief that the substance is needed to maintain emotional balance, and that it will improve social functioning, relieve boredom or anxiety, lead to pleasure and excitement, or have a soothing effect. In addition, a number of 'permission-giving beliefs' may arise, such as 'If I give in this time, I will make sure that I resist temptation next time'. Such beliefs need to be carefully explored and modified if long-term success in achieving abstinence is to be obtained.

> The pleasant effects of drugs and the enhanced social status that they produce may act as positive reinforcers to further use. Cravings and urges are also important, as are dysfunctional beliefs.

16.3.3 The addictive personality

There is no one type of personality more likely to misuse substances or develop dependence, but aspects of personality have been linked to substance misuse. Some individuals are novelty seekers or risk takers, and others find that they need to 'self-medicate' with psychoactive substances when they experience stressful situations. There is evidence for a link between alcohol misuse and aggressive, antisocial, and impulsive personality characteristics or behaviour.

Research studies involving the long-term follow-up of children have examined personality attributes that predict substance use at a later stage. Alcohol problems in later life are more likely in those who display unrestrained aggression, hyperactivity, denial of their fears, or feelings of inferiority in childhood.

However, the large number of potential variables listed above means that it does not appear to be possible to predict 'addictive' personality traits that inevitably lead to addiction.

16.3.4 Environmental factors

Availability

In order for a person to become addicted to a substance they must first be exposed to it. For legal substances such as alcohol, cost, taxation, income, and legislation all help determine *per capita* consumption and so the incidence of problems. There is considerable evidence from many countries that reducing the real price of alcohol tends to increase its overall consumption by a population. Furthermore, measures that make alcohol easier to obtain (such as longer opening hours for bars or more retail outlets) also tend to increase consumption.

At present, UK consumers spend more of their disposable income on alcohol than they do on personal goods and services, fuel and power, or tobacco. The manufacture and distribution of alcohol is therefore a hugely profitable business, and it is estimated that the drinks industry generates approximately 1 million jobs in the UK. Political decisions about alcohol therefore involve a difficult balancing act between pleasure and profit on the one hand, and **harm reduction** on the other.

In a similar way the distribution of illicit drugs is a business and so subject to supply and demand. 'Droughts' and 'floods' of a particular substance can occur naturally or deliberately, and trends, fashions, and new technology are also important (for example, the emergence of ecstasy in the 1980s linked to the club scene).

Governments spend large sums of money in attempting to reduce the entry of illegal drugs into their countries, and such initiatives vary in success. The way a society views the use or misuse of a substance is another important factor in determining accessibility, and this may change in a relatively short space of time. The debate in the UK and other western societies about the legalization or decriminalization of cannabis is a good example.

Occupation

Occupation is linked to both opportunity and likelihood of substance use. For example, jobs where alcohol is readily available (such as publicans, bar staff, or waiters) are linked to higher levels of death from liver cirrhosis. Jobs that require frequent periods of absence from home, long and irregular working hours, very high or very low income, social pressure to drink at work, or very high stresses or hazards in the workplace, may all be linked to an increased likelihood of alcohol problems.

Family environment

The family environment that a person grows up in plays a crucial part in their likelihood of developing addiction problems. Psychological effects such as modelling of substance-using behaviour are important from an early age. Use of alcohol or drugs may be a way of escaping from social deprivation or physical, emotional and sexual abuse. However, it is hard to separate these causes from the fact that a person shares much of their genetic make-up with their biological family. Furthermore, effective parenting involving warmth, affection, consistency, and boundaries can be a strong protective factor.

Peers and friendship

Friendships and peer relationships are an important moderating influence on the behaviour of individuals. An individual may develop a peer group as a result of shared substance use, and may misuse substances as a result of the influence of the peer group. The idea of 'peer pressure' is often mentioned in association with initiation into drug use, but friends can have both positive and negative influences on each other. This may be particularly important in situations where parental influence is perceived as inadequate.

Stress and life events

External events that lead to aversive emotional states may become the stimulus to which substance use is a reinforced, learned response. Various sorts of stressors appear to increase alcohol consumption, but substance use generates its own stresses and life events, and so the picture is often hard to interpret. Life events can often be linked to periods of lapse back to substance use in abstinent individuals, and an awareness of this problem forms the basis of the 'relapse prevention' strategy of management described in section 16.6.1 below.

> **SELF-CHECK 16.3**
>
> List ten potential factors in the causation of an addiction problem.

16.4 What harm is caused by substance misuse?

Dependence on a substance may cause a range of harms to the individual, including physical and psychological problems, disruption to relationships, unemployment, and the need to commit crime to make money to pay for drugs.

16.4.1 **Physical effects**

Alcohol

Alcohol consumption is a major cause of health problems, and the **mortality** rate of heavy drinkers is at least twice that of the normal population. The cost to the NHS of treating the effects of alcohol misuse is up to £1.7 billion per year. Intoxication with alcohol increases the risk of soft-tissue injuries, fractures, head injuries, and other trauma, and short-lived episodes of memory loss (or 'blackouts') are particularly associated with binge drinking.

Withdrawal effects may follow a bout of acute intoxication, although it is difficult to predict the severity of symptoms, as variation occurs between one episode and the next. Weakness, faintness, sweating, and insomnia may occur within a few hours of the blood alcohol levels declining sharply, and may be accompanied by a tremor.

The most severe form of alcohol withdrawal is known as **delirium tremens**, and is characterized by severe tremor, agitation, disorientation, confusion, sweating, a racing heartbeat, delusional beliefs, and visual hallucinations. These symptoms may last for up to 7–10 days and are associated with a fatal outcome in a small percentage of patients.

A range of other physical complications associated with alcohol are listed in Table 16.3. In addition, heavy drinking can contribute to anxiety and depression, and can lead to non-compliance with medical treatment for these conditions.

Opioids

Large doses of opioids cause a reduction in the rate of breathing and ultimately respiratory arrest, but tolerance develops rapidly with repeated doses. Physical dependence becomes obvious when the person stops taking the opioid drug, leading to a characteristic withdrawal syndrome, as described in Table 16.1. These symptoms peak after 3–4 days and rarely last more than a week, although insomnia may persist for several weeks. Although unpleasant, opioid withdrawal is not usually life threatening.

Most problems with opioid use come not from the drug itself, but the unstable patterns of use. Once dependent, maintaining a supply of opioids is often a full-time occupation, leading to neglect of physical health. The drug suppresses appetite and causes constipation, leading to weight loss and nutritional deficiencies. Suppression of the respiratory centres and the cough reflex leads to an increased risk of respiratory problems, including aspiration pneumonia. Tuberculosis is a growing problem among opioid users worldwide. Insomnia can be a debilitating problem, making it hard to work or study.

Opioid overdose can be precipitated by fluctuations in the purity of the drug bought on the street. It often follows a period of abstinence, when tolerance to the drug's respiratory depressant effects falls, and may lead to slow, shallow breathing, low blood pressure, a reduced level of consciousness, and ultimately coma and death.

Stimulants

Use of amphetamines produces elevated mood and increased alertness and self-confidence. As the dose increases there may be restlessness, rapid speech, muscle twitching, nausea, vomiting, and irregular breathing. Large doses may lead to very high blood pressure which, in turn, can cause cerebral haemorrhage and stroke, and both amphetamine and cocaine can lead to psychotic reactions.

Table 16.3 The effect of alcohol on various body systems

Nervous system	Wernicke's encephalopathy—confusion, double vision, and unsteadiness
	Korsakoff's syndrome—profound impairment of recent memory and disorientation in time.
	Peripheral neuropathy—numbness and altered sensation in the hands and feet
	Muscular weakness
Liver	Liver damage—fatty change (usually asymptomatic), alcoholic hepatitis (abdominal pain, jaundice or fever), and ultimately cirrhosis and liver failure
	Complications of cirrhosis—fluid collection in the abdomen (ascites), encephalopathy (confusion and disorientation), liver cancer
	Inflammation of the pancreas—severe pain, nausea and vomiting
Gastrointestinal system	Excess acid production can lead to reflux from the stomach to the oesophagus and inflammation of both
	Carcinoma of the oesophagus is associated with alcohol and heavy smoking
	Poor small bowel functioning, diarrhoea and difficulty absorbing food
Cardiovascular system	'Low risk' alcohol consumption (up to 3 units per day) protects middle-aged men against coronary heart disease
	'High risk' alcohol consumption (more than 5 units per day in women and 7 units per day in men) increases the risk of stroke, high blood pressure, and abnormalities of the heart rhythm (cardiac dysrhythmia)
Endocrine system	Men can experience reduced testicular size and impotence
	Women may experience irregular menstrual bleeding, reduced fertility, and recurrent abortion
Skin	Facial flushing
	Alcohol-related psoriasis

A period of low mood and lifelessness usually follows a period of heavy stimulant use, which tends to promote use in binges. Large or frequent doses over 24–48 hours may lead to abnormal cardiac rhythms, chest pain, and epileptic seizures. Longer periods of use lead to malnutrition, vitamin deficiencies, weight loss, exhaustion, and dental problems.

The effects produced by cocaine are similar to those described with amphetamine use. Chronic 'snorting' can lead to the formation of a hole between the two nasal cavities as a result of a perforation of the nasal septum.

A number of deaths have been reported in occasional users of ecstasy, many after taking only one tablet. The cause of death is variable, but a very high temperature (hyperthermia) is a characteristic feature. Tiredness, muscle aching, and headache may be present 24 hours after taking the drug, and both depression and cognitive impairment have been associated with longer-term regular use.

Benzodiazepines

Central nervous system (CNS) depressants such as benzodiazepines, barbiturates, and gamma-hydroxybutyric acid (GHB) result in a reduction of the activity of excitable neuronal tissues. Benzodiazepine drugs work as **anticonvulsants**, muscle relaxants, anti-anxiety agents, and **hypnotics**. However, they lose their effectiveness as 'sleeping tablets' if taken every night for more than 2–3 weeks.

Benzodiazepine drugs are also taken to enhance the high from alcohol and opioid drugs, to alleviate withdrawal symptoms from alcohol and other illicit drugs, and in high doses (and often intravenously) they may give a feeling of euphoria or 'high'. The risk of accidental overdose from opioid drugs is much increased if CNS depressants are also taken at the same time.

Cannabis

Although widely considered to be a drug with few harmful effects, evidence for the long-term effects of cannabis is emerging, with respiratory diseases such as chronic bronchitis associated with smoking as the method of administration. There is an increased risk of cancers of the mouth, oesophagus, and possibly lungs, and a risk of exacerbating the symptoms of heart disease, such as high blood pressure and coronary artery disease. Road traffic accidents may be also be increased by cannabis use. The link between cannabis and severe mental illness is only now being unravelled, and there are strong associations with psychosis in some users.

The risks of injecting

Many of the negative physical effects of drugs of abuse are a direct result of injecting, a practice that becomes more common when supplies of the drug are limited. Opioids, amphetamines, cocaine, and benzodiazepines can all be injected. The repeated injection of drugs and adulterants using unsterile, contaminated equipment can lead to scars or 'tracks' along the path of veins. Other complications include inflammation of the veins (thrombophlebitis) or local infections, abscesses, and ulcers.

However, the greatest public health concern comes from the transmission of a variety of blood-borne bacterial and viral infections via shared injecting equipment, including hepatitis B, hepatitis C, and HIV.

Research has suggested that over 60% of heterosexually acquired HIV is related to injecting drugs. Around 5% of those infected with hepatitis B become chronic carriers of the virus, and around 15–25% of carriers develop an active inflammation of the liver which progresses to cirrhosis or liver failure. Chronic hepatitis B carriers with liver disease are at increased risk of developing cancer of the liver.

Between 30% and 80% of past and current injecting drug misusers may be infected with hepatitis C. Again there is a range of severity, but about 20% of those chronically infected develop cirrhosis, and 25% of these may develop liver cancer. These serious complications can take 20–30 years to develop.

16.4.2 Criminal activity

It is estimated that there are 1.2 million incidents of alcohol-related violence each year in the UK, 360 000 alcohol-related incidents of domestic violence, and 85 000 cases of drink driving. This may cost up to £7.3 billion, with further human or emotional costs that are hard to quantify.

The mechanism of action of benzodiazepines is described in Box 6.9 on page 125, and their use for the treatment of anxiety is discussed in section 13.5.1 on page 278.

SELF-CHECK 16.4

List three negative effects each of alcohol, opioids, cocaine, and cannabis on the health of users.

Many illicit drug users become involved in crime to support their drug use. It is estimated that half of all recorded crime is drug related, with associated costs to the criminal justice system alone reaching £1 billion a year.

16.4.3 Social functioning

Alcohol has a huge impact on workplace productivity. Up to 17 million days are lost each year in the UK as a result of alcohol-related absence, with a cost of up to £6.4 billion. Those with severe alcohol problems become socially withdrawn, which may lead to relationship breakdown, homelessness, and social isolation.

The nature of drug withdrawal syndromes and the associated psychological craving for the drug may mean that the need to obtain supplies takes precedence over all other priorities. This may lead to mistakes at work, lost productivity, or unemployment. Personal relationships are placed under considerable strain by dependent drug use, and problems with accommodation are common. Parenting may become severely compromised by heavy alcohol or drug use.

16.5 How is addiction assessed?

Patients with a range of substance misuse problems may present to their doctor, and often the substance misuse problem is not the primary reason for consultation. Therefore screening and assessment questionnaires may help to pick up potential problems. One simple example is the CAGE questionnaire for alcohol problems, as shown in Table 16.4, and this is made up of four questions that can be incorporated into a standard health screen. If the answer is 'yes' to two or more of the questions, it is likely that an alcohol problem exists, and further questioning is necessary.

Once a potential problem has been identified a detailed assessment of substance use in both the past and the present (that is, in the last month) is important, and corroboration may need to be sought from the individual's family or friends. The quantity used, as well as the route, length, pattern and context of use, and the development and severity of withdrawal symptoms are useful in the identification of the degree of problematic use. The previous treatment history, including any attempts to cut down substance use and any periods of abstinence, is a further pointer to the readiness or motivation of the patient for change.

It is also important to consider the range of potential co-existing physical, psychological and social problems. A proper initial assessment will ensure adequate estimation of

Table 16.4 The CAGE screening questionnaire for alcohol problems

1	Have you ever felt you ought to **C**ut down on your drinking?
2	Have people **A**nnoyed you by criticizing your drinking?
3	Have you ever felt **G**uilty about your drinking?
4	Have you ever had a drink first thing in the morning to steady your nerves (an **E**ye opener)?

risk, the safe initiation of effective therapies, appropriate referral to specialist services, and provide a baseline against which treatment outcomes may be measured.

In the case of the heavy drinker, blood tests to measure liver function and other bio-chemical parameters may be useful to gauge the extent of physical damage. Blood or breath alcohol levels may help to confirm a history of recent use from the patient. Urine may be also be tested for a variety of substances, both legal and illegal. Testing for HIV, hepatitis B, and hepatitis C may also be important. However, physical tests usually only serve to complement a verbal history.

SELF-CHECK 16.5

Why is it important to detect people with substance misuse problems early?

> Simple screening tests for heavy alcohol use may detect a substance misuse problem before dependence fully develops and allow an early and effective intervention.

16.6 What can be done to treat addiction?

Many people resolve their addiction problems without recourse to specialist treatment. However, different approaches have been tried to help those who cannot manage alone, and treatment for drug and alcohol problems needs to be tailored to the individual. In some cases the objective will be to achieve and maintain abstinence from the substance of abuse. For example, patients with a long history of alcohol dependence, medical or psychiatric problems, or poor social support do better in the long term if they aim to remain abstinent.

However, this approach may not always be acceptable to the individual, and attempting to enforce abstinence as the only possible goal may lead to a missed opportunity to bring about improvements in physical, psychological or social conditions. Setting more limited treatment targets can be effective at both an individual and population level, and the **harm reduction** model has become more popular recently.

The spread of the HIV virus in the early to mid-1980s, and the associated risk of blood-borne infection via sharing needles, led to the development of a 'hierarchical health message'. People were discouraged from taking drugs, but if they did so, it was suggested that they avoid injecting them. If they did inject, then it was suggested that they use sterile equipment and avoid sharing this with other drug users.

16.6.1 Alcohol

Psychosocial interventions

If alcohol is being consumed at harmful levels, opportunistic 'brief interventions' by front-line health-care staff may be extremely effective. The simplest of these involves the use of a screening tool (such as we saw in Table 16.4), or a blood test, to identify harmful patterns of alcohol use, followed by personalized feedback about the results and information about safe levels of drinking.

More extensive interventions may take place over 3–5 further sessions with a counsellor, allowing a more detailed assessment of the pattern of alcohol consumption, the range

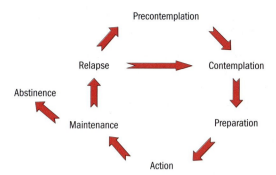

Figure 16.2 The transtheoretical (stages of change) model of addiction.

of alcohol-related problems, and the degree of alcohol dependence. The use of a drinking diary can help to increase motivation for change and allow the therapist to compare the patient's drinking level with the rest of the population. Information booklets and worksheets are often provided. Such interventions are based on a public health model of care in which clinicians actively seek health risk factors among their patients. Their potential effectiveness has been demonstrated in a large number of clinical trials.

The **stages of change** model can be helpful in understanding substance misuse problems, and this is shown in Figure 16.2. The authors, Prochaska and DiClemente, studied people who had changed their smoking behaviour without treatment and found that change is rarely a sudden event, but instead occurs in steps or stages. This challenged the view that motivation to change behaviour is an all-or-nothing phenomenon, and that people who failed to benefit from help were 'lacking motivation'. Knowledge of the stages of change model may be used to employ a range of different treatment strategies at different stages of the problem.

Motivational interviewing is well suited to moving patients towards a firm decision to stop drinking. It involves a discussion about the personal costs and benefits of continued drinking when balanced against the health and social benefits that would follow a reduction in consumption or abstinence. Once a person has accepted the need to change (and so moved into the action stage of the stages of change model), it is possible to work with them to generate realistic goals and to offer a menu of strategies to help reach these.

A range of cognitive behavioural strategies can be used at this stage, including self-monitoring (diary keeping), setting drinking limits, controlling the rate of drinking, drink refusal skills, assertiveness training, relaxation training, and the development of alternative coping skills and rewards. A careful evaluation is made of the short-term and long-term benefits and disadvantages of drinking, and the individual is helped to find more satisfactory ways of coping with problems and unpleasant feelings. An attempt is made to structure the person's life so that alternative sources of pleasure are available.

Once withdrawal from alcohol is complete (see the section on medical treatments below), **relapse prevention** strategies can help support the person to remain abstinent. The most common treatment outcome for addicts is relapse, with approximately two-thirds of all research participants returning to drinking by the 90-day follow-up assessment. Relapse prevention aims to offer alternative strategies to the 'revolving door' phenomenon of relapse and withdrawal. The strategy teaches the person to anticipate relapses, and if possible to prevent them from occurring. However, it also accepts that

SELF-CHECK 16.6

How does a motivational interviewing approach differ from a traditional confrontational approach to addiction?

if a return to drinking does happen, it is possible to minimize the negative consequences and maximize learning from the experience.

Alcoholics Anonymous is a self-help organization that utilizes a 12-step programme towards recovery from alcohol problems. The **12-step model** is one of the most widely used treatment philosophies for substance use problems around the world, with an estimated 3.5 million people attending AA meetings at one of over 100 000 different meeting locations. The model has a number of important therapeutic elements, including providing strategies that promote the development of spirituality, and the use of practical strategies to combat dependence. Self-referral to AA is simple, and the only requirement for membership is a desire to stop drinking.

> Even brief interventions involving screening for alcohol misuse and providing individually tailored feedback can be very effective in reducing consumption.

Medical treatments

Once an individual has developed physical dependence on alcohol, stopping drinking abruptly will lead to withdrawal symptoms, which may even be life threatening. In 'medicated' detoxification the severity of withdrawal symptoms is minimized (or completely suppressed) by the administration of a drug (for example benzodiazepines, such as chlordiazepoxide or diazepam), with gradual reduction of the substitute medication after the peak of the withdrawal syndrome has passed. Such detoxification can usually be done safely, successfully and cost-effectively at home, although people with a history of withdrawal fits or delirium tremens, severe medical or psychiatric problems, or few social supports, are likely to require admission to hospital.

Detoxification is best seen as the start of the therapeutic process rather than a treatment on its own. Although psychosocial methods are the most commonly used treatment modalities for alcohol problems, there is a growing body of evidence for new forms of medication such as acamprosate or naltrexone to reduce drinking in the rehabilitation phase of management. It should be noted that these medications are likely to be enhanced in combination with psychosocial interventions, and they should not be viewed as a simple answer to a complicated problem.

16.6.2 Drug misuse

One of the key aims of treatment for drug misuse problems is the reduction of associated medical or social harms. Injecting any illicit drug carries a significant risk of infection, particularly when equipment is shared or poorly cleaned. Advice about improved injection technique and cleaning of equipment can be effective in reducing this risk, particularly when combined with the provision of clean needles and syringes by local needle exchange schemes.

Opioids—detoxification

Individuals using small amounts of heroin may be able to stop abruptly using medication to relieve the symptoms of opioid withdrawal, such as muscular aches, diarrhoea, vomiting, and agitation. This is normally accompanied by an explanation of the likely withdrawal side effects and their time course, to help to clarify any misunderstandings.

Those with dependence on higher doses of heroin, or with longer histories of drug use, may not be able to tolerate such a simple detoxification process, and may require a more complex medical regime. Lofexidine is an effective non-opioid method of reducing heroin withdrawal symptoms, but it also causes low blood pressure and so the dose needs to be built up slowly and monitoring by a nurse may be necessary. The opioid drug buprenorphine is also an effective detoxification agent.

Opioids—maintenance

'Substitute' prescribing implies the use of a legally prescribed drug of known purity and quality, instead of an illegal drug. **Methadone maintenance therapy** (MMT) has been used for over 30 years in the management of heroin dependence, and research has demonstrated clear benefits in reducing illicit opioid use, HIV infection, and criminal activity. There is evidence to suggest that the regimes most successful at reducing illicit drug intake are those involving higher daily doses of the substitute drug (approximately 60–120 mg of methadone), but retention in treatment and the provision of psychosocial interventions are also important factors.

Methadone maintenance may last indefinitely, but the aim is to use the period of stability that the methadone allows to work on other important issues such as tackling housing, employment, and relationship difficulties. Ultimately reduction of the dose of methadone and detoxification will be possible, followed by the relapse prevention strategies outlined above.

Buprenorphine is a partial opioid agonist, and so produces less euphoria, sedation, or respiratory depression than heroin. It also has a longer half-life, and discontinuation leads to less severe withdrawal symptoms. It appears to be as effective as methadone as a maintenance and detoxification agent.

> Maintenance treatment with a drug such as methadone enables a person to swap illicit street drugs of unknown purity for a reliable pharmaceutical alternative. This allows them time to tackle other psychosocial issues without having to worry about opioid withdrawal effects.

SELF-CHECK 16.7

What might be the potential arguments against maintenance treatment?

Stimulants

The problem of stimulant (such as amphetamines, cocaine, and crack cocaine) abuse has tended to receive less attention than heroin abuse in the UK, and there is little agreement on the best management strategy.

Antidepressants have been advocated to manage the craving and depressive symptoms of the stimulant withdrawal syndrome, with limited success. The psychosocial strategies outlined above may offer the most promising treatment strategy. Stimulant use may also carry a risk of precipitating psychiatric symptoms such as psychosis or depression, and these will also need assessment and adequate treatment.

Benzodiazepines

Dependence on benzodiazepines may be tackled by prescribing an initial 'maintenance' period while other factors are stabilized, followed by a planned slow reduction of the benzodiazepine. The starting dose and reducing regime are negotiated between doctor and patient, aiming to minimize withdrawal symptoms. Clear criteria for review and goals of progress are also established before starting.

SUMMARY

- Humans have a unique capacity to seek out and use psychoactive or mind-altering substances.

- Problems with addiction occur on a spectrum of severity.

- In the UK, the rate of substance misuse has increased dramatically over recent decades.

- All drugs of abuse affect the so-called reward pathway in the brain, which is a dopaminergic pathway.

- Twin studies suggest that there is some genetic contribution to the development of dependence on alcohol.

- The reinforcement of substance misuse by its pleasant effects, cravings, and dysfunctional beliefs

are important aspects of psychological explanations of substance use.

- Drugs of abuse have a variety of different and potentially harmful physical effects. The process of injecting drugs is particularly likely to lead to physical harm.

- The detection of substance misuse problems before the development of dependence is likely to allow more effective treatment.

- Strategies for reducing substance misuse commonly involved a strategy known as motivational interviewing. For opiates, maintenance treatment may allow the secondary effects of addiction to be addressed before the addiction.

FURTHER READING

J. P. Allen and V. B. Wilson. *Assessing Alcohol Problems: A Guide for Clinicians and Researchers*, 2nd edn. Bethesda, MD: National Institute on Alcohol Abuse and Alcoholism, 2003.
Practical guide to the assessment of alcohol problems and brief clinical interventions in general medical practice.

A. Lingford-Hughes and D. Nutt. Neurobiology of addiction and implications for treatment. *British Journal of Psychiatry* 2003; **182**: 97–100.
A review of the neurobiological basis of addiction and suggestions for how this understanding may lead to the development of new therapeutic interventions.

A. R. Lingford-Hughes, S. Welch, and D. J. Nutt. Evidence-based guidelines for the pharmacological management of substance misuse, addiction and comorbidity: recommendations from the British Association of Pharmacology. *Journal of Psychopharmacology* 2004; **18**(3): 293–335.
Summarizes the evidence base for pharmacological strategies in the management of substance misuse.

W. R. Miller and P. L. Wilbourne. Mesa Grande: a methodological analysis of clinical trials of treatments for alcohol use disorders. *Addiction* 2002; **97**: 265–277.
Summary of the evidence for psychological interventions for alcohol use problems.

S. Wanigaratne, P. Davis, K. Pryce, and J. Brotchie. *The effectiveness of psychological therapies on drug misusing clients. Research briefing*. London: National Treatment Agency for Substance Misuse, 2005.
Summarizes the evidence base for psychological strategies in the management of substance misuse.

J. Ward, W. Hall, and R. P. Mattick. Role of maintenance treatment in opioid dependence. *Lancet* 1999; **353**: 221–226.
Review of the role of substitute prescribing in the management of opioid dependence.

Working Party of the Royal College of Psychiatrists and the Royal College of Physicians. *Drugs. Dilemmas and Choices*. London: Gaskell, 2000.
An excellent and readable introduction to the scope of addiction problems in the UK.

Glossary

Abscess A localized collection of pus. *See also* cerebral abscess.

Absence epilepsy A form of generalized epilepsy, most common in children, during which patients lose consciousness for a few seconds whilst maintaining posture. Often mistaken for daydreaming, it is associated with characteristic 3 cycles/s spike and wave activity on the EEG.

Acetylcholine A neurotransmitter present in the autonomic nervous system, in the central nervous system where it may regulate learning and memory, and at the neuromuscular junction where it controls the actions of skeletal muscle.

Action potential Electrical impulse that can travel down the axon to trigger the release of neurotransmitter.

Action potential propagation The rapid spread of the action potential along the membrane.

Acute Transient, short lasting, or rapid onset; the opposite of chronic. Note, acute does not mean severe.

Addison's disease An endocrine disorder caused by insufficient cortisol produced by the adrenal glands.

Adoption studies A study which investigates whether the familiality of a disorder is likely to be determined by genes, by comparing rates of the disorder in biological and adoptive relatives of a proband and controls.

Adrenaline A hormone released from the adrenal medulla into the bloodstream in response to stress.

Adrenergic *See* noradrenergic.

Aetiology Cause of a condition.

Affect A person's present emotional responsiveness, usually inferred from their facial expression and the amount and range of emotional expression.

Affective blunting Reduction in normal variations of mood.

Afferent Neuronal information which travels towards the brain.

Agitated depression Depression characterized by mental anguish and restlessness.

Agnosia Inability to recognize people or objects even when basic sensory modalities, such as vision, are intact.

Allodynia Pain caused by a stimulus that is not normally painful.

Ambidextrous Equally skilled with both hands, that is, not left or right hemisphere dominant.

Amino acid The basic building block of proteins.

Amnesic syndrome A selective impairment of new learning in the presence of unimpaired attention and concentration.

AMPA receptor Cation channel briefly opened upon binding of glutamate or AMPA.

Amyloid angiopathy Beta-amyloid deposition in the wall of blood vessels.

Amyloid cascade hypothesis Historically, the earliest and best known hypothesis which attempted to explain how Alzheimer's disease develops.

Amyloid plaques Deposition of beta-amyloid between nerve cells.

Amyloid precursor protein A transmembrane protein, a small part of which, when cut out, may produce the undesirable beta-amyloid protein.

Anaerobic metabolism Metabolism that can occur without the presence of oxygen.

Anergia Loss of energy.

Aneurysm Balloon on the side of an artery due to a weakened wall.

Angiography X-ray based technique in which an injection of contrast or dye into an artery outlines the inside of the vessel and shows up blockages. The image produced is called an angiogram.

Anhedonia Loss of pleasure or interest in things that normally give pleasure.

Annual incidence The number of new cases of a disease in a population over a 1-year period.

Anterograde amnesia The period of time between a head injury and the resumption of normal continuous memory.

Antibodies Soluble proteins produced by B lymphocytes after stimulation by antigens and acting specifically against those antigens in an immune response.

Anticonvulsant A medication that prevents epileptic seizures.

Antigen Any substance foreign to the body that provokes a response from the immune system.

Anxiolytics Drugs which are effective in treating anxiety.

Apathy Absence of emotion, motivation or enthusiasm.

Aphasia Loss of ability to speak or to understand speech.

Apolipoprotein E A protein which binds to fat molecules to facilitate their transport.

Apoptosis A process of cell death by a series of genetically programmed steps.

Apraxia *See* dyspraxia.

Arterio-venous malformation Abnormal blood vessels of medium calibre that are formed in a cluster within the substance of the brain, which act as a direct communication from the arterial to the venous part of the circulation and divert blood from the brain substance.

Asociality Avoiding the company of other people.

Assembly A group of neurons that together respond to the same feature and hence have established strong interconnections.

Association areas Regions of the cortex which interconnect with primary cortical regions to allow the integration of diverse information needed for complex sensory and motor functions.

Astrocyte Type of glial cell primarily responsible for controlling the environment surrounding the neurons.

Ataxia Unsteady broad-based gait, usually due either to intracranial pathology, particularly affecting the cerebellum, or a side effect of certain medication.

Atheroma Fatty deposits which block arteries.

Atherosclerosis The process by which atheroma develops in arteries.

Atonic seizures A form of generalized seizure characterized by a sudden loss of muscle tone.

Atrial fibrillation Irregular fast beating of the atria of the heart leading to turbulence and possibly clotting of blood. Can be a source of cardiac emboli to the brain.

Atrophy Tissue wasting, shrinkage.

Auditory hallucinations Hallucinations occurring in the auditory modality, commonly hearing voices speaking in psychiatric disorder, but also including hearing other sounds or occasionally music.

Aura Sensory, motor or cortical symptoms in the early phase of a migraine attack or preceding some forms of epileptic seizures.

Autoimmune disease A disorder in which the body directs an immune response against its own tissues.

Autonomic dysfunction Abnormal function of the autonomic nervous system.

Autonomic nervous system The portion of the peripheral nervous system that innervates smooth muscle, cardiac muscle and glands thereby facilitating control of their activity, albeit subconsciously.

Autosomal A characteristic encoded on one of the 22 chromosomes that is not a sex chromosome.

Autosomal dominant inheritance Inheritance of a disease due to a single mutant gene being passed to the offspring from either affected parent.

Avolition Lack of initiation or persistence in goal-directed activities.

Axon Very fine and long process originating at the soma of the neuron. Functionally acts to convey information in the form of electrical signals from the soma to the target tissue.

Axon reflex In sensory neurons, refers to the conduction of nerve impulses in a direction opposite to normal from an excited branch of the neuron to a non-excited branch, leading to the release of neuropeptides and other inflammatory mediators.

Baby blues Transient, mild depression occurring in the first few days after childbirth.

Bacteria Very small, single cell microorganisms capable of rapid reproduction.

Basal ganglia A group of structures below the cerebral hemispheres, playing a critical role in movement control.

Behaviourism An atheoretical psychological approach in which mental or psychological processes are investigated through observation of behaviour alone, and the importance of conscious will is denied.

Benign Non-malignant.

Benzodiazepines A class of drugs which are very effective anxiolytics, but whose clinical use is limited by their tendency to induce tolerance and dependence.

Beta-amyloid (β-amyloid) A short segment of the amyloid precursor protein that has a tendency to aggregate.

Beta-pleated sheet (β-pleated sheet) A protein molecule that is folded into a relatively rigid and stable shape or secondary structure (the primary structure is defined by the sequence of amino acids). The other common motif in secondary structure of proteins is the alpha-helix (α-helix).

Biopsy Procedure to take a tissue sample from an organ.

Bipolar affective disorder A major mood disorder characterized by at least one episode of mania and usually one or more episodes of depression.

Bipolar I disorder A psychiatric diagnosis for a mood disorder characterized by at least one episode of mania and usually one or more episodes of depression.

Bipolar II disorder A psychiatric diagnosis for a mood disorder characterized by at least one episode of hypomania and usually one or more episodes of depression.

Blood–brain barrier A physical barrier between the blood vessels in the CNS and the brain tissue itself that acts as a selective filter to limit the passage of substances into the brain.

Bottom-up Information processing from lower sensory cortex to higher association cortex.

Bradykinesia Slowness of movement.

Brain stem Part of the brain linked to the spinal cord controlling respiratory and cardiovascular function.

Brodmann's areas Numbered areas of the cortex which can be distinguished on the basis of histological appearance.

Burr hole A small opening in the skull made with a drill.

Capacitor The neuronal membrane acting as an electrical storage device.

Carbonic anhydrase The enzyme that converts CO_2 and water to bicarbonate: important in the transport of CO_2 in blood, and has some effect on inhibitory synapses because the bicarbonate ions can get through the chloride channels of $GABA_A$ receptors.

Cardiac arrhythmias Changes in the normal regular heart beat, caused either by some disease process or by certain medications.

Cardiac syncope A faint, or loss of consciousness and loss of muscle tone, caused by transient stopping or irregularity of the heart beat.

Carotid artery A major blood vessel supplying oxygenated blood to the head and neck.

Carotid endarterectomy *See* endarterectomy.

Carotid ultrasound *See* ultrasound.

Cartesian dualism Refers to Descartes' idea that there is a fundamental distinction between the brain (or body) and the mind.

Catatonia Catatonic stupor involves loss of volitional movement and speech, unresponsiveness and waxy flexibility. Catatonic excitement involves hyperactive behaviour and unexplained shouting.

Catecholamine A class of neurotransmitter molecules that includes noradrenaline, adrenaline, and dopamine.

Cavernous angioma Abnormal collection of small calibre vessels that forms a small mass within the brain substance.

Central nervous system The brain and spinal cord.

Cephalgia A general term for headache, regardless of cause.

Cerebellum Part of the brain situated above the brain stem responsible for balance and coordination of movement.

Cerebral abscess Collection of pus within the substance of the brain because of infection.

Cerebral hemispheres The two halves of the brain; consisting of the overlying cortex and deeper structures. Functionally are connected together via tracts.

Cerebrospinal fluid (CSF) The fluid which surrounds the brain and the spinal cord, and which is also present within the ventricles of the brain.

Channelopathies Abnormal ion channels in neuronal membranes that lead to diseases such as epilepsy.

Channels *See* ion channels.

Chemotherapy The treatment of disease by the use of chemical agents toxic to malignant cells.

Chlamydia pneumoniae A bacterium that causes a type of pneumonia.

Cholinergic Describing neurons or synapses that utilize the neurotransmitter, acetylcholine.

Cholinesterase inhibitors Molecules that inhibit the activity of the enzyme that breaks down acetylcholine.

Chorea Brief, twitchy movements of the limbs, trunk or face.

Chromosome A single piece of DNA containing many, many genes. Human cells all contain 23 pairs of chromosomes.

Chronic Persistent or long-lasting, or slowly developing. The opposite of acute.

Circle of Willis The connection of certain blood vessels at the base of the brain which can, in some circumstances, allow blocked arteries to be bypassed.

Clang associations Thoughts linked by rhyme.

Clipping Surgical technique to treat intracranial aneurysms.

Cluster headache A rare form of primary headache disorder, so named because the attacks usually come in clusters lasting for a month or two with a gap for several months before another bout.

Cognitive behavioural therapy A psychological approach to treatment which examines and modulates maladaptive thoughts (cognitions) and behaviours which may be leading to symptoms.

Cognitive style An individual's characteristic way of thinking.

Coiling Radiological technique to treat intracranial aneurysms.

Coincidence detector The mechanism, mediated by the NMDA receptor, which determines that calcium influx sufficient for long-term synaptic modulation only takes place when pre- and post-synaptic neurons are depolarized simultaneously.

Co-morbidity The presence of more than one disease in an individual at any one time.

Computed tomography (CT) A diagnostic imaging procedure that uses a computer to generate a three-dimensional image of the brain structure using a series of X-ray images.

Concordance The odds of the second twin of a pair having a disease if the first twin of the pair suffers from that disease.

Confounder A factor or variable which may affect other variables.

Congenital malformations Abnormal deformities of parts of the body that are present at birth.

Consolidation The process that makes changes in connectivity permanent.

Contralateral Affecting the opposite side of the body.

Contusion (brain) Damage of the brain parenchyma, without a big collection of blood.

Cortex The outer surface of the cerebral hemispheres of the brain.

Cortical spreading depression A wave of depolarization which propagates across the cerebral cortex. It is implicated in the causation of migraine.

Corticospinal tracts Nerve pathways transmitting impulses from the motor cortex to the spinal cord, involved in the control of voluntary movement.

Craniectomy Surgical removal of part of the skull.

Cushing's syndrome An endocrine disorder caused by too much cortisol produced by the adrenal glands.

Cytokine A soluble protein secreted by cells of the immune system.

Cytoskeleton The skeleton of the cell.

Cytotoxic drug A drug that has a toxic effect on cells. Such drugs are commonly used in cancer therapy to kill rapidly dividing cancerous cells.

Declarative memory Memory for specific pieces of information such as facts and places which an individual can consciously recount.

Deep brain stimulation Stimulation of specific regions of the brain via electrodes implanted using neurosurgical procedures.

Defence mechanisms Unconscious psychological strategies used to reduce anxiety.

Delirium An acute reaction of the brain to a wide variety of insults, which is characterized particularly by gross impairment of attention and concentration, leading to disorientation and a variety of other, often florid, psychological symptoms.

Delusion A false belief that is held with conviction despite evidence to the contrary, and which is out of keeping with the person's educational, cultural and social background.

Delusional misidentification A belief of a change of identity either in the self or in others. The most common type is a belief that (usually) a close relative has been replaced by an identical-looking impostor (known as Capgras syndrome).

Delusion of passivity The belief that some aspect of oneself (will, actions, emotion, thoughts, handwriting, voice) is under the external control of another or others.

Delusion of reference The belief that events, objects or people have a special personal significance.

Delusional mood An overwhelming feeling of apprehension, that something unspecific and unusual is about to happen, which will be of special significance for that person.

Delusional perception A normal perception which has become highly invested with significance and which has become incorporated into a delusional system, such that the perception is given as evidence to support a delusional belief.

Dementia An acquired and progressive impairment of cognitive functioning, memory, personality and intellect.

Dendrite Protrusion from neurons that receives most of the synaptic input. The dendritic trees of some neurons can be very complex geometrically, and may receive tens of thousands of synapses.

Deoxyribonucleic acid (DNA) The molecule which stores all genetic information.

Depolarize Membrane potential becomes more positive.

Depressogenic attributional style A psychological state in which events are attributed to external factors outside of one's control, the consequence of which is helplessness.

Dexamethasone suppression test A clinical investigation of endocrine function. The subject is given an infusion of dexamethasone (an exogenous steroid). In normal subjects this leads to reduced production of endogenous steroids by the adrenal glands.

Diabetes Pancreatic insufficiency leading to high blood sugar.

Diathesis An inborn, genetically mediated predisposition to develop some particular disease or abnormality.

Diathesis-stress model A theory that explains behaviour as a result of both genetic factors (nature) and life experiences (nurture).

Differentiation The process by which cells mature to become specialized in form and function.

Diffuse Axonal Injury Severe injury of the white matter tracts within the brain that happen as a result of intense acceleration–deceleration injury of the head, during which the poles of the brain rotate within the head and the white matter tracts are severed.

Diplopia Double vision.

Disc prolapse Prolapse of part of a spinal disc that usually presses against the spinal cord or nerve roots.

Disorder A morbid state that is manifested by a characteristic set of symptoms and signs (syndrome). Pathology and prognosis may be known or unknown.

Disposition Relating to an individual's personality. An intrinsic aspect of that individual.

Dissociation In terms of psychopathology, this refers to a separation of mental functions which would normally be integrated.

Diuretic 'Water tablet' to get rid of excess body fluid.

Diurnal mood variation A mood state which varies according to a daily pattern. Classically this occurs in depression with a mood which is worse in the morning than at other times of the day.

Dizygotic twins Non-identical twins derived from separate eggs.

DNA methylation Chemical modification of DNA which results in inactivation of genes.

Dominant A dominant characteristic is apparent if an individual inherits a gene for that characteristic from only one parent. This is in contrast to recessive characteristics, which are only apparent if an individual inherits genes for that characteristic from both parents.

Dopamine Neurotransmitter found in several pathways in the brain which have extensive connections to many regions. Two particularly important pathways are the one originating in the substantia nigra which is important for movement control and the one originating in the ventral tegmental area which is part of the reward pathway.

Dopamine hypothesis of schizophrenia The theory that schizophrenia is caused by increased transmission of the neurotransmitter dopamine.

Dopaminergic Describing neurons or synapses that utilize the neurotransmitter dopamine.

Downward social drift hypothesis of schizophrenia The theory that patients with schizophrenia become more socially deprived because they are unable to function in daily life.

Dualism *See* Cartesian dualism.

Dysarthria Slurred speech.

Dyskinesia Involuntary writhing movements of the limbs, trunk, or face.

Dysphagia Difficulty in swallowing.

Dysphasia Disorder of language affecting the generation of speech and its understanding.

Dyspraxia Impairment of planning, executing and sequencing motor movements. Also known as apraxia.

Dystonia Painful involuntary muscle spasm of a body part.

Echocardiography An ultrasound-based imaging technique which provides images of the heart and its valves.

Efferent Neuronal information which travels away from the brain.

Electroencephalogram (EEG) Electrical recordings of brain activity from electrodes placed on the scalp (brain waves).

Embolism Particle blocking an artery.

Empyema A localized collection of pus in a body cavity.

Encephalitis Inflammation of the substance of the brain.

Endarterectomy Surgical removal of plaque or blood clots from the inner lining of an artery.

Endemic Present in a geographical area or population at all times.

Endocrine Relating to the hormonal systems of the body.

Endogenous features Biological features.

Endotoxin A toxic component of the cell wall of certain bacteria that when released causes fever and inflammation.

Engram The permanent change in a neuronal network that embodies memory.

Enterovirus A type of virus that lives in the gut and is usually transmitted via the faeco-oral route.

Eosinophil A type of white blood cell that plays a major role in the body's defence against parasites and is also important in allergic reactions.

Epidemiology Study of the frequency of a condition in the population, its mortality and the prognosis.

Epilepsy A group of diseases which result in seizures that cannot be explained by clinical problems outside the brain.

Episode of illness A specific period of illness.

Epstein–Barr virus A virus that causes many disorders, including glandular fever.

Erotomania The delusional belief that one has a lover, usually of higher status (also known as de Clerambault syndrome).

Erythrocyte sedimentation rate Blood test used to show evidence of inflammation in the body. Particularly high in temporal arteritis.

Essential tremor Condition of older people in which they develop a tremor of the upper limbs when performing tasks.

Excitable Describing a membrane capable of generating action potentials.

Excitatory Increasing the chance that a neuron fires an action potential.

Excitatory postsynaptic potential A change in the membrane potential of a post-synaptic neuron, as a result of synaptic neurotransmitter release, that increases the likelihood of that neuron generating an action potential.

Excitotoxicity Excessive release of neurotransmitter, usually glutamate, causing damage to nerve and glial cells by overstimulation of excitatory receptors such as the NMDA receptor.

Exogenous Arising outside the body.

Exotoxin A soluble toxin that is excreted by living bacteria.

Expressed emotion Type of negative communication involving excessive criticism, hostility and emotional over-involvement directed at a patient by family members.

Extradural haematoma Collection of blood between the skull and the dura, the covering of the brain.

Extraversion A personality trait involving sociability and optimism.

Family study A study which is able to demonstrate whether a disorder tends to run in families. Family studies cannot distinguish between genetic causes and environmental influences common to all members of a particular family.

Family therapy A psychological therapy where more than one member of a family is treated in the same session. Family relationships and processes are explored as potential causes of mental disorder in one or more of the family members.

Fasciculations Spontaneous, involuntary, painless, rapid twitches in muscle fibres due to impaired nerve supply.

Firing threshold The membrane potential above which an action potential will be generated.

First-rank symptoms of schizophrenia Symptoms that are highly predictive of the presence of schizophrenia (proposed by the German psychiatrist, Kurt Schneider).

Flight of ideas An abnormality of the flow of thought in which a patient cannot maintain the overall direction of thinking, the links between sequential thoughts being tenuous and difficult to follow. It is often associated with pressure of speech

Free association The technique employed by Sigmund Freud to investigate a patient's subconscious mind. He would ask the patient to report all thoughts that entered the patient's mind.

Frequency coding The degree to which depolarization is translated in the frequency of firing.

Frontal lobe That part of the cerebral cortex responsible for cognitive functions and movement control.

Functional magnetic resonance imaging (fMRI) A technique which measures regional cerebral blood flow as a proxy for cerebral function. It is based on the same principles as magnetic resonance imaging.

Fungus A plant-like organism lacking in chlorophyll.

GABA$_A$ receptor A chloride channel, opened upon binding of GABA.

GABAergic Describing neurons or synapses that utilize the inhibitory neurotransmitter, GABA.

Gamma aminobutyric acid (GABA) Major inhibitory neurotransmitter in the brain.

Gate control theory The modulation of incoming pain signals by a neuronal gate in the spinal cord. The gate can also be opened or closed by messages from the brain.

Gene A region of DNA which encodes an entire protein.

Genetic linkage studies Process for identifying disease-causing genes by tracking the inheritance of the disease and genetic markers through large pedigrees.

Genetic polymorphism The variation found within individual genes.

Genome The complete set of chromosomes containing all the genes of an organism.

Genotype The genes possessed by an organism.

Glasgow Coma Score Scale used to score the clinical state of a patient with brain injury. Varies from 3 to 15.

Glia Collective name for the various types of non-neuronal cells of the nervous system. They are critical for the optimal functioning of neurons.

Gliosis An excess of glial cells in damaged areas of the CNS forming scar tissue.

Glutamate Major excitatory neurotransmitter in the brain.

Glutamatergic Describing neurons or synapses that utilize the excitatory neurotransmitter, glutamate.

Grand mal An alternative name for tonic-clonic seizures.

Grandiose delusions False beliefs that one has a highly elevated identity or extraordinary abilities.

Grandmother cell A theoretical neuron that only responds to a specific complex feature.

Grey matter Part of the central nervous system containing a mixture of dendrites, somata and axons, where most of the processing takes place. Looks darker than the white matter which mainly contains axons.

Gyrus Fold of cortical tissue, facing the outside of the brain, gives the human brain its characteristic appearance.

Haematogenous spread The spread of infectious agents via the blood stream.

Haemorrhage Leakage of blood.

Hallucination An abnormal sensory experience that arises in the absence of a direct external stimulus, and which has the qualities of a normal percept and is experienced as real and usually in external space. Hallucinations may occur in any sensory modality.

Harm reduction A strategy that acknowledges the continued drug use of individuals, whilst seeking to minimize the harm that such behaviour causes. Examples of harm reduction activities include exchanging used needles and syringes for clean ones, and providing free condoms.

Hebbian plasticity The increase in synaptic strength achieved when pre- and post-synaptic neurons fire together.

Hebbian synapse A synapse that has the ability to detect coincidence of pre- and post-synaptic firing and to modulate its strength accordingly.

Hemianopia Loss of vision to one side. This involves the temporal field of one eye and the nasal field of the other eye.

Hemiparesis Weakness of one side of the body involving the face, arm and leg.

Herpes virus A family of viruses that includes varicella, which causes chickenpox and shingles.

Hierarchy of anxiety provoking situations A feature of graded exposure therapy for phobic anxiety disorders. A series of situations, each leading to a little more anxiety than the last.

Hippocampus Part of the temporal lobe of the human cortex, playing a role in learning and memory.

Histology The study of tissues and cells at a microscopic level.

History Account of a patient's clinical background gained by interview.

HLA region Region on human chromosome 6 that encodes many genes involved in the immune response.

Homunculus Reconstruction of the body in which the size of the body parts is proportional to the area of cerebral cortex that either receives information from that part (sensory homunculus) or controls the movement of that part (motor homunculus).

Horner's syndrome Ptosis, miosis and reduced sweating on the face due to sympathetic nervous system under activity.

Hydrocephalus An abnormal increase in the volume of CSF within the ventricles of the brain.

5-Hydroxytryptamine *See* serotonin.

Hyperalgesia An increased response to a stimulus that is normally painful.

Hypercarbia Refers to increased levels of carbon dioxide.

Hypercortisolaemia An excess of plasma concentrations of cortisol.

Hyperpolarize Membrane potential becomes more positive.

Hypersomnia Excessive sleeping.

Hypertension High blood pressure.

Hyperthyroidism A state characterized by overactivity of the thyroid gland.

Hyperventilation Overbreathing.

Hypnosis An induced state of altered consciousness, particularly characterized by increased suggestibility.

Hypnotic A medication that induces sleep, commonly referred to as a 'sleeping tablet'.

Hypofrontality hypothesis of schizophrenia The hypothesis that schizophrenia is associated with reduced activity in the left dorsolateral pre-frontal cortex of the brain.

Hypokinesia Poverty or loss of movement.

Hypomania A less severe form of mania which does not cause impairment in social and occupational activities.

Hypothalamic–pituitary–adrenocortic system A major part of the neuroendocrine system that controls reactions to stress.

Hypothalamus A small structure at the base of the brain regulating body temperature and food intake amongst other functions.

Hypothyroidism Underactivity of the thyroid gland.

Hypotonia Abnormally low muscle tension, making an affected individual floppy.

Hypoxia Reduced oxygen content.

Iatrogenic Arising as the result of the action of a doctor, usually because of the effect of a prescribed drug.

Identical twins Twins that develop from fertilization of a single egg. They share the same genome.

Idiopathic Disease with no identifiable cause.

Idiopathic intracranial hypertension Condition presenting with headaches and papilloedema associated with a rise in intracranial pressure.

Illusion A false perception arising from an external stimulus.

Immediate memory Retention of unprocessed information for less than 1 second duration.

Immune system The body system that protects the body from foreign substances and tissues by producing the immune response. It includes the spleen, lymph nodes and lymphocytes.

Immunocompromised A state in which the body's immune system is not functioning normally, for example because of the action of certain drugs or illness.

Immunoglobulin Another term for antibody.

Immunosuppressant drug A drug that reduces the activity of the immune system.

Imprinting The differential expression of a gene in an offspring depending on which parent it was inherited from.

Inappropriate affect A show of emotion that is incongruous to the circumstances.

Incidence The rate of occurrence of new cases of a disease in a population.

Incontinence Inability to control urination and/or defecation.

Incubation period The time interval between exposure to an infectious organism and the appearance of the first symptom or sign of the disease.

Indoleamine hypothesis of depression Theory that depression is caused by low synaptic concentrations of serotonin.

Infantile sexuality The idea that sexuality is expressed from the first year of life in a series of stages—oral, anal, phallic, followed by latency and pubertal.

Infarction Death of tissue due to loss of blood supply.

Inhibitory Decreasing the chance that a neuron fires an action potential.

Inhibitory postsynaptic potential A change in the membrane potential of a post-synaptic neuron, as a result of synaptic neurotransmitter release, that decreases the likelihood of that neuron generating an action potential.

Initial insomnia Difficulty in falling asleep at night.

Insight The ability of a patient to understand the pathological nature of their symptoms and appreciate the presence of their illness.

Insomnia Difficulty in falling asleep.

Interictal Referring to the period between seizures.

Interpersonal psychotherapy A psychological therapy which uses relationships with other people as a medium through which neurotic mental illness, particularly depression, is treated.

Intracranial Within the skull cavity.

Intracranial pressure The pressure within the skull cavity.

Intracerebral haematoma Collection of blood within the substance of the brain.

Intubation The insertion of a tube into the trachea (windpipe) to assist breathing.

Ion channels Specialized proteins in membranes that allow selected ions to cross the otherwise impermeable lipid (fatty) membrane. Ion channels that are controlled by the voltage across the external membrane, or by neurotransmitters, are essential for neuronal function.

Ion pump An enzyme that consumes metabolic energy to transport ions across a cell membrane.

Ipsilateral Affecting the same side of the body.

Ischaemia Reduction in blood flow to an organ.

Ischaemic penumbra Area of brain adjacent to the dead tissue due to a stroke.

Jacksonian march A progression of a focal seizure that follows a characteristic pattern of spread to other parts of the body. Most commonly seen, but not exclusively, in motor seizures.

Kinases Enzymes that facilitate phosphorylation.

Labile mood Unstable, changing mood state such as the co-occurrence of elation and irritability.

Late insomnia Waking up very early in the morning.

Leak channels Proteins in the membrane that form pores that allow ions to cross the membrane.

Learned helplessness A psychological state in which patients with depression learn that they cannot control unpleasant events, give up trying to help themselves, and become helpless.

Lesion Area of damaged tissue.

Levodopa The main drug treatment for Parkinson's disease; it is metabolized in the brain into dopamine.

Lewy body Intraneuronal inclusion body found in Parkinson's disease.

Limbic leucotomy A psychosurgical technique in which lesions are produced within the limbic system nuclei.

Limbic system A phylogenetically old part of the brain, within the temporal lobes. It consists of a number of linked nuclei and neuronal pathways, and is considered to be the anatomical seat of human emotion.

Lobe One of four areas of a cerebral hemisphere. *See* frontal lobe, parietal lobe, occipital lobe and temporal lobe.

Long-term memory Retention of information over long periods of time. The duration and quantity of information is not limited. In terms of the neuronal basis of memory, this is the permanent change in connectivity between cells in an assembly that form the engram for a feature and allow for the perception of that feature long after.

Long-term potentiation Long-lasting enhancement of synaptic strength.

Loosening of associations Reduced associations between thoughts, which are reflected in disorganized speech.

Lumbar puncture Investigative technique in which a needle is inserted in the lumbar region of the back between the spinous processes of the vertebrae and pushed through into the subarachnoid space. CSF can be obtained and analysed by this method.

Lymphocyte A specialized type of white blood cell particularly important in the immune response and defence against infection.

Macrophage A specialized type of white blood cell particularly important in phagocytosis.

Magnetic resonance imaging (MRI) A non-invasive imaging technique based on computerized analysis of the interaction between magnetic fields generated by hydrogen atoms in body tissues and fluids and radio waves. Detailed three-dimensional images are produced by varying the magnetic fields and radio waves used.

Maintenance medication Long-term medication taken to reduce the risk of relapse of illness.

Malignant Cells or tumours growing in an uncontrolled and aggressive fashion that may spread to and disrupt other normal tissue, either locally or at distant sites via the blood stream.

Mannerisms Strange, repetitive goal-directed movements.

Medication overuse headache A common form of secondary headache disorder, usually related to the overuse of analgesics.

Medulla The lowermost segment of the three regions of the brain stem, attached to the spinal cord.

Meiosis Cell division to form an egg or a sperm cell, which results in the new cell having only 23 chromosomes (one from each pair).

Membrane potential The electrical potential difference across a cell membrane.

Mendelian genetics Inheritance of characteristics as described by Gregor Mendel. Dominant characteristics are evident if an individual has only one gene for that character; recessive characteristics require a gene to have been inherited from both parents. Mendelian genetics does not allow for interactions between different genes, which modifies the expression of most characteristics.

Meninges Membranes around the brain and spinal cord that contain the blood supply and provide nutrients to the brain.

Meningism The term used to describe the three clinical features of neck stiffness, intolerance of bright lights and headache. It is a sign of meningitis.

Meningitis Inflammation of the meninges, the membranous coverings of the brain.

Mental disorder A very general term which encompasses all psychiatric disorders, including mental illnesses and personality disorders.

Messenger ribonucleic acid (mRNA) A form of RNA that serves as a template for protein synthesis.

Microtubule The building block of the cytoskeleton of nerve cells.

Midbrain The uppermost segment of the three regions of the brain stem.

Middle insomnia Bouts of waking up during the night.

Migraine Paroxysmal disorder with moderate to severe unilateral throbbing headaches.

Migration The movement of newly created neurons to their final positions.

Miliary deposit Small, widespread deposits.

Miosis Constricted pupil.

Mixed mood state Co-occurrence of symptoms of mania and symptoms of depression.

Molecular biology The study of structure and function of biological molecules.

Monoamine hypothesis of mood disorders Theory that mood disorders are caused by altered levels of monoamine activity in the brain.

Monoamine oxidase inhibitors A class of antidepressant drugs which reduce the enzymatic breakdown of noradrenaline, dopamine and serotonin resulting in an accumulation of monoamine transmitters in the synapses.

Monozygotic twins Identical twins derived from the same fertilized egg.

Mood A pervasive and sustained (prolonged) prevailing state or disposition.

Mood congruent psychosis The content of psychosis is consistent with the current mood state.

Mood incongruent psychosis The content of psychosis is not consistent with the current mood state. This includes neutral themes.

Morbid jealousy The delusional belief of infidelity of a spouse or sexual partner.

Morbidity Suffering due to disease.

Mortality The rate of death from a disease within a given population.

Mosaicism A situation seen for example in some cases of Down's syndrome, in which some cells in the body have an abnormal number of chromosomes, whereas other cells are normal.

Motivational interviewing A style of counselling that aims to elicit behaviour change by helping individuals to explore and resolve ambivalence. It encourages the person to consider the pros and cons of continuing a behaviour, whilst systematically encouraging talk of change.

Motor complications Complications of therapy seen in the later stages of Parkinson's disease. Comprised of dyskinesia and fluctuations in motor response (switching between on and off).

Multiinfarct dementia Dementia due to multiple small infarcts.

Mutation A change in the DNA sequence.

Mute Unable to speak.

Myalgia Muscle pain.

Myelin sheath Electrically insulating layer surrounding axons formed from the membranes of oligodendrocytes.

Myelination The process by which oligodendrocytes wrap membranous processes around axons to form the myelin sheath.

Myelitis Inflammation of the spinal cord.

Myelopathy Disease to or damage of the spinal cord.

Myocardial infarction Permanent blockage of artery to the heart leading to death of heart muscle. Analogous to stroke in the brain and referred to as 'heart attack' by the public.

Myoclonic seizures A form of generalized seizure characterized by brief sudden jerking of one or more limbs.

Myopathy A disorder in which the primary abnormality is degeneration of muscle fibres.

Narcolepsy Neurological disorder characterized by inappropriate sudden attacks of sleep.

Necrosis Cell death whereby cells break open, release their contents and can damage neighbouring cells and provoke inflammation.

Negative recall bias Preferential recall of unpleasant memories rather than pleasant memories.

Negative symptoms Symptoms present in schizophrenia that involve a loss of normal functions, such as avolition, apathy, asociality and affective blunting.

Neocortex *See* cortex.

Neurodegenerative diseases Conditions in which neurons die over some years leading to a slowly progressive clinical course.

Neurofibrillary tangle Flame shaped intraneuronal inclusion.

Neurofilament Specialized fibrous structure within a nerve cell with many important functions including the transport of proteins along the nerve.

Neurogenic inflammation Inflammation arising from noxious stimulation of peripheral sensory neurons resulting in the release of neuropeptides and other inflammatory mediators.

Neuroimaging Investigation of the structure and function of the nervous system using methods such as PET and NMR that reconstruct internal anatomy from measurements taken outside the body.

Neuromuscular junction A specialized synapse where a nerve connects with a muscle fibre.

Neuron A cell type that is the fundamental functional unit of the nervous system, being able to generate and propagate electrical signals.

Neuronal migration Process by which neurons find their way from where they are born to their correct locations in the brain during development.

Neuropathic pain Pain in which nociceptive activity causes changes to occur in the peripheral or central nervous system, often without obvious associated tissue damage.

Neuroprotective therapy A treatment which will slow or halt the underlying pathophysiological process of a neurodegenerative condition.

Neurosurgery Surgery of the central nervous system.

Neurotic Describes psychological symptoms which are extreme variations of normal experience into which the patient retains insight.

Neuroticism A characteristic of individuals, reflecting the degree to which they exhibit neurotic symptoms. Such people may be worriers or tend to experience frequent low mood. They are also at greater risk of developing neurotic mental illnesses, such as depression or anxiety disorders.

Neurotransmitter A chemical messenger used by neurons to transmit signals from one nerve cell to another.

Neurotrophic factor Substance that promotes nerve growth and survival.

Neurotrophin Proteins that regulate the growth, differentiation, function, plasticity, and survival of nerve cells.

Neurotropic Having an affinity for the nervous system.

Neurulation The embryonic formation of the neural tube which subsequently develops into the central nervous system.

Neurulation defect Developmental defects that occur before the central nervous system has been shaped to its final form.

NMDA receptor A cation channel opened upon binding of glutamate or NMDA.

Nociceptive pain Pain in which nerves endings (nociceptors) are activated by inflammation or damage to tissues in the body thereby transmitting pain signals via the peripheral nerves and the spinal cord to the brain.

Nociceptors Peripheral nerve pain sensors.

Nodes of Ranvier Regularly spaced gaps in the myelin sheath that encases an axon.

Non-identical twins Twins developed from 2 eggs fertilized at the same time. They have different genomes.

Non-shared environmental factors Environmental factors that contribute to differences between family members.

Noradrenaline A catecholamine neurotransmitter in the central and sympathetic nervous systems. Also released from the adrenal medulla as a hormone into the blood.

Noradrenaline reuptake inhibitors A class of antidepressant drugs that inhibit the reuptake of noradrenaline by the pre-synaptic cell.

Noradrenergic Describing neurons or synapses that utilize the neurotransmitter, noradrenaline. Sometimes described as adrenergic.

Nucleic acids Organic substances found in living cells that contain information to direct protein synthesis and determine hereditary features. The two main types are deoxyribonucleic acid, DNA, found mainly in the nucleus, and ribonucleic acid, RNA, found mainly in the cytoplasm.

Nucleus A collection of neuronal cell bodies in the central nervous system that have the same function and connectivity. Also describes the membrane-bounded compartment of eukaryotic cells containing the genetic material.

Occipital lobe That part of the cerebral cortex primarily associated with the processing of visual information.

Oedipus complex This refers to Freud's idea that a male child has an unconscious need for his mother to love him exclusively, leading to jealousy directed towards his father. Oedipus was a figure in Greek mythology who, without knowing it, killed his father and then married his mother.

Oligoclonal bands Group of immunoglobulins with activity against a few antigens.

Oligodendrocyte Type of glial cell primarily responsible for myelination of axons.

Ophthalmoparesis Eye movement disorder.

Ophthalmoscope Instrument for looking at the back of the eye.

Opportunistic infection An infection that occurs due to a compromised immune system.

Optic atrophy Degeneration of the optic nerve.

Pain An unpleasant sensory and emotional experience associated with actual or potential tissue damage and expressed in terms of such damage.

Palpitations Feeling of rapid heart beat.

Panic attacks Symptoms of anxiety developing over a short space of time.

Papilloedema Swelling of the optic disc in the back of the eye due to raised intracranial pressure.

Paracentral scotoma Loss of a small part of vision near to the centre of the visual field.

Paraesthesiae Pins and needles.

Paraparesis Weakness of both legs.

Paraplegia Complete paralysis of both legs.

Parasite An organism that lives on or in a host organism, obtaining nourishment from the host but without providing any benefit.

Parenchyma The tissue or functional components of an organ.

Parietal lobe That part of the cerebral cortex primarily associated with sensory processes.

Parkinsonian syndrome Combination of rigidity and bradykinesia, one cause of which is Parkinson's disease.

Pathogen A disease-causing organism.

Pathology To describe something as pathological is to consider it abnormal in a medical sense, indicative of illness or disorder, or in need of treatment.

Pathophysiology The physiological or functional characteristics of a disease state.

Penetrance The likelihood that a particular gene will affect the overall phenotype. Genes or mutations with high penetrance are very likely to affect phenotype.

Perception The process by which sensory data are formed into meaningful percepts.

Peripheral nervous system The nerves that connect the central nervous system to the tissues and organs of the body thereby allowing the CNS to control the activity of these tissues.

Periventricular Brain region surrounding the cerebral ventricles.

Persecutory delusion A belief that one (or someone to whom one is close) is being attacked, harassed, cheated, persecuted, or conspired against.

Personality disorder This refers to a particular type of mental disorder, in which the patient has not developed some acute mental illness. Rather their whole personality has developed abnormally, probably as a result of their upbringing, life experiences, and perhaps some genetic influences.

Petit mal An alternative name for absence epilepsy.

Phagocytosis The term to describe the engulfing, ingestion and digestion of microorganisms and foreign matter by cells such as macrophages.

Phenotype The structure and behaviour of an organism.

Phenotypic heterogeneity Variations between individuals in key clinical characteristics of a disease.

Phonophobia Aversion to noise.

Phosphatases Enzymes that detach phosphate groups from molecules.

Phosphorylation Chemical process by which phosphate groups are attached to a molecule.

Photophobia Aversion to light.

Photopsia Visual sensation of flashing lights.

Pill rolling tremor Classical rest tremor of Parkinson's disease.

Pituitary gland The small gland situated at the base of the brain that secretes and controls many hormones involved in key metabolic processes.

Plaque Deposition of amorphous insoluble material between cells.

Plasticity The ability of a neuronal network to adapt to new situations.

Point prevalence The number of cases of a disease in a population at a given point in time.

Polymerase chain reaction A laboratory method used to amplify specific sequences of DNA.

Polymorph (polymorphonuclear leucocyte) A specialized white blood cell that is activated during inflammation and rapidly phagocytoses foreign antigens.

Polypeptide A molecular chain of amino acids.

Pons One of three regions of the brain stem, located between the medulla and the midbrain.

Positive formal thought disorder Abnormalities in the form of thoughts, which are reflected in disorganized speech.

Positive symptoms Symptoms present in schizophrenia that are not present in healthy individuals, such as hallucinations and delusions.

Postnatal depression An episode of major depression starting within 3 months of childbirth.

Postneurulation defect Developmental defects that occur after the brain and spinal cord have partially developed.

Post-traumatic amnesia Amnesia to events that happened after head injury.

Postural hypotension The fall in an individual's blood pressure when he or she stands up, leading to feelings of lightheadedness, dizziness and perhaps fainting. Common side effect of various medications.

Potassium channel A protein spanning the cell membrane that is selectively permeable to potassium ions.

Poverty of content of thought Vague, uninformative speech, which reflects vagueness of thoughts.

Poverty of thought Reduction or slowness in the stream of thoughts.

Premonitory phase Warning symptoms before a migraine attack.

Premorbid Prior to the occurrence of disease.

Presenilin A protein involved in the rare inherited form of early onset Alzheimer's disease.

Pressure of speech Fast, uninterruptible speech, which is usually increased in quantity. It is commonly associated with flight of ideas.

Prevalence Percentage of a population who have a particular disease over a specific time. Lifetime prevalence is the percentage of a population who have the disease at some stage in their lives. Not to be confused with incidence.

Primary brain injury Damage to a group of neurons and supporting cells as a direct result of an insult such as trauma or haemorrhage.

Prion protein A protein normally found in neurons and some other cells, with uncertain function but is responsible for making animals susceptible to transmissible spongiform encephalopathies.

Proband A term usually used in the context of genetic studies into causes of illness. It refers to an individual who has the disorder under investigation.

Progenitor A partially specialized foetal cell that can divide and give rise to differentiated cells.

Prognosis Long-term outcome of a condition.

Progressive muscular relaxation A way of helping patients to recognize and relieve tension, by progressively tensing and then relaxing different muscular groups.

Prolactin A hormone produced by the pituitary gland which is attached to the hypothalamus. Normal role is to promote lactation, but can be released following some kinds of seizure.

Prophylactic Treatment intended to prevent illness.

Proprioception Collective term for the sensory information originating in the muscles and joints.

Proteasome Organelle that removes unwanted proteins from a cell.

Proxy measure A variable which is used in place of the variable which is really under investigation. The proxy measure is likely to be more easily measured, but the investigation then assumes that the relationship between the proxy and the true variable is reliably understood.

Pseudoseizures Non-epileptic attacks with behavioural rather than neurological causes.

Psychomotor retardation Slowed thoughts and actions.

Psychotic Symptoms which are qualitatively different to normal human experience. The sufferer does not usually realize that they are abnormal symptoms.

Ptosis Drooping of eyelid.

Puerperal psychosis A severe psychiatric disorder, involving symptoms of mania, psychosis, confusion and disorientation, which occurs after childbirth.

Radiotherapy The treatment of disease by the use of high energy radiation.

Rapid cycling Four or more episodes of major mood disorder in a 12-month period.

Receptors Specialized proteins that become active when a specific molecule (agonist) binds to it.

Recovered memories The remembering of stressful events that have previously been forgotten, particularly (and controversially) relating to childhood sexual abuse.

Recurrent unipolar depression A major mood disorder characterized by two or more episodes of depression.

Red flags Symptoms or signs that would alert a doctor to the possibility of a more serious pathology in any condition.

Rehabilitation Therapeutic process which aims to improve function, where possible, and minimize the effects of loss of function on patient's everyday life.

Response fluctuations Predictable wearing off of medication effect or unpredictable on/off switching in Parkinson's disease.

Resting membrane potential The membrane potential of a cell when it is not conducting nerve impulses.

Retrograde amnesia The period of time between a head injury and the last clear memory preceding the head injury.

Rigidity Stiffness of the limbs in Parkinson's disease.

Saltatory conduction Literally 'jumping conduction'. Process in which the action potential jumps from node to node along a nerve axon.

Scarring hypothesis The theory that episodes of mood disorders result in lasting personality changes that persist beyond recovery from the mood disorder.

Schizoaffective disorder A disorder with symptoms of schizophrenia and symptoms of major mood disorder of equal prominence.

Schizoid personality traits Detachments from social relationships and a restricted range of interpersonal emotional expression.

Schizophrenia A complex, severe mental illness characterized by the presence of positive and negative symptoms.

Schizophrenogenic mother An outdated concept in psychiatry of a mother who causes schizophrenia in her child by being hostile and overprotective.

Schizotypal personality traits Eccentricities of thought and behaviour, and social anxiety and/or withdrawal.

Sclerosis A hardening of tissue, usually resulting from inflammation.

Seasonal affective disorder A disorder in which the mood change of the sufferer occurs in relation to the season of the year. Typically, depression occurs in autumn/winter.

Secondary brain injury Damage to neurons and supporting cells surrounding an area of primary injury due to lack of oxygen and other vital substances, leading progressively to cell death.

Secondary generalization The spreading of a focal seizure to the whole cortex.

Secondary prevention Treatments to reduce the risk of further transient ischaemic attacks or stroke.

Seizure Abrupt disruption of brain function associated with abnormally synchronous and intense activity of cortical neurons.

Selective serotonin reuptake inhibitors A class of antidepressant drugs which inhibit the reuptake of serotonin to the pre-synaptic cell.

Sensation seeking A personality trait involving the desire to seek out new and varied, often risky, experiences.

Sensory memory *See* immediate memory.

Serotonergic Describing neurons or synapses that utilize the neurotransmitter, serotonin.

Serotonin A neurotransmitter (also known as 5-hydroxytryptamine) involved in many functions, including mood, behaviour, sleep and appetite.

Short-term memory Retention of about 6–7 items of information for 15–30 seconds. In terms of the neuronal basis of memory, this is the transient increase in activity in a cell assembly that forms the engram for a feature and allows for a short-lasting increase in the perception of that feature.

Sinuses These are gaps within the bones of the skull. It is possible to place recording electrodes within certain sinuses. These are closer to the brain than surface electrodes and therefore are more sensitive. Not to be confused with venous sinuses which drain blood from the cranium.

Skull fracture Break of the skull bones. When the skin over it is broken, it is called a compound fracture.

Smiling depression Depression in which patients try to mask their underlying low mood by trying to appear apparently cheerful.

Sodium channel A protein spanning the cell membrane that is selectively permeable to sodium ions.

Soma The widest part of the neuron, containing its nucleus and other intracellular apparatus, where the inputs from the dendrites converge and are integrated. The axon also arises from the soma. The plural of soma is somata.

Somatic nervous system The portion of the peripheral nervous system that innervates the skeletal muscles to allow conscious control of movement.

Somatosensory system Collective term for the sensory information originating largely from the skin, such as temperature, touch and pain.

Somatotopy Map whereby regions of the body are represented by discrete regions of the cerebral cortex.

Spatial summation The reinforcement of synaptic potentials by the addition of the effects of several synapses active at the same time.

Spinal cord compression Pressure put upon the spinal cord, perhaps by a tumour or a fragment of bone from the spine.

Spongiform Sponge-like appearance of brain tissue down a microscope resulting from swelling of neurons. Characteristic of prion disease.

Spurious association Association that has arisen by chance rather than representing a true biological relationship.

Statins Drugs that reduce plasma cholesterol levels.

Status epilepticus A prolonged seizure (usually defined as lasting longer than a couple of minutes) or a series of repeated seizures. This is a serious medical emergency.

Stem cell An unspecialized cell that has the ability to transform into a specialized cell and also the ability to regenerate itself.

Stenosis The narrowing or constriction of an opening.

Stereotactic equipment Equipment that allows the precise placement of an electrode in deep parts of the brain based on radiological images.

Stereotypies Odd, repetitive movements that do not appear to be goal-directed.

Striated muscle The main type of muscle in the body, so-called because of the striped appearance of the muscle fibres when viewed under a light microscope.

Striatum A region of the brain that forms part of the basal ganglia.

Stroke Sudden loss of brain function lasting for more than 24 hours resulting from perturbation of its blood supply.

Subarachnoid haemorrhage Bleeding into the subarachnoid space.

Subdural empyema Collection of pus over the brain but underneath the dura, the covering of the brain, because of infection.

Subdural haematoma Collection of blood between the dura and the surface of the brain.

Substantia nigra A region of the brain that forms part of the basal ganglia containing black pigmented nerve cells that produce dopamine.

Suicidal ideation Thoughts about taking one's own life.

Sulcus Groove between adjacent gyri.

Symptomatic seizures Seizures due to identifiable problems outside the brain.

Symptomatic treatment One which improves the symptoms of a condition, but does not affect the underlying disease progression.

Synapse Site of functional connection between two neurons, which communicate by one releasing a transmitter which diffuses the short distance to the other where it binds to receptors which produce an effect on the target or post-synaptic neuron.

Synaptic plasticity Variation in the strength of a signal transmitted through a synapse.

Synaptic terminal The end of an axon specialized to release neurotransmitter.

Synaptic vesicles Small spheres filled with neurotransmitter that will be emptied by a process triggered by an action potential.

Synaptogenesis The formation of synapses between neurons.

Synchrony Simultaneous occurrence of events, or at least the occurrence of events within a short time of each other. In the EEG this means many neurons doing the same thing at the same time and producing a bigger voltage. Desynchrony is the opposite process in which many smaller groups of neurons work relatively independently of each other.

Syncope A faint, or loss of consciousness and loss of muscle tone. *See also* cardiac syncope and vasovagal syncope.

Syndrome A combination of signs and symptoms that forms a distinct clinical picture indicative of a particular disorder.

Systematic doubt The philosophical method employed by Descartes, according to which he searched for absolute certainty by rejecting everything which could in any way be doubted.

Tangentiality Illogical, irrelevant responses to questions.

Tangles *See* neurofibrillary tangle.

Tau A microtubule-associated protein.

Tedium vitae Passive desire to be dead because life holds nothing of interest and no possibility of improving.

Teichopsia Visual hallucination in a migraine attack of zigzag lines like an old map of a walled city.

Temporal arteritis Inflammatory condition of the temporal and other arteries leading to headache and other symptoms.

Temporal gradient This refers to the tendency of patients with dementia to be able to remember things from the distant past more effectively than recent events.

Temporal lobe That part of the cerebral cortex primarily associated with the auditory senses.

Temporal summation The reinforcement of synaptic potentials by the addition of successive activations of the same synapse, where the next synaptic potential starts before its predecessor ends.

Tension-type headache The most common of all headache disorders; frequently associated with anxiety and depression. Depending on frequency, may be subdivided into episodic and chronic forms.

Terminal The end process of the axon which can release chemical substances known as neurotransmitters to allow communication between one neuron and another.

Tetraplegia Paralysis of all four limbs.

Thalamotomy Surgical operation involving lesioning the thalamus to interrupt pathways involved in control of movement.

Thalamus Brain structure that links sensory organs (for touch, vision, and hearing) to the cortex.

Thought block The unpleasant experience of having one's train of thought curtailed absolutely so that no thoughts are left in the mind.

Thought broadcasting The experience that thoughts are leaving the mind and being broadcast to everyone.

Thought echo The experience of thoughts being repeated out loud.

Thought insertion The experience of alien thoughts being inserted into the mind.

Thought withdrawal The experience of thoughts being removed or extracted from the mind.

Thrombolysis Process by which a blood clot is broken down.

Thrombolytic therapy Drugs that promote the breaking down of blood clots.

Thrombosis Blood clot.

Thyroid stimulating hormone *See* thyrotropin.

Thyrotropin A neurochemical which acts on the pituitary gland, stimulating the release of thyroid stimulating hormone, which in turn causes the thyroid gland to produce the hormones thyroxine and triiodothyronine.

Tolerance A pharmacological phenomenon whereby identical doses of a drug induce decreasing levels of effect, or higher doses are required to produce the same level of effect.

Tonic seizures A form of generalized seizure during which widespread muscular contraction usually leads to falling.

Tonic-clonic seizures A form of generalized seizure in which the patient becomes rigid and may fall during the tonic phase, followed by a clonic phase during which the muscles rhythmically contract and relax.

Top-down Information processing from 'higher' association cortex to 'lower' sensory cortex.

Tract A bundle of axons in the central nervous system.

Transient ischaemic attack (TIA) Cerebral ischaemic event with all symptoms and signs disappearing within 24 hours.

Translocation The movement of genetic information from its normal site on the chromosome to a different location on the same, or a different, chromosome.

Transmissible spongiform encephalopathy Degenerative disease of the brain transmitted by prion proteins and characterized by cellular changes giving the appearance of a sponge.

Transporters Membrane proteins specialized in removing the neurotransmitter from the synaptic cleft.

Tremor An involuntary, rhythmical, alternating movement of a body part.

Tricyclic antidepressants A class of antidepressant drugs, with a basic chemical structure of three rings, which inhibit the reuptake of noradrenaline and serotonin to the presynaptic cell.

Trigeminal autonomic cephalgias A small group of headache disorders, that includes cluster headache, and that share similar clinical features such as pain in the trigeminal nerve territory and autonomic disturbance.

Trisomy The condition of having three copies of a particular chromosome.

Tryptophan An essential amino acid and the precursor of serotonin.

Tumour Mass created by abnormal uncontrolled growth of cells within an organ. *See* benign, malignant.

Twin studies A study which investigates whether the familiality of a disorder is likely to be determined by genes, by comparing rates of disorder in identical and non-identical twins.

Ultrasound Imaging technique in which high-frequency sound waves are used to outline part of an organ. Carotid ultrasound outlines narrowing in the carotid artery and gives detail of the flow within it.

Unipolar depression A major mood disorder characterized by at least one episode of depression, and the absence of episodes of mania.

Vasculitis Inflammation of blood vessels.

Vasospasm Spasm in a cerebral artery after subarachnoid haemorrhage.

Vasovagal syncope A faint, or loss of consciousness and loss of muscle tone, caused by sudden reduction in blood pressure due to decreased resistance of peripheral blood vessels and slowed heart rate.

Ventral tegmental area Region of brain containing the dopaminergic neurons which form the reward pathway.

Ventricle One of four cavities in the brain containing cerebrospinal fluid.

Ventriculo-peritoneal shunt Surgically implanted tube which relieves intracranial pressure. The tube is inserted into a lateral ventricle at one end then tunnelled under the skin to the abdominal cavity at the other.

Vertigo Sensation of spinning.

Virus An infectious agent that can replicate itself only within the cells of a living host.

Visual obscurations Short-lived loss of vision caused by postural changes in idiopathic intracranial hypertension.

Voltage-gated channels Ion channels that open dependent on the membrane potential.

Waxy flexibility Rigid maintenance of awkward and uncomfortable body position over an extended period of time.

White matter Regions of the central nervous system that contain bundles of myelinated axons which make them appear pale in colour to the naked eye.

Wide dynamic range neurons Neurons present in the deeper layers of the spinal cord that receive sensory input from both noxious and innocuous stimuli, and that can change properties (such as decreasing their firing threshold) as a result.

Wind-up The nociceptive neurons in the dorsal horn of the spinal cord become progressively amplified in response, after a primary stimulation.

Withdrawal A collection (or syndrome) of symptoms and signs resulting from reduction in, or cessation of, heavy and/or prolonged psychoactive substance use. It is often divided into psychological and physical withdrawal.

Word salad A severe form of positive formal thought disorder where there is a mixture of words and phrases that lacks comprehensive meaning or logical coherence.

Xanthochromia Yellow colour of CSF due to red blood cell breakdown products following subarachnoid haemorrhage.

Answers to self-check questions

Chapter 1

1.1 To perform its role, a neuron needs to have regions which are specialized to (1) receive information, (2) process that information, and (3) pass on appropriate messages to other neurons.

1.2 The most important differences are that neurons are able to generate and propagate electrical signals, whereas glia perform a more supporting role; for example, producing myelin and forming the blood–brain barrier.

1.3 The frontal lobes are responsible for a huge range of diverse functions, all of which are critical for normal human functioning. The best studied of those functions are motor control (by several regions of the frontal lobe) and functions often lumped together as 'higher cognitive functions', such as problem-solving and planning.

1.4 Three regions that we have covered in this chapter are the motor cortex of the frontal lobe, the cerebellum and the basal ganglia.

1.5 The short answer is yes. Brains show remarkable degrees of flexibility or 'plasticity'. On a microscopic level brains change every time we learn something new, such as a new phone number or a new skill such as playing a musical instrument or learning a new language. More extreme examples include the ability of large brain regions to take on new functions, for instance after a stroke, or after the loss of the sense of vision.

1.6 There are two main kinds of neuronal death: apoptosis and necrosis. In necrosis the neurons break down and release their contents, which cause inflammation and further damage to the neighbouring tissue. Apoptosis is a controlled or programmed cell death which uses energy to keep the cell contents within intact membranes so that they do not damage the surrounding tissue. During apoptosis the contents of the cell break down and the cell itself breaks up into smaller fragments that can be taken up by specialized scavenger cells. Apoptosis occurs during normal development as well as during some diseases.

Chapter 2

2.1 The presence of voltage-gated Na^+ and K^+ channels enables the neuronal membrane to generate action potentials.

2.2 The message is coded by the firing frequency, which is determined by the level of membrane depolarization.

2.3 Action potentials propagate like a wave along the axonal membrane towards the synaptic terminal. There they trigger the calcium-dependent release of neurotransmitter.

2.4 The binding of glutamate to its receptor causes influx of sodium ions, which depolarizes the membrane. The binding of GABA to its receptor causes influx of chloride ions, which hyperpolarizes the membrane.

2.5 Every time the spatial and temporal summation of many glutamatergic synaptic inputs, counteracted by GABAergic synaptic inputs, depolarizes the membrane above firing threshold, one or more action potentials will be generated.

2.6 Associative learning requires functional reorganization of neuronal connections, through the principle that 'neurons that fire together, wire together'.

2.7 'Neurons that fire together wire together'. Glutamatergic synapses can strengthen when glutamate release coincides with a postsynaptic action potential. All glutamatergic synapses that contribute to the firing will have their influence strengthened.

2.8 The NMDA receptor needs glutamate release coinciding with a postsynaptic action potential that removes the Mg^{2+} plug, in order to activate Ca^{2+}-dependent processes.

2.9 Strengthening of synapses can last if cyclic AMP is increased in the postsynaptic cell, in response to modulatory neurotransmitters released in situations of behavioural relevance.

2.10 In Barlow's view, neurons are organized in a hierarchical fashion with increasingly complex and specific response properties, activating ultimately a 'grandmother cell' that responds to one specific feature. In Hebb's view, both simple and complex features activate large interconnected neuron assemblies.

2.11 The memory trace, or engram, of a feature is formed by strengthening connections (through LTP) between all neurons activated by the feature, forming a unique assembly of interconnected neurons for each feature.

2.12 Neuron assemblies forming an engram receive inputs from neurons forming an engram in 'higher' cortical areas. When the latter fire, it helps to activate the right engram in the 'lower' cortex.

Chapter 3

3.1 Chromosomal abnormalities are problems with the chromosomes that can be visualized under the microscope in the process known as karyotype analysis. Chromosomal abnormalities may occur as a result of mis-sorting of the chromosomes during cell division, giving rise to an extra copy, or a missing copy, of the chromosome. They may also occur as a result of damage to a particular chromosome, so that part of the chromosome is missing, or translocated to a different chromosome. Chromosomal abnormalities can even be due to mutations in a single gene, so long as this causes a visible change in the structure of the chromosome; this is what happens in fragile X syndrome.

3.2 Huntington's disease is caused by a mutation in a single gene: *huntingtin*. Possession of a single copy of the mutant gene is enough to cause the condition, so Huntington's disease is said to be a 'dominant' disorder. The mutant gene contains a greatly expanded CAG triplet repeat region, which gives rise to an elongated chain of glutamine residues in the huntingtin protein. What is not yet clear is how this mutation is related to the development of the symptoms of Huntington's disease.

3.3 Multifactorial disorders are due to the effect of multiple genes along with environmental factors, such as smoking or a viral infection. It may well be that the expression of the genes involved in the disease is not sufficient to cause the disease, unless the environmental factors are also present; schizophrenia appears to be this type of condition. Multifactorial disorders can also arise as the result of a mutation in any one of several different genes, or as the result of an environmental factor such as injury; epilepsy seems to be this sort of multifactorial disorder.

3.4 Linkage studies are used to try and pinpoint the location of a disease-causing gene on the chromosome. They rely on the principle of genetic linkage: that two fragments of the genome which are found close to each other on a parental chromosome will be found together in the offspring more often than predicted by chance. These studies are easiest to perform when you have a large family in which there is a frequent incidence of the disease in question; large families from isolated communities are especially highly prized, as these are expected to have rather limited genetic variation.

3.5 The advantage of microarrays is that they allow the analysis of thousands of genes at once, in a rather simple manner. Thus they are particularly useful for studying multifactorial conditions.

3.6 Understanding the genetic basis of a brain disorder can potentially aid treatment in three main ways: (1) providing the basis for a diagnostic test, (2) revealing information about the cause of the disease which should in turn allow the rational development of new targets for drug treatment, and (3) allowing treatment or cure of the disease using gene therapy, to replace or repair abnormal genes.

Chapter 4

4.1 The mind may be considered to be the functional activity of the brain.

4.2 Psychiatry relies on syndromal diagnoses and cannot fall back upon physical investigations to validate its diagnoses. In addition, the boundaries of psychiatry are less clear than for other branches of medicine, potentially encompassing all aspects of human existence. This leads to potential conflict with other disciplines such as psychology, philosophy, anthropology, and religion, in a way that is less prominent in other medical specialities.

4.3 This model holds that every individual has a level of predisposition to develop a particular disorder. So individual X may have a high propensity, while individual Y has a low propensity. This intrinsic predisposition may be genetically mediated and is known as a diathesis to develop the disorder in question. But whether the individual actually does go on to develop the disorder is dependent upon other, probably environmental factors, or stresses. Individual X may develop the disorder consequent to some minor stress, while individual Y, who has a much lower propensity, would only develop the disorder after some much greater stressor.

4.4 Cognitive theory holds that there is a link between what we think and how we experience emotion or how we behave. So therapies based upon cognitive theory aim to bring about therapeutic effects on emotion by manipulating our thoughts or thinking patterns. Behavioural theory in its purest form is atheoretical, holding that there is no need to consider anything beyond the behaviour itself, and denying the importance of free will or thought.

4.5 Disorders which are long standing, perhaps clearly developing during adolescence, which are characterized by neurosis rather than psychosis, and which particularly cause difficulties in terms of interpersonal relationships, tend to be best suited to psychodynamic psychotherapy.

4.6 Psychotic symptoms are qualitatively different from normal experience and are phenomena that most of us have never experienced. Neurotic symptoms, on the other hand, tend to be extremes of normal emotions or subjective experiences, which are considered pathological because they are extreme, rather than just because of their presence.

4.7 A hallucination is perception without an external stimulus. In every other respect it is, to the person experiencing it, identical to a normal perception.

4.8 There is no single symptom which in itself allows the diagnosis of schizophrenia to be made, but delusions of reference and delusions of control are particularly characteristic. Persecutory delusions are also very common in schizophrenia, but also occur commonly in other psychotic mental illnesses.

4.9 Delusions and loosening of association are the psychotic abnormalities of thought.

Chapter 5

5.1 The frontal, parietal, and temporal cortex are supplied with blood from the right and left internal carotid arteries. The occipital cortex, the brain stem, and the cerebellum are supplied by the right and left vertebrobasilar arteries.

5.2 Strokes are caused by cerebral infarction (blockage of vessel) and intracerebral haemorrhage. Arteries are blocked by fatty deposits or plaques of atheroma on which blood clots (thromboses) can form. Clots can dislodge forming emboli which lead to blockage of an artery downstream. Emboli can also form in the heart and pass to the brain causing infarction. In intracerebral haemorrhage, an artery in the brain ruptures, usually as a result of high blood pressure, causing a leakage of blood into the brain substance.

5.3 In a total anterior circulation syndrome (TACS) stroke, the patient develops severe hemiparesis, hemisensory loss, hemianopia, and cortical dysfunction.

A partial anterior circulation syndrome (PACS) stroke is similar but less severe.

In a lacunar (LACS) stroke, the patient develops hemiparesis and/or hemisensory loss which is equal in the face, arm, and leg.

In a posterior circulation syndrome (POCS) stroke, the patient develops contralateral hemiparesis and/or hemisensory loss which is usually combined with brain-stem signs such as cranial nerve palsies or cerebellar signs.

5.4 CT is used in suspected stroke and TIA patients to exclude other diagnoses, not necessarily to show the actual stroke itself.

5.5 A stroke producing a severe clinical deficit is usually treated with hospital admission, supportive measures (e.g. intravenous fluids, urinary catheter), immediate aspirin, rarely thrombolysis, secondary prevention measures (i.e. treatment of hypertension, diabetes, hyperlipidaemia, smoking, and antiplatelet agents) and rehabilitation.

5.6 Subarachnoid haemorrhage occurs when blood leaks into the subarachnoid space. In 90% of cases, it is caused by rupture of an intracranial aneurysm. Rarer causes include arteriovenous malformations.

5.7 Subarachnoid haemorrhage most commonly presents with sudden, severe headache. This can be associated with stiff neck, brief loss of consciousness, nausea, and vomiting.

5.8 The initial investigation in suspected subarachnoid haemorrhage should be CT followed over 12 hours later by lumbar puncture if the scan is normal.

5.9 Intracranial aneurysms are treated by either intra-arterial coiling or surgical clipping.

Chapter 6

6.1 An EEG may show interictal epileptiform discharges and distinguish between generalized and focal epilepsies. An MRI may show a structural abnormality which is causing seizures.

6.2 In a generalized seizure, epileptic discharges are generated simultaneously through both hemispheres and the patient loses consciousness. In a focal seizure, epileptic discharges are localized to one part of the brain and the clinical features depend on the site of the abnormal discharge. For example, epileptic activity in the temporal lobe may result in a sensation of *déjà vu* and automatisms, while epileptic activity in the motor strip may cause tonic or clonic contractions restricted to the opposite side of the body.

6.3 In most patients, there is no known cause (the epilepsy is said to be idiopathic). Symptomatic epilepsy may result from inborn abnormalities such as neuronal migration disorders and specific genetic defects, or from disorders developed later in life such as head injury or brain tumour.

6.4 An epileptic discharge (the spike in the human EEG) requires the simultaneous discharge of large numbers of pyramidal neurons. The 'chain reaction' model explains how this can be achieved by a relatively small number of excitatory interconnections. The model requires (1) recurrent local excitatory synapses, (2) burst discharges (to allow temporal summation), and (3) a loss of inhibitory control by interneurons.

6.5 Absence epilepsy is a generalized epilepsy, and the synchronized discharges seen in both cerebral hemispheres are thought to be coordinated by the thalamocortical projection. IPSPs in thalamic neurons open T-type Ca^{2+} channels; the depolarization results in action potentials which are projected to the cortex; excitation of cortical neurons results in the spike discharge; intracortical connections result in a wave of inhibition (the slow wave).

6.6 Antiepileptic drugs aim to reduce the excess excitability associated with the hypersynchronous neuronal discharges which cause seizures. Some act to increase synaptic inhibition (for example by activating GABA receptors or enhancing the effectiveness of normally released GABA); others reduce the response to synaptic excitation (for example, by limiting the opening of Na^+ channels or, in the case of absence epilepsy, Ca^{2+} channels).

Chapter 7

7.1 AD is the third most common cause of death in the developed world after heart disease and cancer. Patient numbers are rising very sharply and it is believed that this number will reach 50 million by 2050 (from 12 million in 2000).

7.2 AD starts with simple forgetfulness often associated with depression. Later on, all functions relating to intellect and personality are affected.

7.3 AD can be mistaken for depression in the early stages of the disease. Later on, AD can look very similar to other dementia disorders, such as multi-infarct dementia, hypothyroidism, and Lewy body dementia.

7.4 AD is characterized by the accumulation of plaques and tangles in the brain. Additionally there is extensive death of nerve cells and loss of synapses. The amyloid angiopathy does not appear in all patients.

7.5 AD is a multifactorial disease. Advanced age is the strongest risk factor. Diabetes, atherosclerosis, high blood pressure, vitamin deficiencies, and low education are known to increase the risk of developing AD. Genetic factors, such as ApoE4, may also contribute.

7.6 There is no treatment for AD. The only available medication is symptomatic (cholinesterase inhibitors), and preventive measures can be taken to reduce the risk of AD.

Chapter 8

8.1 The cause or causes of Parkinson's disease are unknown but possible candidates are environmental triggers (e.g. pesticides) and genetic predisposition.

8.2 The main clinical features of Parkinson's disease are tremor, rigidity, bradykinesia, and hypokinesia. Later problems include imbalance and falls, dementia, and depression.

8.3 The most common tremulous condition simulating Parkinson's disease is essential tremor. Conditions presenting with a parkinsonian syndrome include multiple cerebral infarction, drug-induced parkinsonism, progressive supranuclear palsy, and multiple system atrophy.

8.4 Levodopa is metabolized into dopamine which is deficient in the brain in Parkinson's disease. Dopamine itself cannot be used as it does not cross the blood–brain barrier.

8.5 Smoking is the only environmental factor that has consistently been reported to increase the risk of MND. Other proposed risk factors include high levels of sustained physical exercise, service in the military, particularly in the Gulf War in the 1990s, and exposure to certain metals such as iron, mercury, and manganese or to certain viruses, but the evidence for each of these factors being important is not strong.

8.6 Key pathways thought to be important in MND include excitotoxicity mediated via glutamate, the brain's major excitatory neurotransmitter, excess oxidative damage to proteins and DNA, impaired cellular transport by neurofilaments, and abnormalities in mitochondrial function. Ultimately intracellular regulation of Ca^{2+} is disrupted and the affected motor neurons are thought to die by apoptosis.

8.7 Therapies being tested in MND include the use of drugs targeted to reduce glutamate excitotoxicity and oxidative stress, and drugs to improve mitochondrial function. Trials of various nerve growth factors, delivered with gene therapy using viruses to target the factors to the CNS, and of stem cell therapy, are likely to be undertaken in the future.

8.8 Huntington's disease is caused by an autosomal dominant genetic mutation on chromosome 4 leading to an abnormality in the protein huntingtin.

Chapter 9

9.1 In children younger than 3 months, group B streptococci, *Escherichia coli*, and *Listeria* are the most common causes. *Neisseria meningitides*, *Pneumococcus*, and *Haemophilus* are common causes in children aged 3 months to 17 years. *Pneumococcus* and *Neisseria meningitides* are the most common causes in those aged 18–50 years, while *Pneumococcus*, *Listeria*, and gram-negative bacilli are the most common causes in those over 50 years old.

9.2 The key features of bacterial meningitis are rapid onset of generalized headache, fever, photophobia and meningism developing over a day or two. Other symptoms include irritability and confusion, decreased consciousness, myalgia, anorexia, tachycardia, and nausea and vomiting.

9.3 Normal CSF is clear and contains no, or very few, cells. If cells are present these are lymphocytes. In bacterial meningitis the CSF is cloudy and yellow, with >1000 neutrophils/mL and decreased glucose and increased protein levels compared to normal. In viral meningitis the CSF is clear or only slightly turbid, with 10–2000 lymphocytes/mL, a normal glucose level, and a normal or only slightly raised protein level.

9.4 Bacterial meningitis is diagnosed on the basis of a typical history and the typical findings of increased cells, increased protein and low glucose on CSF examination. Staining of the CSF with stains to detect organisms may allow the species of bacteria causing the meningitis to be determined.

9.5 Bacterial meningitis is treated with intravenous antibiotics. Empirical treatment with ceftiaxone or cefotaxime and vancomycin should be started without delay and then refined once the infecting organism is known.

9.6 Vaccines are available to prevent *Haemophilus influenzae* and pneumococcal meningitis.

9.7 Viral meningitis presents with fever, headache, and neck stiffness, and sometimes a rash, enlarged lymph glands or enlarged salivary glands depending on the specific virus involved.

9.8 Most cases of viral meningitis are diagnosed clinically with no specific tests performed to confirm the diagnosis. Examination of the CSF may show the typical features of viral meningitis (raised lymphocyte cell count, normal glucose, slightly raised protein level) and sometimes PCR tests on CSF will allow the specific virus to be identified.

9.9 Sexual stages of the malaria parasite are present in the blood of individuals with malaria. When a mosquito bites an infected person the male and female stages fuse in the mosquito's gut and penetrate the wall. Daughter parasites grow within a cyst which eventually bursts and the resulting sporozoites migrate to the mosquito's salivary glands. When the mosquito next bites a human these sporozoites enter the person's blood stream and travel to the liver where they undergo asexual reproduction to form merozoites. After 1–3 weeks the merozoites burst through the liver cells and invade red blood cells where they mature. Symptoms occur when the merozoites are in the red blood cells.

9.10 Encephalitis means inflammation of the brain tissue and is most frequently caused by viruses.

9.11 Examination of the CSF will show a modest rise in the lymphocyte cell count and a slight rise in the protein content, with a normal or only slightly reduced glucose level. Specific viral antibodies or viral DNA may also be found in the CSF. An EEG may show widespread slowing of the normal brain wave patterns.

9.12 Usually many different bacteria are found within a brain abscess. The most common are *Streptococcus milleri*, *Pneumococcus*, *Bacteroides*, and *Staphylococcus aureus*.

9.13 The clinical features are those of a space-occupying lesion at the particular site where the abscess has formed. For example features may include motor symptoms, sensory symptoms or disturbances of speech, vision or hearing and epileptic seizures. Diagnosis is usually made on either CT or MR brain imaging.

9.14 A pathogenic form of a normal protein called prion protein or PrP^C. (The mis-folded form known as PrP^{Sc} can link up to form aggregates which accumulate more PrP^C until they are so big they resist digestion by enzymes). No effective treatment is available at present. Pentosan polysulfate, injected directly into the brain, seems to slow the disease, but does not cure it.

Chapter 10

10.1 The cause of MS is unknown, but thought to involve both environmental and genetic factors. One proposed mechanism is that the disease is triggered in genetically susceptible people in childhood by viral infection, and that the neurological disability results from abnormal reactions in an individual's immune system throughout life.

10.2 The most common pattern is relapsing and remitting MS in which symptoms occur for about 4–5 weeks, corresponding to disruption of neuronal conduction due to inflammatory plaques forming on particular myelinated nerves in the CNS. As the inflammation resolves and the myelin reforms, nerve conduction is restored and the symptoms disappear. Further episodes of relapse and remission occur with the individual making a full recovery each time. In secondary progressive MS, symptoms occur due to plaques forming and then partially resolve as remyelination begins to occur. In these cases remyelination and recovery of nerve transmission is incomplete, and individuals are left with some residual symptoms. In primary progressive MS, patients never make a full recovery, even after the first attack of the disease. This reflects a failure of remyelination and subsequent scarring and loss of nerve axons. These patients have disability from the onset, which gradually worsens.

10.3 Optic neuritis usually presents as blurred vision in one eye that gradually increases over the course of about a week and may result in complete blindness. There is often also pain in the eye, particularly on movement. Vision usually recovers within a month or so. The symptoms arise due to an inflammatory demyelinating plaque forming on one of the optic nerves.

10.4 There is no single correct answer to this question, with advice being tailored to an individual patient. Brain MR imaging and evoked potential studies could be undertaken to determine the likelihood of the individual subsequently developing MS. If both the brain MRI scan and CSF examination are normal, there is only a 15% chance that the individual will go on to develop MS compared to a 70% chance if both the MRI brain scan and CSF findings are abnormal and compatible with MS.

10.5 Corticosteroids are the main symptomatic therapy in MS. They are given in high doses intravenously for short periods of time and hasten remission from acute relapses. Muscle spasms can be treated with baclofen, tizanidine, or diazepam, urinary symptoms with anticholinergic drugs, and paroxysmal pain with various antiepileptic drugs and possibly, and controversially, with cannabis.

10.6 Both interferon beta and glatiramer acetate reduce the number or relapses in relapsing remitting MS by about 30%. No agents have as yet been shown to be effective in influencing the course of the progressive phase of the disease.

Chapter 11

11.1 The warning signs with headaches are: headache wakes the patient in the early hours of the morning; twitching of the face, arm, or leg (epilepsy); loss of consciousness (epilepsy); progressive weakness or sensory loss of the face, arm, or leg; swollen optic disc (papilloedema); sudden severe headache; scalp tenderness; clusters of short-lived attacks with watering of eye or nose.

11.2 Tension-type headache presents as a mild to moderate pressing or tightening feeling which is felt all over the head. Patients often describe it as though 'my head will explode' or as though 'there is a tight band around my head'. In patients with a typical history of tension-type headache and normal examination, there is no need for further investigations.

11.3 Migraine presents with a severe, throbbing, unilateral headache which is often associated with photophobia, phonophobia, nausea, and vomiting. Some patients have a preceding aura of an evolving visual disturbance or rarely weakness, sensory loss, or vertigo. Clinical examination is normal, as is imaging which should be avoided if the history is typical and examination normal.

11.4 Cluster headache presents with unilateral, ocular and/or frontal headache. The duration of the attacks is short compared with migraine; each lasts for around 30–90 minutes. The diagnostic feature is watering of an eye and unilateral nasal discharge. Attacks are usually repeated several times in the day, often at night. It is called 'cluster' headache as attacks come in clusters lasting for a month or two with a gap of several months before another bout.

11.5 Acute pain is closely linked to tissue damage and related to sensory stimulation. Chronic pain arises from complex interneuronal connections, sometimes in the absence of tissue damage, and requires multidisciplinary management.

11.6 We know that acute tissue damage activates sensory nerve fibres that respond to painful stimuli in the periphery. Nerve impulses pass to the dorsal horn of the spinal cord. The neurons of the dorsal horn of the spinal cord can become sensitized to pain impulses, and the patient becomes hypersensitive to noxious stimuli. This means the patient can ultimately experience pain more severely.

11.7 Chronic pain has a nociceptive and a neuropathic form. Both require escalating medication and a multidisciplinary approach including behaviour modification.

Chapter 12

12.1 Primary brain injury leads to direct physical damage to neurons and supporting cells. Secondary brain injury causes damage to, or destroys, neurons and supporting cells surrounding the area of the primary injury due to lack of oxygen and other vital substances.

12.2 The Glasgow Coma Score is a universal grading scale that describes and grades the motor, verbal, and eye-opening functions of a patient with a brain abnormality. It is used to describe patients who are ill with head injury or other serious neurosurgical conditions.

12.3 If rising intracranial pressure is left untreated it will lead to severe neurological deficit or even death. It can be treated with medication that reduces brain swelling (e.g. mannitol) or surgical procedures designed to remove fluid or blood collection from the head.

12.4 Benign tumours compress and displace normal brain or spinal cord tissue. Malignant tumours destroy and invade the surrounding brain or spinal cord.

12.5 Brain tumours can be treated with a combination of surgery, radiotherapy, and chemotherapy depending on their histological type.

12.6 Hydrocephalus is the accumulation of CSF inside the brain. In most cases it is treated with insertion of a plastic tube and valve system, a shunt. In some forms it can be treated with an internal redirection of the fluid using neuro-endoscopic techniques.

Chapter 13

13.1 In dispositional anxiety, the tendency to experience anxiety and tension is a feature of personality, and an intrinsic characteristic of the individual. Therefore it will be evident throughout their life, from adolescence onwards. An acute anxiety disorder, on the other hand, will have a clear beginning, before which the individual did not experience such high levels of anxiety or tension.

13.2 The pathological nature of anxiety may be signified by the precipitating situations, the anxiety being out of proportion to the demands of the stimulus. In other cases it is simply the degree of anxiety which is pathological.

13.3 In GAD, the anxiety is often not extremely severe or acute, as it is in panic disorder for example. Rather it is its persistence and all-pervading quality which over time leads to a deterioration in personal and social functioning.

13.4 Typically panic attacks peak within about 10 minutes and start to subside after about 30 minutes.

13.5 There are only three categories of phobic anxiety disorder. They are agoraphobia, social phobia, and specific phobia.

13.6 Re-experiencing symptoms, hypervigilance, avoidance, and associated problems, particularly depression and substance misuse.

13.7 Common themes include dirt and contamination, obscenities and blasphemies, abhorrent sexual practices, orderliness, and tidiness.

13.8 Serotonergic, dopaminergic, and noradrenergic systems.

Chapter 14

14.1 Normal sadness is usually related to some unhappy event or circumstance. The low mood of depression is experienced as qualitatively different to normal sadness by the sufferer, and it is persistent and all-pervading, in a way that normal sadness is not. Furthermore, low mood in depression is associated with the other symptoms that go to make up the syndrome of depression, such as lack of energy, reduced interest in life, impaired sleep and impaired appetite.

14.2 Such patients may have delusions of grandiose ability, leading them to believe that they can fly or that they are invincible. Also it is common for manic patients to have persecutory ideas or delusions, which may lead them into conflict with others.

14.3 It may be that some of this observed discrepancy is caused by differing behaviours between men and women. Women may be more likely to articulate their distress in terms of low mood, and may be more likely to seek help from the medical profession when unwell. In contrast, it may be that men are more likely to 'put on a brave face' and try and fulfil the expectations of society in terms of machismo. It may also be that aspects of women's traditional role in society make them more vulnerable to stressful life events.

14.4 Twin studies have demonstrated that the monozygotic concordance for depression is significantly greater than the dizygotic concordance. Studies of adoptees show that individuals whose biological parents have a history of mood disorder but whose adoptive parents do not, have a higher rate of mood disorder than individuals who were born to parents without mood disorder, and raised by sufferers of mood disorders.

14.5 Research studies examining personality and cognitive style associated with mood disorders are usually cross-sectional. Therefore they cannot demonstrate that one leads to the other. In addition it may be that both the personality or cognitive style and the mood disorder are each consequent to some third factor.

14.6 When considering an individual case such factors are often considered to be either predisposing or precipitating factors. A predisposing factor is one which increases the likelihood of an individual suffering from a mood disorder. A precipitating factor is one which causes the individual to develop an episode of illness at this particular time.

14.7 Essentially, the monoamine hypothesis of depression postulates that depression is caused by reduced activity of monoamine systems, and mania is caused by increased activity. This is undoubtedly a gross simplification of the true picture.

14.8 Changes in levels and function of cortisol are established in mood disorders. It might be that this influences mood by affecting central serotonergic function.

14.9 By directly interviewing and examining the patient, and often by taking a history from an informant.

14.10 CBT assumes a relationship between thoughts, emotions, and behaviour, and attempts to affect emotional experiences by influencing habitual ways of thinking and behaving.

14.11 Some of the treatments used have unpleasant side effects. Also, patients with bipolar disorder may miss the feelings of mild elation that they may experience without maintenance treatment.

Chapter 15

15.1 Auditory hallucinations; persecutory delusions, particularly delusional perceptions; delusions of passivity; thought insertion, withdrawal and broadcast; thought disorder.

15.2 Avolition; apathy; asociality; affective blunting; poverty of thought.

15.3 Because schizophrenia is a chronic, lifelong disorder.

15.4 This would provide a major focus for research investigating the pathogenic mechanisms underlying schizophrenia, because the functions of those genes implicated could be targeted as potential causes. This in turn would be likely to lead to improved treatment of schizophrenia. But before improvements in treatment, identification of susceptibility genes would be likely to lead to better ability to predict risk of developing schizophrenia for individuals, and better illness education for sufferers and their relatives.

15.5 Patients with schizophrenia have increased rates of obstetric complications, developmental delays during childhood, and soft neurological signs. The anatomical cerebral changes associated with schizophrenia tend to be static and do not progress.

15.6 Schizophrenia often has a very gradual and insidious onset, and in populations of high-risk children, behavioural and cognitive problems are present from an early stage in sufferers. Therefore, it is often difficult to be certain when the effects of the illness began, and to identify a reliably premorbid period.

15.7 A predisposing factor is a factor which leads to an individual having a greater likelihood of developing a particular disorder. A precipitating factor is one which is influential in causing the development of the disorder, or episode of illness, at that particular time.

15.8 People who smoke cannabis often begin to do so in late teenage years, about the time that the effects of schizophrenia may begin to affect them. So it is difficult to distinguish between cannabis misuse being a cause of subsequent schizophrenia and cannabis misuse being a consequence of a developing mental illness.

15.9 The side effects of antipsychotic treatments vary between particular drugs and classes of drugs, but common side effects include (1) extrapyramidal side effects including dystonia, tremor, parkinsonism, and tardive dyskinesia; (2) sedation; (3) weight gain; and (4) changes in heart rate and blood pressure.

15.10 Family therapy aims to provide education to families about mental illness, improve communication between family members and the patient, help the family develop shared coping strategies, and generally involve the family in caring for the patient. These approaches may exert their effect partly through reducing expressed emotion and levels of criticism, which have been observed to be associated with higher rates of relapse.

15.11 The central symptoms in delusional disorder are delusions. Such patients do not suffer from the other common symptoms of schizophrenia such as auditory hallucinations or passivity experiences.

Chapter 16

16.1 As defined by ICD-10, they are:

- A strong desire to take the substance.
- Difficulties in controlling the use of the substance.
- A withdrawal syndrome when substance use has ceased or been reduced. The physical symptoms of withdrawal vary across drugs, but psychological symptoms include anxiety, depression, and sleep disturbance. The individual may also report the use of substances to relieve the withdrawal symptoms.
- Evidence of tolerance, i.e. higher doses are required to achieve the same effect.
- Neglect of interests and an increased amount of time taken to obtain the substance or recover from its effects.
- Persistent substance use despite evidence of its harmful consequences.

Dependence gives some indication of the severity of the addiction problem, and this may have implications for the treatment strategy adopted. For example, someone who is heavily alcohol dependent should be advised to remain abstinent from alcohol for life in order to achieve the best outcome. In contrast someone who has experienced alcohol-related problems, but doesn't meet the criteria for dependence, may be able to return to non-problematic drinking in the future.

16.2 Many neurotransmitters have been implicated but the one for which there is the most consistent evidence for involvement in the neurobiology of drug abuse is dopamine.

16.3 These include:

- genetic factors
- personality traits e.g. impulsivity
- positive reinforcement of substance use
- psychiatric co-morbidity, e.g. depression or anxiety
- cost of the substance
- income of the individual
- legislation, e.g. pub opening hours, illegality of certain drugs
- supply and availability of substance
- cultural factors—attitudes towards substances, adjustment factors
- trends and fashions
- occupation
- family environment—modelling or social learning, deprivation or abuse, disruption of family rituals
- peer pressure
- stress and life events.

16.4 Alcohol has a potentially negative effect on every system in the body, including memory impairment and dementia; muscular weakness; loss of sensation in the hands and feet; high blood pressure leading to increased risk of stroke and myocardial infarction; gastric inflammation and ulcers; liver disease; and increased risk of accidents.

Regular use of opioids leads to problems sleeping and can disrupt the menstrual cycle. Accidental overdose can lead to respiratory failure, coma, and death. Injecting drug use causes abscesses and deep vein thrombosis, and leads to the transmission of blood-borne viruses such as hepatitis B or C, or HIV.

Snorting cocaine can lead to a perforated nasal septum due to constriction of blood vessels. Rapidly raised blood pressure may lead to intracranial bleeding or stroke, and a rapid onset of an increased heart rate can result in abnormal cardiac rhythms and myocardial infarction. Inhaling crack cocaine may lead to local irritation and bronchitis. Anxiety and nervousness can be associated with regular stimulant use, and stimulant psychosis is manifested by a high level of suspiciousness and paranoid delusions. Severely lowered mood, excessive sleep and appetite may occur after a cocaine binge.

Cannabis may cause feelings of depression and difficulty sleeping, increased risk of cancer and precipitation of psychotic symptoms.

16.5 From a public health perspective, it would be better to reduce the amount the whole population drinks by an average of 1 unit per day than to reduce an individual's average daily consumption by 20 units. If less people drank at dangerous levels there would be a massive national saving in terms of lives lost, hospital stays, criminal justice expenditure and other social costs. From an individual perspective, early assessment and intervention may prevent the development of a wide range of physical, psychological, and social problems associated with addiction. Self-perpetuating vicious circles can maintain the addiction, e.g. drinking to prevent alcohol withdrawal symptoms, and early intervention can prevent these cycles forming.

16.6 Although a confrontational approach—trying to 'wake the person up' and make them see their problems—seems logical, there is a lot of evidence to suggest that it usually has the opposite effect. A common reaction to confrontation and being told what to do is to argue and so do the opposite. Motivational interviewing takes a different approach, aiming instead to 'roll with resistance' by reflecting it back to the client. The emphasis is put on personal choice regarding future substance use, and the therapist focuses on eliciting the client's own concerns. A key goal is to evoke from the addicted person statements of problem perception and a need for change. This is the conceptual opposite of an approach in which the therapist takes responsibility for persuading the client to change.

16.7 Giving people a prescribed version of heroin can be seen as giving them what they want, and therefore the 'easy way out' of the problem. This is consistent with the idea that drug taking is wrong and entirely under voluntary control, and therefore should be punished. Another commonly voiced view is that it is 'just swapping one addiction for another', and that it doesn't cure the person of their problem. This is of course true, but the goal is not cure (at least initially) but rather reduction of harm. By using the 'carrot' of maintenance prescribing to engage the drug user in treatment, services hope to then use other effective psychosocial interventions to bring about change in behaviour.

Index